# ADVANCED
# C
## TIPS AND TECHNIQUES

# ♯♯♯
# HOWARD W. SAMS & COMPANY/HAYDEN BOOKS

# ADVANCED C

# C

# TIPS AND TECHNIQUES

**Paul L. Anderson**
**Gail C. Anderson**

## HAYDEN BOOKS

*A Division of Howard W. Sams & Company*
*4300 West 62nd Street*
*Indianapolis, Indiana 46268 USA*

FIRST EDITION
THIRD PRINTING — 1989

International Standard Book Number: 0-672-48417-X
Library of Congress Catalog Card Number: 88-61226

Acquisitions Editor: *Jim Hill*
Development Editor: *Jennifer Ackley*
Cover Art: *Visual Graphic Services, Indianapolis*
Typesetting: *Pipeline Associates, Inc.*

This entire text was edited and processed under UNIX. The text was formatted using `troff`, with the assistance of `tbl` for the tables and `pic` for the figures. The `troff` output was converted to PostScript using `devps`. The camera ready copy was printed on an Apple LaserWriter Plus, with no pasteup required.

*Printed in the United States of America*

# Hayden Books
# C
# Library

The C Library is an integrated series of books covering basic to advanced topics related to C programming. The books are written under the direction of Stephen G. Kochan and Patrick H. Wood, who worked for several years teaching introductory and advanced courses at Bell Laboratories, and who themselves have written many books on C programming and the UNIX system.

The first book in the series, *Programming in C*, teaches the fundamentals of C programming. All aspects of the language are covered in this text, and over 90 *complete* program examples are shown with their output.

*Topics in C Programming* takes up where *Programming in C* leaves off. In this advanced-level book you'll learn more about the subtleties of working with structures and pointers in C. The book also covers the functions provided in the Standard C and Standard I/O Libraries. Of special interest to UNIX programmers are the chapters on the UNIX System Interface Library and on the `curses` routines for writing terminal-independent programs. The `make` program is also covered in the text, and the book describes in detail how to debug programs using tools like `lint`, the preprocessor, `ctrace`, and `sdb`.

*Advanced C: Tips and Techniques* is an in-depth book on advanced C programming, with special emphasis on portability, execution efficiency, and application techniques. Among the things you'll learn about are: C's run-time environment, debugging techniques, fast array transfers, multidimensional arrays, and dynamic memory allocation. Practical examples are given to demonstrate these techniques.

*Programming in ANSI C* is for people who want to learn how to write programs in the new ANSI standard C. Using the same approach as *Programming in C*, the book covers all of the features of ANSI C. Over 90 program examples are presented with step-by-step explanations of all the procedures involved.

# ◆ Acknowledgements ◆

Our thanks to Tim Dowty for reviewing the entire manuscript and providing countless valuable suggestions. Thanks to Steve Kochan and Pat Wood for their C expertise, editorial assistance, and the great set of macros they gave us to typeset the book. This, of course, makes us solely responsible for any errors and not someone else. Thanks to Marty Gray, Bob Long, and Bill Barton of Overland Data Inc., who provided time and encouragement. Dave Atkins gave us AT&T System V insights and Bob Goff supplied Berkeley 4BSD and SUN details. Marty Gray contributed many techniques and is a virtual wizard when it comes to using C in interesting ways. Thanks to Jennifer Ackley, Jim Hill, Wendy Ford, and Lou Keglovits of Howard Sams for their support and assistance. Last, thanks to Sara and Kellen for cooperating (as much as kids can) while we wrote this book.

# C O N T E N T S

# P R E F A C E

C is over fifteen years old now and yet it's as popular as ever. What originally began in the early seventies as a systems programming language for mini-computers has evolved to a standard for programming in the eighties. We have the microprocessor industry to thank for that, since software has to keep up with new hardware technology. C has risen above the other languages because it's nitty-gritty enough to handle machine level operations, yet portable enough for most applications.

Naturally, when a language has been around as long as C, someone's bound to come up with a few techniques. *Advanced C: Tips and Techniques* is for the legion of C programmers who are interested in learning more about C and how to use it effectively. The techniques in this book are the outgrowth of our efforts to write applications programs in C and our development of course materials for seminars on C programming. Many people, therefore, contributed to the wealth of information we present, making this book very much a group project.

A major goal of our book is to present advanced techniques often shared by experienced C programmers but that have little or no documentation. Our approach to advanced C, by the way, is somewhat different than other books on the subject. Instead of showing you how to *port* techniques from other languages to C (like doubly linked lists, binary trees, and so forth), we *develop* techniques from parts of C that don't exist in the other languages. Although this makes some of our techniques not applicable to other languages, it doesn't make them any less valuable.

We assume you already know C and have written modest programs with the language and the library functions. Although we are primarily versed in UNIX and its derivatives (XENIX, Berkeley 4BSD, and others), we've tested all of our programs under two popular MS-DOS C compilers as well. By the way, our techniques should apply equally well to C compilers running under Microsoft's new operating system, OS/2. Specifically, we compiled every program in this book with the following systems, representing 16- and 32-bit integer sizes:

| | |
|---|---|
| UNIX Standard C Compiler | (AT&T PC 6300+, AMDAHL UTS) |
| Microport System V/AT | (IBM 286 PC/AT) |
| SCO XENIX 286 | (IBM 286 PC/AT) |
| SCO XENIX 386 | (COMPAQ 386) |
| Sun 3.4 OS C Compiler | (SUN 3/260 68020) |
| Microsoft C 5.0 under MS-DOS | (IBM 286 PC/AT) |
| Turbo C under MS-DOS | (IBM 286 PC/AT) |

We made every effort to write programs as portable as possible. If your compiler or machine is not a member of this list, the details of our discussions may differ but the concepts should still apply. At the least, our programs should perform satisfactorily with minor modifications. In any event, we encourage you to experiment with our techniques to see how they behave on your machine.

In situations where we discuss C compiler implementation, (*e.g.*, assembly code generation and stack frames), we use the INTEL architecture. This includes the 8086, 186, 286, and 386 processors. We chose this architecture because many of you probably have access to a machine based on one of these chips due to the proliferation of PC's in the marketplace. And besides, we are most familiar with these machines.

We have also included discussions of how the upcoming ANSI C standard impacts the techniques in this book. Most chapters contain footnotes where an ANSI C feature affects the discussion, and the appendices show you how several commercial C compilers are currently implementing features from the proposed standard. As of this writing, the standard has not been ratified, but "it's only a matter of time."

The book is divided into six chapters with five appendices. Each chapter is self-contained, so experienced C programmers can read only the sections of interest. At the end of each chapter is a set of exercises that augment the material. The appendices discuss specifics from each of the above compilers as they relate to the material from the chapters.

Chapter 1 is a refresher of the C language. Obviously this is not a comprehensive treatment (entire books exist on the subject), but this chapter provides the foundations for the techniques that the rest of the book develops. Experienced programmers, who will most likely want to skip over most of this material, may want to glance at the programs since many include advanced techniques.

Chapter 2 is C's run time environment, or what goes on "behind the screen" when a C program executes. Knowledge of the text, stack, data, and heap areas help determine how much memory a program requires as well as how efficiently you can write a program.

Chapter 3 merges the concepts of arrays and pointers. Here you'll find techniques to help you interpret pointer expressions, declare multidimensional arrays at run time, and increase program performance with pointers.

Chapter 4 takes a closer look at the C language. Topics like sequence guarantee points and the right-left rule help you work with C expressions more confidently. Fast array transfers, passing entire arrays to functions, and calling functions with a variable number of arguments give you more insight into how C works.

Chapter 5 shows you how to use C for debugging. Topics like command line flags, assertions, and selective debug prints are independent of a debugger and help you track down those "tough-to-find" bugs.

Chapter 6 contains the source code for a memory object allocator. C programs may use the allocator to dynamically allocate, resize, and deallocate objects from the heap.

The appendices organize information that you need to use the C language with many of the popular C compilers. The first three appendices discuss the AT&T Standard C, Microport System V, and SCO 286 and 386 C compilers under UNIX and XENIX, and the last two appendices cover Microsoft C 5.0 and Turbo C under DOS. If you're shopping for a C compiler, we hope you'll find the compiler flags in the appendices useful, since you can tell a lot about a C compiler from the options it provides. If you already own one of these compilers, having this information in one place should be handy. You'll also find discussions of ANSI C features and how our techniques work with the compilers in the appendices. A floppy disk with all of the programs from this book is available for a nominal charge, should you decide that typing them in is too arduous a task. A booklet and diskette with the exercise solutions are also available.

We hope you'll find the information in this book useful and informative. Good luck in your C travels.

Paul L. Anderson
Gail C. Anderson
Leucadia, California

*To our parents...*
  Jane and Charles H. Anderson
  Jean D. Campbell
*and in memory of...*
  Graham F. Campbell

Life is what happens to you
While you're busy
Making other plans . . . .

— John Lennon, *Double Fantasy*, 1980

# 1

# C Refresher

This chapter is a whirlwind tour of the C language. It's more of an advanced C warmup than a comprehensive treatment of the language. We assume you already have a working knowledge of C and have written C programs. The chapter addresses C's major topics and provides the groundwork for the techniques we show in subsequent chapters.

As you work through the techniques and example programs later in the book, you may refer to the tables and reference charts from this chapter. Our approach is *C by example*. The programs review the basics but show advanced techniques as well.

## ◆ Data Representation ◆

The C compiler manipulates data types. A program's variables and constant data have *attributes*, which include word length (in bits), data format (integer or floating point), and sign (positive or negative). Attributes affect how the C compiler passes parameters to functions and how it performs arithmetic and assignment conversions. The compiler assigns attributes to variables from program declarations, and to constant data from their use in program statements.

Word length is machine dependent, but popular machine architectures use 16 and 32 bits. Data formats have two forms: integer and floating point. Bit patterns for integers differ from floating point representations, and C supports several data types with different word lengths for each format. Integer formats (one's complement or two's complement) and floating point formats are machine dependent.

C also supports sign bits for integer variables and data. To elaborate, suppose we examine all of the possible data representations for eight bits.

```
     bit pattern              value

0 0 0 0 0 0 0 0                 0
0 0 0 0 0 0 0 1                 1
0 0 0 0 0 0 1 0                 2
0 0 0 0 0 0 1 1                 3
 .  .  .  .  .  .  .  .        .  .
1 1 1 1 1 1 0 0               252
1 1 1 1 1 1 0 1               253
1 1 1 1 1 1 1 0               254
1 1 1 1 1 1 1 1               255
```

The range spans a positive (*unsigned*) set of numbers between 0 and 255. Suppose, however, we rearrange the bit patterns, as follows.

```
     bit pattern              value

0 1 1 1 1 1 1 1               127
0 1 1 1 1 1 1 0               126
0 1 1 1 1 1 0 1               125
 .  .  .  .  .  .  .  .
0 0 0 0 0 0 1 1                 3
0 0 0 0 0 0 1 0                 2
0 0 0 0 0 0 0 1                 1

0 0 0 0 0 0 0 0                 0

1 1 1 1 1 1 1 1                -1
1 1 1 1 1 1 1 0                -2
1 1 1 1 1 1 0 1                -3
 .  .  .  .  .  .  .  .        .  .
1 0 0 0 0 0 1 0              -126
1 0 0 0 0 0 0 1              -127
1 0 0 0 0 0 0 0              -128
```

The pattern of all zeroes appears in the middle. Bit patterns whose leftmost bit (this is called the *most significant bit*) is 0 appear above the zero pattern. Each subsequent bit pattern is 1 more than the previous pattern as you move up through the table. Similarly, bit patterns whose leftmost bit is a 1 appear below the zero pattern. Starting with a pattern of all ones, each bit pattern is 1 less than the previous pattern as you move down through the table. Using two's complement notation, we can assign positive or negative values to each bit pattern.

If you interpret the most significant bit as a sign bit, each pattern becomes a signed quantity. Patterns above the zero pattern are positive items, and those below are negative. This arrangement allows the compiler to interpret bits as signed data. Note, however, the allowable range for positive numbers decreases since one bit of the eight is now being used to store the sign. For 8 bits, therefore, the range of positive values is only 0 to 127. This same notation applies to 16 bits and more.

C's basic data types are char, int, float, and double. Each size is machine dependent, but typical machines use 8 bits for a char, 32 bits for a float, and 64 bits for a double. The size of an int reflects the word size of the machine and is typically 16 or 32 bits.

C provides long, short, and unsigned qualifiers for integer data types. A long is usually twice the size of an int on 16-bit machines, but long's and int's are often the same length for 32 bits and more. Going the other way, a short is half the size of an int on 32-bit machines, and short's are typically the same length on 16-bit machines. unsigned treats the most significant bit as a data bit and applies to char, int, short, and long data types. C integer data types are signed by default.†

# ♦ Functions ♦

C programs are lists of function declarations. Execution starts at main(). C doesn't allow you to declare a function inside another function, and there are two basic function usage rules to remember:

1. The compiler does *not* convert function parameters from floating point to integer and vice versa.

2. If a function returns a data type other than an integer, you must inform the compiler of the return data type *before* you call it.

The following three programs show the importance of the two rules.

**Program 1-1**

```
/* sqrt1.c - parameters passed to functions - incorrect */

main()
{
    printf("%.8g\n", sqrt(25));
}
```

```
$ sqrt1
g
```

---

† ANSI C supports a long double data type and void is a basic data type. ANSI C also allows you to explicitly declare data types as signed (signed char, for instance).

**Program 1-2**

```
/* sqrt2.c - parameters passed to functions - incorrect */

main()
{
    printf("%.8g\n", sqrt(25.));
}
```

$ **sqrt2**
1.1561338e-05

**Program 1-3**

```
/* sqrt3.c - parameters passed to functions - correct */

#include <math.h>

main()
{
    printf("%.8g\n", sqrt(25.));
}
```

$ **sqrt3**
5

Each program requires the -lm command line option to link the C library math function sqrt() with main().† sqrt() returns a double and expects a double for an argument. Each program attempts to calculate the square root of 25. sqrt3.c is the only one to display the correct answer, because the first two violate the rules for C functions. sqrt1.c, for example, passes an integer constant to sqrt(). C does not convert the integer to floating point; hence, the compiler generates assembly code which interprets the integer bit pattern as a floating point number. This produces a meaningless result.

sqrt2.c passes a valid floating point bit pattern (25.) to sqrt(). The return value from sqrt(), however, is interpreted incorrectly because the compiler generates assembly code for an int instead of a double. The program should tell the compiler that sqrt() returns a double before it is used. Otherwise, the compiler passes an integer to printf(), which displays a meaningless value.

sqrt3.c uses the include file <math.h> to provide the correct function return type for the compiler. Inside this file is the definition

---

† For example, sqrt1.c was compiled as follows:
    $ cc sqrt1.c -o sqrt1 -lm

```
double sqrt()
```

which informs the compiler that `sqrt()` returns a double. Note that it's not necessary to include `sqrt()`'s argument in the definition.

C function declarations have the following format:

```
retype func(arg1, arg2, . . .)
type arg1;
type arg2;
. . . .
{
     local declarations;
     . . . .
     return statements;
}
```

`retype` (the function's return data type) is optional. Without it, the compiler assumes `func` returns an integer. Otherwise, `retype` is any C data type or the keyword `void`. The use of `void` in a function declaration, by the way, makes the compiler report an error if the function's return value is used in an expression. The arguments `arg1, arg2, ...` are optional and if a function has no arguments, the lines

```
type arg1;
type arg2;
. . . .
```

may be omitted for function parameter data types.†

Local declarations and return statements appear inside a function block, delimited by braces. *Local declarations* are optional, and their scope is confined to the function block where they are declared. *Return statements* are also optional and have the following formats:

```
return;
return expr;
return (expr);
```

There is an implicit return at the end of every function block.

C allows you to omit type declarations for function parameters, in which case the compiler assumes the parameters are integers. With some compilers, you'll have to be careful with the following:

---

† The ANSI C Standard provides *function prototypes* that perform type checking of function parameters. For more information, see Appendices D and E.

```
long timer(count)
{
long count;
    . . .
}
```

Function `timer()` returns a `long` and expects a `long` argument. By mistake, we switch the first two lines after the function definition, which is not difficult to do if you're in a hurry. The compiler assumes the function parameter `count` is an integer. The line with `long count` becomes a local declaration. The mistake is particularly annoying, because `timer()` cannot access its own argument! `count` (which is a `long`) has a separate memory location from the function parameter (which is an `int`).

C also allows you to call functions with a variable number of arguments. We examine this technique in Chapter 4.

## ◆ Operators and Expressions ◆

This section reviews C's building blocks for programs. We present operators and expressions first, followed by control flow constructs.

As we discuss C operators, we'll use the term *operand*. Many operators have restrictions that apply to an operand's data type. An operator has at least one operand. We group most of the operators into separate tables according to their precedence, or order of evaluation. A precedence table for all C operators appears at the end of the chapter (Table 1-7).

### Arithmetic Operators

Let's begin with the C arithmetic operators from Table 1-1.

**TABLE 1-1. Arithmetic operators**

| Operator | Meaning | Example |
|----------|---------|---------|
| – | unary minus | –x |
| * | multiplication | x * y |
| / | division | x / y |
| % | modulus | x % y |
| + | addition | x + y |
| – | subtraction | x – y |

The compiler generates assembly code for integer or floating point arithmetic based on conversion rules. Floating point arithmetic is normally done in double precision. `char` and `short` promote automatically to `int`. `float` promotes to `double`. Arithmetic expressions have two operands, and C converts an operand to a `double` if the other one is a `double`, making the result a `double`. C handles operands with `long` and `unsigned` in the same way. The mod operator (%) does not apply to `floats` or `doubles`.

Refer to Table 1-7 for operator precedence. Addition and subtraction have lower precedence than the other arithmetic operators. With an expression containing operators at the same precedence level (*e.g.*, multiplication and division), Table 1-7 shows the order of evaluation. Arithmetic operators, for example, evaluate left to right. This implies that the expression

```
40 / 4 * 5
```

evaluates to 50 and not 2.

Arithmetic operators are legal with character data. Suppose c, for example, contains an ASCII character between '0' and '9'. The following statements

```
char c;
int digit;
. . . .
digit = c - '0';
```

convert the character to a decimal digit without calling a conversion function.

## Relational Operators

Table 1-2 lists C's relational operators.

**TABLE 1-2. Relational operators**

| Operator | Meaning | Example |
|----------|---------|---------|
| < | less than | x < y |
| <= | less than or equal to | x <= y |
| > | greater than | x > y |
| >= | greater than or equal to | x >= y |
| == | equals | x == y |
| != | not equals | x != y |

These six operators produce a zero result if logically FALSE, and a nonzero result if logically TRUE. Equals (==) and not equals (!=) have lower precedence than the other four.

Note that relational operators that compare character pointers with constant strings do not produce valid results. Suppose, for example, `p` is a pointer to a character. The declaration

```
char *p = "string";
```

assigns the address of `"string"` to the character pointer `p`. The expression

```
p == "string"
```

attempts to compare `p` to the address of `"string"`. The compiler, however, may allocate memory for a separate copy of the same constant string at a different address to perform the comparison. (See Chapter 2 for a discussion of constant strings.) Hence, the expression never evaluates to TRUE.

The C library function `strcmp()` compares character strings. `strcmp()` returns 0 if two strings are the same. Hence, the expression

```
strcmp(p, "string") == 0
```

is TRUE (nonzero) if `p` points to `"string"`.

## Logical Operators

Table 1-3 lists the C logical operators.

**TABLE 1-3. Logical operators**

| Operator | Meaning | Example |
|----------|-------------|--------------------|
| ! | logical NOT | !x |
| && | logical AND | x >= 3 && y <= 5 |
| \|\| | logical OR | x == 3 \|\| y == 5 |

`!` has higher precedence than the other two and converts a nonzero result (TRUE) to zero (FALSE), and a zero result (FALSE) to 1 (TRUE). `&&` evaluates before `||`, which eliminates extra parentheses from some expressions. For example,

```
c >= '0' && c <= '9' || c >= 'a' && c <= 'f' ||
      c >= 'A' && c <= 'F'
```

evaluates to TRUE if a character variable `c` is a hexadecimal character. With subexpressions separated by logical operators, as in the following,

```
expr1 && expr2
expr1 || expr2
```

`&&` and `||` always evaluate left to right. For `&&`, C guarantees that `expr2` evaluates only if `expr1` is TRUE. Similarly, `expr2` evaluates only if `expr1` is FALSE for `||`.

## Bitwise Operators

Table 1-4 lists C's bitwise operators.

**TABLE 1-4.  Bitwise operators**

| Operator | Meaning | Example |
|----------|---------|---------|
| ~ | one's complement | ~x |
| << | left shift | x << n |
| >> | right shift | x >> n |
| & | bitwise AND | x & 3 |
| ^ | bitwise Exclusive-OR | x ^ 3 |
| \| | bitwise OR | x \| 3 |

These operators manipulate bits (1 or 0). With the exception of `~`, which inverts all bits from 1 to 0 and 0 to 1, each operator requires two operands. `&` (bitwise AND), for example, operates on two operands a bit at a time. The result is a new integer where each bit is a 0 unless both corresponding bits of its operands are 1. Likewise, `|` (bitwise OR) produces a 1 unless both corresponding bits of its operands are 0. `^` (bitwise Exclusive-OR) is like `|` (bitwise OR), except that it produces a 0 if both corresponding bits of its operands are 1.

`<<` and `>>` shift bits left and right, respectively. The left operand shifts by the number of bits specified by the right operand. Left shifts fill vacated bits with zero. Right shifts fill with zeroes if the left operand is unsigned; otherwise, the result may not be portable. (Some machines shift the sign bit, an *arithmetic* shift, and others shift zero bits, a *logical* shift.)

C's bitwise operators provide alternatives to assembly language routines for manipulating bits. Although C doesn't provide operators to *rotate* bits, we can write our own functions to rotate integers using the bitwise operators. The following program called `rotate.c`, for example, prompts for a hexadecimal integer and displays the result after we rotate the bits. Here's the program and the output on a 16-bit machine.

**Program 1-4**

```
/* rotate.c - integer rotations */

#include <stdio.h>

#define WORDSIZE sizeof(unsigned int) * 8

unsigned int rol(), ror();

main()
{
    unsigned int num;

    printf("Input a hex integer: ");
    scanf("%x", &num);

    printf("rotate left 8 bits = %x\n", rol(num, 8));
    printf("rotate right 4 bits = %x\n", ror(num, 4));
}

unsigned int rol(word, n)        /* rotate left */
unsigned int word, n;
{
    return word << n | (word >> WORDSIZE - n);
}

unsigned int ror(word, n)        /* rotate right */
unsigned int word, n;
{
    return word >> n | (word << WORDSIZE - n);
}
```

```
$ rotate
Input a hex integer: abcd
rotate left 8 bits = cdab
rotate right 4 bits = dabc
```

rol() rotates bits left and ror() rotates bits right. Using the sizeof() operator, a #define sets WORDSIZE to the number of bits in an unsigned int (usually 16 or 32). Function parameters are unsigned int's, and both functions return an unsigned int result. Neither routine modifies the original value, and we include the parentheses in each return statement for clarity, since precedence rules do not require them. Shift counts larger than the number of bits in an unsigned int make rotate.c produce meaningless results, but it's straightforward to add these checks (see Exercise 1).

## Assignment Operators

Table 1-5 lists C's assignment operators.

**TABLE 1-5. Assignment operators**

| Operator | Meaning | Example |
|----------|---------|---------|
| = | assignment | x = 7 |
| += | addition update | x += 7 |
| -= | subtraction update | x -= 7 |
| *= | multiplication update | x *= 7 |
| /= | division update | x /= 7 |
| %= | modulus update | x %= 7 |
| <<= | left shift update | x <<= 7 |
| >>= | right shift update | x >>= 7 |
| &= | bitwise AND update | x &= 7 |
| \|= | bitwise OR update | x \|= 7 |
| ^= | bitwise XOR update | x ^= 7 |

Assignment operators have low precedence. Simple assignment (=) evaluates right to left, making expressions like

```
x = y = z = 1;
```

convenient. The remaining operators are compressed forms of assignment updates. That is, `x >>= 7` is the same as `x = x >> 7`, which updates `x`.

The following program uses a bitwise Exclusive-OR operator with an assignment update (^=).

**Program 1-5**

```
/* swap.c - interchange two integers with Exclusive-OR */

#include <stdio.h>

main()
{
    int a = 3, b = 4;

    a ^= b;
    b ^= a;
    a ^= b;

    printf("a = %d  b = %d\n", a, b);
}
```

```
$ swap
a = 4   b = 3
```

The program swaps two integers without a temporary variable.

## Conditional Operator

The conditional operator has the following format:

```
expression1 ? expression2 : expression3
```

If *expression1* evaluates to nonzero, *expression2* evaluates; otherwise, *expression3* evaluates.  Conditional operators may be nested.

Suppose, for example  c is a character with values in the ASCII ranges ′0′ to ′9′ and ′a′ to ′f′.  The following expression converts  c to a decimal number with a conditional operator.

```
c >= ′0′ && c <= ′9′ ? c - ′0′ : c - (′a′ - 10)
```

If  c is between ′0′ and ′9′ inclusive, the expression evaluates to a decimal number between 0 and 9.  Otherwise, the expression evaluates to a decimal number between 10 and 15. This type of expression is useful in function parameters,  return statements, and macros.

## Increment and Decrement Operators

Table 1-6 lists C's increment and decrement operators.

**TABLE 1-6.  Increment and decrement operators**

| Operator | Meaning | Example |
|---|---|---|
| ++ | pre increment | ++x |
| | post increment | x++ |
| -- | pre decrement | --x |
| | post decrement | x-- |

Both operators expect single operands.    ++ increments its operand by one, and -- decrements it by one.  When the operand increments (or decrements) depends on which side of the operand you place the operator.  For example,

++x increments x before it's used in an expression, whereas x-- decrements x after it's used. Increment and decrement operators are useful in for statements and with pointers inside loops.

The following expression, for example, performs two operations in one inside a loop.

```
a[++i]
```

The expression updates i before referencing an array element. This format eliminates a separate statement to increment i before the array reference.

# ♦ Control Flow Constructs ♦

Semicolons terminate C statements. C allows null statements (*i.e.*, a semicolon with nothing else). Braces form program *blocks* and variable declarations are optional at the start of a block. A variable's scope is defined only within the block where it is declared.

## if and if-else

if statements have three formats. The first format is

```
if (expression) {
    statements;
}
```

*Expression* requires parentheses. If *expression* evaluates to nonzero, one or more *statements* execute; otherwise, the next statement following the if executes. Braces are optional if there is one statement.

The second format is

```
if (expression) {
    statements1;
}
else {
    statements2;
}
```

If *expression* evaluates to nonzero, *statements1* execute; otherwise *statements2* execute. Braces are optional for single statement blocks.

The last format is

```
if (expression1) {
    statements1;
}
else if (expression2) {
    statements2;
}
. . . .
else {
    statements3;
}
```

`else-if`'s may nest. The last `else` is optional and executes only if all previous expressions fail. An `else` associates with the nearest `if` which does not contain an `else`. Braces may override the association, if necessary.

Suppose, for example, `c` is a character that takes on hexadecimal values in the ASCII ranges `'0'` to `'9'`, `'a'` to `'f'`, and `'A'` to `'F'`. The following `if-else` converts `c` to a decimal number and displays the result.

```
if (c >= '0' && c <= '9')
    printf("%d\n", c - '0');
else if (c >= 'a' && c <= 'f')
    printf("%d\n", c - ('a' - 10));
else if (c >= 'A' && c <= 'F')
    printf("%d\n", c - ('A' - 10));
else
    printf("Invalid hex char\n");
```

If `c` is `'8'` the program displays `8` and if `c` is `'e'` or `'E'` the program displays `14`, and so on. If `c` is not in the allowable range, the program displays an error message. Note that in time-critical code, you should pay attention to the order of expressions that evaluate with an `if-else`. If you know, for example, that certain conditions appear more often than others, place them near the beginning of an `if-else`.

## while

The format for a `while` is

```
while (expression) {
    statements;
}
```

*Statements* execute if *expression* evaluates to nonzero. The code evaluates *expression* each time at the beginning of the block. It's possible to not execute *statements* if *expression* evaluates to zero when the block is first executed, and braces are optional for a single statement.

Suppose c is an integer. The following while loop does all the work in the expression rather than the body of the loop.

```
while ((c = getchar()) != ' ' && c != '\t' && c != '\n' && c != EOF)
    ;
```

The code skips input characters until it encounters white space (a space, tab, or newline) or the end of file.

## do while

The format for a do while is

```
do {
    statements;
} while (expression);
```

*Statements* execute if *expression* evaluates to nonzero. The code evaluates *expression* each time at the end of the block. *Statements* always execute at least once. Braces are optional for a single statement.

do while statements are useful when you need to prompt for input or access data and repeat the process if necessary. Suppose, for example, c is an integer. The following do while loop continues to prompt politely for a digit until you get it right.

```
do {
    printf("Please input a digit: ");
    c = getchar();
} while ((c < '0' || c > '9') && c != EOF);
```

## for

The format for a for statement is the following:

```
for (expression1; expression2; expression3) {
    statements;
}
```

However, it's better visualized as a while:

```
expression1;
while (expression2) {
    statements;
    expression3;
}
```

*Expression1* evaluates only once. If *expression2* evaluates to nonzero, *statements* execute; otherwise, the loop exits. *Expression3* does not execute until *statements*, if any, complete. *expression2* usually contains a relational operator. *expression1*, *expression2*, and *expression3* are all optional.

for statements are useful for looping through arrays and maintaining counts, but they have other applications as well. The following program, for example, performs integer to hexadecimal conversion with a for loop.

**Program 1-6**

```
/* itoh1.c - integer to hex conversion */

#include <stdio.h>

main()
{
    unsigned int num, d, i = 0;
    char buf[10];

    printf("Input a number: ");
    scanf("%u", &num);

    for (; num; num /= 16) {
        d = num % 16;          /* next digit */
        buf[i++] = (d <= 9) ? d + '0' : d + 'a' - 10;
    }

    while (i)                  /* output hex chars backwards */
        putchar(buf[--i]);
    putchar('\n');
}
```

```
$ itoh1
Input a number: 23456
5ba0
```

The for loop divides num by 16 using a division update (/=) after the modulus operator (%) extracts the rightmost digit. The for loop exits when num becomes zero. The program uses a while to loop backwards and display hexadecimal digits from buf.

C allows the *comma operator* (,) in any expression. Comma operators are useful inside `for` statements. The following code, for example, initializes integers `i` and `j` and increments them each time through a `for` loop.

```
for (i = 1, j = 2; i * j < MAX; i++, j++)
```

## switch

The format for a `switch` is

```
switch (expression) {
    case constant1:
        statements;
        break;
    case constant2:
        statements;
        break;
    . . . . . . .
    default:
        statements;
        break;
}
```

*Constant1*, *constant2*, etc. are constant integer expressions. C allows operators inside constant integer expressions, but they must evaluate to integer constants at compile time. Variables and noninteger data types produce compilation errors.

The compiler evaluates *expression* and compares it to the constant integer expressions. There can be at most one match, whereupon the corresponding *statements* execute. Omitting `break` makes execution fall through to the next `case` statement. The keyword `default` is optional, and its statements execute if none of the other `case` expressions match. `case` and `default` statements may be in any order inside a `switch`.

The following code demonstrates a `switch`. Suppose we name primary colors with preprocessor defines as follows:

```
#define RED     1
#define YELLOW  2
#define BLUE    4
```

If `color` is an integer between 0 and 7 inclusive, the following `switch` statement displays color names.

```
switch (color) {
  case RED:
      printf("red\n");
      break;
  case YELLOW:
      printf("yellow\n");
      break;
  case BLUE:
      printf("blue\n");
      break;
  case RED + YELLOW:
      printf("orange\n");
      break;
  case BLUE + YELLOW:
      printf("green\n");
      break;
  case BLUE + RED:
      printf("violet\n");
      break;
  case RED + BLUE + YELLOW:
      printf("black\n");
      break;
  default:
      printf("white\n");
      break;
}
```

The + operators inside case statements distinguish the color black and the secondary color names (orange, green, and violet) from the primary colors (red, yellow, and blue). Note that it's legal to use operators here as long as they evaluate to constant expressions.

The implementation of switch statements is compiler dependent. C compilers generate assembly code based on the number of cases in a switch and the values of the case labels. If the number of cases is small, many compilers treat a switch like a nested if statement. If the number of cases is large, however, the compiler may take two approaches, depending on the values of the case labels. Suppose, for example, the case labels are "sparse" (20, 40, 60, etc.). In this situation, the compiler may generate a series of *value-address* pairs that are searched during the execution of a switch. If, on the other hand, case labels are not "sparse" (0, 1, 2, ..., 15, for instance) the compiler may produce a *jump table*. In assembly code, the switch expression becomes a base address and *case* labels are offsets (integers). A "jump" instruction in assembly code transfers execution to the *case* statement that matches.

These approaches help explain why C demands unique constant integer expressions in *case* statements. It also means you should investigate the assembly code that your compiler generates for a switch when you write time-critical programs. With a jump table, for instance, the execution time to "branch" to any `case` statement is the same. Contrast this to an `if-else` construct, where execution times depend on the number of expressions to evaluate. `switch` statements, therefore, may be a viable alternative to `if-else` statements when there are many cases in time-critical programs.

## break and continue

The `break` and `continue` statements appear inside loops and `switch` statements. `break` terminates control flow prematurely, and `continue` statements cause the next loop iteration to execute immediately. Both constructs affect only the innermost loop.

Suppose `choice` is an integer. The following loop handles screen menu selections.

```
for (;;) {
    printf("Selection: ");
    if ((choice = getchar()) == 'q')          /* quit? */
        break;
    menu(choice);
}
```

The program uses an infinite `for` loop. If the user types 'q' after the prompt, `break` terminates the loop. Otherwise, the program calls `menu()` to process a selection.

The following `for` loop uses a `continue` statement inside a `switch`.

```
for (nchars = 0; ;) {
    printf("Input a char: ");
    switch (getchar()) {
        case '\033':      /* ESC */
            continue;
        case '\n':        /* newline */
            break;
        . . . .
    }
    nchars++;             /* increment character count */
    . . . .
}
```

The loop increments `nchars` unless the input is an escape character (ESC). `continue` makes the `for` loop input another character instead of including it in the character count. Note that in this example, `break` is a part of the `switch` statement and not the `for` loop.

Most algorithms don't require `break` and `continue` statements (a `do while`, for example, eliminates `break` from our screen menu example). For loops that have a large number of statements, `break` and `continue` provide worthwhile alternatives to setting flags and testing their values.

## goto

The format for a `goto` is

```
goto label;
```

`goto` is one word. The *label* must appear in the same function as the `goto`, and has the format

```
label:     statements
```

Structured programming dictates prudent use of `goto` statements, since they tend to obscure the logical flow of programs. Perhaps a worthwhile application for a `goto` is inside deeply nested loops where error checking and quick response is mandatory. The following function called `servo()`, for example, shows you how to transfer control to a single entry point from different places in the same function to handle an error condition.

```
servo()
{
. . . .
while (. . . .) {
    if (error) goto stop;
    for (. . . .) {
        if (error) goto stop;
        while (. . . .) {
            if (error) goto stop;
            . . . .
            goto stop;
. . . .
stop:
        /* handle error condition */
}
```

Without a `goto`, `servo()` must set flags and test them inside each loop. A `goto` transfers control quickly to statements in `servo()` that handles the error condition. Arguably, there is a trade-off between handling time-critical error conditions and unstructured program flow. Jumps between functions are also possible and desirable for the same reasons. See Chapter 2 for a discussion of nonlocal control transfers using `setjmp()` and `longjmp()`.

# ◆ Arrays and Pointers ◆

This section reviews the basics of arrays and pointers. We present single and multidimensional arrays first, followed by pointer concepts.

## Single Dimension Arrays

The format for declaring a single dimension array is

```
type name[size] = { initialization list };
```

*Type* is a C data type. Square brackets surround *size*, which is the number of elements in the array. *Initialization list* sets array elements to specific values and is optional. The number of values in the initialization list may be less than *size*, but not more. *Size* is optional if you include *initialization list* and explicitly initialize all values. You must use the keyword `static` before *type* if you initialize an array inside a function. †

Single dimension array references have the format

```
name[expression]
```

*Expression* must be an integer expression. Array subscripts start at 0 and end at one less than the number of elements in the array.

The following declarations are examples of single dimension arrays.

```
char buf[80];
char greeting[] = { 'h', 'e', 'l', 'l', 'o', '\0' };
float parms[5] = { 6.23, 18.5, -4.7, .722, 1.6 };
long terms[10] = { 6, 8, 10 };
```

`buf` is an 80-character array. `greeting` is a 6-character array containing the string `"hello"` (including a NULL byte). C provides an easier way, however, to initialize character arrays with

```
char greeting[] = "hello";
```

Here the compiler automatically includes the NULL string terminator. `parms` is an array of 5 floats, initialized to five floating point constants. `terms` is an array of longs. Only the first three elements have specified values.

---

† This is no longer true in ANSI C, but many compilers still require it.

## Multidimensional Arrays

C views a multidimensional array as a one dimensional array whose elements are arrays. The format for a multidimensional array is

```
type name[size1][size2] ... [sizen] = { initialization list };
```

Square brackets surround each size. *Initialization list* is optional and may contain inner braces. Multidimensional array references have the format

```
name[expression][expression]. . .[expression]
```

Each *expression* references an array subscript and must be an integer expression. The range of array subscripts follows the same rules as single dimensional array references. We'll have a lot more to say about multidimensional arrays in Chapter 3.

## Pointer Concepts

A pointer is a variable that contains an address in memory. Addresses are used to reference objects; thus, pointers provide an indirect access mechanism. Pointer declarations use * and have the format

```
type *pname;
```

for a pointer to C data types, and the format

```
type *parray[size1][size2] ... ;
```

for arrays of pointers. Pointers should contain valid addresses before expressions use them, and the compiler requires a data type for pointer operations. The declaration

```
char *p = "databytes";
```

for example, creates a pointer to a character (p) and initializes it to point to the first character in the string "databytes".

Pointers use the *indirection* operator (*) to access objects. *p from above, for example, produces the character 'd'. Pointers may be NULL, or they may point to the same address as another pointer of the same data type. Pointers typically have the same word length as integers, but you should never write code that relies on this. On the INTEL 286, for example, far pointers are 32 bits and integers are 16 bits.

The declarations

```
int i = 3;
int *p = &i;
```

use the *address* operator (&) to initialize  p  to the address of the integer  i. Pointer concepts extend to pointers to *pointers* as well.  In the following declarations

```
int i = 3;
int *p = &i;
int **q = &p;
```

for example,  q points to  p, which points to  i.  *p yields an integer.    *q, however, produces a pointer to an integer, and  **q yields an integer.

## Pointers as Function Arguments

The following program calls  xchg()  to swap two integers in memory.  The function uses pointers and the assignment operator (^=).

**Program 1-7**

```
/* xchg.c - exchange two integers with a function */

#include <stdio.h>

main()
{
    int a = 45, b = 53;

    xchg(&a, &b);   /* pass pointers to a, b */

    printf("a = %d  b = %d\n", a, b);
}

xchg(pa, pb)            /* exchange integers using pointers */
int *pa, *pb;
{
    *pa ^= *pb;
    *pb ^= *pa;
    *pa ^= *pb;
}

$ xchg
a = 53  b = 45
```

main() uses  &  to pass the addresses of  a and  b to  xchg(), respectively. Inside  xchg(),  pa points to  a and  pb points to  b.  The output shows the function swaps the integers in memory.

## Command Line Arguments

C allows programs to access command line arguments with arrays and pointers using the following format:

```
main(argc, argv)
int argc;
char *argv[];
```

The first argument is the number of command line arguments (including the command name), and the second argument is a pointer to an array of character pointers to each argument. By convention, these names are `argc` and `argv`, respectively.

Suppose, for example, `com.c` takes one argument with two valid options (-b and -s). The command line

```
$ com -b
```

sets `argc` to 2. The array pointed to by `argv` contains pointers to each argument. `argv[0]` points to "com" and `argv[1]` to "-b". `argv` allows programs to access arguments by their names or by individual characters.†

The following code determines `com.c`'s options and checks for errors.

```
if (argc != 2) {
   fprintf(stderr, "Usage: %s -[bs]\n", argv[0]);
   exit(1);
}
switch (argv[1][0]) {
   case '-':
      switch (argv[1][1]) {
         case 'b':
            printf("-b option\n");
            break;
         case 's':
            printf("-s option\n");
            break;
         default:
            fprintf(stderr, "%s: illegal option\n", argv[0]);
            exit(1);
      }
      break;
   default:
      fprintf(stderr, "%s: no option specified\n", argv[0]);
      exit(1);
}
```

---

† ANSI C requires `argv[argc]` to be a NULL pointer. This provides a redundant check for the end of the argument list.

If `argc` is not 2, the program displays a usage message and terminates. Otherwise, two `switch` statements process the options. `argv[1][0]` is the first character of the second command line argument. The first `switch` verifies the character is `'-'`; otherwise, the program displays an error message and exits. The program uses `argv[1][1]` in the second `switch` statement to access the second character of the second command line argument. The program displays correct options and prints error messages for incorrect ones.

Note that the program writes error messages to standard error with `argv[0]` in place of the program name. This is a good idea if you pipe a C program's output. For example, the command

```
$ com -x | sort -b
com: illegal option
```

makes `sort` take its input from `com`. `sort` won't process error messages because they appear on standard error. Furthermore, error messages contain the command name (`com`), which identifies which program the error belongs to. The technique also allows you to change the program name without modifying error messages.

## ♦ Structures and Unions ♦

Structures allow members of different data types to become one object. Unions are like structures, but members overlay memory and the same data can have different data types. C provides special operators to access members of structures and unions.

### Structures

Structures have four formats and members may have arbitrary data types (including structures themselves). In the following examples, we look at a structure that contains two elements: an array of integers and a pointer to a character.

The first format is commonly called a *template* and is useful in header files.

```
struct block {
    int buf[80];
    char *pheap;
};
```

The compiler does not allocate storage for the structure template `block` because there is no variable name following the right brace.

The second structure format is of the form

```
struct block data = { initialization list };
```

The compiler allocates storage for variable `data`. The structure template `block` must be previously defined. The *initialization list* is optional. The keyword `static` must precede `struct` if you initialize a structure inside a function.† Arrays of structures are possible.

The third format

```
struct block {
    int buf[80];
    char *pheap;
} data = { initialization list };
```

is a combination of the first two, and the fourth format

```
struct {
    int buf[80];
    char *pheap;
} data = { initialization list };
```

omits the template name.

C has two operators for structures. The `.` operator provides a mechanism to reference structure members with a structure name. `data.pheap`, for example, is a pointer to a character. C also allows pointers to structures. For example, the declaration

```
struct block *ps = data;
```

makes `ps` point to structure `data`. C provides the `->` operator to access structure members with a structure pointer. `ps->buf[5]`, for example, evaluates to an integer. Arrays of structure pointers are also possible.

## Unions

Unions have the same formats and operators as structures. Unlike structures, which reserve separate chunks of memory for each member, unions allocate only enough memory to accommodate the *largest* member. On 16-bit and 32-bit machines, for example, the declaration

```
union jack {
    long data;
    char a[4];
} chunk;
```

---

† As with the initialization of automatic arrays, this is no longer true in ANSI C, but many compilers still require it.

allocates only 4 bytes of storage.    `chunk.data` is a `long` and `chunk.a[2]` is a `char`.

C allows pointers to unions, but you may not initialize unions.† Maintaining data integrity for union members is the programmer's responsibility.

The following program is a second version of integer to hexadecimal conversion.

**Program 1-8**

```
/* itoh2.c - integer to hex conversion with unions -
   not portable */

#include <stdio.h>

main()
{
   union {
      unsigned short num;       /* 16 bit integer */
      unsigned char s[2];       /* array of hex chars */
   } val;

   char *p = "0123456789abcdef";

   printf("Input a number: ");
   scanf("%hd", &val.num);    /* input as a short */

   /* high byte */
      putchar(p[val.s[1] >> 4]);
      putchar(p[val.s[1] & 15]);

   /* low byte */
      putchar(p[val.s[0] >> 4]);
      putchar(p[val.s[0] & 15]);

      putchar('\n');
}

$ itoh2
Input a number: 23456
5ba0
```

`itoh2.c` uses a union to manipulate bits as two different data types. The program stores keyboard input into memory as an `unsigned short` (assuming a `short` is 16 bits) and uses the same memory as a character array to convert high

---

† The ANSI C standard allows programs to initialize the *first* member of a union. Many current C compilers already provide this capability.

and low bytes. Right shifts produce the leftmost 4 bits of each byte, and bitwise &'s deliver the rightmost 4 bits. The result (an integer between 0 and 15) is a subscript for p, which points to a string of 16 hexadecimal characters. putchar()'s display each character.

Unions make itoh2.c execute faster than itoh1.c (from a previous section). itoh2.c has no loops and uses bitwise operators, while itoh1.c includes arithmetic operators for the conversion and two loops to store and display the data. This technique, on the other hand, is not portable because some machines store bytes in memory differently than others. In fact, we ran itoh2.c on an INTEL 286 machine to show you the result, but the same program displays the bytes in *reverse* order (a05b) on a Motorola 68020 machine. Using the preprocessor, we show you how to make the program portable in a later section.

## ◆ Storage Classes ◆

C has storage classes in addition to data types. This section reviews auto, static, register, and extern.

### auto

auto (short for *automatic*) is the default storage class in C. Statements like

```
auto int i, j;
```

compile in C, but auto is optional. Automatic declarations appear inside functions and blocks.

Automatic variables have undefined initial values by default, and their scope applies only to the block in which they are declared. The following program, for example, creates four uninitialized automatic variables with different data types.

```
main()
{
    int i;
    float f;
    char buf[80];
    struct complex {
        float imag, real;
    } val;
    . . . .
}
```

Auto declarations may appear anywhere a block is legal in C. The following statements

```
if (i > MAX) {
   char buf[80];
   . . . .
}
. . . .
while (i++ < MAX) {
   char buf[80];
   . . . .
}
```

for example, declare two automatic character arrays with the same name (buf). Each array has its own separate memory location, and the scope of each one is limited to its own block.　auto variables inside functions do not retain their values the next time a program calls the function.

Before a program uses an automatic variable's value, it should have an initial value. Declarations may initialize automatic variables, including arrays and structures if you have an ANSI C compiler.

## static

The storage class static provides a way to retain a variable's value throughout program execution. A static variable has value zero before a program starts running if a program does not explicitly initialize it. C allows two types of static variables. A variable is *internal static* when you declare it inside a block with the keyword static. The following function called readf(), for example, uses a static variable as a flag.

```
readf()
{
   static int once = 1;       /* set flag */

   if (once) {
      once = 0;                /* reset flag */
      openfiles();
   }
   . . . .
}
```

readf() declares once static and initializes it to 1. The first time a program calls readf(), the function resets the flag and calls openfiles(). Subsequent readf()'s do not call openfiles() because once retains its value between calls. If once were auto this scheme wouldn't work, since the flag would reset to 1 every time a program calls readf().

Note that the static storage class does not affect a variable's scope. In readf(), once is unknown outside the function, even though its value is retained between function calls.

Internal statics also allow initialization of arrays and structures that are declared within blocks. The statements

```
{
    static char buf[] = "fountain";
    static struct complex {
        float real, imag;
    } val = { 2.3, 1.7 };
    . . . .
}
```

for example, initialize an array `buf` and a structure `val` inside a block. `buf` contains the string `"fountain"` and `val` contains the floating point numbers 2.3 and 1.7, organized as a structure of template `complex`.

The second type of static variable (called *external static*) applies to variables and functions. External statics appear outside blocks with the keyword `static` in front of the declaration. For example, the statements

```
static cling;          /* local to this file */
long fellow;           /* known to another file */

f ()                   /* known to another file */
{
    . . . .
}

static g()             /* local to this file */
{
    . . . .
}
```

make the integer `cling` and the function `g()` external static. `cling` and `g()` have scope only inside this file. Other files can't reference `cling` or call `g()`.

The opposite occurs if you omit the keyword `static`. A program in another file, for example, may reference `fellow` or call function `f()`.

Note that external statics make declarations local (we call this *private*), whereas declarations outside blocks and without the keyword `static` are global (we call this *public*). This often confuses newcomers to C. In a large software system with many modules, you may have to choose which variables and functions are public and which are private. It's good practice to name all functions and (nonlocal) variables `static` unless you intend on making them accessible to other compilation modules. This prevents unintended name conflicts when linking program modules written by different programmers.

The preprocessor helps carry this philosophy a step further. Suppose we create a header file called defs.h containing the following definitions:

```
$ cat defs.h
#define PRIVATE static
#define PUBLIC
```

We use PRIVATE for external statics and PUBLIC to share variables and functions between modules. If we include this header file in our previous program, here's what it would look like with the new definitions:

```
#include "defs.h"
 .  .  .  .

PRIVATE cling;
PUBLIC long fellow;

PUBLIC f()
{
 .  .  .  .
}

PRIVATE g()
{
 .  .  .  .
}
```

The labels PRIVATE and PUBLIC aid in documenting the use of a variable or function in a program. This makes the meaning and intentions clearer to someone who didn't write the code.

## register

C makes hardware CPU registers available to programs that use the register storage class. Only local variables can reside in registers, and C uses the same rules for variable scope and initialization with registers as it does with autos. The address operator (&) cannot be applied to a register variable.

The use of register variables is highly machine and compiler dependent. Many compilers, for instance, allocate registers for only pointers and the int and char data types. Furthermore, the compiler may choose to ignore *all* of your register declarations, or give you a register even if you don't ask for one! You'll need to consult your compiler's documentation to see how to use this storage class effectively.

Register variables are handy for time-critical code. Arithmetic and array subscripting operations with register variables execute faster inside loops than with auto or static variables. Loop variables, pointers, and function parameters are suitable candidates for register variables. Registers are a limited resource, so you'll want to allocate them carefully. When the compiler runs out of physical CPU registers, variables that you declare `register` become automatic.

The following code uses a register variable to loop through a large array if it's time to process data.

```
if (process) {
    register int i;
    for (i = 0; i < HUGE; i++)
        . . . a[i] . . .
}
```

Inside the block, the program declares `i` as a register variable before it loops through the array. If a register is available, the loop executes faster.

It's often a good idea to declare the most important register variables first when declaring multiple register variables of the same type. With this approach, the least important ones become autos if the compiler cannot provide a register. A good application for this technique is with multidimensional array subscripts. The following code, for example, loops through all the elements of a two dimensional array of integers named `b`.

```
register int j;
register int i;
int b[IMAX][JMAX];
. . . .
for (i = 0; i < IMAX; i++)
    for (j = 0; j < JMAX; j++)
        . . . . b[i][j] . . . .
```

The second `for` loop executes more often than the first. It's more important, therefore, for the compiler to provide a register for `j` than for `i`. In the declarations we declare `j` as a register variable before `i`, and on a separate line. This is more portable than

```
register int j, i;
```

which may not allocate a register (if available) for `j` on all machines. If only one register is available, the code runs faster because the compiler allocates a register to the correct variable.

## extern

C provides the `extern` storage class for programs to reference functions and variables in separate modules. Variables and functions that files do not declare static are accessible to other modules. The file that references variables and functions from other modules uses the keyword `extern`.

Suppose, for example, `mod1.c` calls a function defined in `mod2.c` which, in turn, references data declared in `mod1.c`. Here's the code for `mod1.c`.

```
/* mod1.c */
#include <stdio.h>
#include "global.h"
int nitems;
double servo[100];
struct something s;
double f();

main()
{
    . . . .
    servo[5] = f();
    . . . .
}
```

`mod1.c` defines an integer (`nitems`), an array of 100 doubles (`servo`), and a structure (`s`), whose template definition is defined in `global.h`. These variables are available to `mod2.c`, because none are static. `main()` calls a function `f()`, which returns a `double` and is not defined in `mod1.c`.

Here's the code for `mod2.c`.

```
/* mod2.c */
#include <stdio.h>
#include "global.h"
extern int nitems;
extern double servo[];

double f()
{
    extern struct something s;
    . . . .
}
```

`mod2.c` uses `extern` to reference `nitems`, `servo`, and `s` from `mod1.c`. Note that a program may place `extern` statements anywhere a declaration is legal, as long as the reference appears before it's used. The compiler requires only square brackets (`[]`) for the array `servo` (100 is optional).

`extern`'s for function names are optional. C allows

```
extern double f();
```

in `mod1.c`, although it's not necessary. Without the keyword `static`, all function declarations are external.

## ◆ Preprocessor Directives and Macros ◆

The preprocessor is separate from the C compiler and has its own syntax rules. Programs use the preprocessor to include header files and provide textual substitutions before compilation. The preprocessor provides a mechanism for macros and contains directives to conditionally compile lines of code.

### Preprocessor Directives

Preprocessor directives start with a # as the first character on a line. To continue a directive on the next line, a backslash (\) precedes a carriage return. The preprocessor accepts directives anywhere in a source file, and a directive may appear inside another directive.

The directives

```
#include "file"
#include <file>
```

make the lines from `file` appear as though they are part of a C program. The first directive searches your current directory for `file` before it searches standard directories in the file system. The second directive fetches files only from the standard directories.

The directives

```
#define name text
#undef name
```

enable and disable textual substitution, respectively. `#define` substitutes *text* for *name* in all lines of a source file, except within quoted strings. This directive centralizes parameter values and is useful inside array declarations and loops. `#undef` undefines *name* and terminates textual substitution.

The directives

```
#if constant_expression
. . . .
#endif

#if constant_expression
. . . .
#else
. . . .
#endif

#if constant_expression
. . . .
#elif constant_expression
. . . .
#endif
```

conditionally compile lines of code. If *constant_expression* evaluates to nonzero, the first format makes the lines between `#if` and `#endif` compile. Otherwise, the preprocessor eliminates them from the source file, and the compiler never sees them. The second format is like the first, except the preprocessor includes lines after the `#else` if *constant_expression* evaluates to zero. The third format is like a C `if-else-if` construct.

The directives

```
#ifdef name
. . .
#endif

#ifndef name
. . .
#endif
```

check *name*'s definition. When *name* from the first format appears with a `#define` in a source file or with a `-D` option on the command line, the preprocessor makes the lines after `#ifdef` compile. Likewise, the second format includes lines if *name* has not been defined.

Recall that `itoh2.c` from a previous section performs integer to hexadecimal conversion correctly on our INTEL 286 processor but is not portable. The Motorola 68000 family, for example, stores bytes in reverse order compared to the INTEL processors. Inside `itoh2.c`, we add preprocessor directives before `main()` to make `itoh2` run correctly on both machines.

```
#ifdef M68000
#define SWAPBYTES 1
#else
#define SWAPBYTES 0
#endif
```

Inside the program, we make the following changes:

```
/* high byte */
    putchar(p[val.s[SWAPBYTES ? 0 : 1] >> 4]);
    putchar(p[val.s[SWAPBYTES ? 0 : 1] & 15]);

/* low byte */
    putchar(p[val.s[SWAPBYTES ? 1 : 0] >> 4]);
    putchar(p[val.s[SWAPBYTES ? 1 : 0] & 15]);
```

`SWAPBYTES` is 1 for a 68000 and 0 for INTEL machines. The preprocessor substitutes 1 or 0 for the high and low bytes, according to the value of `SWAPBYTES`.

The command

```
$ cc -DM68000 itoh2.c -o itoh2
```

compiles `itoh2.c` for a 68000 based machine.

## Macros

Macros use the `#define` directive and have the following format.

```
#define name(arg1, arg2, . . ., argn) text
```

The preprocessor performs textual substitution in the source file by substituting *arg1, arg2, ...* for all their occurrences in *text*. *Text* typically contains C expressions with operators and conditional (? :) constructs. More complex macros, however, include blocks with local variables and control flow constructs.

Let's look at several macro examples. The first one, called ELEMS, produces the number of elements of an array of any C data type.

```
#define ELEMS(A) (sizeof(A) / sizeof A[0])
```

The macro uses the `sizeof()` operator, which produces the number of bytes in its argument. ELEMS divides the total number of bytes in an array by the number of bytes in the array's first element. This produces the number of elements in the array, regardless of the array's data type (the array may be an array of characters or an array of structures, for instance).

The next group of macros allows programs to set, reset, and test individual bits within an integer. The macros use C's bitwise operators and include parentheses to insulate the text and each parameter. This allows them to appear in arbitrary C expressions.

```
#define SET(X,N) ((X) |= (1 << (N)))

#define RESET(X,N) ((X) &= ~(1 << (N)))

#define TEST(X,N) ((X) & (1 << (N)))
```

Suppose a is an `int`, for example. `SET(a, 5)` turns on bit 5 and `RESET(a, 7)` turns off bit 7. The expression

```
if (TEST(a, 4)) {
    . . . .
}
```

executes statements inside the `if` construct if bit 4 of a is 1.

The last macro example swaps `char`, `short`, `int`, and `long` C variables.

```
#define SWAP(A, B) {\
    long t;\
    (t) = (A);\
    (A) = (B);\
    (B) = (t);\
}
```

The macro uses a temporary variable inside a block to swap two arguments. `t` is a `long` to accommodate the size of the largest integer data type. For readability, backslashes (\\) allow macro text to appear on separate lines. Note that programs that use `SWAP` never have name conflicts with `t`, since its scope is defined inside the block of the macro.

Macros execute faster than equivalent functions because the compiler doesn't have the overhead of pushing parameters on the stack and returning values. Macros, on the other hand, increase code size and have some restrictions. For example, you can't call a macro from another language, and pointers may address functions but not macros. Furthermore, not all functions will convert to macros. Macros also have possible side effects with arguments that use the `++` and `--` operators. The following statements, for example,

```
FILE *fp;
char *p;
. . . .
putc(*p++, fp)
```

use `putc()` from the C library to output a character to a `FILE` pointer `fp`. The code executes incorrectly because `putc()` is a macro (defined in `stdio.h`) and `p` may increment more than once during macro expansion. To eliminate the problem, you need to increment `p` outside the function call or use `fputc()`, which is a function.

## ◆ Casts ◆

The format for C's cast operator is

```
(type) expression
```

Casts convert the result of the evaluated *expression* to the specified data type *type* at run time. The values of variables inside *expression* are unaffected. Casts have many applications in C. Perhaps their most valuable use is converting function parameter data types and function return values. In addition, they affect arithmetic conversions and help make programs portable.

Suppose, for example, i and j are integers. The statement

```
pow((double) i, (double) j);
```

calls pow() from the C math library to calculate i to the jth power. The casts convert i and j to the required doubles without affecting their values.

Casts apply to function return values as well. The statements

```
struct block *bptr;
. . . .
bptr = (struct block *) calloc(10, sizeof(struct block));
```

for instance, call the C library routine calloc() to allocate 10 structures of type block on the heap and assign the heap address to bptr. The cast converts calloc()'s character pointer to a structure pointer.†

return statements may use casts. The following program calls a function to calculate the square root of a floating point number and truncates its fractional part before returning.

```
/* cast.c - casts in return statements */

#include <math.h>

double calc();

main()
{
    printf("%f\n", calc(85.66));
}

double calc(v)
double v;
{
    return (int) sqrt(v);
}
```

```
$ cast
9.000000
```

The cast converts sqrt()'s return value (double) to an int. This truncates the fractional part before calc() returns it as a double. In the main program, printf() displays the double result.

---

† In ANSI C, calloc() returns a void pointer and a cast is unnecessary.

Programs may also use casts to control the compiler's arithmetic conversion rules. Suppose `val` is a float and `num` is an integer. The expression

```
val/num
```

makes the compiler generate a floating point division in assembly code. The following expression

```
(int) val/num
```

however, uses a cast to make the compiler perform integer division.

More advanced uses of casts are possible. Assuming `b` and `e` are `double`'s, for example, the expression

```
pow((double) (long) b, e)
```

applies two casts to truncate `b`'s fractional part before calling `pow()`.

The following program uses casts to swap 8 bit bytes in a 16-bit `short`.

**Program 1-9**

```
/* swab1.c - Swap bytes in a short, not portable */

unsigned short swapb();

main()
{
    unsigned short num = 0xabcd;

    printf("%4x\n", swapb(&num));
}

unsigned short swapb(pnum)
register unsigned short *pnum;
{
    return  *((unsigned char *) pnum + 1) |
                  *((unsigned char *) pnum) << 8;
}

$ swab1
cdab
```

`swapb()`'s cast of characters has many stars. Try to work through the `return` expression assuming the compiler stores the two byte `short` num as 'cd' followed by 'ab' in memory. Each cast works with byte pointers and bitwise operators to swap bytes and construct a new 16-bit `short`. The function is fast and compact, but it's not portable. It runs on INTEL architectures because of the assumption we make about byte layout in memory. On other machines (like the Motorola 68020), swapb() produces a different result.

We conclude this review chapter with a portable version of swapb() using unions for 16-bit shorts. The program uses techniques from earlier parts of the chapter.

**Program 1-10**

```
/* swab2.c - Swap bytes in a short,
             portable for 16-bit shorts */

unsigned short swapb();

main()
{
    unsigned short num  = 0xabcd;

    printf("%4x\n", swapb(&num));
}

unsigned short swapb(pnum)
register unsigned short *pnum;
{
    union {
        unsigned short n;
        unsigned char c[2];
    } word;

    word.n = *pnum;               /* get the bytes */

    word.c[0] ^= word.c[1];
    word.c[1] ^= word.c[0];
    word.c[0] ^= word.c[1];

    return *pnum = word.n;        /* change permanently */
}

$ swab2
cdab
```

The union makes a 16-bit short appear as a two-byte character array. Exclusive OR's perform the swap, and memory byte layout does not affect the union. This version of swapb() also shows you how to modify the original value as well as return the new result. A similar approach works for 32-bit integers (see Exercise 11).

### TABLE 1-7. C operator precedence

| Operator | Description | Associativity | Precedence |
|---|---|---|---|
| ()<br>[]<br>-><br>. | Function call<br>Array element<br>Structure pointer member<br>Structure member | Left to right | Highest |
| -<br>++<br>--<br>!<br>~<br>*<br>&<br>sizeof<br>(type) | Unary minus<br>Increment<br>Decrement<br>Logical NOT<br>One's complement<br>Indirection<br>Address<br>Object size<br>Cast | Right to left | |
| *<br>/<br>% | Multiplication<br>Division<br>Modulus | Left to right | |
| +<br>- | Addition<br>Subtraction | Left to right | |
| <<<br>>> | Left shift<br>Right shift | Left to right | |
| <<br><=<br>><br>>= | Less than<br>Less than or equal to<br>Greater than<br>Greater than or equal to | Left to right | |
| ==<br>!= | Equals<br>Not equals | Left to right | |
| & | Bitwise AND | Left to right | |
| ^ | Bitwise XOR | Left to right | |
| \| | Bitwise OR | Left to right | |
| && | Logical AND | Left to right | |
| \|\| | Logical OR | Left to right | |
| ?: | Conditional | Right to left | |
| =<br>*= /=<br>%= +=<br>(etc.) | Assignment | Right to left | |
| , | Comma | Left to right | Lowest |

# ♦ Summary ♦

- The compiler treats the most significant bit as data in `unsigned` data types.

- Integers have different formats than floating point. If the compiler interprets an integer for a `float` (or vice versa), programs may produce incorrect results.

- C does not convert function parameters from integer to floating point and vice versa.

- If a function returns something other than an integer, you must inform the compiler of the function's return data type before it's used.

- C provides operators for arithmetic, relational, and logical expressions. Bitwise operators manipulate bits, and compound assignment operators provide compact expressions. Conditional operators are useful in function parameters and macros.

- C provides control flow constructs for decisions, loops, and multiway branches. `if-else` statements evaluate successive expressions until one, if any, evaluates to nonzero. A `switch` with a large number of `case` labels may be more efficient than an equivalent `if-else` when the compiler produces jump tables in assembly code.

- `break` and `continue` provide control over loop processing. `goto`'s should be used sparingly but may be helpful to quickly exit from a deeply nested construct.

- C supports single and multidimensional arrays. Arrays may contain aggregate types as well as simple data types.

- Pointers are variables that contain addresses of memory objects. C provides the operators `*`, `&`, `->`, `++`, and `--` to manipulate pointers in programs.

- C programs begin execution at `main()`, which is a function with two arguments. The first argument is the number of arguments on the command line which invoked the program, and the second argument is a pointer to an array of character pointers that contain each argument's address.

- Structures group different members into a single object. The size of a structure is the amount of space required to store all the members. Unions are like structures, but the compiler allocates only enough space to hold the largest member of the union. Structures and unions have the same syntax.

- C provides storage classes so that programs may control where variables reside in the run time environment. The four storage classes are `auto`, `static`, `register`, and `extern`.

- A function or block should declare the most important register variables first and put each register declaration on a separate line for portability.

- Preprocessor directives allow conditional compilation of lines in a source file. The preprocessor has a separate syntax from C.

- Macros execute faster than functions but take more code space. Not all functions convert to macros.

- Casts change data types at run time. Programs use casts for function parameters, return values, and arithmetic conversions.

## ◆ Exercises ◆

1. Include error checks in `rotate.c` for illegal shift counts. Make each routine display a message on standard error before terminating the program, or optionally, return from the routine with the integer unchanged.

2. `rol()` and `ror()` return rotated integers and leave their arguments unchanged. Modify `rotate.c` from the previous exercise to *modify* the integer. This involves passing pointers to `rol()` and `ror()`, so the routines may change them.

3. It's possible to write pseudo random number generators in C using bitwise operators. Suppose, for example, `i` is a 16-bit `short`. The following expression

   ```
   i = (i & 0x8000) ? (i << 1) ^ 0x100b : (i << 1);
   ```

   generates a new bit pattern for `i` from a previous one. Inside a loop or function call, the expression generates 65,535 different bit patterns before repeating. Write a function called `rnd()` using this expression to generate random bit patterns. Initialize `i` to a nonzero value to start the sequence. Devise a way to test for unique bit patterns.

4. Write a function called `zerocnt()` that takes an integer for an argument and returns the number of zero bits in the integer.

5. Write a program to reverse characters in a string. Input the character string from the command line and use `argv` to access it.

6. Modify `xchg.c` to swap floats without a temporary variable. This is not as easy as it looks, since C doesn't allow Exclusive-OR's between floats. What restrictions, if any, would this new function have and how portable is the code?

7. Modify the `SWAP` macro so that it doesn't use a temporary variable. What is the disadvantage here?

8. Compile and run the following program on your machine.

   ```
   /* sizeof.c - show examples of sizeof operator */

   main()
   {
       long walk[50];
       double *p;
       struct something {
           char buf[80];
       } s;
   ```

```
    printf("%d\n", sizeof(int));
    printf("%d\n", sizeof(double));
    printf("%d\n", sizeof(double *));
    printf("%d\n", sizeof(struct something));

    printf("%d\n", sizeof walk);
    printf("%d\n", sizeof walk[2]);
    printf("%d\n", sizeof walk + 1);
    printf("%d\n", sizeof s.buf);
}
```

Can you explain the output?

9. The following program uses a stack and two functions named push() and pop() to reverse characters in a string.

```
/* stack.c - function calls */

#include <stdio.h>

#define NSTACK 20          /* depth of stack */
char stack[NSTACK], *stackp = stack;

main()
{
    char *p = "draw emit";
    int c;

    /* push string on stack */

    while (c = *p++)
        push(c);

    /* pop characters in reverse order */

    while ((c = pop()) != EOF)
        putchar(c);
    putchar('\n');
}
```

```
/* place char d on stack */

push(d)
char d;
{
    if (stackp >= stack + NSTACK)
        exit(1);                    /* stack overflow */
    *stackp++ = d;
}

/* pop char from top of stack */

pop()
{
    if (stackp <= stack)
        return EOF;                 /* stack underflow */
    return *--stackp;
}
```

```
$ stack
time ward
```

Rewrite push() and pop() as macros.

10. Include preprocessor directives to make stack.c use either functions or macros for push() and pop(). Use a command line option flag called MACROS to compile stack.c. For example, the command

    ```
    $ cc -DMACROS stack.c -o stack
    ```

    compiles stack.c with macros, but the command

    ```
    $ cc stack.c -o stack
    ```

    compiles push() and pop() as functions.

11. Write a function called swapw() that uses unions to swap 16 bits in a 32-bit int or long.

# The Run Time Environment

**C** provides features not found in other programming languages. When you declare variables, for example, you choose a name, the class of variable (array, structure, union, etc.), and a data type, as in most other languages. C is special in that you tell the compiler *where* to place a variable in the *run time environment*. The compiler doesn't decide, you do. This is a bonus, because it gives you more control of your executing program. The other side of the coin is that the programmer must have a clear idea of what he or she intends to do. This is why it makes sense to find out how C programs execute. Understanding the run time environment helps you diagnose run time bugs and write faster-executing code.

This chapter looks at the run time environment from the C compiler's perspective. We discuss program areas and how they relate to C's storage classes. We show ways to reduce a program's run time overhead and estimate its memory requirements. We examine program variables in the context of their run time environment; that is, where and when storage allocation occurs, and what choices you have for specifying storage classes. Although your program's environment is often machine dependent, it still makes sense to understand C's run time philosophy. This helps you design programs that run faster and require less memory.

## ♦ Program Areas ♦

We've mentioned the importance of understanding the run time environment. This is where the declarations in your program are put into action. Whether you're running under UNIX, DOS, OS/2, or another operating system, the system first allocates a chunk of memory for your program. The executing code and associated system structures make up what's called a *process* (as in UNIX or OS/2), and the operating system copies the executable program from disk to memory. As we will see, this means more than just the executable statements.

The system has to allocate memory for other parts of the program, too.

Fig. 2-1 shows the four program areas of the run time environment: the *text area*, the *stack*, the *data area*, and the *heap*.

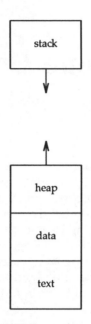

*Fig. 2-1.* Program areas at run time

We don't make any assumptions about how memory is arranged here. That is, the system may place the stack in upper memory and the text area at the bottom (or vice versa). What's important is determining how much memory a program requires. This sometimes aids in debugging run time errors, like stack overflows and "out of heap space" messages. If you're targeting C code for ROM (read-only memory) applications, you'll also need to estimate a program's memory requirements. Naturally, the total memory required depends on the requirements of each of the four program areas.

Let's discuss memory allocation for program areas first. The text and data areas are fixed. This makes sense, since the size of a program's instructions and its data are known at load time. The stack and heap, however, are dynamic. A program uses these areas as it runs, allocating memory based on the logic of your program, I/O, and function calls. At load time, their sizes are unknown.

Fig. 2-1 shows the stack and heap at opposites ends of memory. As each increases in size, they "grow" towards each other. While this opposing relationship may hold in some run time environments, it's certainly not always true. Frequently the stack and heap are in separate areas and saving stack space may or may not affect the storage available for the heap. Furthermore, the space required to hold a program's data may also affect storage for its text, stack, or heap areas. Again, these implementation details depend on the underlying machine architecture, the operating system, and the compiler and loader command line flags. As we mentioned, the most important thing to understand is which parts of the run time environment are dynamic and which parts are fixed.

## Text Area

When we use the word *text area* we mean an area of memory reserved for the executable instructions of a program and not the ASCII characters that make up its source file. This memory area is usually considered read only by the system and is often called *program text*. C compilers typically have compiler options to place text and data in separate spaces; this is sometimes called *pure*, since the text area may not be writable. If, on the other hand, text and data share the same address space, it's possible for *impure* programs to modify themselves! The size of the text area is fixed, determined at the time the program is compiled and linked. As we will see, the only time a program should access data in this area is with pointers to functions.

## Data Area

The second program area is the data area (also called *static data*). This contains the C static variables (internal and external) as well as the global variables from your program. There's nothing dynamic about these items, and the system knows just how much memory to allocate when it's time to run your program.

The data area is divided into two parts: *initialized* data and *uninitialized* data. Where the system stores a variable depends on how you declare it. If you initialize a static or global variable in a declaration, the system places it in the initialized data area. Otherwise, it goes in the uninitialized data area. The uninitialized data area is sometimes called the *BSS* area (for "Block Started by Symbol"). The system fills the BSS area with zeros.

Because the system determines sizes and values from these data, we refer to variables in the data area as *load-time* variables. That is, these variables exist at the point where the system initially loads the program into memory, until the program terminates. When the system allocates memory for the load-time variables, it sets the initialized variables to their respective values and fills the BSS area with zeros. This guarantees that load-time variables have predetermined values when your program begins running.

## The Stack

The third program area is the stack, which has two important uses. The stack is the basis for what's called a *stack frame*, which is a mechanism that many compilers use to implement function calls. When you pass a parameter to a function, for example, the stack frame makes the data accessible to the function. We look at stack frames in a later section.

The stack is also a place for the compiler to store automatic variables. Since this happens at run time, the system can't determine the size of the stack before your program runs. This is because its size changes as a program executes. As we will see, the stack is constantly growing and shrinking during the life of a program.

## The Heap

Programs may declare variables at compile time or at run time. Should you decide to allocate storage at run time, however, you need memory from a place other than the stack or the data area. A program area called the *heap* provides storage for this purpose. A heap manager, separate from your program, provides C library functions that allocate and deallocate storage. Pointers allow you to access heap memory as if it were an array, a structure, or any C data type.

The heap is under programmer control. It's dynamic, and like the stack, doesn't have a fixed size. It's possible to use up all the heap space when a program runs, and it's your responsibility to address heap data properly and detect heap overflow errors. Let's look at each of these program areas now in detail.

## ◆ The Text Area ◆

We'll begin our discussion of the run time environment with the program text area. This is where your program's object code resides. In most cases, the operating system decides the layout of allocated memory for the text area, but you can control memory layout to some extent with loader options. The *-i* loader option, for example, separates instructions and data in memory. This helps the operating system detect write operations to the text area, and allow multiple instances of a program to share the same text area (as in multitasking operating systems like UNIX and OS/2).

### Pointers to Functions

As your program executes, instructions are fetched from the text area. C programs don't usually access the text area unless you use *pointers to functions*. In this situation, a pointer contains an address of a function in the text area. Programs call a function with the pointer, which means your program must fetch addresses from the text area.

Let's review pointers to functions. Suppose you want a pointer to contain the address of a function that returns an integer. Here's how you declare it:

```
int (*p)();   /* ptr to function that returns an integer */
```

Note the parentheses surrounding the pointer variable and indirection operator. Once you've declared the pointer you must initialize it. This is done in two steps. First, you tell the compiler the name of the function you wish to assign to the pointer. For example, the statement

```
int func();   /* tell the compiler about the function */
```

informs the compiler that `func` is a function that returns an integer. It's not necessary to specify function parameters here. The compiler just needs to know the name of the function and what data type it returns.

The second step is to assign the address of the function to the pointer. There are two ways to do this. The first is with an assignment statement:

```
p = func;    /* assign func address to pointer */
```

Note that `p` must be a pointer of the same data type that `func()` returns; otherwise a cast is necessary. Parentheses do not appear after the function name. If you use them, the compiler tries to *call* the function. Using the name of a function without parentheses makes the compiler interpret it as a pointer. Therefore, the address operator (`&`) is not needed.

The second way to assign a function address to a pointer is with a declaration. We could, in fact, combine all the previous steps into one:

```
int func(), (*p)() = func;
```

In this case we're declaring a pointer and initializing it in the same statement. Regardless of how you do it, the pointer contains an address from the *text* area.

Once you have the pointer set, you'll want to call the function. To do this, you use the pointer name, the indirection operator, and the function's arguments. For example,

```
result = (*p) (arg1, arg2,...);      /* call the function */
```

invokes `func()` with its arguments (if there are any) and stores the return value in `result`, which is an integer. The parentheses are required for the pointer name and indirection operator as well as for the optional argument list, even if the function has no arguments.

Let's look at a program that uses pointers to functions to maintain a table of mathematical functions. We declare an array of pointers to functions and use an array reference to call the function. In the following example, we only show one mathematical function. You could easily extend it to hold more.

**Program 2-1**

```c
/* pow.c - power function */

#include <stdio.h>
#include <math.h>

main(argc, argv)
int argc;
char *argv[];
{
    double base, power;
    double (*mtab[10])();    /* array of ptrs to functions */

    if (argc != 3) {
        fprintf(stderr, "Usage: %s base power\n", argv[0]);
        exit(1);
    }

    base  = atof(argv[1]);   /* command line argument 1 */
    power = atof(argv[2]);   /* command line argument 2 */

    mtab[0] = pow;           /* address from text area */

    printf("%g\n", (*mtab[0]) (base, power));
}
```

Inside the program, we declare an array of pointers to functions. The declaration

```c
    double (*mtab[10])();    /* array of ptrs to functions */
```

makes mtab an array of 10 pointers to functions that return doubles. (Refer to Chapter 4 for the *right-left rule*, which helps sort out complex declarations like this.) We assign the address of the power function pow() to the first element of the array. The expression

```c
    (*mtab[0]) (base, power)
```

calls the pow() function with two arguments. The atof() function converts the command line character strings to doubles before we pass them as parameters to pow(). Here's how to compile pow.c and run it.

```
$ cc pow.c -o pow -lm
$ pow 3 4
81
$ pow 2.5 3.5
24.7053
```

Note that we tell the linker to search the math library (-lm) for pow(). The first argument to pow() is the base and the second is the power. We display the result using the g format for printf(). This prints digits to the right of the decimal point only if there's a fractional part in the result.

In the next example, we create a table of trigonometric functions from the math library. We'll use a structure with two pointers: one for the name of the function, and one that *points* to it. Here's the program, called trig.c:

**Program 2-2**

```
/* trig.c - trig functions */

#include <stdio.h>
#include <math.h>

main()
{
    struct trig {
        char *name;
        double (*ptr)();
    };

    static struct trig tbl[10] = {
        "acos",   acos,
        "asin",   asin,
        "atan",   atan,
        "atan2",  atan2,
        "cos",    cos,
        "cosh",   cosh,
        "sin",    sin,
        "sinh",   sinh,
        "tan",    tan,
        "tanh",   tanh
    };
    int i;

    for (i = 0; i < 10; i++)
        printf("%04x\t%s\n", tbl[i].ptr, tbl[i].name);
}
```

Inside main(), we declare a structure trig that holds two pointers. The first one points to the name of a function as a character string, and the second one is a pointer to a function which returns a double. Next, we declare an array of these structures called tbl, and initialize each one. The program loops through the array to display the function address and its name. All names are from the standard C math library.

To demonstrate this program, let's run it under XENIX on a 286-based machine.

```
$ cc trig.c -o trig -lm
$ trig
00dd     acos
00d7     asin
00e2     atan
00e7     atan2
00f3     cos
0103     cosh
00ed     sin
00fd     sinh
00f8     tan
0108     tanh
```

The output is in two columns. Before each function name, we display its address in hexadecimal. These (16-bit) addresses live in the text area, and it's possible to make the loader provide the same information with a *loadmap*. Under UNIX, for instance, the nm (namelist) command displays such a loadmap. Here's the one from our XENIX system (showing only the trigonometric functions):

```
003f:00dd   T _acos
003f:00d7   T _asin
003f:00e2   T _atan
003f:00e7   T _atan2
003f:00f3   T _cos
003f:0103   T _cosh
003f:00ed   T _sin
003f:00fd   T _sinh
003f:00f8   T _tan
003f:0108   T _tanh
```

All numbers are in hexadecimal. The number before the colon is a segment number, part of the 286 architecture of our XENIX system. (See Appendices B, C and D for more details on Intel 286 memory models.) The second hexadecimal number is an address followed by a T, which means text area. As you can see, these addresses and function names in the namelist match the output from trig.c.

Up to this point, we've shown examples of programs that read from the text area. Suppose a program tries to write there instead? There's no reason to ever do this; it's just that since C allows pointers to point to so many things, it's possible to use a pointer incorrectly. The following program writes over its text area on purpose. We use it for demonstration only. Here's the code:

**Program 2-3**

```c
/* mod.c - self modifying code */

#include <stdio.h>

main()
{
    void func();

    strcpy((char *) func, "clobber");
    printf("function address = %04x\n", func);
    func();
    printf("I'm ok.\n");
}

void func()
{
}
```

The program is a main program that calls a function that doesn't do anything. We call strcpy() with a pointer to a function as the first argument, which we cast as a pointer to a character. This makes strcpy() overwrite the text area with the string "clobber". We display the function address and call it. When we return from the function, the program displays a small message. Let's compile mod.c on a 286 machine with XENIX and see what happens.

```
$ cc mod.c -o mod
$ mod
function address = 00c9
mod: Segmentation violation -- Core dumped
```

On our system, the XENIX kernel terminates the program and dumps core. Although the function address appears, we never return after we call func() to print the message. The program fails because the text area was changed at run time.

mod.c's behavior is not always predictable, however. In fact, it depends on the loader options you use as well as the operating system and machine that you run it on. Under DOS, for instance, we've seen the program's output look like this:

```
> mod
function address = 00a3
I'm ok.
```

In this case, `mod.c` appears to work correctly. This is disturbing, since the program gives no hint that something is amiss. On your system, you'll probably want to run `mod.c` to see what happens. If `mod.c` runs without error, you need to be aware that write operations to the text area (which should never happen) could go unnoticed on your system.

# ♦ The Stack ♦

The stack is dynamic and its behavior depends on how your program executes. Whereas the text area never changes in size, the stack grows and shrinks. A program may not even use the same amount of stack space each time it runs. Function calls, program flow, and variable declarations all play a part in how the compiler reads and writes to stack memory. It's worthwhile understanding how C uses the stack for several reasons. First, you can effectively use the auto storage class to conserve memory and estimate a program's stack requirements. Second, you can use this knowledge to help debug programs.

This section looks at how C uses the stack when C programs execute. We'll discover how the system allocates and initializes automatic variables and how the stack behaves inside functions, blocks, and loops. We'll also discuss the run time issues that relate to initializing automatic arrays and structures (which is legal in ANSI C), and how this fits in with C's run time philosophy.

## What Is the Stack?

The stack is a simple data structure that stores information. In C's run time environment, the stack is used most often to store addresses or data. The system typically pushes and pops items on and off the stack in a *last in/first out* manner. This means that the most recent item put on the stack is removed first. A common analogy to explain stack behavior is a stack of spring-loaded cafeteria trays. Patrons remove a tray from the top. This is the tray placed most recently, hence the term last in/first out.

What does C store on the stack?

1.  Automatic variables

2.  Function parameters

3.  Return addresses of functions

4.  Temporary variables during expression evaluation

You should be knowledgeable with most, if not all, of the ways C uses the stack. Let's look at how a typical C compiler stores stack information and find out how this affects the run time environment.

## Stack Frames

When your program calls a function, the system pushes important information like the function's arguments, local variables, and return address on the stack. We call this information a *stack frame*. There's a separate stack frame each time the system calls a function. The stack program area is a series of stack frames as a program executes.

Not all C compilers use stack frames. Some compilers pass function parameters in registers, since this is faster than accessing stack memory. There's nothing that says C *has* to use stack frames; however, a stack frame is a suitable mechanism used by most compilers to implement recursive functions and local variables declared inside functions. The details of your particular compiler's function call mechanism may differ, but the concepts of saving and restoring local variables should be the same. For more information, consult your compiler's documentation.

To demonstrate, suppose a C compiler uses stack frames for function calls. We'll look at two examples of passing function parameters using a stack frame. The first example is a function that passes the *address* of a variable. The following program (addr.c), for example, calls function func() with the addresses of two integer variables. Inside func(), we declare two local integers. Here's the code:

**Program 2-4**

```
/* addr.c - pass the address */

main()
{
    int a = 3, b = 4;

    func(&a, &b);
}

func(pa, pb)
int *pa, *pb;
{
    int m = 5, n = 6;
}
```

The compiler stores the function's arguments, local variables, and return address in the stack frame. In Fig. 2-2, we look at a snapshot of the stack frame just after the call to func(). For simplicity, we assume that addr.c runs on a 16-bit machine and that the stack is consecutive words of memory that are all 16 bits in length. Furthermore, higher addresses are at the top and lower addresses are at the bottom. Each stack frame's memory slot contains 16 bits of data displayed in hexadecimal. Memory addresses (also in hexadecimal) appear to the left of the stack frame. Program variable names and frame addresses are shown on the right.

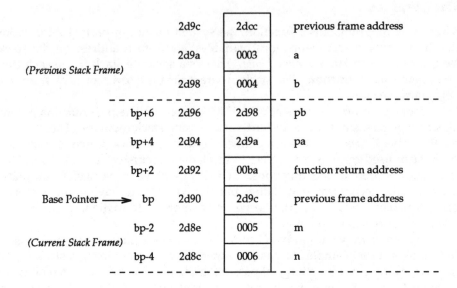

| | | | | |
|---|---|---|---|---|
| | | 2d9c | 2dcc | previous frame address |
| *(Previous Stack Frame)* | | 2d9a | 0003 | a |
| | | 2d98 | 0004 | b |
| | bp+6 | 2d96 | 2d98 | pb |
| | bp+4 | 2d94 | 2d9a | pa |
| | bp+2 | 2d92 | 00ba | function return address |
| Base Pointer ⟶ | bp | 2d90 | 2d9c | previous frame address |
| | bp-2 | 2d8e | 0005 | m |
| *(Current Stack Frame)* | bp-4 | 2d8c | 0006 | n |

*Fig. 2-2.* Stack frame - pass the address

Fig. 2-2 shows you what a stack frame would look like if addr.c was compiled on a machine with an INTEL architecture. The compiler uses a *base pointer* to access information from the stack frame. In the diagram, we use bp as the base pointer, and it points to the current stack frame. Since func() was just called, bp points to address 2d90, the current frame address. The address just above it (2d92) contains the return address (00ba). Execution resumes at this text address inside main() when we return from func().

Note that bp+4 is the address of the function's first argument, pa. Since it's a pointer to an integer, the memory location contains the address of variable a in the main program (address 2d9a). Similarly, bp+6 points to variable b. Note that with this arrangement, the compiler can use the base pointer with a *positive* offset to access function parameters.

Let's turn our attention now to the local variables declared inside func(). Here, m and n are automatic variables that appear in the stack frame at addresses 2d8e and 2d8c, respectively. Their memory locations are *negative* offsets from the base pointer (bp-2 and bp-4, respectively).

The current frame address contains the address of the previous stack frame, (2d9c) in this example. This is the current frame address for main(). Addresses 2d9a and 2d98 contain the data for main()'s local variables, a and b, respectively. This organization is similar to the local variables m and n inside the current stack frame. Note that func() doesn't need to access memory locations above bp+6, since they are a part of the previous stack frame.

Let's use this stack frame implementation to discuss the sequence of events that takes place during a function call. When your program calls a function, the system creates a stack frame and sets the base pointer to the stack frame's address after it generates code to load the arguments onto the stack, followed by the return address. The compiler generates assembly code using the base pointer of the current stack frame to reference function arguments with a positive offset and automatic variables with a negative offset. If the first function calls another function, the system creates a new stack frame and the whole process repeats. When a function returns, the system fetches the return address from the current stack frame, and the previous stack frame becomes the current one. In our example, the base pointer is set to address 2d9c when func() returns. The compiler accesses main()'s local variable a using bp-2 (address 2d9a), and so on.

Let's use this same approach to show a stack frame for passing the contents of a variable instead of its address. Again, we declare a simple function func() with two local variables, m and n. This time, however, we pass the *values* of variables a and b to func() rather than their addresses. Here's the code:

**Program 2-5**

```
/* val.c - pass the value */

main()
{
    int a = 3, b = 4;

    func(a, b);
}

func(c, d)
int c, d;
{
    int m = 5, n = 6;
}
```

Fig. 2-3 shows the stack frame for this program.

The new stack frame is essentially the same as before, except that the parameters c and d (addresses 2d94 and 2d96) now contain copies of the *values* of a and b, respectively. The base pointer still references the function arguments and automatic variables. However, the data in a and b is now insulated from func(). The function uses the copies stored in the current stack frame and has no way to reference or alter a and b. This is the main difference between passing the address of a variable and passing its value.

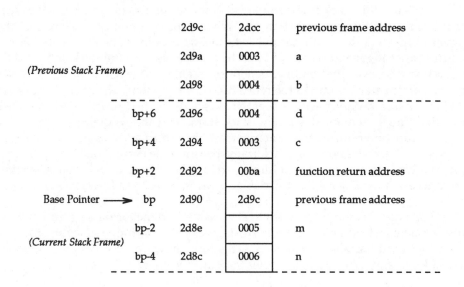

*Fig. 2-3.* Stack frame - pass the value

Note that in Fig. 2-2 and Fig. 2-3, parameters passed to functions appear in both stack frames in *reverse* order. On our machine, the Microsoft C compiler pushes the rightmost parameter first and the leftmost parameter last. This means that the first argument is always at address bp+4 (the "top" of the stack) when func() executes. Although not all C compilers handle function parameters this way, it does help explain how scanf() and printf() are implemented on some machines. For example, look at the following use of printf():

```
int val;
char buf[80];
. . . .
printf("%d %s", val, buf);
```

How does printf() access the *value* of val and the *address* of buf? Since we assume function arguments are pushed in reverse order on the stack, a pointer to the format string "%d %s" appears on top. Note that printf() can use this information to determine how many arguments were passed and whether to interpret them by address or value. This is how printf() and scanf() accept a variable number of arguments. Chapter 4 shows you how to write your own functions that take a variable number of arguments with different data types.

What about stack requirements? In Fig. 2-2, we pass pointers to integers. Suppose we pass a pointer to a structure or some other object instead. It turns out that no matter what type of pointer we pass, the number of bytes the stack frame requires is always the size of a pointer to the specified data object. Passing the address of an object, therefore, saves stack space and minimizes the execution time to set up a stack frame.

Contrast this to Fig. 2-3, where we pass integer values. What happens when we pass a structure? In this case, the system duplicates the *entire* structure, resulting in a larger stack frame. Not only does this increase stack space, but the compiler generates assembly code to *copy* all of the data to the new stack frame as well. This can slow down a program that passes large structures to functions. The problem doesn't exist for arrays, since C always passes the address.

By the way, if you want to pass a small array with all of its elements to a function in C, we present the technique in Chapter 4.

## Stack Allocation

As we mentioned, the stack contains the automatic variables that you declare in your C programs. The details of how the C compiler allocates stack space for automatic variables is implementation dependent, but we can still make some general comments that will be true for most systems. First, an automatic variable's data type determines the number of bytes that the compiler allocates on the stack. Assuming your machine has 8 bits per byte, a char takes one byte and a double allocates eight bytes. The number of bytes for an int will be two or four, depending on the size of an integer on your machine. If the variable you declare is an automatic array or a structure, the number of bytes on the stack also depends on the size of the array or structure.

Your compiler will most likely allocate memory for automatic variables when you *call* a function. With this knowledge, it's possible to make fairly good estimates of how much stack space a function might require. For example, the following program contains a main program and two functions. Here, main() calls f1(), which in turn, calls f2(). All functions declare automatic arrays.

**Program 2-6**

```
main()
{
    char buf1[1000];

    f1():
}

f1()
{
    char buf2[500];

    f2();
}

f2()
{
    char buf3[500];
}
```

How much stack space does this program use? Excluding function call overhead, we can say that the program needs at least 2000 bytes. The total number of bytes should be the sum of all the arrays in the program because f1()'s stack frame uses 500 bytes that can't be released until f2() returns. Note that buf1 (inside main()) remains allocated for the life of the program.

Suppose we modify this program and have main() call f2() instead of f1().

**Program 2-7**

```
main()
{
    char buf1[1000];

    f1():
    f2():
}

f1()
{
    char buf2[500];
}

f2()
{
    char buf3[500];
}
```

This change should make the program require less memory. You may find, for instance, that the amount of stack space is at least 1500 bytes, since f1() and f2() can use the same 500 bytes of stack memory.

Recall that C allows declarations inside any block. It's legal, therefore, to declare automatic variables inside blocks formed by loops and if statements. It turns out that on many systems the declaration of an automatic variable inside a block affects a variable's *scope*, not the program's stack space requirements. To illustrate, let's see what happens on machines with an INTEL architecture (using the Microsoft C compiler) when you declare automatic variables inside blocks.

The following function, for example, uses an if statement to check its argument. If mode is 1, the function declares an 80-byte character buffer.

```
process(mode)
int mode;
{
    if (mode == 1) {
        char buf[80];
        .  .  .  .
    }
    .  .  .  .
}
```

At first glance, one might think that C allocates stack space for `buf` only if `mode` is `1`. The Microsoft C compiler, however, allocates memory in the stack frame for *all* automatic variables whether or not their scope ever becomes active. This helps the operating system (XENIX or DOS) detect stack overflows before a program calls a function. † The following function, therefore, requires the same stack space:

```
process(mode)
int mode;
{
    char buf[80];

    if (mode == 1) {
        .  .  .  .
    }
    .  .  .  .
}
```

The only difference between the two functions is `buf`'s scope. In the first function, `buf` is known only inside the block. In the second one, it's known everywhere in `process()`. The stack space requirements are the same. This analysis should also be true with variables inside loops. Again, these details are compiler and machine dependent, so you may want to find out how automatic variables are allocated on your machine.

## Initializing Automatic Variables

You're expected to initialize automatic variables yourself. If you don't, their values are undefined. Why is this? To explain, let's look at several programs.

The following program declares one automatic variable.

---

† Stack overflow checks are called *stack probes*. The Microsoft C compiler has command line options to eliminate stack probes from programs to reduce function call overhead. See Appendices C and D.

**Program 2-8**

```
main()
{
    int i;
}
```

The assembler code from this program reveals that the variable i resides in a stack frame.† There are no assembly instructions to initialize it. The following program, however, produces different assembler code:

**Program 2-9**

```
main()
{
    int i = 3;
}
```

This program initializes i to the constant 3. The compiler generates assembly code to allocate i in a stack frame *and* load the constant 3 into its memory location. This two-step operation is the result when you explicitly direct the compiler to initialize an automatic variable.

If you think about it, C's treatment of automatic variables makes sense. Automatic variable declarations make the compiler generate code to place the automatic variables on the stack. When you also initialize an automatic variable, the compiler generates additional assembly code to load the variable with a value. Otherwise, the compiler skips this step. This arrangement minimizes run time overhead, since the compiler generates the extra assembly code only for variable initializations.

There's another reason why C doesn't initialize automatic variables. C allows goto's to jump into the middle of a block inside the same function. This raises an interesting question. If a variable has been declared inside that block, what is its value? If the compiler initialized all automatic variables, it would have to take this special case into account. This would be messy, to say the least, and take execution time to handle properly. It's best left alone.

For these reasons, C does not initialize automatic variables by default. Their values are simply what's on the stack at run time. This illustrates one of C's basic philosophies — *reducing run time overhead*. In accordance with this philosophy, the compiler tries to minimize certain operations that it has to do repeatedly. Reduction of run time overhead is a part of the design of the C language and not simply compiler optimization.

---

† To look at the assembler code from a C program, compile it with the −s flag. This compiler option produces a .s file under UNIX and a .asm file under DOS containing assembly language instructions.

Programmers new to C learn quickly that this philosophy can appear unforgiving at times. For example, the next function loops through an integer array and counts the number of array elements that are a certain value.

```
int count(buf, nitems, value)
int *buf, nitems, value;
{
    int i, nc;

    for (i = 0; i < nitems; i++)
        if (buf[i] == value)
            nc++:
    return nc;
}
```

The function count() has a subtle run time bug. The automatic variable nc is uninitialized, yet we assume that it's zero when we start the loop. If the program works correctly, it's because the value on the stack for nc happens to be zero at run time. This may not always be the case, since the program may fail the next time it runs or when we port it to a different machine.

Let's look at initializing automatic variables inside loops. The following program, called loop.c, declares two automatic variables i and j. Variable i's value is undefined until we enter the for loop. Inside the loop, we initialize j to 10. We display the values of i and j. Here's the program and its output:

**Program 2-10**

```
/* loop.c - creates auto variable */

#include <stdio.h>

main()
{
    int i;

    for (i = 0; i < 3; i++) {
        int j = 10;
        printf("i = %d\tj = %d\n", i , j);
        j++;
    }
}

$ loop
i = 0    j = 10
i = 1    j = 10
i = 2    j = 10
```

The program initializes  j  to  10  inside the loop. This makes the compiler generate code to load an integer constant into the variable. Suppose, for example, we run this program on a PC AT with the Microsoft C compiler. If  j  is stored at  bp-4  in the stack frame (see Fig. 2-2 and Fig. 2-3), you would see the following instruction in assembly code:

```
MOV [bp-4], 10
```

MOV is the assembler mnemonic for moving data to memory on an INTEL processor.   [bp-4] refers to the *contents* of address  bp-4. This instruction places  10  into the stack frame each time through the loop. The amount of run time overhead may be small for this instruction, but the total time is the sum of the number of times through the loop. Depending on the situation, you may not need to initialize an automatic variable inside a loop each time if you can make it  static, which we discuss in the next section.

What about initializing automatic arrays and structures? Traditionally C did not let you do this, but the new ANSI C standard now allows you to initialize *any* automatic variable, including arrays and structures. Because this new feature was not part of the C language originally, it makes sense to discuss what happens when you initialize automatic arrays or structures. Although it's certainly convenient there are some run time issues that you should be aware of.

For the time being, let's assume your C compiler does not allow you to initialize automatic arrays and structures, and then we'll return to ANSI C later. Let's begin with a program that declares a  double  and sets it to a value. The statement

```
double talk = 56.56;
```

for example, makes the compiler allocate storage for a  double  on the stack and generate code to load the floating point constant  56.56  in the memory location for  talk. C allows you to initialize  talk  because its data type (a  double) has a fixed size and the time it takes to initialize it is small. A  double, therefore, is the *largest* data type that you can initialize as an automatic variable.

Now consider the initialization of an automatic array of doubles:

```
double vision[6] = { 1.2, 3, 6.7, -12.34, 88.7, 12 };
```

This statement won't compile inside a function. The compiler is willing to allocate storage for the automatic array but not initialize the values. This is because the compiler has to initialize the elements at run time, since  vision  is an array on the stack. The compiler must generate code to copy all of the constants to the stack frame. In this case, the array has only 6 elements, but what if the array had 600 elements, or 6000? Although no one would initialize all the elements of an array that big, the compiler still has to generate code to set the initialized elements to specific values (the remaining elements would have undefined values). The assembly code to do this can introduce a significant amount of run time overhead.

When you use `static` to initialize an array inside a function, as in

```
static double vision[6] = { 1.2, 3, 6.7, -12.34, 88.7, 12 };
```

the array contains the initialized values before your program runs. This is the only way to initialize an array without changing the array's scope. More importantly, declaring an array `static` eliminates the overhead of initializing it at run time.

Now let's find out how ANSI C affects this discussion. If you have an ANSI C compiler that allows the initialization of an automatic array, the first declaration for `vision` (the one without `static`) is legal. You should realize, however, that your program now contains run time overhead to initialize the elements in the automatic array. This is not necessarily bad; it just depends on how large the array is, how many elements you initialize, and if execution time is important. You'll have to judge for yourself whether the convenience is worth the run time overhead. This trade-off applies to the initialization of automatic structures with ANSI C compilers as well.

## Recursive Functions

An interesting example of stack usage occurs with recursive functions. Each time you call a function recursively, the system creates a new set of automatic variables on the stack. As you might imagine, the size of the stack grows in relation to the number of times you call the function. Although recursive functions sometimes implement elegant algorithms, you should be aware of their stack requirements. If you call a recursive function too often you may run out of stack space (a condition called *stack overflow*).

Let's return to the integer to hexadecimal conversion routine called `itoh()` from Chapter 1 and make it recursive. Now, `itoh3.c` takes an `unsigned` integer command line argument, converts it to hexadecimal, and displays the result. To show you how recursion uses the stack, we include additional function calls that are not part of the algorithm. These functions, called `showpush()` and `showpop()`, display a recursion *level* number and the current value of the conversion. This is shown in Program 2-11.

Instead of a loop, `itoh()` calls itself. First, we divide the number by `16` and test it for nonzero. As long as this number is not zero, we call `itoh()` again. Otherwise, the statement

```
putchar(hex[n % 16]);
```

displays a hexadecimal digit. How is this done? The expression

```
n % 16
```

evaluates to an integer between 0 and 15. The program uses this value as a *subscript* for a character string that `hex` points to. This provides a hexadecimal character for `putchar()` to display.

**Program 2-11**

```c
/* itoh3.c - recursive integer to hex conversion */

#include <stdio.h>

int level;                          /* recursion level */

main(argc, argv)
int argc;
char *argv[];
{
   unsigned int num;

   if (argc == 1) {
      fprintf(stderr, "Usage: %s number\n", argv[0]);
      exit(1);
   }
   num = atoi(argv[1]);
   itoh(num);
   putchar('\n');
}

itoh(n)
unsigned int n;
{
   int digit;
   char *hex = "0123456789abcdef";

   showpush(&n);
   if (digit = n / 16)
      itoh(digit);                 /* recursive call */
   putchar(hex[n % 16]);
   showpop(&n);
}

showpush(pv)
unsigned int *pv;
{
   fprintf(stderr, "push level %d:\tdigit = %x\t&digit = %x\n",
           ++level, *pv, pv);
}

showpop(pv)
unsigned int *pv;
{
   fprintf(stderr, " pop level %d:\tdigit = %x\t&digit = %x\n",
           level--, *pv, pv);
}
```

We use special functions to examine the stack. Function `showpush()` displays the current address and value of n before the recursive call, and `showpop()` does the same after the call. The routines write to standard error so we can run the program and save the stack information in a separate file. Here's a sample run.

```
$ itoh3 31759 2> sav
7c0f

$ cat sav
push level 1:    digit = 7c0f    &digit = 2e0a
push level 2:    digit = 7c0     &digit = 2dfe
push level 3:    digit = 7c      &digit = 2df2
push level 4:    digit = 7       &digit = 2de6
 pop level 4:    digit = 7       &digit = 2de6
 pop level 3:    digit = 7c      &digit = 2df2
 pop level 2:    digit = 7c0     &digit = 2dfe
 pop level 1:    digit = 7c0f    &digit = 2e0a
```

The stack information is in three columns. The first four lines are from `showpush()` and the next four are from `showpop()`. The second column shows `digit` divided by 16 each time it's pushed on the stack. We print its value in hexadecimal. Note that `digit` has a new address each time we call `itoh()`.

When n becomes zero, we start popping the stack. The numbers come off in reverse order (that is, last in/first out), as the hexadecimal addresses in the third column show. When we apply the mod operator (%) to the value, we get the rightmost character. The bottom line shows the converted value (7c0f).

## Nonlocal Control Transfers

Before we end our discussion of the stack area, let's look at a way to branch to arbitrary parts of a program. This technique, unlike the others, *changes* your run time environment under program control.

Chapter 1 shows the virtue of using *goto* statements in deeply nested blocks for error checking. C limits the destination of a `goto` to within the same function, however. What happens if you need to transfer program control to a different function? The C library functions `setjmp()` and `longjmp()` provide this capability. They appear to work rather mysteriously, until you understand how they use the run time environment. Let's examine these routines, discuss why they are useful, and how they work.

You'll find these definitions in the C library manual:

```
#include <setjmp.h>
. . . .
int setjmp(env)
jmp_buf env;

void longjmp(env, val)
jmp_buf env;
int val;
```

The header file `setjmp.h` defines `jmp_buf`. Programs must use `setjmp()` and `longjmp()` in pairs. The `setjmp()` routine is called first to save the program environment, and it returns zero the first time you call it. Otherwise, `setjmp()` returns the value of `longjmp()`'s *second* argument, called somewhere else in your program. For this reason, you need to test `setjmp()`'s return value after you call it. This is how you detect if a control transfer (a call to `longjmp()`) has occurred.

How does `setjmp()` save the program environment? This is the machine dependent part, because the routine has to access all the machine registers and save them in the `jmp_buf` array. The first time `setjmp()` is called, the routine returns 0. As you will see, it's not necessary for `setjmp()` to save stack frames or anything else.

How does `longjmp()` restore the program environment? This is the mysterious part, because after the function call, you're in a different place in your program (at the `setjmp()`). Calling `longjmp()` restores all the original machine registers (including the program counter) saved by `setjmp()`, to force the machine to execute a different set of instructions. Instead of executing the next line in your program, the program now returns from `setjmp()` with a nonzero value. This changes a program's execution path, and we call this a *context switch*. Note that `longjmp()` is declared `void` and you never return from a `longjmp()` call.

Let's illustrate the use of these functions. Program 2-12, called `jump.c`, handles keyboard input a character at a time. For simplicity, we use *curses* (a terminal independent screen control package, useful for graphics applications) to set up the terminal properly. We'll use a loop to process keyboard input with two functions, `getline()`, which handles lines, and `mygetch()`, which reads characters. Basically, the program stores an input string of characters into a buffer with a trailing NULL byte. When the program encounters a newline, it increments the line number. If you type more than 10 characters or type `Cntrl-L`, the program discards the input. In these two cases, the line number remains the same. If you press the `<ESC>` (Escape) key, the program prompts "Are your sure?" and terminates if you type `'y'`; otherwise, processing continues. Inside the functions `getline()` and `mygetch()`, we check for error conditions and special keyboard characters. If any are detected, we transfer control (using `longjmp()`) from inside the functions back to the main program.

Before you look at the code, let's look at some sample output. We need to link the curses library when we compile `jump.c†`. Here's several lines of output (we show user input in bold):

```
$ cc jump.c -o jump -lcurses
$ jump
Line  1:          string one
Line  2:          string two
Line  3:          string three      too long - discarding
Line  3:          garbageCntrl-L    start over
Line  3:          hello
Line  4:          <ESC>             quit - Are you sure? n
Line  4:          goodbye
Line  5:          <ESC>             quit - Are you sure? y
$
```

There are three columns in the display. The first column lists the current line number. The second column displays the input strings, and the last column contains messages from the program. The program accepts lines 1 and 2. Line 3, however, exceeds 10 characters, so the program prints a message and discards the buffer. Next, we type `garbage` followed by `Cntrl-L`. This makes you start over. The program accepts `hello` on line 3.

When you type the `<ESC>` key on line 4, the program prompts for you to stop. We type `'n'` to continue. Still on line 4, we type `goodbye`. Line 5 terminates the program when you type the `<ESC>` key followed by `'y'` after the prompt.

Now let's study the code. Here's `main()` from `jump.c`:

**Program 2-12**

```
/* jump.c - setjmp and longjmp */

#include <curses.h>
#include <setjmp.h>

#define MAX 11

jmp_buf jmp_environment;
```

---

† Berkeley and pre-System V Release 2 UNIX systems require the termlib library to be linked as well:
```
cc jump.c -o jump -lcurses -ltermlib
```

```
main()
{
    int retval;
    char buf[MAX], ch;
    int lineno = 1;

    initscr();                     /* initialize curses */
    raw();                         /* process each char */
    noecho();                      /* no echo */
    nonl();                        /* no newline mapping */

    if ((retval = setjmp(jmp_environment)) != 0) {
      switch (retval) {

        case 1:            /* Too many chars input */
            printw("\t too long - discarding\n");
            refresh();
            break;

        case 2:            /* Cntrl-L - start over */
            printw("\t\t start over\n");
            refresh();
            break;

        case 3:            /* ESC - quit program */
            printw("\t\t quit - Are you sure? ");
            refresh();
            ch = getch();
            printw("%c\n", ch);
            refresh();
            if (ch == 'y') {
                endwin();          /* restore terminal */
                exit(1);
            }
        }
    }

    printw("Line %2d:\t", lineno);  /* current line number */
    refresh();

    while (1) {
        getline(buf);                          /* input string */
        printw("Line %2d:\t", ++lineno);  /* current line num */
        refresh();
    }
}
```

To use curses and nonlocal control transfers, you need to include the appropriate header files. In `main()`, we initialize curses, and call the curses routines `raw()`, `noecho()`, and `nonl()` to put keyboard input under program control. This allows you to provide your own echoing, handle newlines, and process each character as it's typed.

Next, we call `setjmp()`. We switch on the return value, which has four values. If `retval` is 0 (which it will be in this case), we bypass the `switch` statement and enter a `while` loop processing input. We print the current line number and call `getline()` for a new string. Now let's look at `getline()`:

```
getline(buf)              /* get a line from the keyboard */
char *buf;
{
    int nc = 0, ch;

    do {
        ch = mygetch();        /* get a char */
        addch(ch);
        refresh();
        if (nc == MAX)         /* too many characters */
            longjmp(jmp_environment, 1);
        buf[nc++] = (ch == '\n') ? '\0' : ch;
    } while (ch != '\n');    /* quit on newline */
}
```

Note that `getline()` processes input characters by calling `mygetch()`. We call the curses routines `addch()` and `refresh()` to echo the character. We store each character into the buffer, unless it's a newline. In this case, we store a NULL byte and return.

Routine `getline()` makes the first call to `longjmp()`. This happens if you type more than 10 characters. When we call `longjmp()`, execution continues at the `setjmp()` in the main program, which returns with a value of 1— `longjmp()`'s second argument. The program displays a message and enters the `while` loop again at the top. This discards the buffer's contents.

`mygetch()` uses the curses routine `getch()` to read a keyboard character. Since we call `nonl()` for keyboard input with curses, `getch()` returns a `'\r'` for a newline. In this case, `getch()` returns a `'\n'` to `getline()`.

`mygetch()` makes two calls to `longjmp()`. Typing `Cntrl-L` or `<ESC>` transfers control back to the main program with different return values. This places you back in the main program's `switch` statement, where we handle each case separately. For a `Cntrl-L`, we display a message and enter the processing loop at the top. The `<ESC>` key makes the program prompt to continue. If you type `'y'`, we restore the terminal with the curses routine `endwin()` and terminate the program. Otherwise, we again enter the processing loop at the top.

Here's the code for `mygetch()`:

```
mygetch()
{
    int c;

    c = getch();            /* get a char from keyboard */

    if (c == '\014')                /* Cntrl-L */
        longjmp(jmp_environment, 2);
    if (c == '\033')                /* ESC - quit */
        longjmp(jmp_environment, 3);

    return (c == '\r') ? '\n' : c;   /* check for newline */
}
```

How do these routines affect local variables? At the point where you call setjmp(), the system has allocated the stack frame and automatic variables. A setjmp() saves the registers that contain this information. After a call to longjmp(), the restored stack frame and auto variables retain their values. This is why lineno in jump.c doesn't change after the calls to longjmp().

As the program shows, you can transfer control from just about anywhere in your program. The only restriction is you can't call longjmp() if the function that contains setjmp() has already returned. This makes sense, since automatic variables and stack frames disappear when a function returns.

Why use nonlocal control transfers? First of all, they are useful in large programs like editors, menus, and window-based managers. Since the routines manipulate machine registers, the execution time to transfer control is small. You may be deeply nested within many function calls, yet branch to one place in the code to handle special input conditions. Without them, we would have to rely on flags and control mechanisms, things that would undoubtedly be clumsy and error prone. Use setjmp() and longjmp() sparingly, if possible. Too many calls make programs hard to follow.

## ♦ The Data Area ♦

The data area holds a C program's data. Whatever variables or data that you place here exist for the life of your program. Unlike variables on the stack that come and go during function calls, static variables retain their values after a function returns. The data area has two sections, one of them set aside for variables that you initialize, the other for ones that you don't. The data area's size is typically fixed throughout program execution.

This section looks at how C uses the data area. We discuss static initializations as they relate to the data area, and how internal and external static variables are used. As we did with the stack, we examine blocks, loops, and functions that use variables from the data area. We'll also look at how C allocates constant strings from the data area. Understanding how a C program uses the data area is helpful in determining its data requirements.

## Allocation

The compiler uses memory from the data area for the following items:

1. Internal and external static variables

2. Global variables

3. Initialized arrays and structures

4. Constant strings

Let's review what this means. Internal static means you place the word `static` in front of a variable declaration inside a function or block. External statics appear outside functions with the keyword `static`, making the variable private to the file where it's declared. Global variables also appear outside functions but without the keyword `static`. Their values are available to other files that wish to access them. Initialized arrays and structures inside a block or function live in the data area when you use `static` in their declarations.

What about constant strings? It turns out that most C compilers place them in the data area, but the location of constant strings may be compiler dependent. It's possible, for example, to place them in the text area, which saves data space if you're targeting C object code for ROM (read-only memory). This implies that constant strings can't be changed, however. Some C compilers give you an option for placing constant strings in text or data space. In the following examples, we assume constant strings appear in the data area, but we'll have more to say about them later.

Let's look at all the ways C uses the data area from the following program:

**Program 2-13**

```
/* data.c - allocate memory in data area */

    /* external static - private integer */
static int status;

    /* external - global array */
char buf[10];

    /* external - global structure */
struct complex {
   float real, imag;
} polar;
```

```
main()
{
        /* internal static - long */
    static long flag;

        /* internal static - array */
    static float vals[] = { 1.2, 3.4, 5.6 };

        /* internal static - structure */
    static struct complex plane;

        /* constant string */
    printf("%f %f\n", vals[1], vals[2]);
}
```

```
$ data
3.400000 5.600000
```

Note that status, buf, and polar reside in the data area because they are outside main(). Inside main(), flag, vals, and plane are internal statics. Array vals lives in the data area, since we declared it static. printf() contains the format string "%f %f\n". This is a constant string; hence, it also lives in the data area. This implies that every time you use scanf() and printf(), you may be using memory from the data area.

## The BSS Area

The data area is divided into two separate sections. Static variables may appear in either one. If you declare a static variable without an initialization, it goes into a special part of the data area called the BSS. Otherwise, it's placed in the other section, sometimes called *initialized data*. Static variables in the BSS may be internal or external. We'll look at BSS variables first, and then discuss initialized variables.

Let's edit the previous program and mark the BSS variables. Here's the code for bss.c.

**Program 2-14**

```
/* bss.c - allocate memory in BSS area */

        /* BSS external static - private integer */
static int status;

        /* BSS external - global array */
char buf[10];
```

```
        /* BSS external - global structure */
struct complex {
   float real, imag;
} polar;


main()
{
        /* BSS internal static - long */
    static long flag;

        /* internal static - array */
    static float vals[] = { 1.2, 3.4, 5.6 };

        /* BSS internal static - structure */
    static struct complex plane;

        /* constant string */
    printf("%f %f\n", vals[1], vals[2]);
}
```

**$ bss**
3.400000 5.600000

Except for array `vals`, all variables reside in the BSS. Constant strings are never placed in the BSS, because they must be initialized. Incidentally, a variable's scope has nothing to do with the BSS.

Now that we understand how C statements map to the BSS area, the next topic is "why bother?". It turns out that separating the uninitialized variables from the initialized ones is done more for the loader than for the compiler. Recall that C guarantees uninitialized statics and global variables have zero values before a program runs. To make this happen, the compiler marks these variables so the loader can group them together at link time. When it's time to run the program, all the system has to do is load the BSS variables into a section of memory and zero-fill it all at once. This is obviously faster than initializing one variable at a time.

What does this mean to you? First of all, you're assured all uninitialized statics and global variables are zero when your program starts running. This implies that initializing a static flag to FALSE (zero), as in

```
static int flag = FALSE;
```

is unnecessary, although it can be argued that this is better programming. Moreover, filling a static array with zeros may also be a waste of time. The following code

```
#define MAX 1000
int buffer[MAX];                    /* BSS */

main()
{
   int i;

   /* initialize the buffer */
   for (i = 0; i < MAX; i++)
       buffer[i] = 0;
   . . . .
}
```

for example, uses a `for` loop to set all the integer elements of an array to zero. Not only is this slow, it's often unnecessary. (Memory resident programs that don't get reinitialized each time they are run might require such an initialization, however.)

As another example, suppose we modify the `count()` function from the previous section. This time we want to maintain a total count of the number of values in an array throughout the life of a program. Here's the old code, which doesn't quite do it.

```
int count(buf, nitems, value)
int *buf, nitems, value;
{
   int i;
   int nc = 0;                      /* auto */

   for (i = 0; i < nitems; i++)
     if (buf[i] == value)
         nc++;
   return nc;
}
```

nc's storage class is automatic. We make sure it's zero before we loop over the array. When we return from the function, `nc` disappears from the stack. The next time we call `count()`, `nc` starts off at zero again. We can't use `count()`'s return value as the total, because it resets after each call.

With this arrangement, we have to maintain a separate count in the function that calls `count()`. Here's the calling program:

```
#define MAX 1000
int databuf[MAX];
int total = 0;                      /* auto */
```

```
while (1) {
    . . . .
    total += count(databuf, MAX, 0x7f);
    printf("%d\n", total);
    . . . .
}
```

This works, but a better solution is to move `total` to `count()` and change its storage class.

```
int count(buf, nitems, value)
int *buf, nitems, value;
{
    int i;
    static int total;                /* BSS */

    for (i = 0; i < nitems; i++)
        if (buf[i] == value)
            total++;
    return total;
}
```

Since `total` is now in the BSS, it's zero when the program runs. It will retain its count after each function call. In the calling program, all we have to do now is:

```
#define MAX 1000
int databuf[MAX];

while (1) {
    . . . .
    printf("%d\n", count(databuf, MAX, 0x7f));
    . . . .
}
```

Inside `count()`, we return `total` each time, so it is available to the calling routine.

## Initialization

The initialized data area contains statics and global variables that you explicitly initialize in a C program. The system initializes each variable in memory before the program runs. Constant strings, if they are stored in the data area, appear in initialized data.

Let's modify `data.c` to create several initialized statics and global variables. The following program called `initd.c` contains only items that do *not* appear in the BSS:

**Program 2-15**

```
/* initd.c - allocate memory for initialized data */

        /* external static - private integer */
static int status = -1;

        /* external - global array */
char buf[] = "worthwhile";

        /* external - global structure */
struct complex {
   float real, imag;
} polar = { -1.7, -4.8 };

main()
{
        /* internal static - long */
  static long flag = 1;

        /* internal static - array */
  static float vals[] = { 1.2, 3.4, 5.6 };

        /* internal static - structure */
  static struct complex plane = { .7, .9 };

        /* constant string */
  printf("%f %f\n", vals[1], vals[2]);
}
```

```
$ initd
3.400000 5.600000
```

All variables have initialized values. The constant string in `printf()` also appears in initialized data.

Why is this important? To investigate, suppose the following declarations appear inside a function or block:

```
{
    int var1 = 3;                 /* automatic */
    static int var2 = 4;          /* internal static */
    . . . .
}
```

Since `var1` is automatic, the compiler allocates storage on the stack. Following this, the compiler generates assembly code to load a constant 3 in that location. This is a two-step process. But `var2`, on the other hand, lives in initialized data. The initialization is the system's job and not the compiler's. The value 4 is loaded in memory for `var2` before your program runs. Initializing a static variable, therefore, is a one-step process.

This implies there is no run time overhead for initializing statics and global variables because the compiler doesn't produce assembly code for the initialization. The declaration

```
static char chargeplate[] = "mastercard";
```

for example, doesn't generate assembly code to load a constant string into the array. Instead, the array contains the characters in the data area before your program runs.

What about static declarations inside loops? Let's return to `loop.c`, which declares an automatic integer inside a block. Here's the program again and its output:

**Program 2-16**

```
/* loop.c - creates auto variable */

#include <stdio.h>

main()
{
    int i;

    for (i = 0; i < 3; i++) {
        int j = 10;
        printf("i = %d\tj = %d\n", i , j);
        j++;
    }
}
```

```
$ loop
i = 0    j = 10
i = 1    j = 10
i = 2    j = 10
```

Even though the declaration for `j` appears inside the loop, the compiler allocates stack storage for it only once. The initialization step, however, is done each time through the loop. This is why the output shows `j` never changes.

We get a different output if we modify this program and make  j static, as in `loop2.c`.

**Program 2-17**

```
/* loop2.c - creates static variable */

#include <stdio.h>

main()
{
    int i;

    for (i = 0; i < 3; i++) {
        static int j = 10;
        printf("i = %d\tj = %d\n", i , j);
        j++;
    }
}

$ loop2
i = 0    j = 10
i = 1    j = 11
i = 2    j = 12
```

Since  j is static, there's no run time code to initialize it.  The system initializes  j to  10 before the program runs.  The output shows that  j retains its previous value each time through the loop.

## Constant Strings

C provides character constants and constant strings.  When you enclose an ASCII character between single quotes, the compiler uses a constant and not a memory location.  For example, the compiler generates  6b (hexadecimal) for the ASCII character  'k'.  What about constant strings?  They can be any length, so the amount of storage allocated varies.  When you enclose a series of characters within double quotation marks, the compiler allocates one byte for each character, with one additional byte at the end.  The last byte contains all zeros (the NULL byte).  As we mentioned, most C compilers store constant strings in the data area.  We use them so often in C programs, it's worthwhile taking a closer look.

C allows constant strings for the following items:

1. Initializing character pointers
2. Assignment statements for character pointers
3. Functions with character pointer arguments
4. Character pointer references

Here are examples showing the first three uses:

```
char *boy = "kellen";   /* initialize character pointer */

boy = "tyler";          /* character pointer assignment */

puts("stephanie");      /* function argument */
```

Strings also appear in the initialization of a character array, as in

```
char girl[] = "sara";   /* initialize character array */
```

but this is just shorthand notation for

```
char girl[] = { 's', 'a', 'r', 'a', '\0' };
```

and will not be treated as a constant string by the compiler.

The fourth use of constant strings (as character pointer references) requires more explanation. To illustrate, study the following program and its output.

**Program 2-18**

```
/* strcon.c - constant strings as arrays and pointers */

main()
{
    printf("%s\n", "hello again" + 6);
    printf("%c\n", *("12345" + 3));
    printf("%c\n", "12345"[1]);
}

$ strcon
again
4
2
```

If this code looks peculiar, don't be surprised. The use of constant strings in place of character pointers is not common. In the first line, the expression

```
"hello again" + 6
```

is a pointer *offset*. This expression produces a pointer to the seventh character (a) of the constant string.  printf() uses this pointer to display the word again. If this is not clear, look at

```
char *p = "hello again";
```

The expression

```
p + 6
```

evaluates to the same pointer.

In the second line, the expression

```
*("12345" + 3)
```

evaluates to the character ′4′. We apply the indirection operator to the pointer offset.  The result is the fourth character of the constant string.

In the third line, the expression

```
"12345"[1]
```

also evaluates to a character.  Here we use a constant string in place of an array name.  It's actually a pointer to the constant string, but we can use square brackets to reference a character (in this case, the second character  2).

We mention this application of constant strings because we can put it to good use in our recursive function itoh() from the previous section.  Here's the old code for itoh():

```
itoh(n)
unsigned int n;
{
    int digit;
    char *hex = "0123456789abcdef";

    showpush(&n);
    if (digit = n / 16)
        itoh(digit);
    putchar(hex[n % 16]);
    showpop(&n);
}
```

Recall that recursive functions allocate new automatic variables everytime we call them. This means the compiler creates digit and hex on the stack for each function call. Using constant strings for array names, we can use the following code for `itoh()` instead:

```
itoh(n)
unsigned int n;
{
    int digit;

    showpush(&n);
    if (digit = n / 16)
        itoh(digit);
    putchar("0123456789abcdef"[n % 16]);
    showpop(&n);
}
```

In place of pointer hex, we use the constant string. This eliminates the pointer from the recursive call and saves stack space.

A second solution (which arguably may be better programming) is to declare hex *static* in the original program. The declaration

```
static char *hex = "0123456789abcdef";
```

retains the readability of the original program and still saves stack space at run time.

Let's return to the difference between initializing a character array and initializing a pointer to a constant character string. Suppose we have a program with the following statements:

```
char buf[] = "hello.";
char *p    = "goodbye";
```

Note that we haven't said where these statements appear. But with the knowledge we've learned so far, we can make several comments. First of all, the line that initializes buf is most likely declared outside a function (unless your compiler supports initializing automatic arrays). Second, buf is the address of a character array of length 7 (including the string terminator character). Third, the array name buf is a constant. This is important because it keeps us from reassigning a new constant string to the array. The assignment statement

```
buf = "newstring";      /* illegal, doesn't compile */
```

for example, produces a compilation error. It's like trying

```
5 = 6;
```

and we certainly don't expect this to compile.

The pointer p, on the other hand, may appear in several places and its storage class may be auto or static. In this case, we declare p as a pointer to a character, initialized to a constant string. If you change the value of p, you change what it points to. Therefore, we can reassign what p points to with the following statement:

```
p = "newstring";
```

Array assignments must occur an element at a time. Thus, the following statements are legal:

```
buf[0] = 'j';
buf[5] = '!';
```

Let's put all these statements into a program (minus the illegal one, of course). We'll make p static and declare an automatic pointer q:

**Program 2-19**

```
/* str.c - show constant strings */

char buf[] = "hello.";          /* static array */
char *p    = "goodbye";         /* static pointer */

main()
{
    char *q = "string";         /* auto pointer */

    printf("buf's address: %x\n", buf);
    printf("p's address:   %x\n", &p);
    printf("q's address:   %x\n\n", &q);

    printf("%s\t\t(len = %d)\t(string's addr = %x)\n",
            buf, strlen(buf), buf);
    printf("%s\t\t(len = %d)\t(string's addr = %x)\n",
            p, strlen(p), p);
    printf("%s\t\t(len = %d)\t(string's addr = %x)\n",
            q, strlen(q), q);

    p = "newstring";
    buf[0] = 'j';
    buf[5] = '!';

    printf("%s\t\t(len = %d)\t(string's addr = %x)\n",
            buf, strlen(buf), buf);
    printf("%s\t(len = %d)\t(string's addr = %x)\n",
            p, strlen(p), p);
}
```

Here's the output on a machine with 16-bit addresses:

```
buf's address:  15ca
p's address:    15d2
q's address:    2e16

hello.          (len = 6)        (string's addr = 15ca)
goodbye         (len = 7)        (string's addr = 1576)
string          (len = 6)        (string's addr = 14be)
jello!          (len = 6)        (string's addr = 15ca)
newstring       (len = 9)        (string's addr = 14c6)
```

First we display the addresses of the array and the two pointers.  p and buf live in the data area, but q lives on the stack (its address is quite different). The next five lines list all the strings from the program (we omit the format strings from the printf() statements). We show the string's length followed by its address. The addresses for the first and fourth strings are the same as the address of buf.

Let's walk through this program as it executes. Fig. 2-4 shows the program areas before the program runs. We have only the data area allocated at this time.

DATA AREA

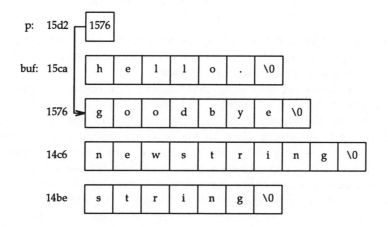

*Fig. 2-4.* Status of str at load time

buf contains the string "hello.", and p points to the string "goodbye". The system has allocated the strings "string" and "newstring" in the data area, but nothing is pointing to them yet.

Fig. 2-5 shows what happens after allocating pointer q on the stack.

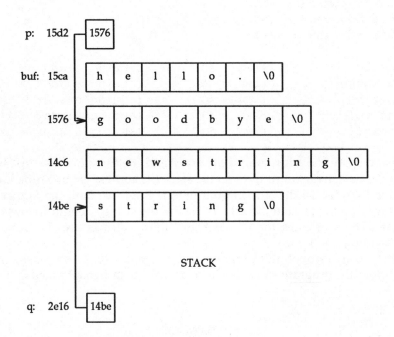

*Fig. 2-5.* Status of str during execution

The program sets its value to 14be, the address of "string". In assembly code, the compiler assigns the address of the string in the data area to the pointer location on the stack. This is pointer assignment.

Fig. 2-6 shows the run time environment just before the program terminates. Now p points to "newstring" and buf is modified.

Several questions arise. What happens to a constant string once a pointer to it has been set to something else? In the previous program, we changed p to point to "newstring" after initially pointing to "goodbye". Not so surprising, the original string becomes an orphan; it can't be referenced again directly. This implies that constant strings don't go away once you're through with them. They occupy memory in the data area for the life of your program.

The next question is even more intriguing. What happens if you use duplicate constant strings in the *same* program? To find out, we ran Program 2-20 on our machine.

DATA AREA

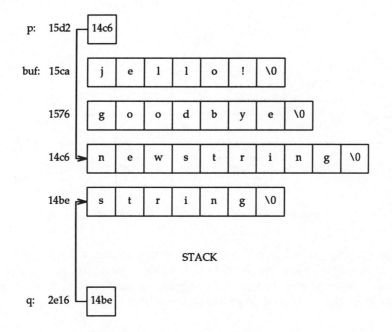

*Fig. 2-6.* Status of str before terminating

**Program 2-20**

```
/* dup1.c - duplicate strings */

main()
{
    char *p = "hello";

    printf("%s's address is %x\n", p, p);

    p = "goodbye";
    printf("%s's address is %x\n", p, p);

    p = "hello";
    printf("%s's address is %x\n", p, p);
}
```

```
$ dup1
hello's address is 1436
goodbye's address is 1450
hello's address is 146c
```

We assign p to three different addresses. Fig. 2-7 shows how our C compiler stores the constant strings from Program 2-20.

DATA AREA

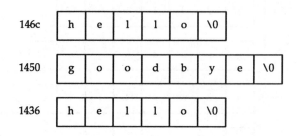

*Fig. 2-7.* Storage allocation for duplicate strings

What this shows is that our C compiler doesn't optimize storage for multiple copies of the same string. With other C compilers, however, the results may be different. You may wish to run this program on your system to find out what your compiler does. And while you're at it, run this program as well:

**Program 2-21**

```
/* dup2.c - duplicate strings */

main()
{
    char *p, *q;

    p = "string";
    q = "string";

    p[3] = 'o';
    printf("%s %s\n", p, q);
}

$ dup2
strong string
```

We don't recommend this type of programming because it's not portable and it's behavior is not predictable.† Nevertheless, `dup2.c` and `dup1.c` tell you a lot about what your compiler does with constant strings. On our system, for instance, two copies of `"string"` live in the data area. Changing the string that p points to has no effect on the other string.

Regardless of how your compiler handles constant strings, it doesn't hurt to follow a few simple guidelines. Here's a tip, for example, that we've found useful with constant strings:

> Use a *pointer* to save a constant string's address if you
> intend to use the same string many times in a program. Only
> one copy of the constant string exists in the data area and
> you reference it with the pointer instead of the string.
> This can save memory and allows you to use a pointer in
> expressions where a constant string is not legal.

Although the concept of saving values is basic to programming, it's not as obvious with the addresses of constant strings. It's far too easy to write (as we did in `dup1.c`):

```
char *p = "string 1";    /* set string's address */
. . . .
p = "string 2";
. . . .
p = "string 1";          /* a different string address */
```

If your compiler creates separate copies of constant strings in the data area, `"string 1"` will appear in two places. The following approach, however, can save memory.

```
char *p = "string 1";    /* set string's address */
char *psav;              /* new pointer */
. . . .
psav = p;                /* save string's address */
p = "string 2";
. . . .
p = psav;                /* restore string's address */
```

Here `psav` contains the address of `"string 1"` and we don't create a second copy of the constant string. This technique is particularly useful for building a set of error messages. Instead of simply passing a constant string at the point the error occurs, you can create an array of error messages. When you need to use the same error message more than once, you avoid duplicating constant strings in the data area.

---

† If constant strings live in the text area, for example, you wouldn't be able to modify them. The ANSI C standard also states that string literals are unmodifiable, so this program may not compile or run with ANSI C compilers.

## ◆ The Heap ◆

Suppose a program needs to reserve storage based on run time events, like user input or I/O requests. These variables can't be automatic, because they need to be allocated and freed under program control. A program area called the *heap* is available for this purpose. The heap allows programmers to allocate memory dynamically.

The heap is kept separate from the stack. It's possible, however, for the heap and stack to share the same memory segment. Recall that Fig. 2-1 shows the stack growing down and the heap growing up in memory. A program that uses a large amount of memory for the stack may have a small amount of memory available for the heap and vice versa. During software development, you need to monitor both of these program areas. Otherwise, you may find yourself out of heap space or overflowing the stack.

The heap is controlled by a heap manager, which allocates and deallocates memory. User programs interface to the heap via C library calls. The following functions are available:

**TABLE 2-1. C library calls for the heap**

| Routine | Meaning |
|---|---|
| `char *malloc(size)` | allocate storage |
| `unsigned size;` | for `size` bytes |
| | |
| `char *calloc(n, size)` | allocate and zero storage |
| `unsigned n, size;` | for n items of `size` bytes |
| | |
| `char *realloc(pheap, newsize)` | reallocate storage |
| `char *pheap;` | for old heap pointer `pheap` |
| `unsigned newsize;` | for `newsize` bytes |
| | |
| `void free(pheap)` | free storage |
| `char *pheap;` | for heap pointer `pheap` |

Bytes of memory are allocated in user-defined "chunks" (sometimes called objects) with `malloc()`, `calloc()`, and `realloc()`. `free()` relinquishes memory. The following program calls `malloc()` to create storage on the heap for a structure called `block`.

**Program 2-22**

```c
/* block1.c - allocate block on heap */

#include <stdio.h>

struct block {
  int header;
  char data[1024];
};

main()
{
  char *malloc();
  struct block *p;

  p = (struct block *) malloc (sizeof(struct block));

  if (p == (struct block *) NULL) {
      fprintf(stderr, "malloc can't allocate heap space\n");
      exit(1);
  }
}
```

sizeof() determines the number of bytes in the structure and makes the code portable. malloc() returns a heap address, and the program casts its return value from a pointer to a char (a byte pointer) to a pointer to a structure (structure block). You should always check the return value from malloc() and the other library calls before you use the heap address. A NULL (defined in stdio.h) indicates that the heap manager was unable to allocate storage. It's usually difficult for a program to continue if this happens, unless you free up some previously allocated space and try again. In our example, we display an error message on standard error and exit from the program.

calloc() is similar to malloc(), but the routine fills heap memory with zeros. calloc(), therefore, runs slightly slower than malloc(). Also, calloc() takes two arguments, which are the number of objects to allocate and the size of each object. calloc() also returns a heap address.

The following code fragment allocates storage for MAXENTRIES structures. The first allocation uses malloc() and the second uses calloc().

**Program 2-23**

```c
/* block2.c - allocate MAXENTRIES blocks on heap */

#include <stdio.h>
#define MAXENTRIES 5

struct block {
    int header;
    char data[1024];
};

main()
{
    char *malloc(), *calloc();
    struct block *p1, *p2;

    p1 = (struct block *)
                malloc (MAXENTRIES * sizeof(struct block));

    if (p1 == (struct block *) NULL) {
        fprintf(stderr, "malloc can't allocate heap space\n");
        exit(1);
    }
    p2 = (struct block *)
                calloc (MAXENTRIES, sizeof(struct block));

    if (p2 == (struct block *) NULL) {
        fprintf(stderr, "calloc can't allocate heap space\n");
        exit(1);
    }
}
```

After the call to `malloc()`, p1 points to the first of five consecutive structures (of type `block`) in memory. Similarly, p2 points to the first of five structures after the call to `calloc()`. The storage that p2 points to is zero-filled. Note that we pass two arguments to `calloc()`, but only one to `malloc()`. Each call allocates the same amount of heap memory.

`realloc()` allows you to change the size of any object on the heap. The routine's first argument is a pointer to a heap address. Presumably, this pointer is initialized from a previous call to the heap manager. The second argument is the number of bytes to reallocate. `realloc()` can increase or decrease an object's size in heap memory.

`realloc()` also preserves data in memory. If the storage space is being increased and there's not enough contiguous space on the heap, `realloc()` returns a different address than the one that you pass as its first argument. This means `realloc()` may have to move data; hence, its execution time varies.

Occasionally, `realloc()` returns the *same* heap address. This is an important point if you're maintaining a table of heap addresses. When you allocate memory from the heap manager using any of the library calls, you should always update your table with the new pointer, even though it may not have changed. Programs that don't do this are not reliable.

The following function, called `readin()`, demonstrates the usefulness of `realloc()`. It answers the question "how much memory should I allocate to store keyboard input if I don't know how many characters will be typed?" `readin()` reacts dynamically to keyboard input and returns a pointer to the input string. The number of bytes on the heap is exactly the number of characters typed.

**Program 2-24**

```
/* readin.c - read in a string using heap */

#include <stdio.h>
#define DELTA 256

char *readin(prompt)
char *prompt;
{
    char *p, *q;
    int nc;
    unsigned size = DELTA;
    char *malloc(), *realloc();

    if ((p = q = malloc (size)) == NULL) {  /* get a chunk */
        fprintf(stderr, "malloc can't allocate heap space\n");
        exit(1);
    }
    printf("%s ", prompt);
    for (nc = 1; (*p = getchar()) != '\n' && *p != EOF; nc++) {
        if (nc % DELTA == 0) {
            size += DELTA;
            if ((p = q = realloc (q, size)) == NULL) {
                fprintf(stderr, "realloc can't allocate heap space\n");
                exit(1);
            }
            p += nc;
            continue;
        }
        p++;
    }
    *p = '\0';
    return realloc (q, nc);
}
```

Here's how it works.  `readin()` allocates 256-byte chunks of memory from the heap.  As the user types in characters, `readin()` allocates additional chunks as required.  When the user types carriage return, `readin()` NULL terminates the input string and reallocates heap memory.

`readin()` has one argument, a character string that is displayed as a prompt.  Character pointer  `q` keeps track of the original pointer returned by `malloc()`.  `*p` stores each keyboard character in heap memory.  `nc` counts the number of characters read.  When we've read in 256 characters, we reallocate the heap for another 256 bytes, passing the original pointer  `q` back to  `realloc()`.  We must increment  `p` by  `nc` after the reallocation to point to the beginning of the unused portion of the new storage (otherwise the subsequent input characters replace the previous input characters).  When we return, we NULL terminate the input string and call  `realloc()` with the number of characters typed to free up any unused space.

The following program calls  `readin()`.

**Program 2-25**

```
/* kbrd.c - uses readin for keyboard input */

main()
{
    char *p, *readin();

    p = readin(">");

    printf("input string = %s\tlength = %d\n", p, strlen(p));
}
```

We use  `>` as a prompt.  Here are two test runs.

```
$ cc kbrd.c readin.c -o kbrd
$ kbrd
> 123456789
input string = 123456789          length = 9

$ kbrd
> abcdefghijklmnopqrstuvwxyz
input string = abcdefghijklmnopqrstuvwxyz          length = 26
```

The program echoes the input string and displays the length.

This version of  `readin()` sets DELTA to 256.  This is more characters than we're likely to type, but it keeps us from calling  `realloc()` too often.  In fact, the larger we set DELTA, the fewer times we call  `realloc()`.

The heap manager frees heap memory with the C library call `free()`. You call it with a heap address returned from a previous call to `malloc()`, `calloc()`, or `realloc()`. The following statements free a structure called `block` from the heap:

```
char *malloc();
void free();
struct block *p;

p = (struct block *) malloc (sizeof(struct block));

if (p == (struct block *) NULL) {
 fprintf(stderr, "malloc can't allocate heap space\n");
 exit(1);
}
. . . .
free(p);                 /* free the structure */
. . . .
```

You must pass a pointer to the start of some previously allocated space to `free()`. Note that `free()` doesn't return anything. Unlike the other routines, you don't know if anything goes wrong. We'll have more to say about the heap in other parts of this book. Chapter 5, for example, presents debugging techniques that provide "front-ends" to the storage allocator routines. Chapter 6 presents a memory object allocator containing additional features.

## ◆ Putting It All Together ◆

This section looks at specific C code related to the run time environment. This includes C programs that produce errors at compile time and run time. To determine the problem and suggest a solution, we'll apply the knowledge we've learned. The chapter concludes with a C program that maps its declarations to all the program areas.

### Initializing Program Variables

The following program produces the compilation error "illegal initialization".

```
main()
{
    char buf[5];                 /* stack */
    static char *p = buf;        /* initialized data */
}
```

Do you see what's wrong? If not, look closely at the storage classes of each variable. buf is an automatic character array, created on the stack when the program runs. p is a pointer in the data area. The program tries to initialize p to the address of the first element of buf. Since p lives in the data area, however, its initial value must be determined before the program runs. How can the compiler do this if buf doesn't exist yet? C reports an error because we're using storage classes incorrectly.

To strengthen this concept, it's worthwhile looking at similar examples. This one correctly initializes a pointer variable at load time.

```
main()
{
    static char buf[5];        /* BSS */
    static char *p = buf;      /* initialized data */
}
```

Fig. 2-8 shows the program's run time environment.

DATA AREA

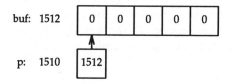

*Fig. 2-8.* Initializing static variables

Both p and buf reside in the data area. buf lives in the BSS, since we didn't initialize it. buf's address (1512) is a constant whose value is known at load time. Before the program runs, p already points to buf. The compiler doesn't generate assembly code for the initialization.

The next example shows you it's possible to initialize an automatic pointer to another automatic variable as long as you're careful of when you do it.

```
main()
{
    char buf[5];        /* stack */
    char *p = buf;      /* stack */
}
```

Fig. 2-9 shows this run time environment.

STACK

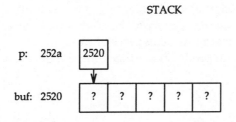

**Fig. 2-9.** Initializing auto variables

Both `buf` and `p` are automatic variables on the stack. To initialize `p`, `buf` must already exist. In other words, the initialization has to follow `buf`'s declaration. This allows the compiler to generate assembly code to load the address of `buf` into `p`, since `buf`'s address on the stack frame is known at the time `p` is created. As Fig. 2-9 shows, the data bytes inside `buf` are not set to anything; they contain whatever happened to be on the stack when the program runs.

The next example initializes variables that have different storage classes. This program, for instance, initializes a stack pointer to the address of a variable in the data area.

```
main()
{
    static char buf[5];         /* BSS */
    char *p = buf;              /* stack */
}
```

Fig. 2-10 depicts this run time environment.

DATA AREA

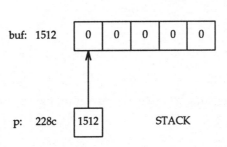

**Fig. 2-10.** Initializing static and auto variables

buf's address is in the BSS and each element has a zero value. When the program runs, the compiler allocates stack space for p. Following this, it generates assembly code to initialize p with the address of buf from the data area. Pointer assignment, therefore, takes place at run time.

The next program produces another compilation error. What's wrong?

```
int block = 1024;                      /* initialized data */

main()
{
    static int tenk = 10 * block;  /* initialized data */
}
```

block and tenk live in initialized data. The program tries to initialize tenk to an expression using block's value. The compiler reports an error on this line because you must use constants or addresses to initialize a static variable.

Changing tenk's storage class to automatic makes it compile, however.

```
int block = 1024;                      /* initialized data */

main()
{
    int tenk = 10 * block;             /* stack */
}
```

The compiler allows expressions with variables if you are initializing an automatic variable. If you declared block inside main() (making it automatic), the program would also compile without error.

Suppose you don't want to change tenk's static storage class to initialize it. In this case, you'll have to use #defines as follows:

```
#define BSIZE 1024
int block = BSIZE;                     /* initialized data */

main()
{
    static int tenk = 10 * BSIZE;  /* stack */
}
```

The compiler accepts this because we are initializing tenk with a constant expression.

## Use with Functions

Suppose you want to declare a variable and initialize it with a function call. With automatic variables, this is legal. The following program

```
main(argc, argv)
int argc;
char *argv[];
{
    int length = strlen(argv[1]);
}
```

for example, initializes `length` to the number of characters in a program's first command line argument. The following program, however, produces a compilation error.

```
main(argc, argv)
int argc;
char *argv[];
{
    /* doesn't compile! */
    static int length = strlen(argv[1]);
}
```

For the same reason we cannot initialize a static variable to the value of another static variable, we can't use a function's return value, either. Both actions are run time events. If your program requires `length` to be static, you'll have to initialize it in a separate assignment statement as follows:

```
main(argc, argv)
int argc;
char *argv[];
{
    static int length;             /* BSS */

    length = strlen(argv[1]);
}
```

In this case `length`'s initial value is zero. In the assignment statement, the compiler generates code to store `strlen()`'s return value into `length` at run time.

What about pointers to functions? You can initialize both automatic and static pointers to functions because function addresses are known at load time. The following program, for example, compiles without error.

```
main()
{
    int f();

    int (*p)() = f;                    /* auto */

    static int (*q)() = f;             /* initialized data */
}

f()                                     /* text area */
{
    . . . .
}
```

Fig. 2-11 shows this program's run time environment.

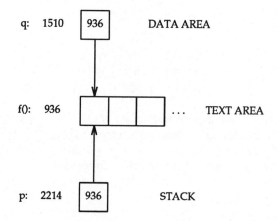

*Fig. 2-11.* Initializing static, auto variables with text addresses

f()'s address (936) is in the text area, p is on the stack, and q is in the data area. Both p and q may be initialized to f()'s address because the address of any function in the text area is known at run time as well as at load time. In this situation, a separate assignment statement is not necessary.

Next, we discuss returning values from functions. How do storage classes and the run time environment affect this? To investigate, let's return to itoh(), our integer to hexadecimal conversion routine. The following version is not recursive and assumes an unsigned short is 16 bits. The program, however, contains a run time bug.

**Program 2-26**

```c
/* itoh4.c - nonrecursive integer to hex conversion
            contains run time bug
*/

#include <stdio.h>

main()
{
    unsigned short num = 1199;
    char *itoh();

    printf("%5d is %s\n",    num,  itoh(num));
    printf("%5d is %s\n", 32767, itoh(32767));
}

char *itoh(num)
unsigned short num;
{
    int digit, nd = 4;
    char buf[5];

    buf[nd] = '\0';                  /* NULL terminate */
    while (nd) {
      digit = num % 16;              /* next digit */
      buf[--nd] = (digit <= 9) ?  digit + '0'
                               :  digit + 'a' - 10;
      num /= 16;
    }
    return buf;
}
```

Inside `itoh()`, we declare an array `buf` to hold the ASCII characters from the conversion. We make its length 5 to hold four characters and a NULL byte. Since the routine is not recursive, we store each converted digit backwards in the array. Here's the output:

```
$ itoh4
 1199 is p,afP,V,.
32767 is p,ffP,V,G
```

This doesn't look promising. What's wrong? If you place debug statements inside `itoh()`, you'll find there's nothing wrong with the conversion steps. The error is the line

```
        return buf;
```

which is returning the address of buf. Let's see if our knowledge of the run time environment helps explain what's wrong.

Since buf is automatic, it lives on the stack. When we return from itoh(), the stack frame disappears. This means the memory used for the old stack frame will be reclaimed. It's possible that the program may work, but this is unlikely. In our case, the data was clobbered.

The example justifies the need for the following rule:

> Do *not* return the address of an automatic variable from a function.

This goes for any automatic variable, not just for arrays. Returning a *value* (and not an address) is never a problem, since the compiler may use a register or copy the automatic variable's data from the stack frame to another location before the function returns. When the stack frame disappears, this has no effect on the return value.

How can we fix itoh()? One way is to call malloc() for heap storage. Since this is not stack memory, we may return a pointer to the main program and know that the data it points to remains valid. A faster executing solution, however, is to make buf static. Here's the modified program:

**Program 2-27**

```
/* itoh5.c - nonrecursive integer to hex conversion
*/

#include <stdio.h>

main()
{
    unsigned short num = 1199;
    char *itoh();

    printf("%5d is %s\n",    num, itoh(num));
    printf("%5d is %s\n", 32767, itoh(32767));
}

char *itoh(num)
unsigned short num;
{
    int digit, nd = 4;
    static char buf[5];              /* BSS - NULL included */
```

```
      while (nd) {
        digit = num % 16;           /* next digit */
        buf[--nd] = (digit <= 9) ? digit + '0'
                                 : digit + 'a' - 10;
        num /= 16;
      }
      return buf;
  }

  $ itoh5
   1199 is 04af
  32767 is 7fff
```

This output looks a lot better. We didn't have to NULL terminate the array in a separate step because buf's memory is zero-filled in the BSS, and the NULL character is already there.

## Program Area Mapping

We conclude this chapter with the following C program, which maps its variables to all the program areas we've discussed.

**Program 2-28**

```
/* map.c - show program area mapping */

#include <stdio.h>

int port = 0x36c;          /* global initialized data */
char cache_on;             /* global BSS */

static char time = -1;     /* private initialized data */

main( )
{
    int i = 0;             /* stack */
    char *malloc();

    static int m;          /* BSS */
    static int k = 20;     /* initialized data */
    static int *ip = &k;   /* initialized data */

    static char buf1[10];  /* BSS */
    static char *q = buf1; /* initialized data */
    char buf2[10];         /* stack */
    char *p = buf2;        /* stack */
```

```
char *pheap =              /* stack */
    malloc(100);           /* heap */

static char Version[] =
    "@(#) example.c";      /* initialized data */

struct record {
    unsigned size;
    char *str;
} rec_buf[10];             /* stack */

struct record *ps =        /* stack */
    (struct record *) malloc(sizeof(struct record));
                           /* heap */

if (k > 10) {
    int j = 1;             /* stack */
}
}
```

Table 2-2 shows the storage allocation for the data area, which includes the BSS variables. Table 2-3 shows the storage allocation for the stack and heap. The program was run on a 16-bit machine.

### TABLE 2-2. Storage allocation for data area

| Initialized Data | | BSS | |
|---|---|---|---|
| *Variable* | *Initial Value* | *Variable* | *Initial Value* |
| port | 36C | cache_on | 0 |
| time | −1 | m | 0 |
| k | 20 | buf1 | 0's |
| ip | &k | | |
| q | &buf1 | | |
| Version | @(#) example.c | | |

**TABLE 2-3. Storage allocation for stack and heap**

| Stack | | Heap | |
|---|---|---|---|
| *Variable* | *Initial Value* | *Address* | *No. Bytes* |
| i | 0 | 7e00 | 100 |
| buf2 | *Undefined* | 8012 | 40 |
| p | &buf2 | | |
| rec_buf | *Undefined* | | |
| j | 1 | | |
| pheap | 7e00 | | |
| ps | 8012 | | |

# ♦ Summary ♦

- C programs use the text, stack, data, and heap program areas of the run time environment. It's possible that a program will not use the data or heap areas.

- The text area is normally write-protected from an executing program. Pointers to functions are addresses from the text area.

- The compiler uses the stack for function return addresses, stack frames, and intermediate storage.

- The compiler also uses the stack for automatic variables and recursive functions.

- The data area contains program variables that store values for the life of your program.

- The BSS part of the data area contains the uninitialized static and global variables from a C program.

- All static and global variables in the BSS have zero values before your program runs.

- Constant strings typically live in the data area, but some compilers may place them in the text area.

- The compiler usually makes separate copies of a single constant string in the data area if you define it more than once. The implementation of constant strings is compiler and machine dependent.

- The heap is memory you control from C library routines. Heap memory is preserved through function calls.

- The heap and stack sometimes share the same memory area; hence, a large amount of heap space may decrease the amount of available stack space, and vice versa.

- The text area and data areas are fixed in size when your program runs. The stack and heap are dynamic.

## ♦ Exercises ♦

1. Write a program called `calc.c`, which reads math function names and arguments on the command line. Use the following structure to create a table of math functions from the standard math library.

```
struct math {
   char *name;          /* name of math function */
   double (*pmf)();     /* ptr to math function */
   int nargs;           /* number of arguments */
};
```

Use only the math functions that take `double` arguments and return a `double` in your table. Here are several sample runs of `calc.c`:

```
$ calc sqrt 25
5
$ calc pow 2.5 3.5
24.7053
$ calc exp .5
1.64872
```

2. Write a function called `itoc()`, which converts an unsigned integer to a binary, octal, or hexadecimal character string. Pass the conversion base as a parameter to `itoc()` and have it return a NULL terminated character string.

3. Rewrite `itoc()` as a recursive function.

4. `itoh3.c` uses `putchar()` to display characters. Suppose we buffer the characters, keeping it recursive. What's wrong with the following version?

```
/* itoh6.c - recursive integer to hex conversion
              with buffering
*/

#include <stdio.h>

main(argc, argv)
int argc;
char *argv[];
{
    unsigned int num;
    char buf[10];
```

```
        if (argc == 1) {
            fprintf(stderr, "Usage: %s number\n", argv[0]);
            exit(1);
        }
        num = atoi(argv[1]);
        itoh(num, buf);
        printf("%s\n", buf);
    }

    itoh(n, s)
    unsigned int n;
    char *s;
    {
        int digit;
        int i;
        static char *hex = "0123456789abcdef";

        if (digit = n / 16)
            itoh(digit, s);
        s[i++] = hex[n % 16];
    }
```

What happens during execution? How would you fix `itoh6.c` to make it work correctly?

5. Modify `jump.c` to handle backspace processing. If the user types the DEL key, terminate the program.

6. Using the techniques shown in program `readin.c`, write new versions of the C library functions `gets` and `fgets`. The synopsis is as follows:

```
    /* in place of gets() */
    char *getstring();

    /* in place of fgets() */
    char *fgetstring(n, infile);


    int n;              /* number of chars to read */


    FILE *infile;   /* file pointer */
```

The important difference is that the new versions don't require character buffers to store the input data. Instead, both functions return pointers to the heap, where the exact number of input characters reside. Make sure your versions mimic what `gets` and `fgets` do. This includes handling EOF and reading less characters than were asked for.

7. Study the following program:

```
/* concat.c - concatenate two strings */

#include <stdio.h>

main()
{
    char *join();

    printf("%s\n", join("duck", "soup"));
}

char *join(s1, s2)      /* join strings */
char *s1, *s2;
{
    char *strcat(), *strcpy();

    struct {
        char buf[256];
    } string;

    return strcat(strcpy(string.buf, s1), s2);
}
```

`concat.c` joins two character strings together. Note that the function `join()` returns a character pointer to an array member of an automatic structure. Compile `concat.c` and run it. Does it work? Does this make sense?

# 3

# An Array of Choices

I f you have a background in other languages, working with arrays in C is bound to cause a few surprises. Initially, newcomers make the transition easily because declaring C arrays and referencing elements is straightforward. You develop new C programs with arrays, and translate programs and subroutines that use arrays from FORTRAN, BASIC, and PASCAL. After a period of time, however, problems begin to appear. The translated programs run slowly. There's no way to declare multidimensional arrays on the fly (*i.e.*, at run time), and you can't pass an entire array to a C function. Most C programmers (even experienced ones) know there is a relationship between arrays and pointers in C, but exactly what that relationship is remains a mystery.

This chapter merges the concepts of arrays and pointers. We show you how the compiler treats different declarations and expressions involving array and pointer notation. First, we describe the fundamental relationship between an array reference and a pointer. This helps you decipher complicated array references using multidimensional arrays, and understand pointer notation for accessing data in memory. Second, we describe how the compiler derives and uses storage map equations to reference elements from multidimensional arrays. Storage map equations are important because they make the compiler generate multiplies (either multiply instructions or "shift and adds" in assembly code), and this plays an important part in slowing down otherwise speedy programs. This chapter shows you how pointer indirection can be used in place of multiplications to dramatically improve the execution speed of many programs.

The rest of the chapter puts these techniques to work. We place pointers in loops and expressions where they execute faster than array references. We speed up programs with multidimensional arrays with a minimum of recoding. The chapter concludes with a technique to create two-dimensional and three-dimensional arrays at run time. You may apply this approach to arrays with four dimensions and more as well.

# ◆ Pointer and Array Fundamentals ◆

As with most things, it's usually best to start on the ground floor to work your way up. C language concepts are no exception. Before we tackle complicated pointer expressions and multidimensional arrays, we need a solid base to work from. The fundamental concepts that we develop now will provide us with the tools to write efficient C code and tune existing programs later.

## The Basic Rule

Let's begin with the following declarations:

```
char a[] = "databytes";     /* array of characters */
char *p = a;                 /* pointer to the array */
```

Fig. 3-1 shows the array and pointer in memory (assume both are in the data area and addresses are 16 bits).

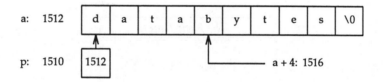

DATA AREA

*Fig. 3-1.* Array and pointer

The compiler treats array names as constants. This means a may be used anywhere a character pointer is legal, except on the left hand side of an assignment statement or with an increment or decrement operator (*e.g.*, a++). The following statements

```
printf("%s\n", a);          /* using the array */
printf("%s\n", p);          /* using the pointer */
```

display the string "databytes" on two separate lines. In the first call to printf() C converts the array name to a pointer. The compiler passes the constant address 1512 (see Fig. 3-1) to printf(). On the second line, p is a pointer. The compiler fetches the same address (1512) from the contents of p's memory location (1510).

The statements

```
printf("%s\n", a + 4);      /* using the array */
printf("%s\n", p + 4);      /* using the pointer */
```

display the string "bytes" on two separate lines. We call both expressions
*pointer offsets*. On the first line, a + 4 points to the fifth character of the string.
The compiler computes address 1516 from the constant address 1512 and the
constant 4. This is the address that's passed to printf(). On the second line,
the compiler fetches p's contents (1512) and adds 4 to get the same address
(1516). Pointer offsets use array names or pointers.

Likewise, the statements

```
putchar(a[4]);              /* using the array */
putchar(p[4]);              /* using the pointer */
```

display 'b' twice. The second line demonstrates that we may use a pointer as
an array reference. Both statements display the fifth byte of the string.

These examples suggest a close relationship between arrays and pointers.
In fact, the compiler treats array names as pointers most of the time. We need to
be more specific, however. To fully understand the relationship, we present the
following (we call it the *basic rule*):

| The Basic Rule |
| :---: |
| a[i]  ≡  (*(a + i)) |
| a    is an array of elements |
| i    is an integer expression |

Simply stated, the basic rule says referencing the i'th element of an array is
equivalent to applying the indirection operator to a pointer offset from the beginning of the array. This implies that anywhere an array reference is legal, we may
substitute an equivalent pointer expression. The basic rule is independent of a's
data type.

Do you notice the outer pair of parentheses? At first glance they seem
unnecessary, but we need them for multidimensional array references. You may
omit these parentheses from expressions where C's precedence rules don't
change their evaluation.

Let's put the basic rule to work. You'll discover it helps explain why many
array and pointer combinations are equivalent.

## There's No Such Thing as an Array Reference

The following program references the same element twice from an array of characters.

**Program 3-1**

```
/* twist.c - strange array reference */

main()
{
    static char a[] = "0123456789";
    int i = 5;

    printf("%c\n", a[i]);          /* sixth element */
    printf("%c\n", i[a]);          /* what is this? */
}

$ twist
5
5
```

The first reference displays the sixth element (5) of a. The second one must be the ultimate in job security. The array reference uses a for the array's subscript and i as the array name. Despite the convolution, the program compiles without error and is portable! It demonstrates that C handles array references in a very different way from other programming languages.

The basic rule explains what's going on. C converts the array reference

```
a[i]
```

to

```
(*(a + i))
```

This expression, however, is equivalent to

```
(*(i + a))
```

This implies that the array reference

```
i[a]
```

is therefore legal. There's no reason to ever do this; it just proves that array references don't really exist because C converts array references to pointer offsets.

Let's use the relationship between array references and pointers in a more useful way. The basic rule helps us derive equivalent pointer expressions from array references. Here's the first derivation:

```
a[i]  ≡  (*(a + i))

&a[i]  ≡  &(*(a + i))
```

We apply the address operator (&) to both sides of the relation. C's precedence rules evaluate & and * from *right to left*, so we can remove the outer parentheses. This leaves us with

```
&a[i]  ≡  &*(a + i)
```

which reduces to simply

```
&a[i]  ≡  a + i
```

Let's explain why.

Suppose you apply the indirection operator to a pointer offset. This evaluates to what the pointer points to. If you subsequently apply the address operator, the compiler produces the pointer offset you started with. They cancel each other out. It doesn't matter if you use an array name or a pointer with the pointer offset. The following program proves this.

**Program 3-2**

```
/* a1.c - shows address and indirection operators */

char a[] = "databytes";
char *p = a;

main()
{
    /* using the array */
    printf("%x %x\n", a+3, &*(a+3));

    /* using the pointer */
    printf("%x %x\n", p+3, &*(p+3));
}

$ a1
142d 142d
142d 142d
```

The output shows that we may use either an array name or pointer to display the same address. This makes sense when you realize that evaluating the address of an object's value after indirection is simply the object. Note that the converse, that is, evaluating an object's value from indirection after taking its address, is *not* the object (see Exercise 1).

Let's return to the previous derivation. The equivalence

```
&a[i]  ≡  a + i
```

applies to many C statements. Suppose, for example, we declare the following:

```
#define MAX 100
int buf[MAX];
int *p;
```

In a `for` statement, we may code

```
for (p = buf; p < buf + MAX; p++)
```

in place of

```
for (p = buf; p < &buf[MAX]; p++)
```

The compiler generates the same assembly code.

Here's another derivation from the basic rule that applies to the first element of any array:

```
a[i]  ≡  (*(a + i))

a[0]  ≡  (*(a + 0))

a[0]  ≡  *(a + 0)

a[0]  ≡  *a
```

This shows one-dimensional arrays use one level of indirection. We will extend this concept to multidimensional arrays shortly.

Using the previous technique, let's apply the address operator to both sides of the last line:

```
&a[0]  ≡  &*a

&a[0]  ≡   a
```

Function arguments make frequent use of the relations

```
a[0]  ≡  *a

&a[0]  ≡   a
```

The function call

```
f(a[0]);
```

for example, is equivalent to

```
f(*a);
```

Both expressions pass the value of the first element of the array. Likewise, the function call

```
f(&a[0]);
```

is a more verbose form of

```
f(a);
```

The compiler passes the address of the first element of the array in both function calls.

The next derivation is a combination of the previous ones:

```
a[i]  ≡  (*(a + i))

&a[i]  ≡  &(*(a + i))

&a[i]  ≡  a + i

&a[i]  ≡  &a[0] + i
```

The last two lines show the equivalence. In a C program, you may use the expressions

```
a + i
```

and

```
&a[0] + i
```

interchangeably. The compiler generates the same assembly code in both cases.

## Command Line Characters

Command line argument processing is another good example that shows the relationship between array references and pointer offsets. This relationship is particularly true when you access command line characters, as the following program shows.

**Program 3-3**

```
/* comc.c - accessing command line characters */

#include <stdio.h>

main(argc, argv)
int argc;
char *argv[];
{
    if (argc == 1) {
        fprintf(stderr, "Usage: %s args\n", argv[0]);
        exit(1);
    }
    printf("%c\n", *(argv[1] + 2));
    printf("%c\n", (*(argv + 1))[2]);
    printf("%c\n", argv[1][2]);
}

$ comc 1234
3
3
3
```

comc.c displays the third character (3) of its first argument (argv[1]) on three separate lines. Recall that argv is a pointer to an array of pointers to characters. Each argument to printf(), however, is different. C allows us to access characters from argv as a one-dimensional array with pointer indirection or as a two-dimensional array. The expressions are equivalent, yet this is not obvious. Let's see if we can apply the basic rule to decipher these expressions.

We start with the easiest one (at least to type, anyway):

```
argv[1][2]
```

We'll derive the other two using the basic rule. To do this, we make a simple substitution:

Let

```
p = argv[1]
```

Then

```
argv[1][2]  ≡  p[2]
```

Marking argv[1] as p makes it easier to apply the basic rule:

```
p[2]  ≡  (*(p + 2))
```

Now substitute argv[1] for p in both sides of the above.

```
argv[1][2]  ≡  (*(argv[1] + 2))

argv[1][2]  ≡  *(argv[1] + 2)
```

We drop the outer parentheses because they're unnecessary. This evaluates to the first expression in comc.c. The pointer expression is clearer than the equivalent two-dimensional notation, because it's easier to visualize the pointer offset. It is, on the other hand, harder to type.

It's more difficult to understand why the second expression in comc.c is equivalent to the other two. All we have to do is apply the basic rule again.

```
argv[1]  ≡  (*(argv + 1))
```

This time, however, we substitute in a different order.

```
argv[1][2]  ≡  (*(argv + 1))[2]
```

Can we remove the outermost parentheses in this expression? The answer is *no*. Precedence rules explain why. Suppose we omit them. The expression

```
*(argv + 1)[2]
```

evaluates differently than the previous one. As an exercise, try and apply the basic rule to this expression. You'll find that instead of accessing the third character of the second command line argument, you'll get the first character of the fourth command line argument (argv[3][0])! The reason is because [] has a higher precedence than *. In sorting out complex looking expressions like this, remember to always include the outer parentheses.

# ◆ Pointer Expressions and Arrays ◆

Understanding the relationship between arrays and pointers is only a beginning. We can develop more concepts from this foundation. It's worthwhile, for example, to investigate how the compiler implements pointer arithmetic and pointer expressions. This will give you a deeper understanding of how pointers work and how to write more efficient C programs.

## Scalars

Pointer arithmetic in C is powerful because the compiler does most of the hard work. Pointer expressions free the programmer from the messy details of addressing memory. To calculate pointer offsets, for example, the compiler uses the size of the pointer's object. To subtract pointers, the compiler produces the number of items between the two pointers. These quantities are called *scalars*. C programs use them in two ways. C's *sizeof()* operator, for one, returns a scalar (the number of bytes of an object at compile time). Let's look at how C uses scalars for pointer offsets and pointer subtraction.

C allows two arithmetic operators (+ and –) with a pointer and an integer expression. Suppose  p  is a pointer to an object in memory and  n  evaluates to an integer. The expressions

```
p + n
p - n
```

represent addresses up or down in memory from the object. To compute the new address, the compiler can't use  n's value. If it did, pointer arithmetic would only access byte offsets. Instead, the compiler uses a scalar that yields the size of the object.

To illustrate these concepts, let's look at several programs. We'll assume that a  char  is one byte, a  float  is four bytes, and a  double  is eight bytes. The first program demonstrates pointer offsets. Program  poset.c  declares two buffers, one  char  and the other a  float. The program displays each buffer's starting address and the address of the sixth element using pointer offsets.

**Program 3-4**

```
/* poset.c - shows pointer offsets */

main()
{
    char cbuf[80], *p = cbuf;
    float fbuf[80], *q = fbuf;

    printf("cbuf = %u &cbuf[5] = p + 5 = %u\n", cbuf, p + 5);
    printf("fbuf = %u &fbuf[5] = q + 5 = %u\n", fbuf, q + 5);
}
```

```
$ poset
cbuf = 11058   &cbuf[5] = p + 5 = 11063
fbuf = 11142   &fbuf[5] = q + 5 = 11162
```

The addresses are 5 bytes apart for the character buffer. The output shows the addresses differ by 20 bytes for the floating point array, however. This means the compiler uses the scalar 4 to compute the correct address for q + 5.

The next program shows how the compiler computes pointer offsets.

**Program 3-5**

```
/* scalar1.c - scalars for pointer offsets */

main()
{
    char  cbuf[80], *p = cbuf;
    float fbuf[80], *q = fbuf;

    printf("cbuf = %u   &cbuf[5] = p + 5 = %u\n", cbuf, p + 5);
    printf("fbuf = %u   &fbuf[5] = q + 5 = %u\n", fbuf, q + 5);

    printf("&cbuf[5] = %u\n", (char *)p + 5 * sizeof(char));
    printf("&fbuf[5] = %u\n", (char *)q + 5 * sizeof(float));
}
```

```
$ scalar1
cbuf = 11120   &cbuf[5] = p + 5 = 11125
fbuf = 11204   &fbuf[5] = q + 5 = 11224
&cbuf[5] = 11125
&fbuf[5] = 11224
```

The first part of the output is similar to the previous program. However, scalar1.c displays the address of each array's sixth element using

```
    (char *)p + 5 * sizeof(char)
    (char *)q + 5 * sizeof(float)
```

These C expressions mimic what the compiler does.  sizeof(datatype) is the scalar. The compiler uses 1 for the character buffer and 4 for the float array. Note that scalar1.c casts p and q to byte pointers. Although this is unnecessary for p (it's already a byte pointer), we must cast q, since it's a pointer to a float. Without it, the program doesn't compute the correct address.

We can generalize this concept for all C data types. Suppose p points to any C object and n is an integer expression. C uses the following formulas for the pointer offsets p + n and p - n:

```
(char *)p + n * sizeof(object)
(char *)p - n * sizeof(object)
```

The compiler uses a byte pointer for the base address and calculates a new address from the pointer offset and the scalar for the object. This works for all C objects, including arrays, structures, and unions.

C allows only one arithmetic operator (−) with two pointers. If p and q point to objects of the same type, the expressions

```
p - q
q - p
```

yield the number of objects between the two pointers. The result is a scalar that you treat like an int or a long, depending on the implementation. Its sign may be negative, depending on which address in memory (p's or q's) is greater.

The following program declares an 80-byte character array and assigns two character pointers to addresses in the array. The program displays the number of characters between the two pointers.

**Program 3-6**

```
/* nchars.c - number of chars in a buffer */

main()
{
    char buf[80], *q = buf, *p = q + 5;

    printf("low address = %u   high address = %u\n", q, p);
    printf("%d\n", p - q);
}
```

```
$ nchars
low address = 11328   high address = 11333
5
```

The difference between the two pointers is 5 bytes.

The next program shows pointer subtraction is independent of a pointer's data type.

**Program 3-7**

```
/* ndoubles.c - number of doubles in a buffer */

main()
{
    double buf[80], *q = buf, *p = q + 5;

    printf("low address = %u  high address = %u\n", q, p);
    printf("%d\n", p - q);
}
```

```
$ ndoubles
low address = 10766  high address = 10806
5
```

buf is an array of doubles and  p and  q are pointers to doubles.  The addresses are 40 bytes apart yet  ndoubles still displays 5.  This shows the compiler scales the pointers' addresses by the data type to produce the number of items between the pointers.

scalar2.c shows how the compiler implements pointer subtraction.  For the purposes of demonstration, we'll assume a pointer fits inside an  int, although this may not always be true.  (Some machines may require a  long, for instance.)

**Program 3-8**

```
/* scalar2.c - scalars for pointer subtraction */

main()
{
    double buf[80], *q = buf, *p = q + 5;

    printf("low address = %u  high address =  %u\n", q, p);
    printf("%d\n", ((unsigned int)p - (unsigned int)q)
                            / sizeof(double));
    printf("%d\n", p - q);
}
```

```
$ scalar2
low address = 10800  high address =  10840
5
5
```

The program shows the pointer addresses (40 bytes apart) and displays the number of items two ways.  The compiler uses

```
((unsigned int)p - (unsigned int)q) / sizeof(double)
```

to compute the number of doubles between the pointers. This expression divides the difference of the addresses by the size of a double in bytes (8). Note that we cast `p` and `q` to unsigned integers to prevent the compiler from performing pointer subtraction (for real).

We can generalize the concept of pointer subtraction for all C data types, as we did with pointer offsets. Suppose `p` and `q` point to the same object. C uses the following formula for `p - q`:

```
((unsigned int)p - (unsigned int)q) / sizeof(object)
```

`sizeof()` is a scalar, and so is the expression's value. This means C allows pointer subtraction anywhere an `int` (or `long`) is legal.

## Compact Pointer Expressions

Most mainframe CPU's and modern microprocessors have addressing modes or instructions that combine indirection with autoincrements and autodecrements. We call pointer expressions that use indirection (*) and autoincrements (++) or autodecrements (--) *compact pointer expressions*. In most cases, the compiler produces assembly code that is smaller in size and runs faster. Let's look at all the formats and show examples that use these pointer expressions.

Suppose `p` points to an object. Table 3-1 lists the eight forms of compact pointer expressions, separated into two groups.

**TABLE 3-1. Compact pointer expressions**

| Expression | Operation | Affects |
|------------|-----------|---------|
| *p++ | post increment | pointer |
| *p-- | post decrement | pointer |
| *++p | pre increment | pointer |
| *--p | pre decrement | pointer |
| ++*p | pre increment | object |
| --*p | pre decrement | object |
| (*p)++ | post increment | object |
| (*p)-- | post decrement | object |

Expressions from the first group modify the pointer and not the pointer's object. Pointers may point to any C data type and typically access elements of an array or the heap inside loops. Compact pointer expressions from the first group improve a program's execution speed if assembly code can access an object and move to another address in the same instruction.

Expressions from the second group affect the pointer's object rather than the pointer. These objects may be simple data types like integers, characters, etc., or array elements of simple types. The compiler applies the increment or decrement operator to the pointer's object and not the pointer. Note that you can't use a pointer to a structure, union, or function with these expressions, however. Although it doesn't make sense to increment or decrement a structure or union, you might want to increment or decrement one of their members.

A pointer's object from the second group may also be a pointer. In this situation, a compact pointer expression affects a different pointer. This improves execution speed inside loops just like pointers from the first group.

Let's look at examples of pointer expressions from both groups. We'll use register pointers to make the compact pointer expressions evaluate as fast as possible. We start with

```
*p++             *p--
```

from the first group. Precedence rules govern the evaluation. The compiler evaluates what p points to and subsequently increments (or decrements) the pointer. This makes the pointer point to the next (or previous) object in memory.

The following program uses compact pointer expressions of this form. Suppose, for example, we maintain a database table of items and prices. The table is an array of character pointers with the last entry set to NULL. fitem.c modifies the table's pointers to print only the items from the table.

**Program 3-9**

```
/* fitem.c - truncate each line to first item */

#include <stdio.h>

main()
{
    static char *lines[] = {
        "Unformatted floppy disks. Pricing: $12.50 a box.",
        "Theft insurance. Coverage premium: $100 per month.",
        "Installation manual. Complete price: $10 with purchase.",
        (char *) NULL
    };
    int i;

    fitem(lines);                   /* pass array of lines */
    for (i = 0; lines[i]; i++)
        printf("%s\n", lines[i]);   /* display modified line */
}
```

```
fitem(pline)                /* first item */
register char *pline[];      /* ptr to line */
{
   register char *pc;        /* ptr to character on line */

   while (pc = *pline++) {   /* point to first char, move line ptr */
      while (*pc++ != '.')    /* move char ptr until '.' */
         ;
      *pc = '\0';            /* NULL terminate first item */
   }
}
```

$ **fitem**
Unformatted floppy disks.
Theft insurance.
Installation manual.

The program is a main program and a function `fitem()`. `main()` mimics the database with an array of character pointers to sample lines of text. The last entry's pointer is NULL (0). `main()` calls `fitem()` with the address of the database table. `fitem()` searches for the first ' . ' in each line and NULL terminates it. The main program prints the modified lines from the table.

The function uses two pointers. `pline` is a pointer to the table. `fitem()` uses `pline` to point to the current line of text. Since the table is an array of pointers, this makes `pline` a pointer to an array of pointers to characters, similar to `argv`. `pc` points to text characters on the current line.

Fig. 3-2 shows memory after `fitem()` executes

```
while (pc = *pline++)
```

the first time. This statement performs three operations in one, so let's break it up into separate steps.

First, we assign the address of the current line to `pc` with

```
pc = *pline
```

Second, we move `pline` by

```
pline++
```

This makes `pline` point to the next line (`lines[1]`). Third, we evaluate `pc`'s newly assigned contents with

```
while (pc)
```

If it's NULL (0), we exit from the loop. Otherwise, we look at each character in the current line (using `*pc`) inside the body of the first `while` loop.

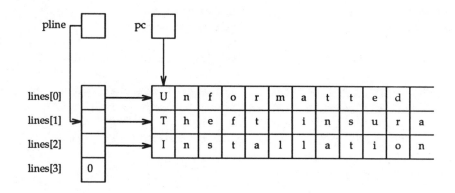

*Fig. 3-2.* while (pc = *pline++)

The second `while` loop contains another compact pointer expression. The code

```
while (*pc++ != '.')
     ;
```

moves the character pointer `pc` until we reach a `'.'`. `fitem()` NULL terminates the line after this character and continues with the next line. Note that we declare `pline` and `pc` in registers, to make the compact pointer expressions run as fast as possible.

The next pair of pointer expressions

```
*++p              *--p
```

makes the compiler increment (or decrement) the pointer *before* it evaluates the pointer's object. This has the same effect as the previous pointer expression, except that the order of evaluation is different.

Program 3-10, called `pricing.c`, uses the autodecrement form. Suppose we process the same table of text as `fitem.c`. We wish to modify the table to delete the prices, so that we may change them later with another program.

`pricing.c` has the same organization as the previous program. The main program calls a function `pricing()` to modify the table. This time the function increments `pc` by the length of the string and then searches backwards for a `'$'` on each line. Admittedly, using the library routine `strlen()` to do this is not very efficient, but the approach shows you different forms of compact pointer expressions. Exercise 5 suggests an alternative method.

## Program 3-10

```
/* pricing.c - trim line for pricing */

#include <stdio.h>

main()
{
    static char *lines[] = {
        "Unformatted floppy disks. Pricing: $12.50 a box.",
        "Theft insurance. Coverage premium: $100 per month.",
        "Installation manual. Complete price: $10 with purchase.",
        (char *) NULL
    };
    int i;

    pricing(lines);                    /* pass array of lines */
    for (i = 0; lines[i]; i++)
        printf("%s\n", lines[i]);    /* display modified line */
}

pricing(pline)                /* delete prices from line */
register char *pline[];        /* pointer to line */
{
    register char *pc;        /* pointer to char on line */

    while (pc = *pline++) {    /* first char, go to next line */
        pc += strlen(pc);      /* end of line to start */
        while (*--pc != '$')   /* go backwards until '$' */
            ;
        *pc = '\0';            /* NULL terminate */
    }
}
```

```
$ pricing
Unformatted floppy disks. Pricing:
Theft insurance. Coverage premium:
Installation manual. Complete price:
```

Inside pricing(), we declare a pointer to the current line (pline) and a character pointer (pc). We loop over the characters on each line backwards, using strlen() to move to the end of the line before we begin processing. At this point, pc points to a NULL byte. The compact pointer expression

```
*--pc
```

decrements the character pointer pc before it accesses a character. This means the first character we examine is the last character on the line. We exit from the second while loop when we reach a '$'. At this point, we NULL terminate the string and continue with the next line. pricing() uses the first while loop to set pc to the current line, move the line pointer, and check for NULL (the end of the table).

Now let's look at compact expressions from the second group. The pair

```
(*p)++              (*p)--
```

affects the pointer's object. The pointer is unaffected. The compiler increments (or decrements) the object *after* the expression evaluates. C requires the parentheses to override default precedence rules; otherwise, the expressions become the first pair of the first group.

The next program, called litem.c, modifies the database table differently. The program displays only the pricing information.

**Program 3-11**

```
/* litem.c - truncate each line to last item */

#include <stdio.h>

main()
{
    static char *lines[] = {
        "Unformatted floppy disks. Pricing: $12.50 a box.",
        "Theft insurance. Coverage premium: $100 per month.",
        "Installation manual. Complete price: $10 with purchase.",
        (char *) NULL
    };
    int i;

    litem(lines);                   /* pass array of lines */
    for (i = 0; lines[i]; i++)
        printf("%s\n", lines[i]);   /* display modified lines */
}

litem(pline)                        /* last item */
register char *pline[];             /* ptr to line */
{
    do {
        while (*(*pline)++ != '.')  /* move ptr to char in line */
            ;                       /* until '.' */
        (*pline)++;                 /* move ptr one more char */
    } while (*++pline);             /* next line, if not NULL */
}
```

```
$ litem
Pricing: $12.50 a box.
Coverage premium: $100 per month.
Complete price: $10 with purchase.
```

The main program calls litem() to modify the table. The algorithm is identical to fitem.c's, except we modify the pointer array (lines) as we search for '.'.

Fig. 3-3 shows memory after litem() executes

```
while (*(*pline)++ != '.')
```

the first time. Let's study the evaluation of this statement.

Note that the compact pointer expression

```
(*pline)++
```

increments a character pointer and not a line pointer. The expression

```
*(*pline)++
```

evaluates to a character on the current line before we increment the pointer to the next character. This code modifies the table so that lines[0] now points to the letter 'n'. The while loop examines the current character, and if it's '.', we exit from the loop. Otherwise, we continue modifying the table entry (lines[0]) as we examine each character.

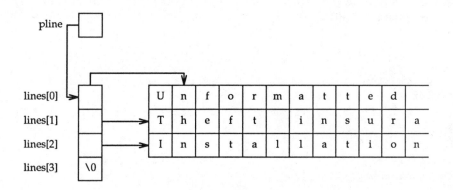

*Fig. 3-3.* while (*(*pline)++ != '.')

The next statement

```
(*pline)++;
```

moves the character pointer one byte past the '.'. The expression

```
*++pline
```

uses a compact pointer expression from the first group to move the line pointer before the  do  while statement checks for a NULL pointer (the end of the table). This allows litem() to modify the next line in the same manner.

The last pair of expressions

```
++*p            --*p
```

pre-increment or pre-decrement the object, not the pointer. The compiler uses the object's value in an expression after it increments (or decrements) the pointer's object. As with the other pair from this group, the compiler reports an error if these pointers point to structures, unions, or functions.

The program  price.c modifies the database table a final time, using the autodecrement expression. The program displays the prices of the items.

**Program 3-12**

```
/* price.c - trim line for price */

#include <stdio.h>

main()
{
    static char *lines[] = {
        "Unformatted floppy disks. Pricing: $12.50 a box.",
        "Theft insurance. Coverage premium: $100 per month.",
        "Installation manual. Complete price: $10 with purchase.",
        (char *) NULL
    };
    int i;

    price(lines);                   /* pass array of lines */
    for (i = 0; lines[i]; i++)
        printf("%s\n", lines[i]);   /* display modified line */
}


price(pline)                        /* prices only */
register char *pline[];
{
    do {
        *pline += strlen(*pline);   /* move line ptr to end of line */
        while (*(--*pline) != '$')  /* go backwards until '$' */
            ;
    } while (*++pline);             /* next line if not NULL */
}
```

```
$ price
$12.50 a box.
$100 per month.
$10 with purchase.
```

The function `price()` uses the same approach as the previous programs. `pline` points to the table and `*pline` is a pointer to the current line. First we move the table pointer to the end of the table (using `strlen()`), and then we search backwards for `'$'`, modifying the table pointer as we go. The compact pointer expression

```
    --*pline
```

decrements a character pointer.   `pline` is unaffected.  The expression

```
    *(--*pline)
```

is tricky.  Precedence rules evaluate right to left, so the expression decrements the character pointer before it produces a character.  The parentheses are not necessary, but we include them for clarity.  With the `while` loop, the expression modifies the current character pointer as we search for `'$'`.  `price()` uses the `do while` loop in the same way as the previous program.

The compact pointer expressions in these programs produce object code that is smaller in size than functionally equivalent programs.  They are, on the other hand, cryptic and difficult to understand.  Try rewriting several of the previous functions using array notation and compare object code sizes and program readability. Based on the situation, you'll have to decide whether code clarity or efficiency is more important.  We'll look at more examples of compact pointer expressions later on.

## Negative Subscripts

Let's combine the basic rule of arrays with the formula the compiler uses for a pointer offset:

$$\&a[n] \equiv a + n \equiv (char *)a + n * sizeof(object)$$

Substituting 0 for `n`, we have

$$\&a[0] \equiv a \equiv (char *)a$$

This explains why array subscripts start at zero.  The compiler always uses the base address for the start of the array.  What happens when `n` is negative?  The formula for a *negative* pointer offset is only slightly different.

$$\&a[-n] \equiv a - n \equiv (char *)a - n * sizeof(object)$$

The pointer offset is below the base address of the array. This shows *negative subscripts* are legal in C.

The following program called `twzone.c` demonstrates out of bounds array references in C. The program uses a negative subscript and also references an array element beyond its last member. Here's the program and its output.

**Program 3-13**

```
/* twzone.c - array out of bounds */

main()
{
    int buf[10];

    buf[-4] = 1;              /* negative subscript */
    buf[10] = 2;              /* one step beyond */

    printf("%d %d\n", *(buf - 4), *(buf + 10));
}

$ twzone
1 2
twzone: Segmentation violation -- Core dumped
```

On our XENIX system `twzone` dumps core, but we've seen it run fine under DOS and other UNIX systems. Note that this program would not compile if rewritten in PASCAL or ALGOL. These languages include compile time checks that complain if an array subscript is out of bounds. In C, however, array references simply convert to pointer offsets. This allows programs with negative subscripts to compile and sometimes run.

Believe it or not, negative subscripts can be put to work in a useful way. In one instance, we use them in a custom version of the C library routine `calloc()`. Our routine (called `xcalloc()`) provides heap memory for data storage at run time and provides features that `calloc()` does not. For one, `xcalloc()` checks for errors instead of leaving this job to the calling routine. This makes it easier to use, and it helps centralize error messages. `xcalloc()` also stores an integer indicating the number of elements you request in heap storage along with the data.

Programs call `xcalloc()` with the same protocols as `calloc()`. `xcalloc()`, however, allocates memory for the integer in addition to space for the data. The routine stores the number of elements allocated from the heap and returns a pointer to the space allocated for the data. Programs use a negative offset from the heap pointer to access the number of elements.

Suppose, for example, we call `xcalloc()` to allocate heap storage for 10 integers and assign the heap address to `p` (a pointer to an integer).

```
int *p;
 . . . .
p = (int *) xcalloc(10, sizeof(int));
 . . . .
```

`xcalloc()`'s arguments are the number of elements and the size of each element, respectively. We use `sizeof(int)` for portability. Fig. 3-4 shows a modified heap configuration for a machine with 16-bit integers and addresses.

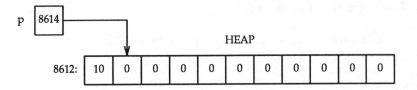

*Fig. 3-4.* Modified heap storage for 10 integers

`p` points to 10 integers (with initial values of zero) on the heap. The number of elements (10) is stored at address `8612`, in front of the data. `p`, however, points to address `8614`, assuming integers are two bytes. Programs use a negative offset from `p` to access the number of elements (10).

The following program called `neg.c` demonstrates `xcalloc()`.

**Program 3-14**

```
/* neg.c - negative subscripts with xcalloc */

#include <stdio.h>

main()
{
    char *xcalloc();
    int *p, *q;

    p = (int *) xcalloc(10, sizeof(int));
    q = (int *) xcalloc(15, sizeof(int));

    fill(p);                /* fill with 10 numbers */
    display(p);             /* print 10 numbers */

    fill(q);                /* fill with 15 numbers */
    display(q);             /* print 15 numbers */
}
```

```
$ neg
  1   2   3   4   5   6   7   8   9  10
  1   2   3   4   5   6   7   8   9  10  11  12  13  14  15
```

neg.c calls xcalloc() twice for heap storage. The first call allocates storage for 10 integers and the second for 15 integers. Note that we can assume the heap pointers p and q are valid because xcalloc() checks for heap errors. The program calls routines to assign integers to the heap and display their values. The first call to fill() stores 10 integer numbers on the heap, and the second call stores 15 integers. display() prints the data from both heap areas. Note that neither of these routines requires the number of elements as a function parameter. This item is available from the heap pointer.

Here's the code for xcalloc():

```
char *xcalloc(nitems, size)          /* custom calloc() */
unsigned nitems, size;
{
    char *pheap;
    char *malloc(), *memset();
    unsigned blksize;

    blksize = nitems * size;        /* size of chunk */

    if ((pheap = malloc(blksize + sizeof(int))) == NULL) {
        fprintf(stderr, "Can't malloc on heap\n");
        exit(1);
    }
    *(int *)pheap = nitems;         /* store no. of items in heap */

    memset(pheap + sizeof(int), 0, blksize);   /* zero the area */

    return pheap + sizeof(int);              /* pointer to data */
}
```

Variable blksize contains the amount of memory you request from the heap. The function calls malloc() from the standard C library to allocate blksize bytes plus one integer (sizeof(int) bytes) from the heap. Note that xcalloc() displays an error message and terminates the program if heap space is not available. The statement

```
*(int *)pheap = nitems;  /* store no. of items in heap */
```

stores the number of elements in the heap. We cast the heap pointer to an integer pointer before we store the size. memset() zeros the heap area to make xcalloc() compatible with calloc(). The statement

```
    return pheap + sizeof(int);      /* pointer to data */
```

returns the heap pointer to the calling routine, offset by the integer containing the number of elements. `sizeof()` makes `xcalloc()` portable.

Let's now turn our attention to the rest of the routines. Here are `fill()` and `display()`, which use negative subscripts.

```
    fill(p)                     /* fill heap with integers */
    int *p;
    {
        int i;
        int nints = p[-1];   /* number of items from heap */

        for (i = 0; i < nints; i++)
            p[i] = i + 1;
    }

    display(p)                  /* display integers from heap */
    int *p;
    {
        int i;
        int nints = p[-1];   /* number of items from heap */

        for (i = 0; i < nints; i++)
            printf("%3d", p[i]);
        putchar('\n');
    }
```

Both routines access the heap to determine the number of elements before they loop through the data. The statement

```
    p[-1]
```

uses a negative subscript. From the basic rule, it's as if you typed

```
    *(p - 1)
```

This evaluates to an integer, which is the number of elements at the heap address.

`neg.c` demonstrates only integer pointers. Note that programs may use `xcalloc()` to allocate heap pointers to any C data type. Suppose, for example, we want to allocate space for 20 structures of type `something`. We call `xcalloc()` as follows:

```
struct something *ps;
 .  .  .  .
ps = (struct something *)
          xcalloc(20, sizeof(struct something));
```

This shows `xcalloc()` is independent of the allocated pointer's data type. The routine still stores the number of elements as an integer, however. This means you have to cast the pointer appropriately to access it. Let's elaborate.

Suppose `sfill()` and `sdisplay()` store data into heap structures and display data, respectively. A call to `sfill()`, for example, looks like

```
sfill(ps);                    /* fill 20 structures */
```

Inside `sfill()`, we access the number of elements with the following statements:

```
sfill(p)                     /* fill structures from heap */
struct something *p;
{
   /* number of items from heap */
   int nitems = ((int *)p)[-1];
    .  .  .  .
}
```

We need to cast `p` before we apply the negative subscript. The parentheses are necessary to make the statement compile. Without them, the compiler tries to cast an array reference. The same changes would apply to `sdisplay()`.

## ◆ Multidimensional Arrays Revisited ◆

Our next task is to tackle multidimensional arrays. The concepts from this section are the foundation for many of the techniques shown later in the chapter. Let's study two-dimensional and three-dimensional arrays, since they are used most often in program applications.

### Two-Dimensional Arrays

C handles multidimensional arrays the same as arrays of one dimension. A two-dimensional array, for instance, is a one-dimensional array whose elements are one-dimensional arrays. It's easy to work with two-dimensional arrays because you may visualize them as grids with rows and columns. By the way, we'll use the term *grid* for a two-dimensional array. Think of it as a checkerboard where rows and columns locate unique elements.

In C, the declaration

```
double mint[3][5];
```

allocates storage for 15 doubles, arranged as 3 rows by 5 columns. (The first subscript of an array reference is the row and the second subscript is the column.)
The following diagram shows how we visualize the array `mint`:

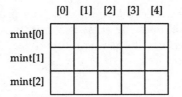

*Fig. 3-5.* Two-dimensional array double mint[3][5]

Rows and columns start at 0.   `mint[0]` is the first row, `mint[1]` the second,
and so on.
     What about two-dimensional array references? C requires the format

        mint [*rown*] [*coln*]

to reference a double from row *rown*, and column *coln*, respectively. Let's look at
a program that displays elements from a two-dimensional array.    `grid.c` uses
an array reference incorrectly, a mistake that beginning C programmers sometimes make:

**Program 3-15**

```
/* grid.c - two-dimensional array reference */

main()
{
    static double mint[3][5] = {
        {  1,   2,   3,   4,   5,  },
        {  6,   7,   8,   9,  10,  },
        { 11,  12,  13,  14,  15   }
    };

    printf("%g\n", mint[1][0]);   /* second row, first col */
    printf("%g\n", mint[1,0]);    /* same thing? */
}

$ grid
6
1.45649e-15
```

The first `printf()` displays a double (6) from the second row and first column. The following `printf()` attempts to do the same thing. It's easy to make the mistake

```
mint[1,0]
```

if you come to C from FORTRAN or BASIC. The program, however, displays something strange. C evaluates the array subscript with the comma operator (,) and discards the first number. It's as if you typed

```
mint[0]
```

It turns out the compiler evaluates the array reference as a *pointer* (because `mint` is a two-dimensional array) and prints it as a floating point number. This is the very small number `grid.c` displays.

The following program provides an insight to pointer expressions like `mint[0]`. `elem2.c` displays two-dimensional array elements and their sizes. Here's the program and its output on a 16-bit machine where a `double` is eight bytes.

**Program 3-16**

```
/* elem2.c - two-dimensional array elements */

main()
{
    double mint[3][5];

    printf("mint   mint[0] &mint[0][0]\n");

    printf("%4x",    mint);             /* addr of entire array */
    printf("%8x",    mint[0]);          /* addr of first row */
    printf("%12x\n", &mint[0][0]);      /* addr of first element */

    printf("%4d",    sizeof(mint));       /* size of entire array */
    printf("%8d",    sizeof(mint[0]));    /* size of row */
    printf("%12d\n", sizeof(mint[0][0])); /* size of element */
}
```

```
$ elem2
mint   mint[0] &mint[0][0]
2c5e    2c5e        2c5e
 120      40           8
```

The memory addresses of the three array references are the same. The `sizeof()` operator produces different sizes, however. As you would expect, mint[0][0]'s size is 8 bytes (the size of a  double). The program reveals something else, however. The compiler treats  mint and  mint[0] as arrays of different sizes. The size of  mint is 120 bytes (15 times the size of a  double), and the size of  mint[0] is 40 bytes (5 times the size of a  double).

When you use these names in expressions, the compiler uses pointers. Each one points to a different object. For example,  mint[0] is a pointer to the first of five doubles in the first row and  mint is a pointer to an *array* of five doubles. Each element of  mint points to a row of the two-dimensional array.

Expressions like these are worthwhile discussing because many similar ones exist. Table 3-2 lists the combinations of pointer indirections and references that C supports for two-dimensional arrays.

**TABLE 3-2. Two-dimensional array and pointer references**

double mint[3][5]

| Expression | Meaning |
| --- | --- |
| mint | pointer to an array of five doubles, first row |
| *mint | pointer to a double, first row, first column |
| **mint | double, value at first row, first column |
| mint[1] | pointer to a double, second row, first column |
| *mint[1] | double, value at second row, first column |
| mint + 1 | pointer to an array of five doubles, second row |
| *mint + 1 | pointer to a double, first row, second column |
| mint[1][1] | double, value at second row, second column |
| mint[1] + 1 | pointer to a double, second row, second column |

The table doesn't list all the possibilities, but you can derive the others. For example,

    mint[0]

is a pointer to a double (the first element). This is the same as

    *mint

because the basic rule shows

    mint[0]  ≡  *(mint + 0)  ≡  *mint

In general, the following hints help decipher two-dimensional (and more) array references:

---
*Array References and Pointer Expressions*
===

1.    A completely specified array reference
      always yields the data type of the array

2.    Substitute a pointer to the data type for
      each incompletely specified array subscript

3.    Evaluate one level of indirection for each
      * in an array reference

---

Let's look at several examples.  The reference

```
mint[1][1]
```

is a double because it's completely specified.  The reference

```
mint[1]
```

is a pointer to a double because it's incompletely referenced.  Likewise,

```
mint
```

is a pointer to a pointer to a double, which is the same as a pointer to an array of doubles.  As we saw earlier with the *sizeof()* operator, the compiler keeps track of the number of doubles in the array.  In this example, *mint* is a pointer to an array of 5 doubles.

Indirection works in an opposite fashion.  The reference

```
*mint
```

is a pointer to a double because we apply indirection to mint.  The reference

```
**mint
```

is a double because we apply two levels of indirection.  The expression

```
*mint[1]
```

is also a double because we apply indirection to a pointer.  This type of analysis also applies to three-dimensional arrays as we'll see shortly.

Table 3-2 shows that the compiler interprets many of the expressions as pointer offsets.  For example, mint + 1 produces a pointer to the second row because the compiler scales the address increment by 40 (5 times 8) bytes.  Likewise, *mint + 1 is a pointer to the next column in the first row because the address increment is only 8 bytes.  We'll use these pointer expressions in our techniques later on.

## Storage Map Equations for Two-Dimensional Arrays

Viewing two-dimensional arrays as grids with rows and columns is for our benefit.  Unfortunately, the compiler has a harder job than we do making the connection between arrays and grids.  Physical memory is accessed as a one-dimensional array, so the compiler *maps* two-dimensional arrays to blocks of memory.  Each time you reference a two-dimensional array element, the compiler calculates an address in the memory block.

Let's investigate how the compiler calculates these addresses.  It's worthwhile discussing because it answers many questions about two-dimensional array usages in C, and it explains why pointer expressions are faster.

Fig. 3-6 shows memory for the declaration `double mint[3][5]`.

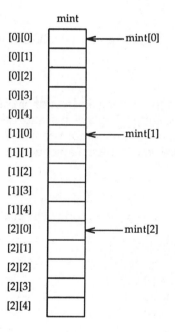

*Fig. 3-6.* Memory block for double mint[3][5]

C stores two-dimensional arrays in memory by rows (this is called *row major form*).  The second subscript varies faster than the first one.  Therefore, `mint[0]` points to the first row, `mint[1]` points to the second row, and `mint[2]` points to the last row.  The compiler calculates the address for an array reference by locating the appropriate row and accessing the correct column within that row.

For two-dimensional array references, the basic rule implies that

```
mint[i][j]
*(mint[i] + j)
*(*(mint + i) + j)
```

are all equivalent. Look closely at the third pointer expression. Recall from Table 3-2 that `mint` is a pointer to an array of 5 doubles. Then, `mint + i` moves the pointer by `i` rows. There are 5 doubles in each row. The compiler, therefore, implements the pointer expression as follows:

```
*(&mint[0][0] + 5 * i + j)
```

Subscript `i` is the row number, subscript `j` is the column number, and `&mint[0][0]` is the base address of the array. We call the above expression a *storage map equation*. Every multidimensional array declaration in a program has one. This particular storage map equation is for

```
double mint[3][5];
```

The compiler uses this formula to translate the array reference

```
mint[i][j]
```

to a pointer offset from the starting address of `mint`.

The following program displays the address of a two-dimensional array reference two ways. The first reference uses a completely specified array reference and the second uses the storage map equation.

**Program 3-17**

```
/* map2d.c - two-dimensional array storage maps */

main()
{
    double mint[3][5];
    int row, col;
    double *address;

    row = 1;
    col = 2;

    /* storage map equation */
    address = &mint[0][0] + 5 * row + col;

    /* address of second row, third col */
```

```
    printf("%u\n", &mint[1][2]);

    /* same address */
    printf("%u\n", address);
}
```

$ **map2d**
```
11332
11332
```

The output shows the addresses are the same. This demonstrates how the compiler computes addresses from two-dimensional array references.

There are additional topics to discuss about storage map equations. First of all, the storage map equation multiplies the first subscript of the array element by the number of columns in the array. In many cases, the compiler will generate a multiply instruction in assembly code for multidimensional array references. Depending on the machine architecture, this may slow down programs.

Secondly, the storage map equation for a two-dimensional array does *not* use the number of rows from the array declaration. This makes sense, since the the starting address of the array and the number of columns is what's important. The compiler locates the appropriate row and column of an array reference by computing a pointer offset in two steps. The row subscript times the number of columns is the first part of the offset. The column subscript is the second part. Depending on the implementation, to calculate the offset the compiler may generate a multiply instruction in assembly code for the first part, and an addition for the second part. Adding this value to the base address of the array is a pointer to an array element.

Most C compilers take a close look at the storage map equation for multidimensional arrays. Suppose, for example, we declare mint as follows:

```
double mint[3][4];
```

The storage map equation for mint[i][j] is now

```
*(&mint[0][0] + 4 * i + j)
```

Some compilers generate *shift* instructions in place of multiplies. Multiplying an integer by a power of 2, for instance, is the same as shifting the bits left by the value of the power. In this example, a compiler could shift i left by 2 bits instead of multiplying it by 4. If the number of columns is not a power of two (like our original declaration of mint[3][5]), some compilers may even generate a set of "shift-and-add" instructions. In other words, shifting i left by 2 bits and adding i is the same as multiplying i by 5. In map2d.c, for example, we could have displayed the same address with

```
/* storage map equation */
address = &mint[0][0] + (row << 2) + row + col;
```

The implementation of storage map equations is therefore machine dependent! For this reason, you shouldn't write programs that rely on how your compiler implements multiplies from the storage map equation. If you declare a two-dimensional array where the number of columns is a power of two, for instance, you're hedging your bets about how smart all C compilers are. Besides, it is not always convenient to declare arrays this way. A better approach is to use *pointers*, which we discuss in the next section.

## Passing Two-Dimensional Arrays to Functions

Storage map equations explain why C allows you to drop the first subscript from arrays that are function parameters and external references. Let's look at an example.

Suppose `extern2d.c` declares a two-dimensional array of doubles and initializes it as follows:

```
double mint[3][5] = {
    {  1,  2,  3,  4,  5 },
    {  6,  7,  8,  9, 10 },
    { 11, 12, 13, 14, 15 }
};
```

Program `pass2d.c` uses this array to pass the starting address of the array to a function, which displays the value of one of its elements.

**Program 3-18**

```
/* pass2d.c - pass two-dimensional array to a function */

main()
{
    extern double mint[][5];
    int row = 0, col = 1;

    printf("%g\n", mint[row][col]);   /* first row, second col */
    pass2d(mint, row, col);           /* two-dimensional array */
}

pass2d(a, row, col)
double a[][5];
int row, col;
{
    printf("%g\n", a[row][col]);      /* first row, second col */
}
```

```
$ cc pass2d.c extern2d.c -o pass2d
$ pass2d
2
2
```

The main program and the function `pass2d()` display the same value.
The statement

```
extern double mint[][5];
```

inside `main()` informs the compiler that `mint` is a two-dimensional array of doubles declared in another file. The compiler does not allocate storage. In this statement, you may omit only the first subscript. C requires `[]` and the number of columns so the compiler can use the storage map equation to compute the appropriate address for a two-dimensional array reference.

C also uses storage map equations for two-dimensional array references inside functions that use the address of the array as a parameter. This is why the statement

```
double a[][5];
```

inside `pass2d()` compiles. C permits function parameter declarations for arrays without the first subscript because storage map equations do not use it. Of course, C always accepts the declaration

```
double a[3][5];
```

but the compiler ignores the 3.

C permits a third way to declare a two-dimensional array as a function parameter. The declaration

```
double (*a)[5];
```

is equivalent to the previous two. This declaration reveals what's really going on when you pass the address of `mint` to a function. The compiler allocates storage for a *pointer* to an array of 5 doubles. Note that C requires the parentheses. Without them, the compiler declares an array of five pointers to doubles, and this makes the program fail. Two-dimensional array references are pointer offsets by rows. C permits array references using two-dimensional notation because of the basic relationship between pointers and arrays. The compiler still requires the storage map equation to compute a pointer offset, however.

## Three-Dimensional Arrays

Three-dimensional arrays add another level to the same concept. The compiler looks at a three-dimensional array as a one-dimensional array whose elements are two-dimensional arrays. For this reason, three-dimensional arrays are more difficult to visualize. The declaration

```
double mint[2][3][5];
```

for example, allocates storage for 30 doubles (240 bytes), arranged as *two grids* of 3 rows and 5 columns each. It's like stacking one two-dimensional array on top of another. Fig. 3-7 shows how we visualize the array `mint`:

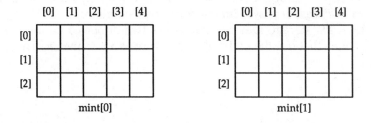

*Fig. 3-7.* Three-dimensional array double mint[2][3][5]

Three-dimensional array references have the following format:

```
mint [gridn] [rown] [coln]
```

*gridn* (the leftmost subscript) references the grid. The second and third subscripts (*rown* and *coln*) are the row and column of the grid, respectively.

Let's extend a previous program for two-dimensional arrays to three. Program `elem3.c` displays three-dimensional array elements and their sizes on a 16-bit machine where a `double` is eight bytes.

**Program 3-19**

```
/* elem3.c - three-dimensional array elements */

main()
{
    double mint[2][3][5];

    printf("mint  mint[0]  mint[0][0]  &mint[0][0][0]\n");

    printf("%4x",    mint);            /* addr of entire array */
```

```
    printf("%8x",    mint[0]);              /* addr of first grid */
    printf("%12x",   mint[0][0]);   /* addr of first grid & row */
    printf("%16x\n", &mint[0][0][0]); /* addr of first element */

    printf("%4d",    sizeof(mint));      /* size of entire array */
    printf("%8d",    sizeof(mint[0]));          /* size of grid */
    printf("%12d",   sizeof(mint[0][0]));        /* size of row */
    printf("%16d\n", sizeof(mint[0][0][0])); /* size of element */
}
```

$ **elem3**

| mint | mint[0] | mint[0][0] | &mint[0][0][0] |
|------|---------|------------|----------------|
| 2c16 | 2c16    | 2c16       | 2c16           |
| 240  | 120     | 40         | 8              |

The addresses are the same, but the sizeof() operator produces different sizes. For a three-dimensional array, mint[0][0] is a row and mint[0] is a grid. Their sizes are 40 bytes (5 doubles in each row), and 120 bytes (15 doubles in each grid), respectively.    mint's size is 240 bytes, or the size of the entire three-dimensional array.

These names have different meanings in expressions, as they did with two-dimensional array references.  The array reference

    mint[0][0]

for example, is a pointer to the first of five doubles. This is the address of the first row in the first grid.  Likewise, the expression

    mint[0]

is a pointer to the first of three rows.  This is also the address of the first row in the first grid.  The pointers contain the same address, but the compiler assigns different meanings to the pointers' objects.  As we will see shortly, the compiler uses this information to compute pointer offsets.

C permits pointer expressions for arrays in three dimensions as it does for two dimensions.  Of course, there are more possibilities.  In fact, C supports all the expressions from Table 3-2 in addition to the following new ones:

```
    ***mint              *mint[1][1]
    **mint[1]            *mint[1] + 1
    **mint + 1           mint[1][1] + 1
```

It's important to understand that two-dimensional expressions have different meanings in three dimensions.  Follow our earlier suggestions for two-dimensional pointer expressions to decipher the new ones.  The compiler interpretations are left as an worthwhile exercise for the reader (see Exercise 6).

## Storage Map Equations for Three-Dimensional Arrays

Just as with two-dimensional arrays, C maps three-dimensional arrays to a single block of memory. Fig. 3-8 shows the layout for the declaration `double mint[2][3][5]`.

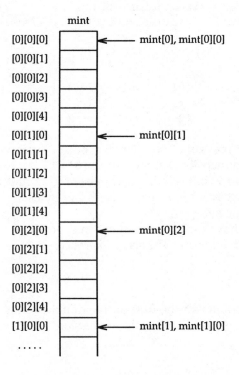

*Fig. 3-8.* Memory block for double mint[2][3][5]

The second 3 by 5 grid follows the first. Memory layout within each grid has the same organization as in the two-dimensional example. Let's now apply the basic rule to derive the storage map equation for three-dimensional arrays.

For three-dimensional array references,

```
mint[i][j][k]
*(mint[i][j] + k)
*(*(mint[i] + j) + k)
*(*(*(mint + i) + j) + k)
```

are all equivalent, according to the basic rule. The last expression reveals how the compiler computes the pointer offset in separate steps. `mint` is a pointer to an array of 15 doubles, `mint + 1` produces a pointer offset 15 doubles from the starting address of `mint,` and `mint + 2` is an address offset by 30 doubles. Therefore, `mint + i` is a pointer offset 15 doubles *times* `i` from the start of the array. After the indirection, this new pointer is a pointer to an array of 5 doubles.

We derive the next pointer offset the same way. The expression `*(mint + i) + j` is an address that's 5 doubles times `j` from the address of `mint + i`. Finally, `*(*(mint + i) + j) + k` is a pointer offset by `k` doubles. This is the address of `mint[i][j][k]`.

This analysis translates to a storage map equation for a three-dimensional array. The declaration

```
double mint[2][3][5];
```

makes the compiler evaluate

```
mint[i][j][k]
```

with the following storage map equation:

```
*(&mint[0][0][0] + 15 * i + 5 * j + k)
```

Subscripts `i`, `j`, and `k` are the grids, rows, and columns, respectively, and `&mint[0][0][0]` is the base address of the array. 15 is the product of the number of rows (3) and the number of columns (5). Pointer offsets for three-dimensional array references require *two* multiplication operations. The number of two-dimensional grids (2) is not used.

## Passing Three-Dimensional Arrays to Functions

The following program called `pass3d.c` contains a main program and two functions. The main program declares and initializes a three-dimensional array of doubles. It passes the starting address of the array to the first function as a parameter. This function calls a second function and passes the address of a two-dimensional array. The program demonstrates several pointer expressions of interest.

**Program 3-20**

```
/* pass3d.c - pass three-dimensional arrays to functions */

main()
{
    static double mint[2][3][5] = {
        { {  1,  2,  3,  4,  5 },
          {  6,  7,  8,  9, 10 },      /* grid 0 */
          { 11, 12, 13, 14, 15 }
        },

        { { 16, 17, 18, 19, 20 },
          { 21, 22, 23, 24, 25 },      /* grid 1 */
          { 26, 27, 28, 29, 30 }
        }
    };

    int grid = 1, row = 0, col = 1;

    printf("%g\n", mint[grid][row][col]);

    pass3d(mint, grid, row, col);      /* three-dim array */
}

pass3d(b, grid, row, col)
double (*b)[3][5];                /* pointer to two-dim array */
int grid, row, col;
{
    printf("%g\n", b[grid][row][col]);

    pass2d(b[grid], row, col);          /* two-dim array */
}

pass2d(a, row, col)
double (*a)[5];                          /* pointer to array */
int row, col;
{
    printf("%g\n", a[row][col]);  /* first row, second col */
}

$ pass3d
17
17
17
```

The program displays the same double from the three-dimensional array `mint`. The extra sets of braces help delineate the separate 3 by 5 two-dimensional grids. Inside the function `pass3d()`, the declaration

```
double (*b)[3][5];    /* pointer to two-dim array */
```

is a pointer to a 3 by 5 grid of doubles. This is equivalent to

```
double b[][3][5];     /* pointer to two-dim array */
```

The statement

```
pass2d(b[grid], row, col);    /* two-dim array */
```

passes the address of the *second* 3 by 5 grid of doubles, since `b[grid]` is a pointer to a two-dimensional array. Inside `pass2d()`, the declaration

```
double (*a)[5];              /* pointer to array */
```

is a pointer to an array of 5 doubles. This declaration is equivalent to

```
double a[][5];              /* pointer to same array */
```

The last `printf()` statement displays the same element as the previous ones. `pass2d()` is therefore identical to the routine from `pass2d.c`.

## ◆ Performance Pointers ◆

It's time to put our knowledge of pointers and arrays to work. The most worthwhile effort, at least in making programs run faster, is to apply pointers inside loops to process array data. To accomplish this, we make the following assumption:

> Pointer indirections are no worse than multiplication
> steps from storage map equations, and they typically
> make loops execute faster.

Our approach eliminates storage map equations and substitutes pointer expressions for array references. This should improve the execution speed of most programs, regardless of whether the compiler uses a shift-and-add algorithm or multiplication in assembly code.

The first part of this section is a suite of C programs that compares the performance of compact pointer expressions to array references. The second part shows the benefits of declaring pointer arrays over multidimensional arrays.

Both sections provide benchmarks that demonstrate how the programs perform on PC's (286 and 386) and a Sun 68020 workstation. You may wish to try several of our programs on your machine and compare the results with ours.

## Compact Pointer Expressions for Array References

There's a total of ten C programs in the benchmark suite, and all of them work with arrays of integers. Here are the machine configurations that we used:

1.  IBM 286 PC/AT running at 8 MHz with SCO 286 XENIX System V.

2.  COMPAQ 386 PC running at 16 MHz with SCO 386 XENIX System V.

3.  SUN 3/260 68020 workstation running at 25 MHz with Sun 3.4 OS.

We compiled the programs with optimization (-o) and ran the programs in single user mode on each UNIX machine. We used the UNIX time command to determine the execution times (real time only) in seconds.

The first program, called a1d.c, declares a one-dimensional array of integers and sets each array element to a different value inside a loop.

**Program 3-21**

```
/* a1d.c - one-dimensional array fill benchmark
          using arrays (pointer offset)
*/

#define IMAX 10
#define LOOP 10000

main()
{
    int a[IMAX];
    register int i;
    int v = 0;

    while (v++ < LOOP)
        for (i = 0; i < IMAX; i++)
            a[i] = v;              /* pointer offset */
}
```

a1d.c (and subsequent programs) fills the array 10,000 times. We declare the array subscript i as a register variable so the program runs as fast as possible. The compiler converts the array reference to a pointer offset.

p1d.c does the same thing, using a compact pointer expression.

**Program 3-22**

```
/* p1d.c - one-dimensional array fill benchmark
            using compact pointer expression
*/

#define IMAX 10
#define LOOP 10000

main()
{
    int a[IMAX];
    register int *p;
    int v = 0;

    while (v++ < LOOP)
        for (p = a; p < &a[IMAX];)
            *p++ = v;                /* compact pointer */
}
```

Pointer p also resides in a register for faster execution. Table 3-3 shows the results.

**TABLE 3-3. One-dimensional arrays**

| Program | Method | 286 (secs) | 386 (secs) | 68020 (secs) |
|---------|--------|------------|------------|--------------|
| a1d.c | array | .9 | .3 | .1 |
| p1d.c | pointer | .7 | .4 | .1 |

Program a1d.c uses a pointer offset and p1d.c uses pointer indirection and autoincrement. On the 286, one-dimensional array references are slower than compact pointer expressions. One-dimensional array references, on the other hand, are faster than a compact pointer expression on the 386. (This has to do with the 386 addressing modes, which are slightly faster than indirection and autoincrements.) On the 68020, there's no apparent difference. The programs do not use storage map equations because they both work with one-dimensional arrays.

Before we continue, we should mention that a one-dimensional array reference in our programs generates shift instructions on these machines to access array elements. That's because we're working with integers whose size (2 bytes or 4 bytes) is a power of two. In general, arrays of objects whose size may not be a power of two (some structures, for example) can make the compiler generate multiplies or shifts-and-adds for one-dimensional array references. In any case, what happens here is machine dependent, so you'll want to study what your compiler does with these programs and the remaining ones in the suite.

The next program fills a two-dimensional array of integers. Program a2d.c has two embedded loops to generate subscripts for the array reference.

**Program 3-23**

```
/* a2d.c - two-dimensional array fill benchmark
          using arrays (storage map equation)
*/

#define IMAX 10
#define JMAX 10
#define LOOP 10000

main()
{
    int a[IMAX][JMAX];
    register int j;
    register int i;
    int v = 0;

    while (v++ < LOOP)
        for (i = 0; i < IMAX; i++)
            for (j = 0; j < JMAX; j++)
                a[i][j] = v;      /* storage map equation */
}
```

Loop variable j increments more often than i, so we use the technique for declaring register variables shown in Chapter 1 (we declare j before i on a separate line). The compiler uses a two-dimensional storage map equation for the array reference.

The following program called p2d.c uses a compact pointer expression in place of a two-dimensional array reference. We use a single for loop to make the pointer access memory in the form of a one-dimensional array.

**Program 3-24**

```
/* p2d.c - two-dimensional array fill benchmark
          using pointers (no storage map equation)
*/

#define IMAX 10
#define JMAX 10
```

```
#define LOOP 10000

main()
{
    int a[IMAX][JMAX];
    register int *p;
    int v = 0;

    while (v++ < LOOP)
        for (p = &a[0][0]; p < &a[IMAX][0];)
            *p++ = v;              /* compact pointer */
}
```

The program sets p to the starting address of the array and terminates the for loop when the pointer reaches the end. The compact pointer expression moves the pointer. The expression

```
p < &a[IMAX][0]
```

tests whether p has accessed all the array elements. Note that the compiler will *not* use a storage map equation for this array reference because both array subscripts are constants and not variables. The last valid address in the array is

```
&a[IMAX-1][JMAX-1]
```

so &a[IMAX][0] is the first invalid one.

By the way, the expressions

```
p < a[IMAX]
```

and

```
p < &a[IMAX][0]
```

are equivalent. We derive it from the basic rule as follows:

$$p < \&a[IMAX][0] \quad \equiv \quad p < \&*(a[IMAX] + 0)$$

$$\equiv \quad p < \&*a[IMAX]$$

$$\equiv \quad p < a[IMAX]$$

Similarly, the expression

```
p < (int *)(a + IMAX)
```

is also equivalent because  a  +  IMAX is a pointer to an array of JMAX integers. We cast the expression as a pointer to an integer and test it against  p.

Table 3-4 shows the results.

**TABLE 3-4. Two-dimensional arrays**

| Program | Method | 286 (secs) | 386 (secs) | 68020 (secs) |
|---------|--------|-----------|-----------|-------------|
| a2d.c | array | 10.4 | 3.5 | 2.1 |
| p2d.c | pointer | 5.5 | 2.7 | .8 |

a2d.c, which uses a storage map equation, makes the compiler generate a multiply instruction in assembly code on the 286 and 386. On the 68020, the compiler produces shifts-and-adds for  a2d.c. The results show that compact pointer expressions are faster than two-dimensional array references with storage map equations on all three machines.

The next pair of programs declares three-dimensional arrays. Program a3d.c has embedded  for loops to fill a three-dimensional array of integers.

**Program 3-25**

```
/* a3d.c - three-dimensional array fill benchmark
         using arrays (storage map equation)
*/

#define IMAX 10
#define JMAX 10
#define KMAX 10
#define LOOP 10000

main()
{
    int a[IMAX][JMAX][KMAX];
    register int k;
    register int j;
    register int i;
    int v = 0;

    while (v++ < LOOP)
       for (i = 0; i < IMAX; i++)
          for (j = 0; j < JMAX; j++)
             for (k = 0; k < KMAX; k++)
                a[i][j][k] = v;      /* storage map equation */
}
```

We declare k, j, and i as register variables. The compiler uses a three-dimensional storage map equation for the array reference.

Program p3d.c has one loop with a compact pointer expression to access memory and does the same job.

**Program 3-26**

```
/* p3d.c - three-dimensional array fill benchmark
            using pointers (no storage map equation)
*/

#define IMAX 10
#define JMAX 10
#define KMAX 10
#define LOOP 10000

main()
{
    int a[IMAX][JMAX][KMAX];
    register int *p;
    int v = 0;

    while (v++ < LOOP)
        for (p = &a[0][0][0]; p < &a[IMAX][0][0];)
            *p++ = v;                /* compact pointer */
}
```

We use the expression

```
p < &a[IMAX][0][0]
```

to exit the for loop when we've reached the end of the three-dimensional array. You should convince yourself that the expressions

```
p < *a[IMAX]
```

```
p < a[IMAX][0]
```

```
p < (int *)(a + IMAX)
```

are all equivalent using the basic rule.

Table 3-5 shows the results.

TABLE 3-5. Three-dimensional arrays

| Program | Method | 286 (secs) | 386 (secs) | 68020 (secs) |
|---------|--------|------------|------------|--------------|
| a3d.c | array | 144.6 | 46.9 | 30.8 |
| p3d.c | pointer | 52.1 | 25.2 | 8.4 |

Program `a3d.c`, which uses a storage map equation, generates two multiply instructions in assembly code on the 286 and 386. As in the two-dimensional case, the 68020 uses shifts-and-adds for `a3d.c`. The results show compact pointer expressions are significantly faster than three-dimensional array references with storage map equations on all three machines.

## Pointer Array Declarations

The previous benchmarks demonstrate the usefulness of compact pointer expressions. Another technique that helps make loops execute faster doesn't have anything to do with the code you place inside a loop. Surprisingly, the approach is based on the *declarations* you use. The key is to declare an array of pointers (we call it a *pointer array*) in place of multidimensional arrays. Pointer arrays eliminate storage map equations and convert array references to pointer offsets. Let's look at several programs and see how this works.

Suppose we are creating a program to maintain a database. The user interface requires codes to access groups of items. The following program stores domestic fruits as character strings inside a two-dimensional array of characters.

**Program 3-27**

```
/* ch2d.c - two-dimensional array of characters */

#include <ctype.h>

main()
{
    static char fruits[6][13] = {
      "avocado", "figs", "lemons",
      "oranges", "strawberries", "watermelon"
    };
    int i;

    for (i = 0; i < 6; i++)
       printf("%c for %s\n", toupper(fruits[i][0]),
                  fruits[i]);
}
```

```
$ ch2d
A for avocado
F for figs
L for lemons
O for oranges
S for strawberries
W for watermelon
```

The program initializes the array with the fruit names and displays the code (the first letter of each name). Fig. 3-9 shows the memory layout for ch2d.c in the data area.

| | [0] | [1] | [2] | [3] | [4] | [5] | [6] | [7] | [8] | [9] | [10] | [11] | [12] |
|---|---|---|---|---|---|---|---|---|---|---|---|---|---|
| fruits[0] | a | v | o | c | a | d | o | \0 | | | | | |
| fruits[1] | f | i | g | s | \0 | | | | | | | | |
| fruits[2] | l | e | m | o | n | s | \0 | | | | | | |
| fruits[3] | o | r | a | n | g | e | s | \0 | | | | | |
| fruits[4] | s | t | r | a | w | b | e | r | r | i | e | s | \0 |
| fruits[5] | w | a | t | e | r | m | e | l | o | n | \0 | | |

*Fig. 3-9.* Two-dimensional array of characters

The number of columns (13) in the array declaration is big enough to hold the number of characters for the largest string ("strawberries") plus one for the NULL byte. The rest of the strings are shorter; hence, the array contains unused bytes.

Inside the for loop, we display the code by converting

```
fruits[i][0]
```

to uppercase, which is the first character of the fruit name. We use

```
fruits[i]
```

to display the fruit name, since this is a character pointer. Both expressions use storage map equations.

The two-dimensional array design for our sample program has several disadvantages. One, it wastes memory bytes since the strings are not all the same length. Two, if you add another name to the list that exceeds the length of the longest string, you must increase the number of columns to accommodate it, further compounding the problem. Three, the compiler uses storage map equations for array references and may generate multiply instructions or shifts-and-adds in assembly code. This list is long enough to suggest another approach.

An alternative to a two-dimensional array of characters is an array of character pointers. The following program's statements are identical to the previous one, except on the line that contains the declaration.

**Program 3-28**

```
/* ch1p.c - one-dimensional array of character ptrs */

#include <ctype.h>

main()
{
    static char *fruits[6] = {
      "avocado", "figs", "lemons",
      "oranges", "strawberries", "watermelon"
    };
    int i;

    for (i = 0; i < 6; i++)
        printf("%c for %s\n", toupper(fruits[i][0]),
                    fruits[i]);
}
```

```
$ ch1p
A for avocado
F for figs
L for lemons
O for oranges
S for strawberries
W for watermelon
```

Fig. 3-10 shows the memory layout for ch1p.c in the data area.

There are no unused bytes in the data area. In fact, with this arrangement, the unused bytes from the two-dimensional design have now been put to better use. Together they form an array of pointers (fruits) to the strings. If we add another fruit name to ch1p.c, we require only enough memory from the data area for one pointer plus the name of the fruit. This solves two of the problems that plague the previous program.

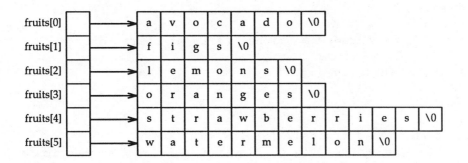

*Fig. 3-10.* Array of character pointers

It turns out the third problem disappears, too. From the basic rule, the expression

```
fruits[i]
```

is equivalent to

```
*(fruits + i)
```

which is a pointer offset. The compiler doesn't use a storage map equation. Likewise, the expression

```
fruits[i][0]
```

is equivalent to

```
*fruits[i]
```

which is the same as

```
**(fruits + i)
```

resulting in double indirection from a pointer offset. (Verify this with the basic rule.) As we will see shortly, this also executes faster on our machine than do two-dimensional storage map equations.

Pointer arrays apply to three-dimensional applications as well. Suppose, for example, our sample program needs to handle tropical fruits in addition to domestic ones. For demonstration purposes, we'll continue to go down the wrong road to discover why we should turn around and try another way. The following program called ch3d.c uses a three-dimensional array to store two groups of fruit names and display the codes.

**Program 3-29**

```c
/* ch3d.c - three-dimensional array of characters */

#include <ctype.h>

main()
{
    static char fruits[2][6][13] = {
        { "avocado", "figs", "lemons",          /* domestic */
          "oranges", "strawberries", "watermelon"
        },
        { "bananas", "coconuts", "guava",        /* tropical */
          "kiwi", "mangos", "papayas"
        }
    };
    int i,j;

    for (i = 0; i < 2; i++) {
        printf(i == 0 ? "domestic:\n" : "tropical:\n");
        for (j = 0; j < 6; j++)
            printf("   %c for %s\n", toupper(fruits[i][j][0]),
                        fruits[i][j]);
    }
}
```

```
$ ch3d
domestic:
    A for avocado
    F for figs
    L for lemons
    O for oranges
    S for strawberries
    W for watermelon
tropical:
    B for bananas
    C for coconuts
    G for guava
    K for kiwi
    M for mangos
    P for papayas
```

The first subscript of the three-dimensional array of characters references the type of fruit and the two-dimensional elements hold the names. Fig. 3-11 shows the memory layout for ch3d.c in the data area.

|     | [0] | [1] | [2] | [3] | [4] | [5] | [6] | [7] | [8] | [9] | [10] | [11] | [12] |
|-----|-----|-----|-----|-----|-----|-----|-----|-----|-----|-----|------|------|------|
| [0] | a | v | o | c | a | d | o | \0 |   |   |   |   |   |
| [1] | f | i | g | s | \0 |   |   |   |   |   |   |   |   |
| [2] | l | e | m | o | n | s | \0 |   |   |   |   |   |   |
| [3] | o | r | a | n | g | e | s | \0 |   |   |   |   |   |
| [4] | s | t | r | a | w | b | e | r | r | i | e | s | \0 |
| [5] | w | a | t | e | r | m | e | l | o | n | \0 |   |   |

fruits[0]

|     | [0] | [1] | [2] | [3] | [4] | [5] | [6] | [7] | [8] | [9] | [10] | [11] | [12] |
|-----|-----|-----|-----|-----|-----|-----|-----|-----|-----|-----|------|------|------|
| [0] | b | a | n | a | n | a | s | \0 |   |   |   |   |   |
| [1] | c | o | c | o | n | u | t | s | \0 |   |   |   |   |
| [2] | g | u | a | v | a | \0 |   |   |   |   |   |   |   |
| [3] | k | i | w | i | \0 |   |   |   |   |   |   |   |   |
| [4] | m | a | n | g | o | s | \0 |   |   |   |   |   |   |
| [5] | p | a | p | a | y | a | s | \0 |   |   |   |   |   |

fruits[1]

*Fig. 3-11.* Three-dimensional array of characters

C does not require the inner pair of braces for the array initialization; we provide them for clarity. This approach, however, suffers the same drawbacks as the two-dimensional version; namely, it's difficult to modify and it wastes memory. Furthermore, the compiler uses three-dimensional storage map equations for array references, which make programs execute slowly.

You can have your fruit and eat it too, however. The following program called `ch1pp.c` uses an array of pointers to pointers to characters to accomplish the same task.

**Program 3-30**

```
/* ch1pp.c - one-dimensional array of pointers
   to pointers to characters */

#include <ctype.h>

main()
{
    static char *domestic[6] = {
      "avocado", "figs", "lemons",
      "oranges", "strawberries", "watermelon"
    };
    static char *tropical[6] = {
      "bananas", "coconuts", "guava",
      "kiwi", "mangos", "papayas"
    };
    static char **fruits[2] = { domestic, tropical };
    int i,j;

    for (i = 0; i < 2; i++) {
       printf(i == 0 ? "domestic:\n" : "tropical:\n");
       for (j = 0; j < 6; j++)
          printf("   %c for %s\n", toupper(fruits[i][j][0]),
                    fruits[i][j]);
    }
}
```

```
$ ch1pp
domestic:
    A for avocado
    F for figs
    L for lemons
    O for oranges
    S for strawberries
    W for watermelon
tropical:
    B for bananas
    C for coconuts
    G for guava
    K for kiwi
    M for mangos
    P for papayas
```

We declare and initialize three pointer arrays. The first two (domestic and tropical) contain pointers to constant strings. The fruits array now holds pointers to the other two character pointer arrays. Note that this arrangement makes `fruits` an array of pointers to pointers to characters. Fig. 3-12 shows the memory layout for `ch1pp.c` in the data area.

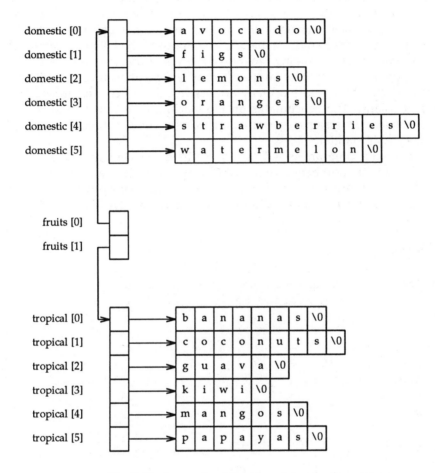

*Fig. 3-12.* Array of pointers to pointers to characters

This pointer hierarchy utilizes memory efficiently and is easy to modify. Array references are pointer offsets (the compiler doesn't use a storage map equation). For example, the expression

```
fruits[i][j][0]
```

is equivalent to

```
*(*(*(fruits + i) + j))
```

from the basic rule.

## Two-Dimensional Array Conversions

The previous programs raise an interesting question. As a rule, are pointer indirections faster than multiplies for two- and three-dimensional storage map equations? To find out, we ran benchmarks on our machines with two pairs of programs that produce different assembly code for array references. The programs illustrate another technique for making program loops run faster by changing a program's declarations. In fact, we have used the following approach to speed up programs by changing program declarations and very little else.

This approach is useful for large software systems that have multidimensional array declarations and too many array references to convert to compact pointer expressions. The benchmarks on the machines we tested confirm that two-dimensional conversions give modest results, while three-dimensional conversions are substantial.

The following program called sm2d.c fills a two-dimensional array of integers with random numbers. We pass the array's address to a function which loops through it to return the maximum number. The main program fills the array and displays the maximum value 10 times in a loop. Here's the code and its output on the 286 machine.

**Program 3-31**

```
/* sm2d.c - two-dimensional array processing
            with storage map equation
*/

#define IMAX      5
#define JMAX   5000
#define LOOP     10

main()
{
    static int a[IMAX][JMAX];
    register int j;
    register int i;
    int n = 0;

    while (n++ < LOOP) {
      for (i = 0; i < IMAX; i++)
        for (j = 0; j < JMAX; j++)
            a[i][j] = rand();        /* random fill */
      printf("max = %d\n", maxv(a));
    }
}
```

```
maxv(b)
int (*b)[JMAX];                 /* equiv to b[][JMAX] */
{
    register int j;
    register int i;
    int mv = b[0][0];           /* first entry to start */

    for (i = 0; i < IMAX; i++)
        for (j = 0; j < JMAX; j++)
            if (b[i][j] > mv)
                mv = b[i][j];
    return mv;                  /* maximum number */
}
```

$ **sm2d**
```
max = 32766
max = 32763
max = 32767
max = 32765
max = 32766
max = 32767
max = 32766
max = 32767
max = 32767
max = 32767
```

All array subscripts reside in registers to make program loops execute as fast as possible. C uses two-dimensional storage map equations in both the main program and the function maxv().

Now let's see how we can eliminate the storage map equations from the array references in sm2d.c. To do this, we'll change just a few lines in the program. Although we could certainly rewrite sm2d.c using compact pointer expressions, this technique applies to larger programs where extensive changes could take a long time and introduce new errors. Here is the technique for *two-dimensional array conversions*:

---

*Two-Dimensional Array Conversions*

1. Rename the original two-dimensional array, keeping the same data type.

2. Declare an array of pointers to the same data type and give it the name of the original array. The size of this new array is the number of rows in the original one.

3. Load the new array with the addresses of the rows of the original array.

---

Program `pi2d.c` shows a two-dimensional conversion for `sm2d.c`. Let's run it again on the 286 machine.

**Program 3-32**

```
/* pi2d.c - two-dimensional array processing
            with pointer indirection
*/

#define IMAX      5
#define JMAX   5000
#define LOOP     10

main()
{
    static int ax[IMAX][JMAX];
    static int *a[IMAX] = {
        ax[0], ax[1], ax[2], ax[3], ax[4]
    };
    register int j;
    register int i;
    int n = 0;

    while (n++ < LOOP) {
        for (i = 0; i < IMAX; i++)
            for (j = 0; j < JMAX; j++)
                a[i][j] = rand();    /* random number fill */
        printf("max = %d\n", maxv(a));
    }
}
```

```
maxv(b)
int *b[];                           /* equiv to **b */
{
    register int j;
    register int i;
    int mv = b[0][0];               /* first entry to start */

    for (i = 0; i < IMAX; i++)
        for (j = 0; j < JMAX; j++)
            if (b[i][j] > mv)
                mv = b[i][j];
    return mv;                       /* maximum number */
}
```

**$ pi2d**
```
max = 32766
max = 32763
max = 32767
max = 32765
max = 32766
max = 32767
max = 32766
max = 32767
max = 32767
max = 32767
```

Fig. 3-13 shows the memory layout for `pi2d.c` in the data area.

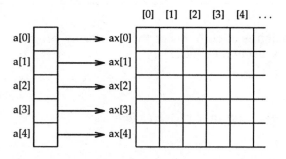

*Fig. 3-13.* Two-dimensional array conversion

Pointer `a[0]` contains the address of the first integer in the first row. Likewise, `a[1]` is a pointer to the first integer in the second row, and so on. Program `pi2d.c` incurs no run time overhead because the static declarations are initialized at load time. For large arrays, however, this approach is not always practical. Macros are possible, but perhaps the best alternative is to write a *function* to load the addresses of the rows into the pointer array. See Exercise 10.

Note that multidimensional array references don't have to change with this technique. Although array references in `pi2d.c` look the same as they do in `sm2d.c`, the compiler uses pointer indirections instead of storage map equations, as we will soon see.

Program `pi2d.c` brings up another point. You'll have to be careful if you *pass* array names to a function or refer to it in another file with `extern` statements. In `sm2d.c`, for example, the declaration inside `maxv()` is

```
int (*b) [JMAX];                    /* equiv to b[] [JMAX] */
```

Variable `b` is a pointer to an array of JMAX integers. In `pi2d.c` the declaration is

```
int *b[];                           /* equiv to **b */
```

Now `b` is a pointer to a pointer to an integer. If you don't declare `b` this way, the program doesn't work properly. The rest of the lines inside `maxv()` do not change.

Table 3-6 shows the benchmark results for the two programs.

**TABLE 3-6. Pointer arrays vs. two-dimensional arrays**

| Program | Method | 286 (secs) | 386 (secs) | 68020 (secs) |
|---------|--------|-----------|-----------|--------------|
| sm2d.c | array | 20.1 | 3.6 | 2.9 |
| pi2d.c | pointer | 19.3 | 3.0 | 2.0 |

The pointer version is slightly faster than the array program on all machines. This is because the array reference

```
a[i] [j]
```

converts to pointer offsets in `pi2d.c` as follows:

```
*(*(a + i) + j)
```

On all machines, assembly code for this expression executes faster than the two-dimensional storage map equation

```
*(&a[0] [0] + JMAX * i + j)
```

for array references in `sm2d.c`.

## Three-Dimensional Array Conversions

The last pair of programs in the benchmark suite applies the conversion technique to three-dimensional arrays. Program sm3d.c fills a three-dimensional array of integers with random data inside a loop.

**Program 3-33**

```c
/* sm3d.c - three-dimensional array processing
            with storage map equation  */

#define IMAX     5
#define JMAX     5
#define KMAX  1000
#define LOOP    10

main()
{
    static int a[IMAX][JMAX][KMAX];
    register int k;
    register int j;
    register int i;
    int n = 0;

    while (n++ < LOOP) {
        for (i = 0; i < IMAX; i++)
            for (j = 0; j < JMAX; j++)
                for (k = 0; k < KMAX; k++)
                    a[i][j][k] = rand();     /* random fill */
        printf("max = %d\n", maxv(a));
    }
}


maxv(b)
int (*b)[JMAX][KMAX];            /* equiv to b[][JMAX][KMAX] */
{
    register int k;
    register int j;
    register int i;
    int mv = b[0][0][0];         /* first entry to start */

    for (i = 0; i < IMAX; i++)
        for (j = 0; j < JMAX; j++)
            for (k = 0; k < KMAX; k++)
                if (b[i][j][k] > mv)
                    mv = b[i][j][k];
    return mv;                   /* maximum number */
}
```

**$ sm3d**
```
max = 32766
max = 32763
```
. . . . .

The program is similar to the two-dimensional version. As before, we show you the output on the 286 machine. All array subscripts reside in registers. Inside `maxv()`, the declaration

```
int (*b)[JMAX][KMAX];    /* equiv to b[][JMAX][KMAX] */
```

makes `b` a pointer to a two-dimensional array. Program `sm3d.c` uses two-dimensional storage map equations in both the main program and the function `maxv()`.

Here now is the technique for *three-dimensional array conversions,* which involves more work:

---

### *Three-Dimensional Array Conversions*

---

1. Rename the original three-dimensional array, keeping the same data type.

2. Declare a two dimensional array of pointers to the same data type. The size of this new array is the number of grids and rows in the original array.

3. Load this pointer array with the rows of the original three-dimensional array.

4. Declare a one-dimensional array of pointers to pointers to the same data type. The size of this new array is the number of grids in the original array.

5. Load the one-dimensional pointer array with the addresses of the previous pointer array's elements.

---

Program `pi3d.c` shows a three-dimensional conversion for `sm3d.c`.

**Program 3-34**

```
/* pi3d.c - three-dimensional array processing
            with pointer indirection
*/
```

```
#define IMAX     5
#define JMAX     5
#define KMAX 1000
#define LOOP    10

main()
{
    static int ax[IMAX][JMAX][KMAX];
    static int *ay[IMAX][JMAX] = {
      ax[0][0], ax[0][1], ax[0][2], ax[0][3], ax[0][4],
      ax[1][0], ax[1][1], ax[1][2], ax[1][3], ax[1][4],
      ax[2][0], ax[2][1], ax[2][2], ax[2][3], ax[2][4],
      ax[3][0], ax[3][1], ax[3][2], ax[3][3], ax[3][4],
      ax[4][0], ax[4][1], ax[4][2], ax[4][3], ax[4][4]
    };
    static int **a[IMAX] = {
      ay[0], ay[1], ay[2], ay[3], ay[4]
    };
    register int k;
    register int j;
    register int i;
    int n = 0;

    while (n++ < LOOP) {
       for (i = 0; i < IMAX; i++)
          for (j = 0; j < JMAX; j++)
             for (k = 0; k < KMAX; k++)
                a[i][j][k] = rand();      /* random fill */
       printf("max = %d\n", maxv(a));
    }
}


maxv(b)
int **b[];                    /* equiv to ***b */
{
    register int k;
    register int j;
    register int i;
    int mv = b[0][0][0];      /* first entry to start */

    for (i = 0; i < IMAX; i++)
       for (j = 0; j < JMAX; j++)
          for (k = 0; k < KMAX; k++)
             if (b[i][j][k] > mv)
                mv = b[i][j][k];
    return mv;                /* maximum number */
}
```

```
$ pi3d
max = 32766
max = 32763
  .  .  .  .  .
```

Fig. 3-14 shows the memory layout for `pi3d.c` in the data area.

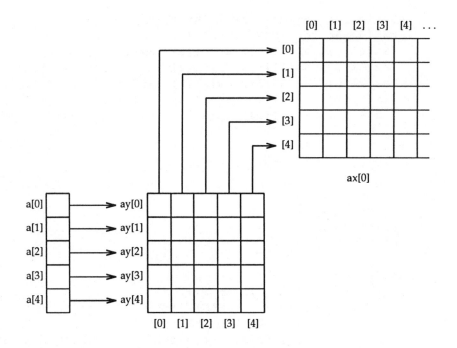

*Fig. 3-14.* Three-dimensional array conversion

We show only the pointers from a to ay, and only the first row of ay (ay[0]) to the first grid (ax[0]). The array reference a[0] is a pointer to the first row of a two-dimensional array of pointers to integers. ay[0][0] is a pointer to the first integer in the first row of the first grid (ax[0][0][0]), ay[0][1] is a pointer to the first integer in the second row of the first grid (ax[0][1][0]), and so on. The original name (a) becomes an array of IMAX pointers to pointers to integers. Note that the three-dimensional conversion technique requires extra memory. For the same reason we gave for two-dimensional conversions, you may write a function to load the two pointer arrays (see Exercise 11).

If you pass the three-dimensional array to a function or reference it with `extern` statements, you'll have to modify the declaration. Inside `maxv()`, the declaration becomes

```
int **b[];                /* equiv to ***b */
```

b is a pointer to a pointer to an integer.

Table 3-7 shows the benchmark results for the two programs.

**TABLE 3-7.** Pointer arrays vs. three-dimensional arrays

| Program | Method | 286 (secs) | 386 (secs) | 68020 (secs) |
|---------|--------|-----------|-----------|--------------|
| sm3d.c | array | 30.3 | 4.3 | 3.3 |
| pi3d.c | pointer | 20.6 | 3.4 | 2.4 |

The pointer version is faster than the array program on all machines. This is because the array reference

```
a[i][j][k]
```

converts to pointer offsets in `pi3d.c` as follows:

```
*(*(*(a + i) + j) + k)
```

Assembly code for this expression executes faster than the three-dimensional storage map equation for `a` in `sm3d.c`:

```
*(&a[0][0][0] + JMAX * KMAX * i + KMAX * j + k)
```

Although performance increases, you'll have to judge whether or not the three-dimensional conversion is worthwhile to implement.

# ◆ Multidimensional Arrays at Run Time ◆

When you declare an array in C, its size remains fixed. You have to decide before your program runs how large an array will be, regardless of whether it lives on the stack or in the data area. What about declaring arrays at *run time*? In this case, you should use the heap manager because it provides library routines to build dynamic arrays. This approach eliminates anticipating array bounds at compile time and makes programs allocate only as much memory as they need. It makes sense, therefore, to explore ways to use the heap for run time arrays.

One-dimensional arrays are easy. The heap manager returns a pointer to a chunk of memory that you may use as a one-dimensional array. You cast the heap pointer to an appropriate data type and use either array notation or pointers to reference the allocated elements.

Multidimensional arrays are more difficult. There's no standard library routine that sets up the heap so that we may use it as a multidimensional array. To the heap manager, heap storage is merely a block of consecutive bytes with no notion of rows, columns, or grids. We need a way to organize the heap for multidimensional arrays. Moreover, we'd like to retain our concepts of rows, columns, and grids so that heap memory will appear like a multidimensional array to our programs.

This section shows you how. We provide C functions and macros that create two-dimensional and three-dimensional arrays at run time. These dynamic arrays may be any data type, including arrays of structures and unions. The technique organizes the heap so that array references are pointer offsets. Furthermore, your program can use array notation with rows, columns, and grids, like it was a declared array. We conclude the chapter with a macro that makes C function calls mimic the same subroutine calling conventions that BASIC and FORTRAN use for multidimensional arrays.

## Two-Dimensional Technique

Let's begin with a 2 by 3 array of integers. The declaration

```
int a[2][3];
```

allocates storage for six integers, organized as two rows and three columns. Fig. 3-15 shows the memory arrangement.

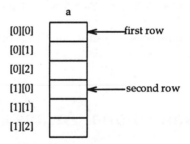

*Fig. 3-15.* Compile time allocation for a[2][3]

The second row follows the first in memory. The compiler calculates the appropriate memory address for each array reference from a storage map equation.

We can allocate the same amount of storage at run time with the C library function `calloc()`. We could use `malloc()` as well, but with `calloc()`, array elements have zero values initially and this may be advantageous in certain situations. The statements

```
char *calloc();
int *p;
    . . .
```

```
p = (int *) calloc(2 * 3, sizeof(int));
    . . .
```

create storage for six integers, as shown in Fig. 3-16.

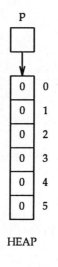

HEAP

*Fig. 3-16.* Run time allocation for six integers

Pointer p contains the address of the first of six integers on the heap. All integers have zero values. p allows us to access the heap as if it were a one-dimensional array. Array references are pointer offsets.

Note that we may *visualize* this memory as an array of two rows and three columns, but we can't use two-dimensional array references to access it. In other words,

```
p[5]
```

is the last element of the array, but

```
p[1][2]
```

won't compile. Why not? From the basic rule, p[1][2] is equivalent to *(p[1] + 2). Since p[1] is an integer, the compiler tries to dereference the integer p[1] + 2, which produces a compilation error. In order to use two-dimensional array notation, we'll need to try another approach.

Suppose we allocate additional heap storage for another array. Rather than have it store data, we use it as a pointer array where each element is an address of a *row* of the data array on the heap. Fig. 3-17 shows the arrangement.

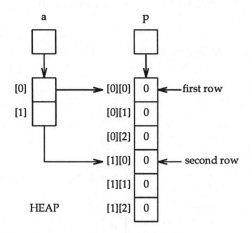

*Fig. 3-17.* Run time allocation for a[2][3]

There are two pointers to heap storage. Note that p points to six integers on the heap as before, and a points to the new pointer array, containing the rows of the data. Here are the C statements to do this, based on the previous declarations:

```
int **a;
   . . .
a = (int **) calloc(2, sizeof(int *));    /* setup ptrs to rows */
a[0] = p;                                 /* first row */
a[1] = p + 3;                             /* second row */
```

This is what we want, because now we can refer to the data as if it were a two-dimensional array. The statement

```
    a[1][2]
```

for example, refers to the last data item, or the third column of the second row of the two-dimensional array. From the basic rule, it's as if you typed

```
    *(a[1] + 2)
```

Here a[1] is a pointer to the second row, and a[1] + 2 is a pointer to the third column in this row. Indirection gives you the data without the compiler using a storage map equation.

Before we put this technique to work, let's make sure we understand the declarations for the pointers. p is a pointer to an integer, since the data is from heap memory. The pointer to the rows (a), however, is a pointer to a *pointer* to an integer. The declarations are

```
    int **a, *p;
```

Both pointers contain heap memory addresses following calls to `calloc()`. Array references use `a` and not `p`. This arrangement makes two memory chunks from the heap behave like a two-dimensional array declaration. The compiler uses pointer offsets for array references in place of storage map equations.

## Two-Dimensional Array Function

Let's apply the code we used to set up the dynamic arrays illustrated in Fig. 3-17. The following program takes two arguments on the command line. The first one is the number of rows of a two-dimensional array, and the second argument is the number of columns. The program creates a two-dimensional array on the heap, fills it with data, displays array elements by rows and columns, and frees heap storage before it exits. Here's the main program and several test runs.

**Program 3-35**

```
/* idim2.c - two-dimensional array of integers at run time */

#include <stdio.h>

int **idim2();
void ifree2();

main(argc, argv)
int argc;
char *argv[];
{
    int **a;                        /* 2D array name */
    int rows, cols;
    int inum = 1;
    register int i, j;

    if (argc != 3) {
        fprintf(stderr, "Usage: %s rows cols\n", argv[0]);
        exit(1);
    }
    rows = atoi(argv[1]);           /* number of rows */
    cols = atoi(argv[2]);           /* number of columns */

    a = idim2(rows, cols);          /* create 2D array */
```

```
    for (i = 0; i < rows; i++)
       for (j = 0; j < cols; j++)
          a[i][j] = inum++;              /* fill 2D array */

    for (i = 0; i < rows; i++)          /* display array elements */
       for (j = 0; j < cols; j++)
          printf("%5d%c", a[i][j], (j + 1) % cols ? ' ' : '\n');

    ifree2(a);                          /* free 2D heap storage */
}
```

```
$ idim2 2 3
    1     2     3
    4     5     6

$ idim2 3 6
    1     2     3     4     5     6
    7     8     9    10    11    12
   13    14    15    16    17    18
```

Pointer a is the name of the two-dimensional array that we're creating, and
idim2() is the function that allocates storage for it at run time. The function's
first argument is the number of rows in the array, and the second argument is the
number of columns. Note that idim2() returns a pointer to a pointer to an
integer, which we assign to a. The program fills a with consecutive integers
and displays all the elements using array notation.

The function ifree2() releases heap storage for the array using a as the
argument. The test runs demonstrate that we've created two separate arrays,
filled them with data, and referenced all the elements using array notation.

Now let's turn our attention to the functions that create and free the two-
dimensional array. Here's the code for idim2() and ifree2():

```
int **idim2(row, col)    /* creates 2D array of integers */
int row, col;
{
   char *calloc();
   int i;
   register int **prow, *pdata;

   pdata = (int *) calloc(row * col, sizeof (int));
   if (pdata == (int *) NULL) {
      fprintf(stderr, "No heap space for data\n");
      exit(1);
   }
   prow = (int **) calloc(row, sizeof (int *));
```

```
    if (prow == (int **) NULL) {
       fprintf(stderr, "No heap space for row pointers\n");
       exit(1);
    }
    for (i = 0; i < row; i++) {
      prow[i] = pdata;              /* store pointers to rows */
      pdata += col;                 /* move to next row */
    }

    return prow;                    /* pointer to 2D array */
}

void ifree2(pa)                     /* frees 2D heap storage */
int **pa;
{
    void free();

    free(*pa);                      /* free the data */
    free(pa);                       /* free the row pointers */
}
```

prow and pdata are similar to a and p from Fig. 3-17. We place them in registers to make idim2() run as fast as possible. The statement

```
    pdata = (int *) calloc(row * col, sizeof (int));
```

calls calloc() to allocate storage from the heap for the appropriate number of integers. We cast the return value since pdata is a pointer to an integer. calloc()'s first argument is the number of objects to create. The expression

```
    row * col
```

gives us the number of integers we need.
    The statement

```
    prow  = (int **) calloc(row, sizeof (int *));
```

calls calloc() a second time to allocate storage for a pointer array on the heap. We cast the return value because prow is a pointer to a pointer to an integer. The size of the pointer array is the number of rows. Each element in the array is a pointer. The statement

```
    sizeof(int *)
```

makes the compiler allocate the number of bytes for a pointer to an integer and is portable for different machines.

Next we use a `for` loop to connect the pointer array elements to the data array. We loop over the number of rows. The statement

```
prow[i] = pdata;              /* store pointers to rows */
```

sets each element of the array pointed to by `prow` to the current value of the pointer `pdata`. The statement

```
pdata += col;                 /* move to next row */
```

uses pointer arithmetic to move the pointer `pdata` to the next row. When we exit the loop, we have set the pointers to all the rows in the data. Fig. 3-18 shows the allocated array for the first test run of `idim2.c` (a 2 by 3 array of integers).

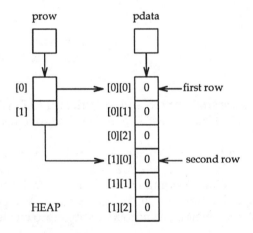

*Fig. 3-18.* Run time allocation for idim2.c

We return from `idim2()` with the pointer to the array containing the pointers to the rows.

Now let's look at `ifree2()`. Recall we made two calls to `calloc()` for storage from the heap, so we need to free both. When we pass the address of our two-dimensional array to `ifree2()`, we use the pointer to access both areas from the heap. The expression `*pa` points to the heap area where the data resides, and `pa` points to the heap area for the array of row pointers. `free()` (from the C library) releases the heap storage for both areas.

## Two-Dimensional Array Macro

The function `idim2()` creates only two-dimensional arrays of integers. To create two-dimensional arrays of any data type, the compiler has to know the data type of the array at compile time. This is not difficult to do and there are several methods. One approach is to make `idim2()` return a character pointer (like `malloc()`) and cast its return value to the data type you want when you call it. Programs call `idim2()` with the `sizeof()` operator as a parameter, which tells the function the size of the object to create as a two-dimensional array on the heap. This involves modifying the `idim2()` function slightly, which we leave as an exercise for the reader. For more information, see Exercise 13.

Another method which also works is a *macro*. This involves some interesting techniques, so we show it here. Keep in mind that this approach makes programs execute faster than ones with function calls, but your code size will also increase. If you're interested in working with two-dimensional arrays of arbitrary data types, you'll have to decide whether a function or a macro best fits your application.

To show you the macro approach, let's enhance the previous program and create two-dimensional arrays of integers and doubles. Program `mdim2.c` is similar to `idim2()`, but it uses one macro to create both arrays. The program fills the arrays with data and displays their contents. Before `mdim2.c` exits, it frees heap storage for both arrays. The next page shows the main program, followed by a test run.

The header file `mdim.h` includes the macros DIM2 and D2FREE, which we'll look at shortly. The program declares two pointers, `a` and `b`, for the two-dimensional arrays of integers and doubles, respectively. `mdim2.c` uses DIM2 to create both arrays. The program fills the first array with consecutive positive integers and the second one with incrementing doubles starting with the number `1.1`. The first five lines show the output of the integer array, and the last five lines show the output for the array of doubles.

The first use of DIM2 creates an array of integers. The macro

```
DIM2(a, rows, cols, int);   /* create 2D array of integers */
```

has four parameters. The first parameter (a) is a pointer to a pointer to an integer. The macro sets it to heap memory that we subsequently use as a two-dimensional array. The second and third parameters are the number of rows and columns in the array, respectively. The fourth parameter is the data type (`int`). We'll see how the macro uses this C reserved word shortly.

Likewise, the statement

```
DIM2(b, rows, cols, double);  /* create 2D array of doubles */
```

uses the same macro to create a two-dimensional array of doubles. `b` is a pointer to a pointer to a double, and the last parameter is the C reserved word `double`. After the program displays all the array elements, it uses the macro D2FREE to release heap storage for the arrays. D2FREE's parameter is the pointer that DIM2 assigns to heap memory.

## Program 3-36

```
/* mdim2.c - macro for two-dimensional arrays at run time */

#include <stdio.h>
#include "mdim.h"                   /* header file for macros */

main(argc, argv)
int argc;
char *argv[];
{
    int **a;                       /* 2D array of integers */
    double **b;                    /* 2D array of doubles */
    int rows, cols;
    register int i, j;
    int inum = 1;
    double dnum = 1.1;

    if (argc != 3) {
        fprintf(stderr, "Usage: %s rows cols\n", argv[0]);
        exit(1);
    }
    rows = atoi(argv[1]);          /* number of rows */
    cols = atoi(argv[2]);          /* number of columns */

    DIM2(a, rows, cols, int);      /* create 2D array of integers */
    for (i = 0; i < rows; i++)
        for (j = 0; j < cols; j++)
            a[i][j] = inum++;      /* fill 2D array with integers */

    for (i = 0; i < rows; i++)     /* display array elements */
        for (j = 0; j < cols; j++)
            printf("%5d%c", a[i][j], (j + 1) % cols ? ' ' : '\n');
    putchar('\n');

    DIM2(b, rows, cols, double);   /* create 2D array of doubles */
    for (i = 0; i < rows; i++)
        for (j = 0; j < cols; j++)
            b[i][j] = dnum++;      /* fill 2D array with doubles */

    for (i = 0; i < rows; i++)     /* display array elements */
        for (j = 0; j < cols; j++)
            printf("%5g%c", b[i][j], (j + 1) % cols ? ' ' : '\n');

    D2FREE(a);                     /* free 2D integer heap storage */
    D2FREE(b);                     /* free 2D doubles heap storage */
}
```

```
$ mdim2 5 9
     1      2      3      4      5      6      7      8      9
    10     11     12     13     14     15     16     17     18
    19     20     21     22     23     24     25     26     27
    28     29     30     31     32     33     34     35     36
    37     38     39     40     41     42     43     44     45

   1.1    2.1    3.1    4.1    5.1    6.1    7.1    8.1    9.1
  10.1   11.1   12.1   13.1   14.1   15.1   16.1   17.1   18.1
  19.1   20.1   21.1   22.1   23.1   24.1   25.1   26.1   27.1
  28.1   29.1   30.1   31.1   32.1   33.1   34.1   35.1   36.1
  37.1   38.1   39.1   40.1   41.1   42.1   43.1   44.1   45.1
```

Now let's look at the header file mdim.h, which contains the macros DIM2 and D2FREE.

```
/* mdim.h - header file for run time multidimensional arrays */

#define DIM2(prow,row,col,type) \
   {\
      char *calloc();\
      register type *pdata;\
      int i;\
      pdata = (type *) calloc(row * col, sizeof (type));\
      if (pdata == (type *) NULL) {\
         fprintf(stderr, "No heap space for data\n");\
         exit(1);\
      }\
      prow = (type **) calloc(row, sizeof (type *));\
      if (prow == (type **) NULL) {\
         fprintf(stderr, "No heap space for row pointers\n");\
         exit(1);\
      }\
      for (i = 0; i < row; i++) {\
        prow[i] = pdata;\
        pdata += col;\
      }\
   }

#define D2FREE(prow) \
   {\
      void free();\
      free(*prow);\
      free(prow);\
   }
```

You'll recognize most of the code from the function `idim2()`. First, let's examine the parameter `type` in the DIM2 macro, which appears in the declaration for `pdata` and the cast statements. At compile time, the preprocessor substitutes the appropriate C reserved word for `type`. In our example, `type` becomes `int` for the first use of DIM2 and `double` the second time.

Did you notice that the macro uses `prow` differently than the function? The `idim2()` routine returns `prow` to the calling program, but DIM2 substitutes array names from your program for `prow`. `prow`, therefore, becomes `a` for the first use of DIM2, and `b` for the second use of DIM2, after macro substitution. This is how the macro sets the pointer array for the row addresses to heap memory.

Study the remaining lines in the header file carefully. You should realize, for instance, that the macro statements for DIM2 are contained within a single block. This hides `pdata` and `i` from the main program. Moreover, the `for` loop that connects the pointer array to the data array is independent of the data type. D2FREE's statements are similar to the function `ifree2()`.

The macro approach supports dynamic two-dimensional arrays of any data type (structures, unions, pointers, etc.). Suppose, for example, a structure template called `something` exists. To create and release a 3 by 4 two-dimensional array of structures, we use the macros as follows:

```
#include "mdim.h"        /* header file for macros */
struct something **c;
   .  .  .  .
DIM2(c, 3, 4, struct something);
   .  .  .  .
D2FREE(c);
   .  .  .  .
```

## Three-Dimensional Technique

The two-dimensional technique for run time arrays shows the benefit of setting up pointer arrays on the heap. The approach makes the compiler use pointer offsets instead of storage map equations with array references. If we extend this technique from two to three dimensions, we'll benefit even more, because array references should execute significantly faster. To do this, we'll create pointer arrays that make the heap look like a three-dimensional array declaration. We can also create a function or a macro to create three-dimensional arrays of different data types as well. The only disadvantage is that the three-dimensional technique requires more memory for the pointer arrays.

Let's begin with a three-dimensional array of integers. The declaration

```
int a[2][3][2];
```

allocates storage for twelve integers, organized as two 3 by 2 two-dimensional arrays (3 rows by 2 columns). Fig. 3-19 shows the memory arrangement.

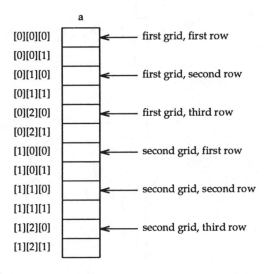

*Fig. 3-19.* Compile time allocation for a[2][3][2]

The second grid follows the first in memory. The compiler uses a storage map equation to address elements. We may use either the array name or a pointer in a three-dimensional array reference.

Let's allocate storage from the heap for the same size array. The statements

```
char *calloc();
int *p;
    . . .
p = (int *) calloc(2 * 3 * 2, sizeof(int));
    . . .
```

create storage for 12 integers as shown in Fig. 3-20.

Memory is allocated consecutively but the concepts of grids, rows, and columns are lost. As in the two-dimensional case, we can't use three-dimensional array notation here. The array reference

```
p[0][2][1]
```

for example, won't compile. We need to allocate additional heap memory to address the data correctly.

We'll use the heap for *two* separate pointer arrays. The first one contains pointers to the rows of heap data and the second one contains pointers for the grids. Fig. 3-21 shows this arrangement of memory.

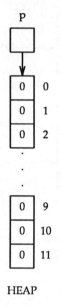

*Fig. 3-20.* Run time allocation for 12 integers

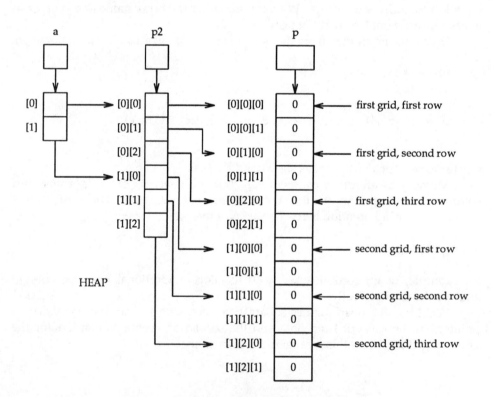

*Fig. 3-21.* Run time allocation for a[2][3][2]

You can place the pointers  a,  p2, and  p anywhere you want (on the stack, heap, or data areas, or in a register).  The arrays reside on the heap.  The size of the array that  a points to is the number of grids (2).  Each element points to an address in the second pointer array that stores the addresses of the rows of each grid.  For this reason, the size of the array that  p2 points to is the number of grids times the number of rows (6).  As an exercise, see if you can come up with the C statements that create this memory arrangement, as we did with the two-dimensional case.  With this configuration, the array reference

```
a[0][2][1]
```

becomes

```
*(a[0][2] + 1)
```

or

```
*(*(a[0] + 2) + 1)
```

according to the basic rule.  The compiler uses pointer indirection and pointer offsets to access heap data like a three-dimensional array reference.

Here are the declarations for the three pointers.

```
int ***a, **p2, *p;
```

Note that three-dimensional array references use pointers with triple indirection. Array references use  a but not  p2 or  p.  Heap storage mimics a three-dimensional array declaration.

## Three-Dimensional Array Function

The following program creates a three-dimensional array of integers at run time. The number of grids, rows, and columns come from the command line.  Program idim3.c creates the array and uses three-dimensional array notation to fill it with consecutive integers and display each element.  The program frees heap storage before it exits.  Here's the main program with a test run.

**Program 3-37**

```c
/* idim3.c - three-dimensional array of integers at run time */

#include <stdio.h>

int ***idim3();
void ifree3();

main(argc, argv)
int argc;
char *argv[];
{
    int ***a;                       /* 3D array name */
    int grid, rows, cols;
    int inum = 1;
    register int i, j, k;

    if (argc != 4) {
        fprintf(stderr, "Usage: %s grids rows cols\n", argv[0]);
        exit(1);
    }
    grid = atoi(argv[1]);           /* number of grids */
    rows = atoi(argv[2]);           /* number of rows */
    cols = atoi(argv[3]);           /* number of columns */

    a = idim3(grid, rows, cols);    /* create 3D array */

    for (i = 0; i < grid; i++)
        for (j = 0; j < rows; j++)
            for (k = 0; k < cols; k++)
                a[i][j][k] = inum++;    /* fill 3D array */

    for (i = 0; i < grid; i++) {    /* display array elements */
        printf("Grid %d:\n", i);
        for (j = 0; j < rows; j++)
            for (k = 0; k < cols; k++)
                printf("%5d%c", a[i][j][k], (k + 1) % cols ? ' ' : '\n');
    }

    ifree3(a);                      /* free 3D heap storage */
}
```

```
$ idim3 2 4 8
Grid 0:
     1      2      3      4      5      6      7      8
     9     10     11     12     13     14     15     16
    17     18     19     20     21     22     23     24
    25     26     27     28     29     30     31     32
Grid 1:
    33     34     35     36     37     38     39     40
    41     42     43     44     45     46     47     48
    49     50     51     52     53     54     55     56
    57     58     59     60     61     62     63     64
```

Function `idim3()` creates the three-dimensional array. The program stores the function's return value in a pointer, `a`, that we subsequently use as a three-dimensional array. Program output displays the number of rows and columns in each grid. The `ifree3()` routine frees heap storage using `a` as the function's argument.

The code for `idim3()` and `ifree3()` is shown on the next page.

The `idim3()` routine uses three pointers. Note that `pgrid` points to the grid pointer array, `prow` points to the row pointer array, and `pdata` is a pointer to the data. All arrays live in the heap. The statements

```
pdata = (int *) calloc(grid * row * col, sizeof (int));
prow  = (int **) calloc(grid * row, sizeof (int **));
pgrid = (int ***) calloc(grid, sizeof (int *));
```

allocate storage and assign addresses to the pointers. We cast `calloc()`'s return value appropriately for each pointer. The first call to `calloc()` allocates heap storage for the data. Function `calloc()` zero fills the bytes. The number of items is the product of its grids, rows, and columns. The next pair of `calloc()`'s allocate storage for the pointer arrays. The row pointer array has `grid * row` elements, and the grid pointer array has `grid` members.

The `idim3()` routine has two `for` loops to connect the pointer arrays to the data. The first one is similar to the one we use in `idim2()` for two-dimensional arrays. Note that the number of elements is

```
grid * row
```

since we need to initialize the pointers to each row in every grid. The second `for` loop sets each element of the grid pointer array to the appropriate row pointer. Study this code carefully. The two `for` loops must be in the order shown (why?) and pointer arithmetic makes it all work. The function returns `pgrid` to the main program.

Routine `ifree3()` is similar to `ifree2()` for two-dimensional arrays. It calls `free()` three times to free heap data and the row and grid pointers, in that order. Routine `ifree()` uses the pointer that `idim3()` returns to release heap storage.

```c
int ***idim3(grid, row, col)          /* creates 3D array */
int grid, row, col;
{
   char *calloc();
   int i;
   register int ***pgrid, **prow, *pdata;

   pdata = (int *) calloc(grid * row * col, sizeof (int));
   if (pdata == (int *) NULL) {
      fprintf(stderr, "No heap space for data\n");
      exit(1);
   }
   prow  = (int **) calloc(grid * row, sizeof (int *));
   if (prow == (int **) NULL) {
      fprintf(stderr, "No heap space for row pointers\n");
      exit(1);
   }
   pgrid  = (int ***) calloc(grid, sizeof (int **));
   if (pgrid == (int ***) NULL) {
      fprintf(stderr, "No heap space for grid pointers\n");
      exit(1);
   }

   for (i = 0; i < grid * row; i++) {
     prow[i] = pdata;             /* store pointers to rows */
     pdata += col;                /* move to next row */
   }

   for (i = 0; i < grid; i++) {
     pgrid[i] = prow;             /* store pointers to grid */
     prow += row;                 /* move to next grid */
   }
   return pgrid;                  /* pointer to 3D array */
}


void ifree3(pa)                   /* frees 3D heap storage */
int ***pa;
{
   void free();

   free(**pa);                    /* free the data */
   free(*pa);                     /* free the row pointers */
   free(pa);                      /* free the grid pointers */
}
```

Routine `idim3()` creates only three-dimensional arrays of integers at run time. The functions and macros to create and free three-dimensional arrays of any data type are left as exercises for the reader (Exercises 14 and 15). You can also extend this technique to four-dimensional arrays, and more.

## Subroutine Calling Conventions

Languages like FORTRAN and BASIC allow you to pass different size multidimensional arrays as arguments to the same function and use array notation to reference elements. In FORTRAN, for example, the statements

```
SUBROUTINE FUNC(A, M, N)
DIMENSION A(M, N)
  .  .  .  .  .
END
```

allow a subroutine called FUNC() to access a two-dimensional array called A with run time values for M rows and N columns. Programs call FUNC() with different sized arrays. FORTRAN libraries use subroutines like FUNC() to invert matrices or calculate mathematical items, such as determinants and eigenvalues. This convention is useful because subroutines may reference elements by rows and columns.

The C language doesn't provide such a built-in feature. Consider what happens, for example, when you pass the address of a multidimensional array to a function. Inside the function, the compiler uses a storage map equation with *fixed* sizes. To illustrate, suppose you declare the following two-dimensional array of integers.

```
int data[5][9];
```

The following statement calls a C function, `func()`, to pass the address of the two-dimensional array along with the number of rows and columns.

```
func(data, 5, 9);
```

Inside `func()` we have the following:

```
func(a, rows, cols)
int a[][9];
int rows, cols;
{
  register int i, j;

  for (i = 0; i < rows; i++)
     for (j = 0; j < cols; j++)
        . . . a[i][j] . . .      /* array references OK */
}
```

The compiler requires 9 in the declaration for a to properly address elements of the array with the storage map equation.

Suppose you have another two-dimensional array as follows:

```
int moredata[4][10];
```

You can't use func() to access data in this array. The function call

```
func(moredata, 4, 10);
```

won't work because func() is compiled with the number of columns set to 9 and not 10. Attempts to do so make func() reference memory incorrectly.

Another alternative is to pass the address of the first element of the two-dimensional array. The statements

```
func(&data[0][0], 5, 9);
func(&moredata[0][0], 4, 10);
```

make func() access the two-dimensional arrays as a one-dimensional array. The code inside func() changes, however. We now have

```
func(a, rows, cols)
int *a;
int rows, cols;
{
  register int *p = a, *end = a + row * cols;

  while (p < end) {
     . . . *p++ . . .       /* Can't use a[i][j] references */
  }
}
```

Parameter a is a pointer to an integer (previously, it was a pointer to an array of integers). This allows you to use compact pointer expressions to access memory as a series of integers whose size is rows * cols. Although this is fast, the concept of rows and columns disappears. Functions that compute matrix inversions and determinants need this information.

In situations like this, we'd like to have C behave like FORTRAN or BASIC. This would help us translate FORTRAN and BASIC subroutines to C more easily. Let's put our knowledge of arrays and pointers together to tackle this problem.

The following main program uses a macro to mimic the subroutine calling conventions of FORTRAN and BASIC for two-dimensional arrays. Program det.c declares two different two-dimensional arrays of doubles. The number of rows and columns in each array is the same. We pass the address of each array and its size to a subroutine that calculates a mathematical quantity called a *determinant*. The details of the algorithm don't concern us here. The technique applies to any subroutine that needs to access two-dimensional arrays of rows and columns that vary at run time. Here's the main program and its output:

**Program 3-38**

```
/* det.c - find determinant of a two-dimensional
           array of doubles */

#include <stdio.h>

double det();

main()
{
    static double f[4][4] = {
        1, 3, 2, 1,
        4, 6, 1, 2,
        2, 1, 2, 3,
        1, 2, 4, 1
    };
    static double g[5][5] = {
        1, 3, 2, 1, 7,
        4, 6, 1, 2, 6,
        2, 1, 2, 3, 5,
        1, 2, 4, 1, 4,
        8, 5, 4, 1, 3
    };

    printf ("determinant of f = %g\n", det(f, 4));
    printf ("determinant of g = %g\n", det(g, 5));
}
```

```
/* calculate determinant for n by n matrix */

double det(arg, n)
double *arg;
int n;
{
    register int i, j, k;
    double **a;             /* this is the array name */
    double ret;             /* determinant */
    double x;               /* temp */

    /* dynamically create 2 dim "array" a from arg */
    DIMENSION2(arg, a, n, n, double)

    /* determinant algorithm using rows and columns */
    for (k = 0; k < n - 1; k++)
        for (i = k + 1; i < n; i++){
            x = a[i][k]/a[k][k];
            for (j = k; j < n; j++)
                a[i][j] = a[i][j] - x * a[k][j];
            }

    for (ret = 1, i = 0; i < n; i++)
        ret *= a[i][i];

    free(a);                /* free heap storage */

    return ret;
}

$ det
determinant of f = 43
determinant of g = 906
```

The arrays of doubles (f and g) have different sizes. The program passes their addresses to a function called det() to calculate the determinant and display the result.

Inside det(), we can't use the array's address (arg) as a two-dimensional array with rows and columns. We use a macro called DIMENSION2 with five parameters to allow us to do so. This macro is similar to DIM2 for two-dimensional arrays, except for one important difference. Since the data already exists, all the macro has to do is set up an array of pointers to the rows. For this reason, the macro needs the address of the two-dimensional array (arg) as the first parameter. The second parameter is a pointer to a pointer to a double (a) that we use in subsequent statements as a two-dimensional array. The third parameter is the number of rows and the fourth parameter is the number of columns. In this example they are the same, but DIMENSION2 can handle different values inside other functions. The fifth parameter of the macro is the data type.

Following the line with the macro, the program loops over the rows and columns to calculate the determinant. We release heap storage with the standard C library routine `free()` before the function returns. This is necessary since heap storage changes every time a program calls `det()`.

All that's left is the macro definition for DIMENSION2.

```
#define DIMENSION2(arga,usera,row,col,type) \
    {\
       int i;\
       usera = (type **) calloc(row, sizeof(type *));\
       if (usera == (type **) NULL) {\
           fprintf(stderr, "No heap space for row pointers\n");\
           exit(1);\
       }\
       for (i = 0; i < row; i++)\
           usera[i] = (type *)((char *) arga + \
                       ((sizeof(type) * i * col)));\
    }
```

The approach is a combination of techniques we've already shown you. The preprocessor substitutes the appropriate C reserved word for `type` in the lines where it appears. DIMENSION2 calls `calloc()` to allocate storage for a pointer array of size `row`. The macro uses a `for` loop to connect the pointer array to the data pointed to by `arga`. The statement

```
usera[i] = (type *)((char *) arga + ((sizeof(type) * i * col)));
```

does the job. Variable `usera` is the pointer array. We cast `arga` to a byte pointer and calculate pointer offsets to the data for each row pointer. Note that the macro declares variable `i` inside a block. This hides it from the main program.

The technique applies to three dimensions as well. The three-dimensional macro DIMENSION3 is left as an exercise for the reader (Exercise 16).

To conclude, we point out that the two-dimensional and three-dimensional macros and functions for declaring arrays at run time (as opposed to the technique presented in Program 3-38 where the arrays are declared) *do* allow you to reference elements with array notation inside subroutines. This is an added bonus, since we already know that array references using pointer indirection typically execute faster than storage map equations. To demonstrate, suppose you call `idim2()` and create two different size arrays of integers and pass the addresses of each array to the same function.

```
int **a;                /* first array name */
int **b;                /* second array name */
. . . .
a = idim2(3, 4)         /* 3 by 4 array of integers */
b = idim2(5, 6)         /* 5 by 6 array of integers */
. . . .
func(a, 3, 4);          /* pass 3 by 4 array to function */
func(b, 5, 6);          /* pass 5 by 6 array to function */
. . . .
```

Inside func(), we have

```
func(c, rows, cols)
int **c;                        /* pointer to 2D array */
int rows, cols;
{
    register int i, j;

    for (i = 0; i < rows; i++)
        for (j = 0; j < cols; j++)
            . . .c[i][j] . . . /* array references OK */
}
```

The function func() can access a two-dimensional array of integers of any size and use rows and columns for array references as long as you create the array with idim2(). Parameter c must be declared as a pointer to a pointer to an integer. The same approach applies when using the macro DIM2.

For three-dimensional arrays created with idim3(), you need only declare the pointer inside the function as

```
int ***c;                       /* pointer to 3D array */
```

Follow the same method when using a three-dimensional macro.

# ♦ Summary ♦

- C converts all array references to pointer offsets.

- The basic rule states a[i] is equivalent to (*(a + i)) for an array a of any data type.

- The basic rule helps decipher array references with pointer indirections. Remember to retain the outer parentheses if C's order of evaluation changes when you omit them in an expression.

- C uses scalars to compute pointer offsets and to subtract pointers that point to similar data types.

- Compact pointer expressions use autoincrement (++) and autodecrement (−−) with pointer indirection (*). Compact pointer expressions fall into two groups. The first group of compact pointer expressions is

    *p++            *p−−            *++p            *−−p

    These expressions change the pointer and not the pointer's object. If the pointers point to arrays, they may be used in place of array references. These expressions improve execution speed inside loops. The second group of compact pointer expressions is

    ++*p            −−*p            (*p)++            (*p)−−

    These expressions increment or decrement the pointer's object. The pointer is unaffected. Pointer expressions in this group are more restrictive. Objects cannot be structures or unions. If the object is a pointer, expressions from the second group improve execution speed inside loops.

- Negative array subscripts are legal. C does no checking for array out of bounds references.

- Two-dimensional arrays have rows and columns. C allocates storage row-wise, so the second subscript varies the fastest.

- If a is a two-dimensional array of integers with n rows and i is an integer, then a[i] is a pointer to an integer (it points to the start of row i).

- Two-dimensional storage map equations have one multiplication step. Depending on the machine, array references with a variable for the row subscript typically make the compiler generate a multiply instruction or shift-and-adds in assembly code.

- When you pass the address of a two-dimensional array to a function, the compiler passes a pointer to the first row.

- Three-dimensional arrays have grids, rows, and columns. Storage is grid-wise, then row-wise, so the third subscript varies the fastest.

- Suppose a is a three-dimensional array of integers with g grids, r rows, and c columns. Assuming i and j are integers, a[i] is a pointer to an array of c integers. a[i][j] is a pointer to an integer.

- Three-dimensional storage map equations have two multiplication steps. Depending on the machine, array references with variables for the grid and row subscripts typically make the compiler generate multiply instructions or shift-and-adds in assembly code.

- When you pass the address of a three-dimensional array to a function, the compiler passes a pointer to the first grid.

- On most machines, compact pointer expressions execute faster than two-dimensional or three-dimensional array references inside loops.

- Declaring pointer arrays in place of two-dimensional and three-dimensional arrays eliminates storage map equations for array references.

- You may convert programs with two-dimensional and three-dimensional array declarations to pointer arrays. This does not affect array notation and the compiler uses pointer offsets in place of storage map equations. Declarations inside functions that access the array must change as well as `extern` statements.

- Run time arrays use heap storage. Programs make one library call to the heap manager for a one-dimensional array. Two-dimensional arrays require a call to allocate the data, and an additional call for a pointer row array. Three-dimensional arrays require a third call for a pointer grid array. Connecting the pointer arrays to the data makes allocated heap storage look like a multidimensional array. The compiler uses pointer offsets for array references.

- Programs may create multidimensional arrays of any size and any type at run time with a macro or a function.

- C functions must use heap storage and pointer arrays to mimic FORTRAN and BASIC subroutine calling conventions. To access elements from different sized arrays declared at compile time, a function must set up pointer arrays on the heap. Functions may access elements of arrays directly, because the pointer arrays are already in place.

- Assume pointers  p,  q, and  r point to arrays  a,  b, and  c, respectively. The following lines show equivalent array and pointer references for one-dimensional, two-dimensional, and three-dimensional arrays.

```
a[IMAX]                 a[i]           *p        p[i]
b[IMAX][JMAX]           b[i][j]        **q       q[i][j]
c[IMAX][JMAX][KMAX]     c[i][j][k]     ***r      r[i][j][k]
```

Array references may use pointers in place of array names. Pointers use one level of indirection for each array dimension. The arrays and pointers may point to any data type.

# ◆ Exercises ◆

1. Compile the following program:

```
/* a2.c - shows address and indirection operators */

char a[] = "databytes";
char *p = a;

main()
{
    printf("%x %x\n", a+3, *&(a+3));    /* using array */

    printf("%x %x\n", p+3, *&(p+3));    /* using pointer */
}
```

   Can you explain the compiler messages? Why doesn't C evaluate the `*&` operators in the same way that it does for `&*`?

2. Study the following program and its output:

```
/* comc2.c - accessing more command line characters */

#include <stdio.h>

main(argc, argv)
int argc;
char *argv[];
{
    if (argc == 1) {
        fprintf(stderr, "Usage: %s args\n", argv[0]);
        exit(1);
    }
    printf("%c\n", argv[0][1]);
    printf("%c\n", *(*argv + 1));
    printf("%c\n", (*(argv))[1]);

    printf("%c\n", argv[1][0]);
    printf("%c\n", *argv[1]);
    printf("%c\n", *(*(argv + 1)));
}

$ comc2 1234
o
o
o
```

```
1
1
1
```

Derive the equivalent pointer expressions using the technique shown in the chapter.

3. Suppose a program has the following declaration:

```
char buf[80], *q = buf, *p = q + 5;
```

Which of the following pointer expressions compile in C?

```
buf[p-q]
p += p - q
q + p - q
p - q + p
q - p - q
```

4. The following program creates a table of commands and arguments. `pointargs.c` calls a function `pointargs()` to modify table pointers. The program displays the command's arguments on each line. Here's the skeletal program with output.

```c
/* pointargs.c - modify table to point to command arguments */

#include <stdio.h>
#define NCOMS 3

main()
{
    static char *table[NCOMS] = {
        "sort -d: -f1",
        "dbase -D12 file.c",
        "backup /dev/mt0 -b20"
    };
    int i;

    pointargs(NCOMS, table);       /* modify table */

    for (i = 0; i < NCOMS; i++)
      printf("%s\n", table[i]);   /* display args */
}

pointargs(tabc, entry)       /* modify each table entry */
{
}
```

```
$ pointargs
-d: -f1
-D12 file.c
/dev/mt0 -b20
```

Using compact pointer expressions, write the function `pointargs()`. Expand the table to test your program more thoroughly.

5. The programs in the section on compact pointer expressions work with an array of character pointers. Consequently, the programs `pricing.c` and `price.c` call `strlen()` to determine the length of each line. Rewrite the programs using a two-dimensional array of characters instead. This eliminates the `strlen()` calls, since the length of each line is fixed. Does this approach make the program faster or slower? Time the two approaches and compare the results, if possible.

6. Table 3-8 contains the three-dimensional array and pointer references for the declaration

```
double mint[2][3][5];
```

Fill in the empty blanks to complete the table of compiler interpretations.

### TABLE 3-8. Three-dimensional array and pointer references

double mint[2][3][5]

| Expression | Meaning |
|---|---|
| `mint` | pointer to a 3 by 5 array of doubles, first grid |
| `*mint` | |
| `**mint` | |
| `mint[1]` | pointer to an array of 5 doubles, second grid, first row |
| `***mint` | |
| `*mint[1]` | |
| `mint + 1` | |
| `**mint[1]` | |
| `*mint + 1` | |
| `mint[1][1]` | pointer to a double, second grid, second row, first column |
| `**mint + 1` | |
| `mint[1] + 1` | |
| `*mint[1][1]` | |
| `*mint[1] + 1` | pointer to a double, second grid, first row, second column |
| `mint[1][1] + 1` | |

7. Enhance `map2d.c` for three-dimensional arrays (call it `map3d.c`). Have this new program display the address of a three-dimensional array reference using storage map equations. Program `map3d.c` should initialize a three-dimensional array with values. How would you use the storage map equation to display the *value* of an element along with its address?

8. Suppose a C program contains the following declarations:

```
int display[23][80];
int colors[23][80][8];
int row = 15, col = 50, pixel = 4;
```

Which of the following array references make the compiler generate multiply instructions or shift-and-adds in assembly code? Use storage map equations to determine how the compiler calculates each address.

```
display[10]
display[row]
display[10][40]
display[row][40]
display[10][col]

colors[15]
colors[15][50]
colors[row][col]
colors[4][col][8]
colors[row][50][4]
colors[row][col][3]
colors[15][50][pixel]
colors[17][col][pixel]
```

9. Rewrite the programs `sm2d.c` and `sm3d.c` using compact pointer expressions. Run the programs and time the results on your machine. How do the execution times compare to `pi2d.c` and `pi3d.c`, respectively?

10. Suppose a program has the following array declaration:

```
static long walk[20][30];
```

Using the two-dimensional conversion technique from the chapter, implement the following code:

```
static long xwalk[20][30];
static long *walk[20];
    . . . .
```

```
load2d(xwalk, walk, 20);
    .  .  .  .
```

`load2d()` loads each element of its second argument with the rows of the two-dimensional array passed as the first argument. Write a program that calls `load2d()` and test the results. Does the new array of pointers have to be declared `static` with this approach?

11. Suppose a program has this array declaration:

```
static long way[20][30][10];
```

Using the three-dimensional conversion technique from the chapter, implement the following code:

```
static long xway[20][30][10];
static long *yway[20][30];
static long **way[20];
    .  .  .  .
load3d(xway, yway, way, 20, 30);
    .  .  .  .
```

`load3d()` performs two tasks. First, it loads each element of its second argument with the rows and columns of the three-dimensional array passed as the first argument. Second, `load3d()` loads the third argument with the pointers to the two-dimensional array passed as the second argument. Write a program that calls `load3d()` and test the results.

12. Rewrite `load2d()` and `load3d()` to use the heap instead of the data area. Pass the address of NULL pointers initially to each routine, so that they may return heap addresses to the main program. Both routines should allocate heap storage for the pointer arrays and load them with the appropriate pointers before returning.

13. Modify `idim2()` to create two-dimensional arrays of any data type. The following code shows you how to call `idim2()` to create a 3 by 5 array of integers and a 4 by 6 array of doubles.

```
    .  .  .  .
char **idim2();
int **a;              /* 2D array of integers */
double **b;           /* 2D array of doubles */

a = (int **) idim2(3, 5, sizeof(int));
b = (double **) idim2(4, 6, sizeof(double));
    .  .  .  .
```

Make sure your version of `idim2()` performs error checking. You can have `idim2()` either terminate with an error message or return a NULL.

14. Write the following macros for creating three-dimensional arrays of any data type:

```
#define DIM3(pgrid,grid,row,col,type)
#define D3FREE(pgrid)
```

Follow the approach used in the chapter for two-dimensional arrays. Include these macros in the mdim.h header file along with the two-dimensional ones.

15. Modify idim3() to create three-dimensional arrays of any data type. The following code shows you how to call idim3() to create a 3 by 5 by 6 array of integers and a 4 by 6 by 8 array of doubles.

```
    .  .  .  .
char ***idim3();
int ***a;              /* 3D array of integers */
double ***b;           /* 3D array of doubles */

a = (int ***) idim3(3, 5, 6, sizeof(int));
b = (double ***) idim3(4, 6, 8, sizeof(double));
    .  .  .  .
```

16. Write the following macro to access a three-dimensional array of any data type.

```
#define DIMENSION3(arga,usera,grid,row,col,type)
```

Assume arga is a pointer to an existing three-dimensional array that has sizes grid, row, and col, respectively. The macro creates a new three-dimensional array of data type type using pointers. Subsequently, programs may use three-dimensional references using usera, similar to the two-dimensional technique shown in the chapter. Add error checking to the macro and include it in mdim.h.

17. Extend the concepts shown in the chapter for two-dimensional and three-dimensional arrays and write a function that creates a four-dimensional array of integers at run time. Implement macros and functions that create and free four-dimensional arrays of any data type.

# 4

# A Closer Look at C

**M**ost high-level languages keep you an "arm's length" from the machine. It's difficult to use a language improperly or write programs that execute unpredictably. C, however, gives you access to a machine's architecture. You may write programs that assign machine registers to variables, manipulate memory addresses, and dynamically change data types. Although these operations make a language powerful, C expects you to apply them correctly. Programmers learn quickly that the absence of compile time errors doesn't necessarily indicate a bug-free (or correct) C program.

This chapter looks at specific areas of the C language. We study how the compiler evaluates expressions: which ones are portable and which ones are "ill-formed." We present a technique for deciphering complex declarations with arrays, functions, and pointers. We also explore unique ways to use arrays in assignment statements and as arguments to functions. Each topic explains why C works a certain way and what the compiler expects you to do.

### ◆ Overview ◆

### Sequence Guarantee Points

You can write C expressions with the ++ and -- operators that won't evaluate the same on different machines. Programs that use these "ill-formed" expressions are not portable. Expressions with *sequence guarantee points*, however, execute consistently and make programs portable.

## Right-Left Rule

C allows complex declarations with pointers, functions, and arrays. C's syntax for these types of declarations can be confusing. The *right-left rule* helps you understand how the compiler parses a complex declaration. This technique allows you to declare complex declarations and decipher existing ones.

## Lvalues in Expressions

The compiler expects you to provide *lvalues* in certain expressions; otherwise, programs do not compile. You need to know what an lvalue is, when you should use one, and why the compiler requires them.

## Fast Array Transfers

C does not allow you to assign one array to another. With one statement, *fast array transfers* move data between arrays of the same size without a function call. The technique provides a method to perform block moves of memory.

## Passing Entire Arrays to Functions

When you call a function with the name of an array as an argument, C always passes the address of the array to the function. There is a way, however, to pass *all* the array elements, which allows the function to modify them without changing the array's original values. Additionally, functions may *return* entire arrays as well. We discuss the pros and cons of this approach as it relates to a program's execution time.

## Functions with Varying Arguments

Programs should call functions with the proper data types and with the correct number of arguments. Otherwise, a program is not portable and may not execute correctly. Some applications may require you to call a function with a *variable* number of arguments and with different data types. We present a portable way to write such a function.

## ◆ Sequence Guarantee Points ◆

Many C expressions have operators that connect *subexpressions*. If one subexpression modifies a variable and the same variable appears in another subexpression, the evaluation of the entire expression is not always predictable. The assignment statement

```
a[i++] = i;
```

for example, may not store the value of `i` that you want into the array `a`, and the expression

```
*p-- + *p
```

may use a pointer to add the wrong two values. The evaluation of the expression

```
*p++ == '\t' ? ' ' : *p
```

is predictable, however. Furthermore, the assignment statement

```
cost[i++].amount += charge;
```

is also predictable, but the (seemingly) equivalent

```
cost[i++].amount = cost[i++].amount + charge;
```

is not. Of course, it's possible for C to evaluate these expressions to produce the result you want, in which case you don't realize that you have a problem. This makes the situation worse, since you won't discover the problem until you port your C code to a machine where the expression evaluates differently.

How does C evaluate these types of expressions? Which ones are portable and which ones are not? Let's review C's operators and see how they affect these types of expressions.

## Sequence Guarantee Operators

C expressions may contain subexpressions separated by operators. If the same variable appears in more than one subexpression, the order of evaluation becomes important if a C operator *changes* the variable. For example, the expression

```
a[i++] + b[i]
```

contains two subexpressions that are both array references. The first subexpression, however, contains the `++` operator and changes `i`. Depending on *when* `i` increments, the evaluation of the entire expression is not unique. The compiler may add `a[i]` to `b[i]` or `a[i]` to `b[i + 1]`, for instance.

Table 4-1 lists the C operators that change variables and produce what we call a *side effect*.

**TABLE 4-1.  Side effect operators**

| Operator | | | | | Meaning |
|---|---|---|---|---|---|
| ++ | -- | | | | pre/post increment/decrement |
| = | | | | | assignment |
| += | -= | *= | /= | %= | arithmetic assignment |
| <<= | >>= | &= | \| = | ^= | bitwise assignment |

If you use a side effect operator in a subexpression, you need to know the order of evaluation that C uses to evaluate the entire expression. Otherwise, the expression is "ill-formed" and is not portable.

A small set of operators connect subexpressions with side effect operators and guarantee that the entire expression evaluates the same on all machines. We call these operators *sequence guarantee operators*. C provides only four, as shown in Table 4-2.

**TABLE 4-2.  Sequence guarantee operators**

| Operator | Meaning |
|---|---|
| && | logical AND |
| \| \| | logical OR |
| , | comma |
| ? : | conditional |

Sequence guarantee operators are important because they evaluate subexpressions *left to right*. The order of evaluation for subexpressions is consistent, and you may use side effect operators in subexpressions. During the evaluation of a subexpression with a side effect operator, C must modify the variable before it *crosses* a sequence guarantee *point*, going left to right. Hence, we'll use the terms "sequence guarantee point" and "sequence guarantee operator" interchangeably. To see how this works, let's discuss each sequence guarantee operator and show examples that use them.

## Logical Operators ( && and | | )

Recall the following format for a logical AND ( &&):

```
expression1 && expression2 && . . .
```

Each subexpression must evaluate to TRUE (nonzero) for the entire expression to be TRUE. There is one additional feature. If any subexpression evaluates to FALSE (zero), no subsequent subexpressions to the right evaluate.

You may use this feature to your advantage in certain expressions. Suppose, for example, b and d are floats. The statement

```
printf("%g\n", b / d);
```

will most likely produce a core dump under UNIX if d is zero. However, the statement

```
d != 0.0 && printf("%g\n", b / d);
```

prevents you from dividing by zero or displaying a meaningless result. This same approach applies to debugging. For example, the statement

```
debug && dump(buf);
```

calls dump() only if a flag called debug is TRUE. We show you a debugging macro like this in Chapter 5.

This feature is also useful for function calls that return TRUE or FALSE. The statements

```
if (check1(buf) && check2(buf) && check3(buf))
    process(buf);
```

for example, won't process the contents of a buffer called buf unless it has passed three error checking routines in succession. The compiler does not call check2() unless check1() returns TRUE, and so forth. When you code process(), you may assume that buf's data has been previously verified by check1(), check2(), and check3(), in that order. It's also possible to write this as a single statement without an if as follows:

```
check1(buf) && check2(buf) && check3(buf) && process(buf);
```

You may do this as long as process() is not declared void.

This next example uses sequence guarantee operators in a set of custom string comparison macros.

```
#define STRCMP(a, b) (*(a) == *(b) && strcmp(a, b) == 0)
#define STRNCMP(a, b, n) (*(a) == *(b) && strncmp(a, b, n) == 0)
```

Each macro tests the first character of a string and calls the C library functions only if they are the same. The macros eliminate function call overhead if the first character of each string is different. Note that these macros rely on the way C evaluates expressions with &&.

Next, let's discuss how C handles the side effect operators `++` and `--` with the logical operator `&&` between subexpressions. Suppose we loop over an array of values, processing array elements as pairs of numbers. When we find an array element which is greater than a certain value, we pass the *next* element to a function called `calc()`. Here's the code:

```
a[i++] > VAL && calc(a[i]);
```

First, we call `calc()` only if the array element's value is greater than `VAL`. Second, the compiler increments `i` before it crosses the sequence guarantee point (`&&`). This ensures that we reference the next array element correctly before we pass it to `calc()`. Using `--` in this expression works in a similar way.

Let's review the logical OR (`||`) format next.

```
expression1 || expression2 || . . .
```

Only one subexpression must evaluate to TRUE (nonzero) for the entire expression to be TRUE. The compiler does not evaluate any further subexpressions to the right once a subexpression evaluates to TRUE.

You may use this feature with `||` in the same way as `&&`. Suppose, for example, you pass a pointer to a routine that saves data in a linked list. The code

```
p == NULL || stuff(p, x, y, z);
```

prevents you from calling `stuff()` if pointer `p` is NULL. This implies that you don't need to check for a NULL pointer in `stuff()`. Moreover, you save a little execution time since there is no function call overhead for a NULL pointer.

## Comma Operator ( , )

C allows expressions to contain any number of subexpressions separated by a comma operator, as follows.

```
expression1, expression2, . . .
```

The compiler evaluates each subexpression left to right. Subexpressions may contain side effect operators.

The program `rev1.c`, for example, reverses characters in a string using a comma operator inside a `for` statement.

**Program 4-1**

```c
/* rev1.c - reverse a string in place */

#include <stdio.h>

main()
{
    char *str = "moorpart";

    reverse(str);
    printf("%s\n", str);
}

reverse(p)
register char *p;
{
    register char *q = p + strlen(p) - 1;

    for (; p < q; p++, q--) {
        *p ^= *q;
        *q ^= *p;
        *p ^= *q;
    }
}
```

```
$ rev1
traproom
```

rev1 uses the Exclusive-OR technique from Chapter 1 to exchange characters in a string. The third expression in the for statement includes the comma operator to increment p and decrement q each time through the loop.

Another use of the comma operator is with subexpressions in a single statement. Suppose, for example, a program loops through elements of an array. The following code exchanges adjacent elements based on a boolean variable called swap:

```c
if (swap)
    tmp = x[i++], x[i-1] = x[i], x[i] = tmp;
```

If swap evaluates to TRUE, we use i to access the desired elements of the x array. We use a variable tmp to swap adjacent elements. The code shows the comma operator is a sequence guarantee point, since i increments before the second subexpression evaluates. Note that we don't need braces with the if here, since the three subexpressions form a single statement.

## Conditional Operator ( ? : )

The conditional operator contains three subexpressions.

```
expression1 ? expression2 : expression3
```

Subexpressions evaluate left to right. If `expression1` evaluates to TRUE (nonzero), `expression2` evaluates, otherwise `expression3` evaluates. Side effect operators may appear in any subexpression.

Conditional operators are handy in return statements, macros, and function arguments. The following `printf()` statement, for example, displays a number in hexadecimal or decimal, depending on a flag called `mode`:

```
printf(mode == HEX ? "%x\n" : "%d\n", num);
```

Here, *expression2* and *expression3* are constant strings. The following example, however, uses the conditional operator in a declaration:

```
unsigned char buf[sizeof(int) == 4 ? 1024 : 512];
```

The `sizeof()` operator determines the word length of the machine. Assuming 8-bit bytes, the declaration declares `buf` as a 1024-byte array on a 32-bit machine and a 512-byte array on others. Subexpressions are integer constants, so a program may declare a different size array based on the word length of the machine.

The compiler uses the conditional operator as a sequence guarantee point for subexpressions with side effect operators. To demonstrate, suppose a program keeps track of time with a pointer to an integer. Once every second, the program increments the time with the pointer and calls a function to display the new time. The counter resets to zero every 60 seconds. Using the conditional operator, we can do all this when we call the function:

```
timer (*p = ++*p < 60 ? *p : 0);
```

This code, while admittedly obscure, combines several operations in one, yet still executes predictably. First, the compact pointer expression

```
++*p
```

increments the time counter with the pointer. If it's less than 60, `timer()` displays the new value; otherwise, the counter is reset to zero before it's displayed. C guarantees that the counter increments before `timer()` displays the new value because the conditional operator has higher precedence than the assignment operator.

By the way, it's important that you don't confuse the comma operator with the comma *separator*. Comma separators appear in function arguments; C guarantees left to right evaluation only with the comma *operator*. This means the code

```
f(row = *p++, col = *p++);
```

is not portable, since C does *not* guarantee that function parameters (separated by commas) evaluate left to right. Problems such as these are not always obvious. The following code compiled and ran correctly on one machine but ran differently on another.

```
int a[MAX];
int i = 0;
 . . . .
while (i < MAX)
    printf("%4d%c", a[i], ++i % 10 ? ' ' : '\n');
```

This tidy bit of code displays an array of 10 integers on one line at a time, separated by spaces and ending with a newline. The problem is with the reference to a[i] and the ++ operator with i. The compiler may increment i *before* we reference an array element. The code is not portable, since the order of evaluation for printf()'s arguments does not execute left to right.

Here's a portable solution (which is probably better programming anyway):

```
int a[MAX];
int i;
 . . . .
for (i = 0; i < MAX; i++) {
    printf("%4d%c", a[i], (i + 1) % 10 ? ' ' : '\n');
```

The program runs predictably because we removed the side effect operator from printf()'s argument list.

## ◆ Right-Left Rule ◆

C has programming features that other languages don't provide. For example, C allows you to create a table of memory addresses that contain pointers to functions. A program may use input data to reference a table element to call an appropriate function. Suppose such a table holds ten addresses of functions that return pointers to integers. The program requires a declaration of an array of ten pointers to functions that return pointers to integers. What does this declaration look like?

C also allows pointers to arrays. Suppose a graphics application requires a function that manipulates double precision data in two dimensions (3 rows by 4 columns). You decide to call such a function with a pointer. The program requires a declaration of a pointer to a function that returns a pointer to a 3 by 4 array of doubles. What does this declaration look like?

The following declaration appears in a program:

```
struct block *(*table())[10];
```

What does this mean?

A simple technique called the *right-left rule*†, helps you interpret advanced declarations like this. There's nothing to memorize here, just a simple rule. Let's find out how this rule works since it allows you to decipher declarations and helps you create your own.

## Complex Declarations

A C declaration may include various combinations of pointers, arrays, and functions. We call this a *complex declaration*. To parse a complex declaration, the compiler has to sort out the attributes listed in Table 4-3.

**TABLE 4-3. Declaration attributes**

| Attribute | Meaning |
|-----------|---------|
| ( )       | function |
| [ ]       | array    |
| *         | pointer  |

Recall that ( ) and [ ] have higher precedence than *. Furthermore, ( ) and [ ] evaluate left to right. With this information, we can make a list of several legal declarations (Table 4-4).

**TABLE 4-4. Legal declarations**

| Attributes | Meaning |
|------------|---------|
| * ( )      | function returns pointer |
| (*) ( )    | pointer to function |
| * [ ]      | array of pointers |
| (*) [ ]    | pointer to an array |
| [ ] [ ]    | array of array |
| **         | pointer to pointer |

Of course, we can extend these concepts to even greater complexity. (* [ ] [ ], for example, is a two-dimensional array of pointers), but the table shows us the

---

† See *C Programming Guide*, Jack Purdum, Que Corporation, 1983.

relationships that we need to understand. We place parentheses around the indirection operator (*) to declare a pointer to a function or a pointer to an array, because * has lower precedence than () and [].

Not all combinations of these operators make legal declarations. Table 4-5 shows you several illegal ones.

**TABLE 4-5. Illegal declarations**

| Attributes | Meaning |
|---|---|
| () [] | function returns array |
| [] () | array of functions |
| () () | function returns function |

You may, however, use *pointers* to these. We'll return to this later and show you how to use pointers to make these declarations legal.

There is one important point that's worth remembering in a complex declaration:

> You must use an intervening parenthesis
> between the () and [] attributes.

This makes sense, since C doesn't allow you to declare an array of functions, or a function that returns an array. When you code complex declarations, remember to place parentheses between these attributes; otherwise, the compiler reports an error.

Here's something else that helps:

> To decipher a declaration, substitute English
> keywords where an attribute appears.

This makes a declaration understandable and also helps you create declarations from an English description. A list of English keywords appears in Table 4-6.

**TABLE 4-6. English keywords for declaration attributes**

| Attribute | English Keyword |
|---|---|
| () | function returns |
| [n] | array of n |
| * | pointer to |

Now let's learn the *right-left rule*.

1. Start with the identifier.

2. Look to the right for an attribute.

3. If none is found, look to the left.

4. If found, substitute English keyword.

5. Continue right-left substitutions as you work your way out.

6. Stop when you reach the data type in the declaration.

This rule applies to any C declaration, simple or complex.

## Example Declarations

Let's begin with a simple declaration:

```
unsigned long buf[10];
```

buf is the identifier. Look to the right for the [] attribute. That's all we have, so

buf is an array of 10 unsigned longs

Here is another example.

```
unsigned long *p[2];
```

p is the identifier. Look to the right for the [] attribute, then to the left for the *. This means

p is an array of 2 pointers to unsigned longs

Remember that multidimensional arrays use the [] attribute more than once. In this case, continue to the right until you've run out of [] before you look left. For example,

```
struct something *ps[3][4];
```

means

ps is an array of 3 arrays of 4 pointers to struct something

This, of course, is better understood as

ps is a 3 by 4 array of pointers to struct something

Now let's try a complex declaration.

```
int (*pf[5])()
```

pf is the identifier. Looking right, we find that pf is an array. Looking left, we see that it's an array of pointers. Looking right, we discover each array element is the address of a function that returns an integer. This means

pf is an array of 5 pointers to functions that return integers.

Note the parenthesis between the [] and () attributes. The declaration

```
int *pf[5]()
```

is illegal and doesn't compile.

We can make a small change to the original declaration as follows:

```
int *(*pf[5])()
```

Another * now appears after the data type. This changes the meaning slightly.

pf is an array of 5 pointers to functions that return pointers to integers.

Now let's see if we can apply the right-left rule to the declarations from the start of this section. In the following declaration

```
struct block *(*table())[10];
```

for example, table is the identifier. Looking right, we know that table is a function. Looking left, we see that this function returns a pointer. Looking right, we find that the function returns a pointer to an array. Looking left again, we discover that each array element is a pointer to a structure. The complete description is

table is a function that returns a pointer to an array
of 10 pointers to structures of type block.

Again, note that C requires a parenthesis between the () and [] attributes.

The right-left rule also helps you construct a declaration from an English sentence. The beginning of this section described several declarations this way. The first example was an array of ten pointers to functions that return pointers to integers. Let's start with the name of the array (buf) and place the first attribute on the right:

```
buf[10]                 array of 10
```

Now we go to the left for the next different attribute:

```
*buf[10]                array of 10 pointers
```

Next, we go to the right for the next attribute.

```
(*buf[10])()            array of 10 pointers to functions
```

Here we remember to place an intervening parenthesis between the `[]` and `()` attributes. Finally, we add the last attribute including the data type:

```
int *(*buf[10])()       array of 10 pointers to functions
                        that return pointers to integers
```

The second example was a pointer to a function that returns a pointer to a 3 by 4 array of doubles. See if you agree with the following steps:

```
          *pf                 pf is a pointer
         (*pf)()               pf is a pointer to a function
        *(*pf)()               pf is a pointer to a function
                               that returns a pointer
double (*(*pf)())[3][4]        pf is a pointer to a function
                               that returns a pointer
                               to a 3 by 4 array of doubles
```

## String Operators

Let's put into an example what we've learned so far. Suppose we use C to implement a language with string operators. The language supports a range of operators, from string assignment to string concatenation. The + operator concatenates strings and the – operator joins strings with an intervening blank. For example, the statement

```
"pop" + "corn"
```

creates the new string

```
"popcorn"
```

and the statement

```
"ice" - "cream"
```

creates the string

    "ice cream"

In our implementation, we'll use an array of pointers to functions. The language translates an operator to an array subscript to access the pointer and calls the function that handles the appropriate string operator. The following example shows how we implement the + and – operators.

**Program 4-2**

```
/* str1.c - join strings with an array of function pointers */

#include <stdio.h>
char *malloc(), *strcpy(), *strcat();

main()
{
   char *join(), *joinb();

   char *(*ps[2])();        /* array of pointers to functions
                               that return pointers to chars */

   ps[0] = join;            /* join strings */
   ps[1] = joinb;           /* join strings with blank */

   printf("%s\n", (*ps[0])("alpha", "bet"));
   printf("%s\n", (*ps[1])("duck", "soup"));
}

char *join(s1, s2)          /* join s1, s2 */
char *s1, *s2;
{
   char *pnew;

   pnew = malloc(strlen(s1) + strlen(s2) + 1);
   if (pnew == (char *) NULL) {
      fprintf(stderr, "Can't malloc for heap space\n");
      exit(1);
   }
   return strcat(strcpy(pnew, s1), s2);
}
```

```
char *joinb(s1, s2)      /* join s1, s2 with blank */
char *s1, *s2;
{
    char *pnew;

    pnew = malloc(strlen(s1) + strlen(s2) + 2);
    if (pnew == (char *) NULL) {
        fprintf(stderr, "Can't malloc for heap space\n");
        exit(1);
    }
    return strcat(strcat(strcpy(pnew, s1), " "), s2);
}
```

$ **str1**
alphabet
duck soup

The functions `join()` and `joinb()` handle the + and – operators, respectively. Both functions return pointers to characters. The declaration

```
char *(*ps[2])();  /* array of pointers to functions
                       that return pointers to characters */
```

creates a table of function addresses (some compilers require `int *(*ps[2])()`). The right-left rule says

> ps is an array of 2 pointers to functions that return pointers to characters.

The statements

```
    ps[0] = join;          /* join strings */
    ps[1] = joinb;         /* join strings with blank */
```

store the function addresses in the `ps` array, and the statements

```
    (*ps[0])("alpha", "bet")    /* call join */
    (*ps[1])("duck", "soup")    /* call joinb */
```

call the functions using the pointers from the `ps` array. Both functions return pointers to new strings, and the program calls `printf()` to display the characters.

Both `join()` and `joinb()` use C library functions. The function `malloc()` allocates heap memory for the concatenated strings. The function `strcpy()` moves string data and `strcat()` joins strings. Note that both `strcpy()` and `strcat()` return heap pointers where the new strings reside. The main program uses these heap pointers to display the new strings.

## Signals

C programs may respond to *signals*. The operating system usually provides function calls for C programs to send and receive signals. In UNIX, for example, the kernel allows C programs to receive a signal from another program or possibly from itself. How a program handles a signal depends on the application. You can choose to ignore a signal, for instance, or you can execute your own function when a signal arrives. Under UNIX, this is done with special header files and operating system calls.

Chapter 5 discusses signals in more detail. Right now, let's look at the UNIX protocols for the signal function. Here's the definition on our XENIX 286 machine:

```
int (*signal (sig, pfunc))()
int sig;
int (*pfunc)();
```

This declaration is enough to make some people decide *not* to use signals. The right-left rule, however, helps decipher it.

signal is a function that returns a pointer to a function
that returns an integer.

The signal() routine is actually a system call to the UNIX kernel. The routine's first argument is an integer signal number (UNIX has over 20 signal numbers) and its second argument is something else. The right-left rule provides the answer.

pfunc is a pointer to a function that returns an integer.

(On some systems, the function returns a void.) This is all the information we need to use signals. Chapter 5 shows you how to use signals for debugging.

## Casts

Let's return to complex declarations. Table 4-7 lists several legal declarations with functions, arrays, and pointers. Although we cannot declare a function, for example, that returns an array, we may create a function that returns a *pointer* to an array. The indirection operator ＊ makes these declarations legal. Table 4-7 lists the legal declarations.

**TABLE 4-7. Legal declarations**

| Attributes | Meaning |
|---|---|
| (*()) [] | function that returns a pointer to an array |
| (*[]) () | array of pointers to functions |
| (*()) () | function that returns a pointer to a function |

The right-left rule and C's precedence rules help interpret them. Let's look first at

    (*()) []

Recall that () and [] evaluate left to right and have a higher precedence than *. There is no identifier here, so we start with the inside () attribute. This attribute is a *function*, so we look right. There's nothing to evaluate, and we look left and find a *pointer* attribute. Looking right we see an *array*. This expression evaluates to a function that returns a pointer to an array. C requires the parenthesis between the () and [] attributes. As an exercise, try and apply the right-left rule to the remaining declarations.

These examples help you apply the right-left rule to *cast* complex objects. To demonstrate, let's return to our discussion of signals. Recall that signal()'s first argument is a signal number and its second argument is a pointer to a function that returns an integer. UNIX allows programs to use the special names SIG_DFL and SIG_IGN in the second argument for signal(). SIG_DFL, for example, resets a signal's action back to the default (which terminates your program). The function call

    signal(SIGINT, SIG_DFL);

makes your program terminate when it receives an interrupt signal (SIGINT). Likewise, SIG_IGN allows a program to ignore a signal. The function call

    signal(SIGQUIT, SIG_IGN);

makes your program ignore a quit signal (SIGQUIT).

Since signal() requires a pointer where these special names appear, you may wonder how they are defined. Here are the UNIX definitions for SIG_DFL and SIG_IGN from the header file signal.h on our machine:

```
#define SIG_DFL (int (*)())0

#define SIG_IGN (int (*)())1
```

This has to be the strangest way to cast the numbers 0 and 1 that anyone could imagine. The right-left rule, however, verifies that these special names agree with the definition of signal()'s second argument. SIG_DFL, for instance, casts 0 as a pointer to a function that returns an int. SIG_IGN casts 1 in a similar fashion. Note that (*) must appear in the cast. The statement

```
(int *())0
```

is incorrect, since this makes 0 a function that returns a pointer to an integer.

Dynamic storage allocation is another important use of casts with complex declarations. Storage allocator calls like malloc(), for example, return character pointers. You may need to cast a heap pointer to match a complex declaration.

The next example returns to our language that implements string operators. Recall that str1.c (Program 4-2) declares an array of pointers (ps) to functions that return pointers to characters as shown in Fig. 4-1.

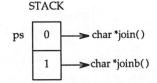

**Fig. 4-1.** Array of pointers to functions

The array ps lives on the stack in the run time environment. Suppose a program requires heap storage for the pointers at *run time*. Now, you would need a pointer instead of an array. Fig. 4-2 shows the new arrangement.

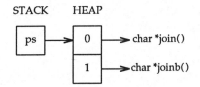

**Fig. 4-2.** Pointer to pointer to functions

The pointer ps lives on the stack and contains a heap address. Therefore, ps is a pointer to a pointer to a function that returns a pointer to a character. The right-left rule gives us the following complex declaration from this English description:

```
char *(**ps)();   /* pointer to pointer to functions
                     that return pointers to chars */
```

When we call malloc() to allocate storage for the pointers from the heap, we can assign the heap address to ps and use the same approach as before.

Here's the modified program, called str2.c:

**Program 4-3**

```
/* str2.c - join strings with function ptrs on the heap */

#include <stdio.h>
char *malloc(), *strcpy(), *strcat();

main()
{
    char *join(), *joinb();

    char *(**ps)();        /* pointer to pointer to functions
                              that return pointers to chars */

    ps = (char *(**)()) malloc(2 * sizeof(char *));
    if (ps == (char *) NULL) {
        fprintf(stderr, "Can't malloc from the heap\n");
        exit(1);
    }
    ps[0] = join;          /* join strings */
    ps[1] = joinb;         /* join strings with blank */

    printf("%s\n", (*ps[0])("alpha", "bet"));
    printf("%s\n", (*ps[1])("duck", "soup"));
}
    char *join(s1, s2)        /* join s1, s2 */
    char *s1, *s2;
    {
        char *pnew;
```

```
    pnew = malloc(strlen(s1) + strlen(s2) + 1);
    if (pnew == (char *) NULL) {
       fprintf(stderr, "Can't malloc from the heap\n");
       exit(1);
    }
    return strcat(strcpy(pnew, s1), s2);
}

char *joinb(s1, s2)        /* join s1, s2 with blank */
char *s1, *s2;
{
    char *pnew;

    pnew = malloc(strlen(s1) + strlen(s2) + 2);
    if (pnew == (char *) NULL) {
       fprintf(stderr, "Can't malloc from the heap\n");
       exit(1);
    }
    return strcat(strcat(strcpy(pnew, s1), " "), s2);
}
```

$ **str2**
alphabet
duck soup

There's not much different except the revised declaration for ps and the new call to malloc(). The statement

```
    ps = (char *(**)()) malloc(2 * sizeof(char *));
```

casts malloc()'s return pointer from a pointer to a character to a *pointer to a pointer* to a function that returns a pointer to a character. Note that this cast is the same as the declaration for ps without the identifier name.

The program allocates heap storage for two pointers, which, as we expected, is the same amount of space we originally reserved on the stack for the array in str1.c. Since ps is a pointer to a pointer, we can still use it as if it were a one-dimensional array. The statements

```
    ps[0] = join;                /* join strings */
    ps[1] = joinb;               /* join strings with blank */
```

make heap space point to the string functions, and the statements

```
(*ps[0]) ("alpha", "bet")     /* call join */
(*ps[1]) ("duck", "soup")     /* call joinb */
```

call the functions to join strings. These statements didn't change from `str1.c`.

## ♦ Lvalues in Expressions ♦

One of the first things C programmers learn is *precedence*, which matches the compiler's actions with how you want an expression to evaluate. There's something else that C programmers sometimes struggle with, and that's the concept of an *lvalue*. This term shows up frequently in the C reference manual as well as in compiler error messages. It's often poorly understood, yet programmers need to grasp the concept to code expressions that compile. This section looks at what an lvalue is, why it's important to the compiler, and what you need to know about it. Once you see how it works, you'll understand more about how C evaluates expressions.

Simply put, an lvalue is usually something that appears on the *left* side of an assignment statement. There's more to it, of course, but C makes a big distinction between an lvalue and something that appears on the *right* side of an assignment statement (appropriately called an *rvalue*). This makes sense if you realize that an lvalue must have storage associated with it, or more specifically, an address in memory. If what you put on the left hand side doesn't have a storage location, you can't expect C to be able to store anything there. For example, the assignment statement

```
5 = 7;
```

does not compile, since the integer 5 has no storage location. Although this is obvious, you might think

```
"dave" = "bill";
```

makes sense, since constant strings could have addresses in memory. This doesn't compile either, so there must be more to the story. Indeed there is, as you will see.

### What is an Lvalue?

The C compiler treats the following as lvalues:

1.  Variable names with data types `float`, `int`, `double`, etc. Also pointers, structures, unions, and array elements.

2.  The result from applying the indirection operator (`*`).

3.  The result from applying the structure member operator (`.`) or the structure pointer operator (`->`), if the member is also an lvalue.

There are, therefore, only four lvalue operators: `[]`, `*`, `.`, and `->`. Once you have an lvalue, you may alter it with any side effect operator listed in Table 4-1.

Let's look at several examples. Suppose we have the following declarations:

```
int num;
char c, *p;
float val[80];
struct s {
    char buf[80];
    float *pd;
} data;
struct s *ps = &data;
```

These are valid expressions with lvalues:

```
num += 5;
p = "new string";
*p = 'x';
val[4] = 6.5;
data.pd = &val[4];
ps->buf[1] = *p;
```

Note that a pointer (`p`) is an lvalue and so is a pointer with the indirection operator (`*p`). Array references like `val[4]` are always lvalues because C converts them to pointer offsets (`*(val + 4)`). Members of structures (and unions) must be lvalues to appear on the left hand side of an assignment statement.

So far so good. The confusing part comes when you look at what's *not* an lvalue. To understand this more completely, let's look at some examples of what the compiler considers as *rvalues*:

1.  Constants

2.  Function names

3.  Enumerated values

4.  Array names

This list implies that rvalues may be referenced but not changed. You cannot, for instance, use a function name as an lvalue, since it doesn't have a memory address that you can change (function addresses in the text area are typically protected from write operations). Furthermore, enumerated values are constants, and programs cannot modify them for the same reason. It's *array names* that confuse C programmers, because the language gives you the notion that arrays and pointers are interchangeable. They are, in fact, but only if they are rvalues.

To demonstrate this, study the following program.

**Program 4-4**

```c
/* lval.c - shows lvalues for pointers and functions */

#include <stdio.h>
void f(), g();

main()
{
    static char a[] = "this is a string";
    char *p = "this is another string";

/* the following statement doesn't compile
    a = "this is a new string";
*/
    p = "this is another new string";

    f(a);                           /* pass pointer to array */
    printf("array a: %s\n", a);

    g(&p);                          /* pass pointer to p */
    printf("pointer p: %s\n", p);
}

void f(a)
char a[];
{
    a = "won't change the array";   /* this compiles OK */
}

void g(ptr)
char **ptr;
{
    *ptr = "changes string pointed to";
}
```

```
$ lval
array a: this is a string
pointer p: changes string pointed to
```

This program makes even experienced C programmers think a little. After initializing a character array (a), we initialize a character pointer (p) to the constant string `"this is another string"`. In the run time environment, a resides in the data area, while p lives on the stack.

What's important to understand in this program is that the statement

```
p = "this is another new string";
```

compiles, but the statement

```
a = "this is a new string";
```

does not (we make it a comment for this reason). Here, p has a storage location, but the compiler doesn't assign one to a. Another way of saying this is that the name of an array is a *constant* (as well as an rvalue). This makes no difference if, say, you pass the address of an array to a function like

```
f(a);                       /* pass pointer to array */
```

because the function uses a pointer that contains the address of the array's first element. However, it does make a difference if you try to use an array name as an lvalue. For the same reason, you can't apply the ++ and -- operators to the name of an array, either. The statements

```
a++     --a
```

for example, produce compilation errors. It's as if you were trying to increment or decrement a constant.

Now let's look inside the function `f()`.

```
a = "won't change the array";   /* this compiles OK */
```

This statement looks just like in the one in the main program, yet it compiles (and the one in `main()` doesn't). Why? Inside `f()`, the function uses a *pointer* called a and the main program refers to a as a *constant*. When `main()` passes a to `f()`, the function allocates a separate storage location for a pointer containing the address of the beginning of the array. Inside `f()`, you can use array notation for a, but it's still a pointer as far as C is concerned.

Thus, a is an lvalue inside `f()` and you can change it. The `printf()` statement following the call to `f()`, however, demonstrates that the program changes only the *local* copy of the pointer inside the function `f()`. When you return to the main program, you haven't changed what was in the original array.

To change it, we call the function  g()  with the address of the pointer to
the string. Note that  g()  declares  ptr  as a pointer to a *pointer* to a character.
The statement

```
*ptr = "changes string pointed to";
```

changes the pointer in the main program to point to a different constant string.
The  printf()  statement following the call to  g()  verifies that the pointer's
address changes.

## Compact Pointer Expressions Revisited

Recall from Chapter 3 that compact pointer expressions use the indirection
operator and the  ++ and  -- operators.  Table 4-8 lists the most commonly used
ones.

TABLE 4-8.  Compact pointer expressions

| Increment | Decrement | Lvalue |
|-----------|-----------|--------|
| *p++      | *p--      | yes    |
| *++p      | *--p      | yes    |
| ++*p      | --*p      | no     |
| (*p)++    | (*p)--    | no     |

Note that the first two compact pointer expressions are lvalues, but the last two
are not.  To illustrate, suppose a program contains the following declaration.

```
int buf[80], *p = buf;
```

Then, in the statements

```
*p++ = 12;
*++p = 6;
```

both compact pointer expressions are lvalues.  The first one (*p++) stores  12
into the first slot of the  buf  array and the second one (*++p) stores  6 into the
third slot of the array.
    The expressions

```
++*p = 12;
(*p)++ = 6;
```

are illegal, however, and produce compilation errors.  Both expressions apply the

++ operator to p's object (an int) instead of the pointer. It's as if you typed

```
++5 = 12;
5++ = 6;
```

as far as C is concerned. The order of the operators that make up a compact pointer expression, therefore, is important if an expression uses one as an lvalue.

The next example uses compact pointer expressions to access command line arguments. Undoubtedly, there are many ways to do this. Here's one that perhaps you haven't seen before:

**Program 4-5**

```
/* com.c - command line arguments */

#include <stdio.h>

main(argc, argv)
int argc;
char *argv[];
{
    if (argc == 1) {
        fprintf(stderr, "Usage: %s args\n", argv[0]);
        exit(1);
    }
    while (--argc) {
      printf("%s: ", *++argv);
      while (**argv)
          printf("%c ", *(*argv)++);
      putchar('\n');
    }
}

$ com one two three
one: o n e
two: t w o
three: t h r e e
```

The program's output is a separate line for each of its arguments. We display the argument, a colon, and each character's argument separated by a space. The program has two while loops. The outer one loops over the number of command line arguments (argc). The compact pointer expression

```
*++argv
```

in the first printf() statement increments argv before it displays the argument with `*argv`. This has the effect of bypassing the first command line argument (the program name). The second loop uses the expression

```
while (**argv)
```

to test whether to exit the loop, using double indirection to examine the *character* that `argv` points to. If its NULL, we're done and we move to the next argument. Otherwise, the compact pointer expression

```
*(*argv)++
```

evaluates to a character in the current command line argument. We looked at this type of expression in Chapter 3, but here are the evaluation steps once again:

1. Evaluate `*argv` to produce a pointer to the current argument.

2. Evaluate `*(*argv)` to produce a character from the current argument

3. Increment `*argv` to point to the *next* character in the current argument.

Fig. 4-3 and Fig. 4-4 show you how all this works. At the start of the second `while` loop, (after `argv` has moved to the second command line argument) `*argv` points to the first character (`'o'`), as Fig. 4-3 shows.

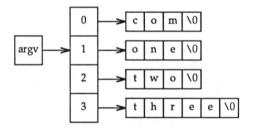

*Fig. 4-3.* Accessing first character of second argument

After one iteration through the second loop, the program modifies `*argv` to point to the second character of the second command line argument. Fig. 4-4 shows the result.

Now, `*argv` points to the character `'n'`. When we reach the NULL character, we move to the next argument. The program terminates when there are no more command line arguments.

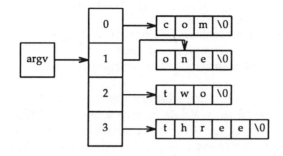

*Fig. 4-4.* Accessing second character of second argument

We show you all this because argv is often mistaken as an array of character pointers, when in fact, it's really a pointer to an array of character pointers, as Figs. 4-3 and 4-4 show. This makes argv an lvalue, so expressions like

```
argv++
```

and

```
*++argv
```

are legal and convenient to use.

## ◆ Fast Array Transfers ◆

The use of arrays in C requires a good understanding of how the language defines them. Chapter 3 justifies why C converts array references to pointer offsets and the previous section shows that both are lvalues. Furthermore, a pointer's name is an lvalue but the name of an array is not.

Suppose a and b are arrays of the same data type and size. The assignment statement

```
a = b;                        /* arrays won't compile */
```

produces a compilation error because a is not an lvalue. Transferring data between arrays (called *array assignment*) is not possible in C.

C does allow you assign one *structure* to another, however. Suppose, for example, s and t are structures of the same type. The assignment statement

```
    s = t;                          /* structures compile */
```

compiles because s is an lvalue. C, therefore, allows you to transfer data from all of the members of one structure to another one with a single assignment statement. This convenient feature is called *structure assignment* (union assignments are also possible).

C allows structures to have arbitrary sizes. A structure, for example, could represent a large record from a data base or a big chunk of memory. You may wonder about the run time efficiency of structure assignment, since execution time could be slow for large structures. On our XENIX 286 machine, for example, the Microsoft C compiler generates the following assembly code for structure assignment:

```
    LEA DI, &s                  ; address of s (destination)
    LEA SI, &t                  ; address of t (source)
    MOV CX, sizeof(s) / 2       ; number of words in s
    REP MOVSW                   ; block move words
```

These instructions make up what's called a *block move* instruction. Execution is fast because there are no loops. You should examine the assembly code on your machine to determine what the compiler does for structure assignment. Of course, your C compiler can't generate block move instructions if the processor you're using doesn't have them. In this case, the compiler probably generates a loop to transfer the data, which is a little slower (but still gets the job done).

If your compiler generates block move instructions as well, then structure assignment is convenient and efficient. Based on this assumption, it's possible to implement *array* assignment if you embed an array as a *member* of two structures (of the same type) and use structure assignment. With this arrangement, the compiler should generate block move instructions as it does with structure assignment.

The following technique, therefore, is an example of how you can use the C language to generate efficient assembly code for certain applications. The technique, which we call *fast array transfers*, is an interesting way of using C, yet its implementation is machine dependent. We'll discuss the pros and cons as we go along and show you a block move function based on the approach.

## The Technique

Suppose a C program declares two arrays of the same data type and size as follows:

```
    type c[SIZE], d[SIZE];
```

SIZE must be a constant integer expression, evaluated at compile time. To use fast array transfers, declare the following structure:

```
struct xfer {
  type buf[SIZE];
};
```

Note that this is a structure *template* and the compiler does not allocate storage. The names `xfer` and `buf` can be anything, but we'll need to use the name `xfer` later (the name `buf` is not used after this).

Now declare the following structures:

```
struct xfer a, b;
```

The statement

```
b = a;
```

for example, moves data from structure `a` to `b`.

Structure assignment is also possible with *pointers* to structures. If we provide the additional declarations

```
struct xfer *pa = &a;
struct xfer *pb = &b;
```

a program can transfer data from structure `a` to `b` with

```
*pb = *pa;
```

Now let's combine these operations into a single statement using casts. The statement

```
*(struct xfer *)d = *(struct xfer *)c;
```

does the job. It's actually a two-step operation. First, we cast the arrays to pointers to the structure template `xfer`. Next, we apply the indirection operator to perform structure assignment using pointers to structures. This should move the data from array `c` to array `d` as if we were doing structure assignment.

Before we continue, we should mention that we don't necessarily recommend this type of C code. We're presenting the technique because we've seen it run on a number of different machines and compilers with good results. The ANSI C standard, however, discourages this type of coding. Why, then, would we want to use C code like this? While there's no guarantee that fast array transfers is portable on all implementations of C, it does provide a technique that:

1. Allows you to learn about the implementation of C.

2. Lets you control the assembly language that is produced on some machines.

3. Moves data between arrays of the same size in one statement without a function call.

4. Possibly runs faster than library calls like memcpy() (since there is no function call overhead).

Clearly, if portability is your highest priority, you should use C library functions like memcpy() in place of fast array transfers. But, like choosing to write some routines in assembly code, we feel the technique still has its place.

## Example

Let's demonstrate the fast array transfer technique in the following program, which moves five integers from array a to array b.

**Program 4-6**

```
/* xfer.c - fast array transfer */

#include <stdio.h>
#define MAX 5

main()
{
  struct nums {
    int buf[MAX];
  };

  static int a[MAX] = {1, 2, 3, 4, 5};
  static int b[MAX] = {5, 4, 3, 2, 1};
  int i;

  *(struct nums *)b = *(struct nums *)a;

  for (i = 0; i < MAX; i++)
    printf("%2d", b[i]);
  putchar('\n');
}

$ xfer
 1 2 3 4 5
```

First, we declare a structure *template* called nums with an array buf. Array a contains five numbers in ascending order, and array b holds five descending numbers. The statement

```
* (struct nums *)b = *(struct nums *)a;
```

moves five integers from a to b. The program displays the contents of b to show it contains the new data.

## A Block Move Function

Now let's apply fast array transfers in a function that moves blocks of data in memory (similar to memcpy()). Suppose we have two large character arrays as follows:

```
unsigned char a[BIG], b[BIG];
```

Here are several calls to a block move function called bmove(), which moves all or part of one array to another:

```
unsigned size, i;
 .   .   .   .
/* move all of a to b */
bmove(b, a, sizeof(a));
 .   .   .   .
/* move 100 elements from b to a */
bmove(a, b, 100 * sizeof(a[0]));
 .   .   .   .
/* move size elements from a[i] to b[i] */
bmove(&b[i], &a[i], size * sizeof(a[0]));
```

The first two arguments of bmove() are character pointers (unsigned char *) and the third argument is the number of elements to transfer. The first call to bmove() transfers all of the data from a to b. The second call moves only the first 100 elements from b to a. The last call moves size elements starting from the address of a[i] to the b array starting at the address of b[i].

Here's the bmove() routine.

**Program 4-7**

```
/* bmove.c - block move function */

#define BSIZE 256

bmove(dest, src, count)
register unsigned char *dest, *src;
register unsigned count;
{
    struct mblock {              /* block size */
        char a[BSIZE];
    };

    while (count >= BSIZE) {     /* transfer blocks */
        *(struct mblock *)dest = *(struct mblock *)src;
        dest += BSIZE;
        src  += BSIZE;
        count -= BSIZE;
    }

    while (count--)          /* transfer remaining bytes */
        *dest++ = *src++;
}
```

bmove() declares a structure template called mblock. The size of the array element is BSIZE (256 bytes), which we'll return to shortly.

Two while loops perform the data transfer. The first while makes sure count is at least BSIZE before it moves a block (256 bytes) one at a time with the fast array transfer technique. Following this, the routine increments both the dest and src pointers and decrements count. The while loop terminates when count becomes less than BSIZE.

Since the argument count is arbitrary, it's possible to have less than BSIZE bytes left after all the preceding BSIZE byte blocks have been moved. A second while loop, therefore, uses compact pointer expressions to transfer the remaining bytes. Register variables for the src and dest pointers make this code execute as fast as possible. Note that bmove() doesn't execute the second while loop if count is zero.

The second while loop also explains why we use 256-byte blocks. Although we're free to use any size block we wish, it's best to keep the number of bytes small to minimize the time spent in the second loop.

The bmove() routine moves data in memory, much like memcpy() from the C library. The statement

```
memcpy(b, a, sizeof(a));       /* move all of a to b */
```

for example, has the same arguments as `bmove()`. As we mentioned, `bmove()` is just an application of fast array transfers and is not meant to replace `memcpy()` in portable C programs. You may, however, want to experiment with `bmove()` and the fast array transfer technique to see how it performs on your machine.

# ♦ Passing Entire Arrays to Functions ♦

C passes all arguments to functions by value. When you call a function, it's up to you to decide whether this value should be the contents of a variable or its address in memory. This is important, because if you pass the contents of a variable to a function that's expecting an address (or vice versa), the program is not going to execute properly.

If a function expects an address for an argument, you typically call the function with an `&` operator in front of the argument name. The function declares a pointer to access the data, and it can modify the original data with the pointer. On the other hand, if a function expects an argument's value, you usually call the function with only the argument's name (no `&` operator). In this case, the function declares a local variable that contains a copy of the data, and the function cannot change the original variable. This mechanism works for simple C data types as well as for structures and unions.

What about arrays? Here's the exception, because when you call a function with an array as an argument, C *always* passes the address of the first array element to the function. This explains why the `&` operator is not required with the name of an array on most compilers. Although passing the address of an array is efficient at run time (the compiler creates only a pointer to the array on the stack), if a function modifies an array element with a pointer, it changes the data in the original array. In C, there is no direct way to create a *copy* of the array for the function to manipulate. There is a method, however, to pass *all* of the array elements to a function. This allows a function to modify array elements without changing their original values.

This section shows you how to pass entire arrays to functions. We recommend that you don't use this approach with large arrays, because it slows down programs, but passing small arrays to functions has certain advantages, as you will see. It's also possible to use the same technique to make a function *return* an array. Let's look at the approach and discuss the pros and cons.

## The Technique

Since we may pass structures to functions, the technique is the same as with fast array transfers. We embed an array as a member of a structure before we pass it to a function. This approach allows you to pass an array to a function as if it were a structure. For example, the program

```
struct buf {
    int s[100];
};

main()
{
    . . . .
    struct buf values;
    . . . .
    f(values);
    . . . .
}

f(s)
struct buf s;
{
    . . . .
}
```

manipulates an array of 100 integers like a structure. This arrangement makes the program pass an entire array to a function.

Note that the technique does not allow you to pass arrays with different sizes. The compiler needs to know the data type of the array and how large it is before your program runs. This is not necessarily a disadvantage, since we plan on using the technique for small arrays anyway.

Let's demonstrate the technique with two C programs. The first program accepts an array of numbers and creates a separate copy when it's called. The second program does the same thing and returns an array as well.

## Arrays as Function Parameters

Suppose you are maintaining a list of disk block numbers in an array. You need a way to access the data as a sorted list without changing the list itself. One solution is to pass the entire array of disk block numbers to a function, which sorts the data from the new copy of the array. When you return from the function, the original list of disk block numbers remains intact.

Let's demonstrate this solution with the following program. sort1.c initializes an array of integers with disk block numbers. We display the list and call a function to sort it. Inside the sort function, we'll display the sorted data before we return. Then we'll display the original list to show it hasn't changed.

Here's the program:

**Program 4-8**

```c
/* sort1.c - sort array by value and display */

#include <stdio.h>
#define MAX 9

struct buf {
  int vals[MAX];
};

display(ps, nc)
struct buf *ps;
int nc;
{
    register int *p = ps->vals;

    while (p < ps->vals + nc)
      printf("%4d", *p++);
    putchar('\n');
}

sort(s, nc)
struct buf s;
int nc;
{
    register int *p;
    int sorted = 0;

    while (!sorted) {
       sorted = 1;
       for (p = s.vals + 1; p < s.vals + nc; p++)
          if (*(p-1) > *p) {
             *p ^= *(p-1);
             *(p-1) ^= *p;
             *p ^= *(p-1);
             sorted = 0;
          }
    }
    display(&s, nc);          /* display sorted data */
}
```

```
main()
{
    static struct buf blocks =
            { 34, 6, 12, 144, 23, 18, 135, 89, 11 };

    display(&blocks, MAX);    /* display original data */
    sort(blocks, MAX);        /* sort data and display */
    display(&blocks, MAX);    /* display original data */
}
```

First, we declare a structure template with an array of nine integers. We load the disk block numbers into a structure of this template type, making it an array, effectively. We display the original list using the routine display(), sort the data with sort(), and display the list again after we return. Both calls to display() pass the address of the structure that contains the data.

The sort() routine does all the work. sort()'s first argument is a structure (with the array of disk block numbers), and its second argument is the number of disk block numbers to sort. This allows us to sort only a part of the list, if we choose (in this program, we sort the complete list). Note that we pass a structure to sort() and not its address.

We use a bubble sort algorithm for the sort. Inside sort(), the structure s contains the array of disk block numbers. We loop through the data looking at pairs of numbers, exchanging them if the first is greater than the second. We use pointers to the data, and swap integers using the Exclusive-OR technique from Chapter 1. When flag sorted remains true, we've sorted the list.

Here's the output from sort1:

```
$ sort1
   34    6   12 144   23   18 135   89   11
    6   11   12   18   23   34   89 135 144
   34    6   12 144   23   18 135   89   11
```

The first line is the unsorted list of disk block numbers. The second line is the sorted list displayed by the sort() routine. The third line is the original list. This proves we haven't changed the original array that we passed to sort().

## Functions Returning Arrays

There's no reason we can't use structures to return an array from a function as well. Using the same approach, a function returns a structure with an array as a member. This has the same compile-time restrictions that we saw with arrays as function parameters.

To demonstrate, let's modify the previous program. sort2.c works the same as before, except that sort() now *returns* a sorted array. This allows us to display the sorted array in the program that calls sort() and not in the sort() routine itself. Here's the code for sort2.c.

**Program 4-9**

```c
/* sort2.c - sort array by value and
             return sorted array  */

#include <stdio.h>
#define MAX 9

struct buf {
  int vals[MAX];
};

display(ps, nc)
struct buf *ps;
int nc;
{
    register int *p = ps->vals;

    while (p < ps->vals + nc)
      printf("%4d", *p++);
    putchar('\n');
}

struct buf sort(s, nc)
struct buf s;
int nc;
{
    register int *p;
    int sorted = 0;

    while (!sorted) {
       sorted = 1;
       for (p = s.vals + 1; p < s.vals + nc; p++)
          if (*(p-1) > *p) {
             *p ^= *(p-1);
             *(p-1) ^= *p;
             *p ^= *(p-1);
             sorted = 0;
          }
    }
    return s;                 /* return sorted data */
}
```

```
main()
{
    static struct buf blocks =
            { 34, 6, 12, 144, 23, 18, 135, 89, 11 };
    struct buf sort();      /* sort returns sorted array */
    struct buf new;

    display(&blocks, MAX);    /* display original data */
    new = sort(blocks, MAX);  /* sort data and save it */
    display(&new, MAX);       /* display sorted data */
    display(&blocks, MAX);    /* display original data */
}
```

First, we tell the compiler that sort() returns a structure of type buf and declare a structure of the same type called new. The first call to display() displays the original data and the second call displays the sorted data in structure new, after we call sort(). The last call to display displays the original data again.

Everything else is the same as in the previous program, except that we return the structure s from inside sort(). The main program stores this return value in new.

Here's the output from sort2:

```
$ sort2
    34    6   12 144   23   18 135   89   11
     6   11   12  18   23   34   89 135 144
    34    6   12 144   23   18 135   89   11
```

Although all this is certainly convenient, you should realize that you are dealing with structures and not simple data types. If you don't use pointers, there is additional run time overhead in passing and returning structures with function calls. Note that we are careful to pass the address of the structure to display() because this routine, unlike sort(), does not need to modify the data. When you pass or return a structure to a function, the compiler copies the data, as it does with structure assignment. This is acceptable for small structures, but you should consider the run time implications when working with larger ones.

## ♦ Functions with Varying Arguments ♦

Unlike many languages, C allows you to call functions with a variable number of arguments that have different data types. The C library routines `printf()` and `scanf()` are good examples. The following program, for instance, reads input data with `scanf()` and displays it with `printf()`.

**Program 4-10**

```
/* varg1.c - scanf() and printf() with variable args */

#include <stdio.h>

main()
{
    int num;
    float val;
    char name[80];

    scanf("%d", &num);
    scanf("%f %s", &val, name);

    printf("%d ", num);
    printf("%g %s\n", val, name);
}
```

```
$ varg1
1234 6.789 something
1234 6.789 something
```

The program `varg1.c` calls `scanf()` and `printf()` differently each time. The first call to `scanf()` has two arguments and the second call has three. Note that `scanf()`'s arguments are all pointers. Likewise, the first call to `printf()` has two arguments and the second call has three. In both calls, `printf()`'s first argument is a pointer to a character, but the remaining arguments all have different data types.

How would you write your *own* function like this? Suppose, for example, you want to display debug information on standard error if a command line flag is set. Instead of calling `fprintf()` directly, you'd like to call a debug routine with a flag. Inside the debug routine, you check to see if the flag is set before you call `fprintf()` to display the debug information. The debug routine, like `fprintf()`, must handle a variable number of arguments with different data types.

One solution is to declare the debug function with more arguments than you're likely to call it with, and make each function argument a `double`. C doesn't convert function parameter data types by default, and a `double` accommodates the largest variable you're likely to have. Here's the approach.

**Program 4-11**

```
/* varg2.c - variable number of args - not portable */

#include <stdio.h>
#include "dbug.h"

main()
{
    int num;
    float val;
    char name[80];

    scanf("%d", &num);
    scanf("%f %s", &val, name);

    debug(1, "%d ", num);
    debug(2, "%g %s\n", val, name);
}

debug(flag, fmt, arg1, arg2, arg3, arg4, arg5)
int flag;
char *fmt;
double arg1, arg2, arg3, arg4, arg5;
{
    . . . . .

    if (flags[flag])
        fprintf(stderr, fmt, arg1, arg2, arg3, arg4, arg5);
}
```

**$ varg2**
**1234 6.789 something**
1234 6.789 something

The header file `dbug.h` declares a `flags` array and sets the flags from the command line. (Chapter 5 shows you a technique for debugging with command line flags.) Inside `debug()`, `fprintf()` displays the debug information if `flag` (in the `flags` array) is set. Each argument, which is a `double`, appears as an argument for `fprintf()` to display. This program demonstrates that it's possible to call C functions with *fewer* arguments than it was declared with.

However, `varg2.c` is not portable. The program may fail if one compiler passes arguments on the stack differently from another. We need a portable way to pass a variable number of parameters with different data types, so that we can write functions like `debug()`.

## The Technique

A special header file called `varargs.h` provides the interface you need. Before
we look at what's inside this file, let's modify the previous program and show
you how to use it.

```
/* varg3.c - variable number of args - portable */

#include <stdio.h>
#include <varargs.h>
#include "dbug.h"

main()
{
    int num;
    float val;
    char name[80];

    scanf("%d", &num);
    scanf("%f %s", &val, name);

    debug(1, "%d ", num);
    debug(2, "%g %s\n", val, name);
}

debug(va_alist)                    /* variable arg list */
va_dcl                             /* NOTE: no semicolon ! */
{
    va_list args;                  /* argument list */
    int flag;                      /* flag number */
    char *fmt;                     /* print format */

    va_start(args);                /* initialize arg list */
    flag = va_arg(args, int);      /* get the flag number */
    fmt  = va_arg(args, char *);   /* get the print format */

    if (flags[flag])
        vfprintf(stderr, fmt, args); /* display remaining args */

    va_end(args);                  /* clean up argument list */
}

$ varg3
1234 6.789 something
1234 6.789 something
```

First, replace debug()'s argument list with the special name va_alist, and substitute the special name va_dcl for the argument declarations. There is *no* semicolon following the word va_dcl, which we will return to shortly. Next, include the statement

```
va_list args;              /* argument list */
```

to use args for the argument list. You must use the special name va_list here, but the second name is arbitrary. Before fetching arguments from the stack, you need to initialize the argument list. The routine

```
va_start(args);            /* initialize argument list */
```

makes args point to the argument list.

The function va_arg() pops arguments off the stack. The routine's first argument is the name of the argument list (args in our case) and the second argument is a *data type*. Your program must provide a variable name of the same data type to hold the return value from va_arg(). The statements

```
flag = va_arg(args, int);      /* get the flag number */
fmt  = va_arg(args, char *);   /* get the print format */
```

for example, store an integer in flag and a character pointer in fmt. In general, you may fetch any data type this way, including structures and unions. Note, however, to access a char or a short, you should use an int data type with va_arg(). Likewise, you need a double data type for a float. The following statements

```
char ch;                       /* character */
short sh;                       /* short */
float fv;                       /* float */
    . . . .
ch = va_arg(args, int);        /* get a character */
sh = va_arg(args, int);        /* get a short */
fv = va_arg(args, double);     /* get a double */
```

show you how to fetch a character, a short, and a float from the argument list. Recall that C promotes these smaller data types to their larger counterparts when you pass them to functions. Unless you access them with the right size, you'll pop the stack incorrectly and get meaningless values.

Your program must also know the number of arguments to fetch from the stack. There is a way to handle this at run time, which we will return to later. The C library, however, provides a set of routines that access arguments from an argument list without you having to specify each argument individually. Here's the list of routines:

```
/* display to standard out */
int vprintf(fmt, args)
char *fmt;
va_list args;

/* display to file stream */
int vfprintf(stream, fmt, args)
FILE *stream;
char *fmt;
va_list args;

/* memory to memory conversion */
int vsprintf(s, fmt, args)
char *s, *fmt;
va_list args;
```

The vprintf() routine is like printf(), and vsprintf() is similar to the memory to memory conversion routine sprintf(). Our debug() routine uses vfprintf() to display debug information on standard error. Note that we fetch the format string with va_arg() before we call vfprintf() to display the rest of the argument list.

The last function call in debug() is va_end(), which cleans up the argument list. You need to pass the same name to this routine that you use with va_start().

## How varargs Works

The varargs.h header file is readable, so let's take a look at it. Here's the one from the /usr/include directory on our XENIX system.

```
typedef char            *va_list;

#define va_dcl          int va_alist;
#define va_start(list)  list = (char *) &va_alist
#define va_end(list)
#define va_arg(list, mode)  ((mode *) (list += sizeof(mode)))[-1]
```

Before we get started, we should mention that yours may look different than ours. Versions of varargs.h can vary from machine to machine and even from one compiler to another. Furthermore, the ANSI C standard uses a different header file called stdarg.h. Let's discuss our version first, which should be similar, if not identical to yours. Appendix E discusses stdarg.h under ANSI C.

The varargs.h file contains the definitions for the special names you use in your programs. The first line typedef's va_list so that the name you choose for the argument list in your program becomes a character pointer. The second line defines  va_dcl as an integer called  va_alist. This is the same special name you use for the argument list in your program. You can't place a semicolon after the word  va_dcl in your program because there's already one in the declaration (two of them produces a compilation error).

The lines

```
#define va_start(list)          list = (char *) &va_alist
#define va_end(list)
```

define what  va_start() and  va_end() do. Actually,  va_end() doesn't do anything on our machine, but  va_start() casts the address of the first argument on the stack (va_alist) to a character pointer and assigns it to your name for the argument list. This is important because subsequent fetches of arguments from the stack use a character pointer to move through memory.

va_arg() does the hard work with the line

```
#define va_arg(list, mode)    ((mode *)(list += sizeof(mode)))[-1]
```

This tidy bit of code pops an arbitrary argument of any size from the stack. Suppose, for example, we call  va_arg() to fetch an integer and store it in  num. The call

```
    num = va_arg(args, int);              /* get an integer */
```

becomes

```
num = ((int *)(args += sizeof(int)))[-1];   /* get an integer */
```

after preprocessor substitution. The compiler evaluates this statement in several steps. First, the argument character pointer  args is incremented by the size of an integer. This makes it point to the next argument, past the one we want. Next, we cast  args as a pointer to an integer and apply a *negative subscript* to move back to the integer argument on the stack. (Chapter 3 discusses negative subscripts.) This positions  args to the next argument on the stack and gives us an integer argument, all in one step.

The technique applies to any C data type. Suppose, for example,  s is a structure of type  something. The call

```
s = va_arg(args, struct something);    /* get a structure */
```

becomes

```
s = ((struct something *)(args += sizeof(struct something)))[-1];
```

This pops a structure from the stack and assigns it to  s. Now  args points to the next argument.

## A Sample Front End

We mentioned earlier that your routine must know how many arguments to pop off the stack. Unless you use one of the C library functions like vprintf(), your function must have access to both the number of arguments and the appropriate data types. Without this information, your routine cannot access each argument individually.

The following program, called mypass.c, provides a simple mechanism to call routines that need this information. The function mypass() is a front end to any routine that needs to access arguments individually from an argument list. Using a format string similar to printf() and scanf(), mypass() knows how many arguments are on the stack and what their data types are. Here's the first part of the code.

```
/* mypass.c - pass variable number of data
                types to one function */

#include <stdio.h>
#include <varargs.h>

main()
{
    static char buf[] = "string of data";
    int num = 44;
    char c = 'X';
    float f = 6.72;

    mypass("%s", buf);
    mypass("%s %d", buf, num);
    mypass("%s %d %c", buf, num, c);
    mypass("%s %d %c %f", buf, num, c, f);
    mypass("%f %c %d %s", f, c, num, buf);
    mypass("%x", num);
}
```

This version of mypass() handles only strings, floats, integers, and characters. The conversion characters inside the format string for mypass() are the same as printf()'s, except that "%x" is illegal (we include it to demonstrate error checking).

Now let's look at the function mypass():

```
mypass(va_alist)              /* front end for variable arg list */
va_dcl
{
    va_list args;                     /* argument list */
    char *fmt, *p;
    int inum;                         /* for integers */
    double fnum;                      /* for floats, doubles */
    char *ps;                         /* for strings */
    int ch;                           /* for a character */

    va_start(args);                   /* initialize arg list */
    fmt = va_arg(args, char *);       /* get the format first */

    printf("\nmypass called with format %s\n", fmt);

    for (p = fmt; *p; p++ ) {        /* loop over format line */
        if (*p == '%')
            switch (p[1]) {
                case 's':
                    ps = va_arg(args, char *);        /* string */
                    printf("    string    = %s\n", ps);
                    break;
                case 'd':
                    inum = va_arg(args, int);         /* integer */
                    printf("    integer   = %d\n", inum);
                    break;
                case 'c':
                    ch = va_arg(args, int);           /* character */
                    printf("    character = %c\n", ch);
                    break;
                case 'f':
                    fnum = va_arg(args, double);      /* double */
                    printf("    double    = %g\n", fnum);
                    break;
                default:
                    printf("   %c is an illegal format\n", p[1]);
                    break;
            }
    }
    va_end(args);                     /* clean up argument list */
}
```

mypass() calls the varargs routines to access the argument list. Note that the function declares an int to fetch a char argument and a double to fetch a float. A for statement loops through the format string and a switch calls va_args() for the appropriate data type. This technique allows you to access an arbitrary number of arguments of any data type.

Let's run the program and show you the output.

```
$ mypass

mypass called with format %s
    string    =  string of data

mypass called with format %s %d
    string    =  string of data
    integer   =  44

mypass called with format %s %d %c
    string    =  string of data
    integer   =  44
    character =  X

mypass called with format %s %d %c %f
    string    =  string of data
    integer   =  44
    character =  X
    double    =  6.72

mypass called with format %f %c %d %s
    double    =  6.72
    character =  X
    integer   =  44
    string    =  string of data

mypass called with format %x
    x is an illegal format
```

The program's output displays the format string as well as the data. Note that we can pass the same number of variables to `mypass()` in any order. Here, `mypass()` considers `"%x"` an illegal format, but the program may be extended to handle this format as well as others. Furthermore, if the arguments are all pointers (like `scanf()` and the UNIX system call `execl()`), `mypass()` could use the convention that the last argument must be a NULL pointer.

Appendix E (Turbo C) contains an ANSI C version of `mypass.c` using `stdarg.h`.

## ♦ Summary ♦

- The operators ++, --, and the assignment operators (=, +=, *=, etc.) produce side effects because they modify variables.

- If an expression has subexpressions with the same variable name and with side effect operators, C may evaluate the expression differently on different machines. The code, therefore, is not portable.

- Sequence guarantee points connect subexpressions and make all expressions with side effect operators execute portably.

- The operators &&, ||, ?:, and the comma operator (,) are sequence guarantee points.

- Complex declarations use arrays, pointers, and functions. The right-left rule helps you to decipher complex declarations and create new ones.

- The compiler requires an lvalue on the left side of an assignment statement and an rvalue on the right side. You may modify lvalues but not rvalues. The name of an array is not an lvalue.

- C allows structure assignment but not array assignment.

- Fast array transfers embed arrays inside structures. Using structure assignment, the technique moves data between arrays of the same size without calling a library function. The implementation is machine dependent.

- Programs may also use a structure with an array member to pass entire arrays to functions. Functions may return arrays with the same approach.

- The include files `varargs.h` and `stdarg.h` (ANSI C) provide a portable way for programs to support functions with a variable number of arguments and varying data types.

# ♦ Exercises ♦

1. Which of the following expressions are portable?

   ```
   *p >= '0' && *p++ <= '9' || *p >= 'a' && *p++ <= 'f';

   a[i] = i++ > 10 ? 10 : i;

   f(++*p, ++p);

   g((++*p, ++p));

   while (++argv, --argc)
   ```

2. The following program increments each element of an integer array.

   ```
   /* table.c - increment each element of a table */

   main()
   {
       static int tbl[2][3] = {
           1, 2, 3,
           4, 5, 6
       };
       int *p;

       for (p = (int *)tbl; p < (int *)tbl + 6;)
           ++*p++;

       for (p = (int *)tbl; p < (int *)tbl + 6;)
           printf("%2d", *p++);
       putchar('\n');
   }

   $ table
    2 3 4 5 6 7
   ```

   Can you explain what ++*p++ does? Is this an lvalue?

3. What is the following declaration?

   ```
   char (*(*pf))()[10];
   ```

   Are there too many parentheses? In other words, does

```
char *(*pf)()[10];
```

compile without error?

4. How would you code the following in a declaration statement?

   `buf` is an array of 20 pointers to functions that return pointers to an array
   of 10 pointers to `float`s.

5. Using the fast array transfer technique for characters, create your own version of the C library routine `strncpy()`. For large strings, which do you
   think is faster? Why is this new version *not* a good replacement?

6. Can fast array transfers be used with *overlapping* memory arrays?

7. Examine the following program and its output:

   ```
   /* fstring.c - fast array transfers for strings */

   #include <stdio.h>
   #define MAX 80

   main()
   {
     struct chars {
       char buf[MAX];
     };

     char a[MAX];

     *(struct chars *)a = *(struct chars *)"hello";

     printf("%s\n", a);
   }

   $ fstring
   hello
   ```

   Does this make sense? Can you explain what is happening at run time?
   How portable is this code?

8. Modify `sort2.c` to pass a *two-dimensional* array to the sort function. Use a
   pointer to an integer in `sort()` to sort the data. Can you think of faster
   ways to pass multidimensional arrays as members of structures?

9. Write your own version of `scanf()` for strings, integers, and floats. The
   new routine, called `myscanf()`, includes error checks that `scanf()`
   doesn't provide (illegal characters, NULL pointers, etc.). The call

```
int *pnum;
 .  .  .  .
myscanf("%d", pnum);
```

for example, should display an error message if pnum is NULL. Likewise, the call

```
float fval;
 .  .  .  .
myscanf("%f", &fval);
```

should display an error message if you pass illegal characters for the float fval. Use either varargs.h or stdarg.h to implement myscanf().

10. Write a version of printf() for strings, integers, and floats called myprintf() that includes error checks where applicable. Implement myprintf() with either varargs.h or stdarg.h.

# C Debugging Techniques

"**A**t the source of every error which is blamed on the computer, you will find at least two human errors, including the error of blaming it on the computer."†

The effort required to debug software is underestimated in a project. Part of the problem is that modifying software is too easy. There are no voltages or currents to correct, no hardware components to replace. You need only an editor, a little time, and, (hopefully) some thought. Once a program's organization and algorithms are in place, it's tempting to apply the "hope for the best" attitude. Programmers often search for debugging tools near the end of a software project (when it may be too late), instead of deciding what tools to use at the start.

We've discovered the development of custom tools is often ignored in large software projects. Custom debugging tools aid the software development cycle in several ways. One, you can apply debugging tools during the design cycle to detect bugs before they show up. Two, you can use the same tools during the software's debugging and maintenance phase. And three, you don't have to worry about someone else's debugging tool not providing you with the information you want.

We call this *defensive programming*. Even time-critical programs have areas that can tolerate embedded debug code. Perhaps the best approach is to combine custom tools with your favorite C debugger.

In this chapter, we look at different ways to use C for debugging. Several techniques use the C preprocessor, and others customize library routines and work with compiler options.

---

† A fortune from the Berkeley 4BSD edition of UNIX.

# ◆ Overview of C Debugging ◆

## C Preprocessor

Preprocessor statements allow debug statements to coexist with production code. This chapter presents several C preprocessor techniques that are helpful for debugging. *Embedded test drivers*, for example, allow modules to test themselves. Header files provide uniform protocols for debug function calls. *Command line flags* affect how a program displays debug output.

## ASCII and Hexadecimal Debug Display

As an example of a custom debugging tool, we present a program that dumps data in hexadecimal and ASCII on the screen. Other sections have programs that include this tool to demonstrate debugging techniques.

## Signals with Debug Output

C programs may receive signals from other programs, or possibly, from themselves. This section shows you how to to display debug output by interrupting an executing program with keyboard characters.

## Assertions

Assertions pinpoint run time errors before a program fails or behaves strangely. Assertions are designed specifically for debugging, yet few people use them. This section shows you what assertions are, how to use them, and how to create your own.

## Selective Debug Prints

Most debugging strategies require recompilation. *Selective debug prints* allow you to display debug output without recompiling any module in your system. This can be a lifesaver for large programs.

## Customized Memory Allocators

Many C programs rely heavily on run time storage management. Bugs are difficult to track down with the standard C library routines. This section presents storage allocator *front ends* that check for errors and display informative error messages when errors occur.

# ◆ C Preprocessor ◆

When you compile C programs, the preprocessor makes the first pass through each source file. The preprocessor, which is usually not part of the C compiler, has a syntax all its own. We assume you already know most of the preprocessor's features, so we'll just look at the ones relevant to debugging.

The preprocessor statement

```
#define NAME string
```

for example, defines NAME as string in a source file. Subsequent C statements may use NAME or test its value.   NAME does not always require a value, however. Recall that the preprocessor statement

```
#define MAX
```

defines MAX as 1.

The C compiler has command line options that are handy for debugging. The C compiler's -D option allows you to define preprocessor symbols without editing your source code.  There are two command line formats.

```
$ cc -DNAME args
```

```
$ cc -DNAME=string args
```

Both formats define NAME (like a #define does in your source file). Let's start with the first format, which defines NAME. Programs use #ifdef to conditionally compile code in source files. Suppose, for example, a program called pgm.c contains the following statements:

```
#ifdef DBUG
    printf("val = %d ptr = %x\n", val, p);
#endif
    . . .
#ifdef DBUG
    printf("servo called\n");
#endif
```

Compiling pgm.c with the -DDBUG option includes the printf() statements. Without the option, they are not compiled.  Note, however, that it's best not to use printf() statements here, because you may want to *redirect* pgm's output. Under UNIX, for example, the command lines

```
$ pgm > file
$ pgm  2> errors
```

make pgm's standard output appear in file and its standard error appear in errors, respectively. The printf() routine writes to standard output and fprintf() writes to a file or to standard error (if you use stderr as the first argument). In any case, you won't see any output on your terminal screen with redirection.

If you make fprintf() write to stderr (standard error), you can save debug output separately from standard output using redirection. fprintf(), therefore, is a better choice for debugging than printf(). Here's the same code again from pgm.c, only this time with fprintf() statements:

```
#include <stdio.h>
    . . . .
#ifdef DBUG
    fprintf(stderr, "val = %d ptr = %x\n", val, p);
#endif
    . . .
#ifdef DBUG
    fprintf(stderr, "servo called\n");
#endif
```

Be sure to include the stdio.h header file, since that's where stderr is defined. With this approach, you can redirect debug output to a separate file when you run your program, as follows:

```
$ cc -DDBUG pgm.c -o pgm
$ pgm  2>  dbug
    . . . program output . . .
$ cat dbug
val = 46 ptr = fa3d
servo called
```

Now let's discuss the command line format

```
$ cc -DNAME=string args
```

This format sets NAME to *string*, which allows programs to use #if's and test NAME's value. The following program called dumpbuf.c, for example, uses DBUG's value to display an array in hexadecimal, octal, or decimal.

**Program 5-1**

```
/* dumpbuf.c - displays buffer in decimal,
               octal, or hexadecimal */

#include <stdio.h>

#define MAXBUF 35
#define DEC 0

main()
{
    unsigned int buf[MAXBUF];
    int i;

    for (i = 0; i < MAXBUF; i++)
        buf[i] = i + 1;

#if DBUG > 0 && DBUG < 3
    printa(buf, MAXBUF, DBUG);
#endif
    putchar('\n');
    printa(buf, MAXBUF, DEC);
}

printa(pb, nitems, debug)
register unsigned int *pb;
int nitems, debug;
{
    register int i;
    static char *pfmt[3] = {"%4d%c", "%4x%c", "%4o%c"};

    for (i = 0; i < nitems; i++)
        printf(pfmt[debug], *pb++, (i + 1) % 10 ? ' ' : '\n');
    putchar('\n');
}
```

dumpbuf.c uses #if instead of #ifdef to test DBUG's value. The program passes DBUG as a parameter to printa() if it's greater than zero. This allows printa() to use it as a local variable called debug. Although printa() could use DBUG directly, this approach allows the function to be in another file that's not compiled with -DDBUG.

  printa() loops through the buffer with a pointer and displays 10 items on a line. The function uses debug as an array subscript to select a hexadecimal, decimal, or octal format for the display.

Here's how we display the buffer in hexadecimal.

```
$ cc -DDBUG=1 dumpbuf.c -o dumpbuf
$ dumpbuf
    1    2    3    4    5    6    7    8    9    a
    b    c    d    e    f   10   11   12   13   14
   15   16   17   18   19   1a   1b   1c   1d   1e
   1f   20   21   22   23

    1    2    3    4    5    6    7    8    9   10
   11   12   13   14   15   16   17   18   19   20
   21   22   23   24   25   26   27   28   29   30
   31   32   33   34   35
```

The first four lines display the buffer in hexadecimal and the last four display it in decimal.

Recompiling dumpbuf.c with DBUG set to 2 displays the same data in octal.

```
$ cc -DDBUG=2 dumpbuf.c -o dumpbuf
$ dumpbuf
    1    2    3    4    5    6    7   10   11   12
   13   14   15   16   17   20   21   22   23   24
   25   26   27   30   31   32   33   34   35   36
   37   40   41   42   43

    1    2    3    4    5    6    7    8    9   10
   11   12   13   14   15   16   17   18   19   20
   21   22   23   24   25   26   27   28   29   30
   31   32   33   34   35
```

The last example compiles dumpbuf.c without debugging and displays the buffer only in decimal.

```
$ cc dumpbuf.c -o dumpbuf
$ dumpbuf
    1    2    3    4    5    6    7    8    9   10
   11   12   13   14   15   16   17   18   19   20
   21   22   23   24   25   26   27   28   29   30
   31   32   33   34   35
```

Note that dumpbuf.c does not conditionally compile printa(). This makes it available to other modules in our system when we are not debugging. In fact, the program calls printa() to display the buffer in decimal in each of the previous examples. This is why printa() writes to standard output with printf() and putchar() instead of standard error.

# ♦ Embedded Test Drivers ♦

Another use of the −D compiler option is to embed *test drivers* in your source code. This allows you to test modules for bugs during development, and more importantly, track down problems later. You'll typically want to include a main() program in the driver that prompts for input or sets certain values. Here's the approach:

**Program 5-2**

```
/* pgm.c - embedded test drivers */

#ifdef DRIVER
main(argc, argv)
int argc;
char *argv[];
{
    /* input test code here */
    subr1();
    subr2();
}
#endif

subr1()
{
  /* subroutine code */
}

subr2()
{
  /* subroutine code */
}
```

The following command line compiles and tests the pgm.c module:

```
$ cc -DDRIVER pgm.c -o pgm
```

You can now supply input to pgm from a file or from the keyboard. When you're satisfied that the subroutines work, recompile it with the −c option.

```
$ cc -c pgm.c
```

This creates a pgm.o module that you can link with other modules to build complete programs.

Let's look at an example. The module `hex.c` contains a function that converts a hexadecimal string to an integer. We embed a test driver for debugging. Here's the file:

**Program 5-3**

```
/* hex.c - hexadecimal to integer conversion */

#include <stdio.h>
#define tolower(c)   ((c) >= 'A' && (c) <= 'Z' ? \
                             (c) - 'A' + 'a' : (c))
#define isxdigit(c)  ((c) >= '0' && (c) <= '9' || \
         (c) >= 'a' && (c) <= 'f' || (c) >= 'A' && (c) <= 'F')

#ifdef DRIVER
main(argc, argv)
int argc;
char *argv[];
{
   unsigned hex();

   if (argc == 1) {
      fprintf(stderr, "Usage: hex <number>\n");
      exit(1);
   }
   printf("%u\n", hex(argv[1]));
}
#endif

unsigned hex(p)
char *p;
{
    unsigned char digit;
    unsigned result = 0;

    for (; *p; p++) {
       if (!isxdigit(*p)) {
          fprintf(stderr, "%c is an illegal hex char\n", *p);
          exit(1);
       }
       digit -= ((digit = tolower(*p)) <= '9') ? '0' : 'a' - 10;
       result = (result << 4) + digit;
    }
    return result;
}
```

The driver allows you to input test data for `hex()` from the command line. It includes a *usage* message if you call it improperly (a good idea if it's been a while since the last test!). The `printf()` statement displays the integer that `hex()` converts from the first argument on the command line.

Note that we define our own macros for `tolower` and `isxdigit` in `hex.c`. On most systems, you can substitute the line

```
#include <ctype.h>
```

for our macro definitions, but some implementations have versions of `tolower` (and `toupper`) that do *not* check if a character is uppercase (or lowercase) before they convert it. Consequently, programs like `hex.c` may convert characters incorrectly. This is a portability issue and one that you'll have to deal with if you compile and run programs with character macros on different machines.

Inside `hex()`, the statements

```
digit -= ((digit = tolower(*p)) <= '9') ? '0' : 'a' - 10;
result = (result << 4) + digit;
```

use a combination of techniques we showed you in Chapter 1 to convert the hexadecimal string to an integer inside a loop. As an exercise, try and work through these statements with several strings to see how it works.

Let's compile the program with the driver and show you the output from several runs.

```
$ cc -DDRIVER hex.c -o hex
$ hex
Usage: hex <number>
$ hex ff
255
$ hex Ff
255
$ hex abc
2748
$ hex dog
o is an illegal hex char
```

Once we convince ourselves that the routine works, we recompile it as follows:

```
$ cc -c hex.c
```

Now we can link `hex.o` with the rest of our system. Later, if we find a bug, we can recompile `hex.c` with the driver and test it against the input that makes it fail.

# ♦ ASCII and Hexadecimal Debug Display ♦

Let's put all this together to produce our first custom tool: an ASCII and hexadecimal display of memory. We have several requirements. First, we make it a function so that other programs may call it. Second, we have the routine display data on standard error. This allows us to capture output separately from the rest of the system.

Let's call our program `adump.c` and use two compile time `-D` options. The first, called `DRIVER`, tests `adump` with a driver program. The second, called `TEST`, produces a table of ASCII characters in ascending order. Here's how we compile `adump.c`.

```
$ cc -DDRIVER -DTEST adump.c -o adump
```

`adump` requires a buffer size as its single argument. For example,

```
$ adump
Usage: adump size
```

produces a usage message.

Let's test `adump.c` with a buffer size of 128. Since we compile it with `TEST` defined, `adump` produces the following table of ASCII characters.

```
$ adump 128
000:    0001 0203 0405 0607 0809 0a0b 0c0d 0e0f    ................
016:    1011 1213 1415 1617 1819 1a1b 1c1d 1e1f    ................
032:    2021 2223 2425 2627 2829 2a2b 2c2d 2e2f     !"#$%&'()*+,-./
048:    3031 3233 3435 3637 3839 3a3b 3c3d 3e3f    0123456789:;<=>?
064:    4041 4243 4445 4647 4849 4a4b 4c4d 4e4f    @ABCDEFGHIJKLMNO
080:    5051 5253 5455 5657 5859 5a5b 5c5d 5e5f    PQRSTUVWXYZ[\]^_
096:    6061 6263 6465 6667 6869 6a6b 6c6d 6e6f    `abcdefghijklmno
112:    7071 7273 7475 7677 7879 7a7b 7c7d 7e7f    pqrstuvwxyz{|}~.
```

The display has three parts. On the left, `adump` displays a decimal offset of memory, starting at zero. The middle part is hexadecimal data and the right part is the same data in ASCII. `adump` prints '.' for unprintable ASCII characters.

The `adump` program writes data to standard error, so we can save it in a file. Let's demonstrate this by saving 58 entries to the file `f1`.

```
$ adump 58 2> f1
$ cat f1
000:    0001 0203 0405 0607 0809 0a0b 0c0d 0e0f    ................
016:    1011 1213 1415 1617 1819 1a1b 1c1d 1e1f    ................
032:    2021 2223 2425 2627 2829 2a2b 2c2d 2e2f     !"#$%&'()*+,-./
048:    3031 3233 3435 3637 3839                    0123456789
```

When you compile `adump.c` without `TEST`, `adump` produces a table of random data. This confirms `adump`'s ability to display arbitrary data from memory. Here are two examples.

```
$ cc -DDRIVER adump.c -o adump
```

```
$ adump 128
000:    5152 201b 5014 5020 1614 4231 0b39 1763    QR .P.P ..B1.9.c
016:    1427 2508 796f 3639 7779 0626 252d 7b1d    .'%.yo69wy.&%-{.
032:    0764 225b 7312 6e16 282f 2f46 276a 5337    .d"[s.n.(//F'jS7
048:    590d 6050 5f2e 2d20 361b 632e 1303 377d    Y.`P_.- 6.c...7}
064:    7864 6561 1938 6b05 725f 0b37 254b 7e7a    xdea.8k.r_.7%K~z
080:    146e 784a 4363 602d 6b5e 4b7e 5d55 3e79    .nxJCc`-k^K~]U>y
096:    1d6b 2005 3a21 0145 6e3b 0d5d 7a74 4e04    .k .:!.En;.]ztN.
112:    4061 254e 1d25 0637 0c5a 766e 7c3a 4667    @a%N.%.7.Zvn|:Fg
```

```
$ adump 77
000:    5e18 1c28 124d 3a5c 0a4d 7217 4c35 1b4c    ^..(.M:\.Mr.L5.L
016:    3734 2e4a 0655 236a 040c 0c7e 0f02 6e79    74.J.U#j...~..ny
032:    4f20 625e 345d 706a 3148 2600 3a54 7c59    O b^4]pj1H&.:T|Y
048:    7e67 6868 6421 3f0e 476c 5202 7248 447e    ~ghhd!?.GlR.rHD~
064:    5a54 2d2a 1e1b 7049 3f24 5c26 1f           ZT-*..pI?$\&.
```

This certainly appears random enough.

We show you `adump.c` in two parts. First, here's the driver.

**Program 5-4**

```
/* adump.c - ASCII to hexadecimal debug display */

#include <stdio.h>
#define HEX   1
#define ASCII 2

#ifdef DRIVER
#ifndef TEST
#define TEST 0
#endif
```

```
main(argc, argv)
int argc;
char *argv[];
{
    char *buf;
    char *malloc();
    int buf_size;          /* holds buffer size */

    if (argc == 1) {
        fprintf(stderr, "Usage: %s size\n", argv[0]);
        exit(1);
    }

    buf_size = atoi(argv[1]);
    buf = malloc(buf_size);
    if (buf == (char *) NULL) {
        fprintf(stderr, "Can't malloc on heap\n");
        exit(1);
    }

    fillbuf(buf, buf_size);    /* fill with data */
    adump(buf, buf_size);      /* ASCII to hex dump */
}

fillbuf(a, size)
char a[];
int size;
{
    register int i;

    srand(i);                      /* plant the random seed */

    for (i = 0; i < size; i++)
      a[i] = (TEST) ? i : rand() & 0x7f;
}
#endif
```

The driver consists of a `main()` program and one function called `fillbuf()`. If TEST is not defined, the driver defines it as 0. Next, the driver allocates memory for a buffer using the size specified on the command line and calls `fillbuf()` to fill it with data. The driver calls `adump()` to display the buffer.

`fillbuf()` looks at TEST to generate the data. If it's zero, the driver calls `rand()` for random data; otherwise, it fills the buffer with sequential numbers. Note that we mask `rand()`'s return value with 0x7f to store each number in the buffer as a 7-bit ASCII character.

Here's the second half of the program, which is part of the same file as the driver.

```
adump(p, size)                    /* ASCII to hex dump */
char *p;
int size;
{
    register int i;
    register char *q = p;

    for (i = 0; i < size; i += 16, q += 16) {
        fprintf(stderr, "\n%03d:\t", i);
        if (i + 16 <= size)
            putbyte(q, 16, HEX);
        else
            putbyte(q, size - i, HEX);
        if (size - i != 1)
            fputc('\t', stderr);
        if (i + 16 <= size)
            putbyte(q, 16, ASCII);
        else
            putbyte(q, size - i, ASCII);
    }
    fputc('\n', stderr);
}

putbyte(p, n, mode)               /* byte display */
char *p;
int n, mode;
{
    register char *q = p;
    register int i;

    for (i = 0; i < n; i++, q++) {
        if (mode == HEX) {
            if (i % 2 == 0)
                fputc(' ', stderr);
            fprintf(stderr, "%02x", *q);
            continue;
        }
        if (mode == ASCII)
            if (*q < ' ' || *q > '~')
                fputc('.', stderr);
            else
                fputc(*q, stderr);
    }
```

```
    if (n != 16) {       /* print the last line */
        for (i = 0; i < 16 - n; i++) {
            fputc(' ', stderr);
            if (mode == HEX) {
                fputc(' ', stderr);
                fputc(' ', stderr);
            }
        }
    }
}
```

This is the nitty-gritty code to produce the display. The `adump()` function uses a `for` loop to display the memory address and calls `putbyte()` to display at most 16 bytes at a time. The `putbyte()` routine uses `mode` (HEX or ASCII) to display the line. Both routines use register variables where appropriate and write data to standard error.

Once we test `adump` thoroughly, we compile it without the driver.

```
$ cc -c adump.c
```

This produces the file `adump.o`. We'll use it in the next section.

## ◆ Command Line Flags ◆

Conditionally compiling `fprintf()` statements in source files is tiresome to type repeatedly. A better technique calls a debug routine with a *flag* as an argument. This allows you to trigger different debug output from programs with command line flags. For example, instead of typing

```
#include <stdio.h>
  .  .  .  .
#ifdef DBUG
fprintf(stderr, "num = %u\n", num);
#endif
  .  .  .  .
#ifdef DBUG
fprintf(stderr, "val[5] = %d\n", val[5]);
#endif
```

you use

```
#include <stdio.h>
#include "debug.h"
 . . . .
DEBUG(1, "num = %u\n", num);
 . . . .
DEBUG(2, "val[5] = %d\n", val[5]);
```

We type the name DEBUG in uppercase, since it stands out more in the source file. And, as we will see shortly, DEBUG is actually a macro.

Let's discuss the approach. You must use a special header file, which we call debug.h. DEBUG calls display only one variable at a time. Each call to DEBUG uses a flag as the first argument. You may use as many debug flags as you want, up to a maximum defined in debug.h.

Suppose a program called pgm.c contains DEBUG calls. You compile pgm.c as follows.

```
$ cc -DDEBUG pgm.c -o pgm
```

This turns on debugging. To set a flag and display debug output, you execute pgm with the -D option. For example,

```
$ pgm arg1 arg2 . . . -D1
```

executes pgm with arguments arg1 arg2 . . . and enables debug flag 1. Inside pgm.c, DEBUG is called with flag 1 to display output on standard error. With this technique, an arbitrary number of debug flags can appear at the *end* of the command line following the arguments, but there are other ways to access the flags in any order (see Exercise 3).

Your program must call a special routine named DEBUGFLAGS to get the flags from the command line. You also need to provide an array to store flag numbers. When you compile a program without the -D option, the preprocessor removes the debug calls from your source code.

The following program (bytes.c) uses adump() from the previous section to demonstrate the technique. The program displays several characters followed by a list of numbers in ascending order. The numbers start at 0 and end with 1 less than the first command line argument. We use both characters and numbers to demonstrate that adump() handles printable as well as unprintable character values. Here's a sample run of bytes with a command line argument of 25.

```
$ bytes 25
000:    5072 696e 7461 626c 6520 6368 6172 7320    Printable chars
016:    2140 2324 255e 262a 2829 5f2b 3d7b 7d3f    !@#$%^&*()_+={}?
032:    556e 7072 696e 7461 626c 6520 696e 7473    Unprintable ints
048:    0001 0203 0405 0607 0809 0a0b 0c0d 0e0f    ................
064:    1011 1213 1415 1617 18                      .........
```

The display shows both the ASCII characters and the hexadecimal values for each byte in the buffer.

Now, let's run the program again. This time we enable flag 1 from the command line (using -D1).

```
$ bytes 25 -D1
buf size = 73

000:    5072 696e 7461 626c 6520 6368 6172 7320    Printable chars
016:    2140 2324 255e 262a 2829 5f2b 3d7b 7d3f    !@#$%^&*()_+={}?
032:    556e 7072 696e 7461 626c 6520 696e 7473    Unprintable ints
048:    0001 0203 0405 0607 0809 0a0b 0c0d 0e0f    ................
064:    1011 1213 1415 1617 18                      .........
```

In this example, flag 1 displays the buffer size. Note that we set the debug flag with -D1 at the *end* of the command line.

Now, let's look at bytes.c. The program calls DEBUGFLAGS to read the flags from the command line and calls adump() to display the data. Here's the code.

**Program 5-5**

```c
/* bytes.c - display bytes with adump() */

#include <stdio.h>
#include "debug.h"

int Debug[NFLAGS];                 /* holds debug flags */

main(argc, argv)
int argc;
char *argv[];
{
    char *s1 = "Printable chars !@#$%^&*()_+={}?Unprintable ints";
    char *buf, *malloc();
    int i, num, nbytes, offset;

    if (argc == 1) {
        fprintf(stderr, "Usage: %s count -Dflag . . .\n", argv[0]);
        exit(1);
    }

    DEBUGFLAGS(&argc, argv);       /* read in the flags */

    num = atoi(argv[1]);
    nbytes = strlen(s1) + num;
```

```
    DEBUG(1, "buf size = %d\n", nbytes);
    buf = malloc(nbytes);
    if (buf == (char *) NULL) {
        fprintf(stderr, "Can't malloc from heap\n");
        exit(1);
    }
    strcpy(buf, s1);
    offset = strlen(s1);
    for (i = 0; i < nbytes; i++)        /* generate data */
        buf[i + offset] = i;

    adump(buf, nbytes);                 /* display data */
}
```

In `bytes.c`, we include `debug.h` and declare an array called `Debug` to hold the flags. The maximum number of flags (`NFLAGS`) is defined in `debug.h`. The program calls `DEBUGFLAGS` to read the flag numbers from the command line (if any). We call `DEBUG` with `1` as an argument to display debug output if this flag is set on the command line.

The number of integers that `bytes` displays is read from the command line. The program calls `malloc()` to acquire memory to store them. The amount of memory we need is the argument number plus the size of the constant string pointed to by `s1`. The program fills heap memory with a constant string of printable characters followed by a set of sequential numbers. The `adump()` routine displays the data.

The call to `DEBUGFLAGS` (defined in `debug.h`) reads the flags from the command line. Note that we pass the *address* of `argc` to `DEBUGFLAGS`, which we will return to shortly.

The following command compiles `bytes.c` and enables debugging.

```
$ cc -DDBUG bytes.c adump.o -o bytes
```

Here's the code for `debug.h`, which does all the work.

```
/* debug.h - debug header file */

#define NFLAGS 16

#ifdef DBUG
#define TRUE 1
extern int Debug[];
#define DEBUG(flag, fmt, arg) \
    if (Debug[flag]) \
        fprintf(stderr, fmt, arg)
#define DEBUGFLAGS(pac, av)  \
    debugflags(pac, av)
```

```
static debugflags(pargc, argv)
int *pargc;
char *argv[];
{
    int argc = *pargc;        /* get argument count */
    int dflag;

    /* loop over command line backwards */
    while (argc-- > 1) {
      if (strncmp(argv[argc], "-D", 2) == 0) {
        if (sscanf(&argv[argc][2], "%d", &dflag) != 1 ||
           dflag >= NFLAGS) {
            fprintf(stderr,
                "%s is a bad debug option\n", argv[argc]);
            exit(1);
        }
        Debug[dflag] = TRUE;
        argv[argc] = NULL; /* put NULL at end of arg list */
        (*pargc)--;           /* decrement argument count */
      }
    }
}
#else
#define DEBUG(flag, fmt, arg)
#define DEBUGFLAGS(pac, av)
#endif
```

The header file `debug.h` allows a maximum of 16 flags. Note that if `bytes.c` is *not* compiled with `-DDBUG`, the preprocessor removes all calls to `DEBUG` and `DEBUGFLAGS` from the program. Otherwise, calls to the `DEBUG` macro check the `Debug` array for the appropriate flag and call `fprintf()` if it's set.

`debugflags()` reads flags from the command line in *reverse* order. When the routine finds a `-D` option, it uses `sscanf()` to get the flag number and set the appropriate flag in the `Debug` array. If the flag number has an illegal character, `sscanf()` returns an error and the program terminates.

Note that `debugflags()` uses the *address* of `argc`. This allows the function to decrement the argument count using the compact pointer expression

```
    (*pargc)--;              /* decrement argument count */
```

With this arrangement, programs that call `DEBUGFLAGS` may access their arguments without having to process (or even know about) `-D` options. Any number of arguments may appear on the command line before the flags. The statement

```
    argv[argc] = NULL;    /* put NULL at end of arg list */
```

stores a NULL pointer at the end of the argument list, which conforms to ANSI C.

We can include DEBUG statements in other modules as well. To demonstrate, let's call DEBUG in adump.c.

```
/* adump.c - ASCII to hexadecimal debug display */

#include <stdio.h>
#include "debug.h"
  . . . . . .
adump(p, size)                  /* ASCII to hex dump */
char *p;
int size;
{
  . . . . . .
    for (i = 0; i < size; i += 16, q += 16) {
        DEBUG(2, "\ni = %d\n", i);
  . . . . . .
putbyte(p, n, mode)             /* byte display */
char *p;
int n, mode;
  . . . . . .
    DEBUG(3, "\nn = %d\n", n);
    if (n != 16) {              /* print the last line */
        for (i = 0; i < 16 - n; i++) {
  . . . . . .
```

Note that adump.c includes the debug.h header file, but it does *not* declare the Debug array. (Debug is shared by all modules using DEBUG and is only declared once.) We recompile as follows.

```
$ cc -DDBUG bytes.c adump.c -o bytes
```

We may now display debug output from bytes in several ways. For example, the commands

```
$ bytes 25 -D2
```

```
$ bytes 25 -D3
```

display only debug output from adump. The command

```
$ bytes 25 -D2 -D3
```

combines two flags to display all debug output from adump.

Since the DEBUG macro writes to stderr, we may save debug display in a file. The command

```
$ bytes 25 -D1 -D2 -D3  2>  display
```

redirects debug output from both bytes and adump to file display.

## ♦ Signals with Debug Output ♦

This section examines how executing C programs may interrupt themselves to display debug output. The approach uses *signals*, which we discuss in Chapter 4. The following programs demonstrate the technique under UNIX.

The UNIX kernel provides the signal() system call for processes (executing programs) to send signals, either to another program or to itself. Programs must include the signal.h header file to use signals. The format is as follows.

```
#include <signal.h>
void func();
 .  .  .  .
signal(sig, func);              /* send a signal */
```

signal()'s first argument is a signal number from a list of integers in signal.h; its second argument is a pointer to a void function.

For debugging, we use a signal number and provide our own function. To illustrate, suppose we have a C program that processes data in a loop construct. We declare a function that the system calls when a predefined signal arrives (called an *interrupt*). The program loops until an interrupt makes the system call our function, which sets a flag and returns.

Inside the loop, the program checks the flag and if it's set, calls a routine to display debug statements. When the program enables the signal again, the scenario repeats. Programs write debug information to standard error, so we can capture output in a separate file.

Which signal number should we use for the interrupt? We don't want to use SIGINT, since that's how we terminate programs. Instead, we use SIGQUIT (called a *quit* signal), which by default terminates a program and creates a *core* file in your current directory. (The UNIX debuggers *adb* and *sdb* interrogate core files.) You may send this signal to your C program by typing control-\. Other signals are possible if you don't want to use SIGQUIT (see Exercise 4).

Here's an example to demonstrate the approach.

**Program 5-6**

```
/*  sig1.c - signals with debug output */

#include <stdio.h>
#include <signal.h>

static int debug;                      /* interrupt flag */

main()
{
   void catch();

   signal(SIGQUIT, catch);            /* enable interrupt */

   printf("running...\n");
   while (1)
     if (debug) {                     /* interrupt? */
        fprintf(stderr, "signal caught\n");
        debug = 0;                     /* reset interrupt flag */
        signal(SIGQUIT, catch);      /* enable interrupt */
     }
}

void catch()                           /* interrupt routine */
{
   signal(SIGQUIT, SIG_IGN); /* ignore further interrupts */
   debug = 1;                          /* set interrupt flag */
}
```

The program includes `signal.h` to use signals. The interrupt flag `debug` is declared `static` to avoid name conflicts with other modules. The first call to `signal()` inside `main()` tells the UNIX kernel that `SIGQUIT` is the interrupt. When we type `control-\`, the system calls `catch()`.

UNIX signals return to their defaults (terminate programs) whenever a signal arrives, so `catch()` calls `signal()` with the special name `SIG_IGN` to ignore more `SIGQUIT` signals. The `catch()` routine also sets `debug` before it returns.

Inside the main loop, the program checks the `debug` flag. If it's set (indicating an interrupt), the program displays the message

```
    signal caught
```

on standard error. After resetting `debug`, the program calls `signal()` to re-enable SIGQUIT as the interrupt, and the whole process repeats.

The `sig1` program writes the message to standard error in case we want to redirect the output to a separate file. To demonstrate, we'll run the program without redirection:

```
$ sig1
running...
control-\
signal caught
control-\
signal caught
control-\
signal caught
DEL
$
```

The output shows that we've caught all the interrupts and displayed the message each time. If we run the program and redirect standard error, we can capture the messages in a separate file.

The next example uses the same technique to dump a buffer to the screen while a program executes. Here's the first part.

**Program 5-7**

```
/*  sig2.c - signals with debug output */

#include <stdio.h>
#include <signal.h>
#define MAX 50

static int debug;                       /* interrupt flag */

main()
{
    unsigned char buf[MAX];             /* data buffer */
    void catch();

    signal(SIGQUIT, catch);             /* enable interrupt */

    printf("running...\n");
    while (1) {
        fillbuf(buf);
        if (debug) {                    /* interrupt? */
            display(buf);
            debug = 0;                  /* reset interrupt flag */
            signal(SIGQUIT, catch);     /* enable interrupt */
        }
    }
}
```

```
void catch()                          /* interrupt routine */
{
    signal(SIGQUIT, SIG_IGN);         /* ignore further interrupts */
    debug = 1;                        /* set interrupt flag */
}
```

It's basically the same, except the processing loop fills a buffer with data. When an interrupt occurs (debug is set), the program displays the buffer's contents and resets the interrupt flag. fillbuf() fills the buffer with data, and display() dumps it to the screen.

Here's the rest of the program.

```
fillbuf(p)                            /* fill data buffer */
unsigned char *p;
{
    register unsigned char *q = p;
    static unsigned char num;

    while (q < p + MAX)
        *q++ = num++;
}

display(pb)                           /* display data buffer */
register unsigned char *pb;
{
    register int i;

    for (i = 0; i < MAX; i++)
        fprintf(stderr, "%4d%c", *pb++,
                        (i + 1) % 10 ? ' ' : '\n');
    putc('\n', stderr);
    fflush(stderr);                   /* flush standard error */
}
```

Inside fillbuf(), num retains its value between function calls because it's declared static. Consequently, the function fills the buffer with different data each time main() calls it. display() prints out decimal data 10 items per line and is similar to the printa() routine discussed earlier in this chapter. The operating system may buffer output, so display() calls fflush() from the C library to flush the buffer and write the data to standard error.

Now let's run sig2 and observe the output:

```
$ sig2
running...
control-\
     88     89     90     91     92     93     94     95     96     97
     98     99    100    101    102    103    104    105    106    107
    108    109    110    111    112    113    114    115    116    117
    118    119    120    121    122    123    124    125    126    127
    128    129    130    131    132    133    134    135    136    137
control-\
     68     69     70     71     72     73     74     75     76     77
     78     79     80     81     82     83     84     85     86     87
     88     89     90     91     92     93     94     95     96     97
     98     99    100    101    102    103    104    105    106    107
    108    109    110    111    112    113    114    115    116    117
control-\
    132    133    134    135    136    137    138    139    140    141
    142    143    144    145    146    147    148    149    150    151
    152    153    154    155    156    157    158    159    160    161
    162    163    164    165    166    167    168    169    170    171
    172    173    174    175    176    177    178    179    180    181
DEL
$
```

The contents of the buffer is displayed each time we type control-\. We terminate the program by pressing the DEL key.

How useful is this technique? Bear in mind that signals do not behave like *real* interrupts, and things can get tricky with multiple processes. It's best to keep the number of debug statements to a minimum, since consecutive signals may scramble the output. Also, if a signal interrupts a system call under UNIX, the system call may fail and make the program terminate or behave strangely. We've found this technique to be most valuable for displaying small amounts of data while monitoring background tasks. You'll probably want to experiment with the approach to suit your application.

## ♦  Assertions  ♦

C program errors occur either at compile time or run time. Compile time errors are the easiest to debug, since the compiler points them out for you. Run time errors, however, are harder to track down. A program that appears to be working fine can suddenly produce strange results due to seemingly unrelated events. Finding these errors can be time consuming.

This section introduces a technique called *assertions* to help detect run time errors. Assertions are useful because they halt your program before a run time error can produce a strange symptom, or possibly terminate your program.

Assertions apply to any C data type, but they are most helpful with arrays, strings, and pointers. This section shows you how assertions work and how to customize them.

## What Is an Assertion?

Many run time errors are the result of reading or writing data from the wrong memory location. This happens, for example, when array elements reference memory outside an array's upper or lower bounds. Recall from Chapter 3 that the compiler can't warn you if you're using an array subscript incorrectly, because C converts array references to pointer offsets. Consequently, you're allowed to access an array with a subscript outside of its upper and lower bounds.

The following program demonstrates the problem.

```
/* field.c - array out of bounds */

#include <stdio.h>

main()
{
    char buf[10];

    putchar(buf[-3] = 'x');         /* dugout */
    putchar(buf[10] = 'y');         /* fence */
    putchar(buf[20] = 'z');         /* bleachers */
    putchar('\n');
}
```

This program compiles fine in C but would not if rewritten in PASCAL, for example. C converts `buf[20]` to `*(buf + 20)` and the program references memory outside of the 10 bytes allocated for `buf`. The same thing happens for the reference `buf[-3]`. The behavior of this program at run time varies. We've seen it display `"xyz"` on some machines but produce core dumps on others.

A remarkably easy technique that helps you locate an error like this is called an *assertion*. The formal definition of an assertion is the evaluation of a boolean expression that is expected to be TRUE at run time. If the expression evaluates to FALSE, the assertion fails. Programs with assertions terminate and display an error message that tells you where in the program the run time error occurred.

C implements assertions with an include file called `assert.h`. Include it in your source file as follows.

```
#include <stdio.h>
#include <assert.h>
    . . . .
```

Don't forget to include `stdio.h`, since `assert.h` uses names defined there. Assertions have the following formats.

```
assert (boolean expression)

assert (boolean expression);

assert (boolean expression) statement
```

If *boolean expression* evaluates to nonzero, the assertion is valid; otherwise, the program terminates with an error message. You may use any valid C expression here, but it's always evaluated as a boolean expression (TRUE or FALSE). You'll typically want to use one with relational and logical operators, although it's possible to use other things like function calls or pointers.

Note that the three different formats for assertions work the same way and it doesn't matter which one you use. A terminating semicolon, for instance, is optional with an assertion. You may also place an assertion on the same line as a program statement or on a line by itself. A command line option removes assertions from programs, to which we will return shortly.

Suppose you have the following declarations.

```
int digit, index, buffer[MAX];
char c;
double *pheap;
```

Here are several examples of assertions.

```
    . . . .
assert (c >= '0' && c <= '9')
digit = c - '0';
    . . . .
assert (index >= 0 && index < MAX);
buffer[index] = digit;
    . . . .
assert(pheap != (double *) NULL)    *pheap = 34.5;
```

The first assertion verifies `c` is an ASCII digit before converting it to a binary number. The second assertion won't allow a program to place `digit` into `buffer` if `index` is outside the bounds of the array. The last assertion makes sure that pointer `pheap` points to a valid memory location (i.e., is not `NULL`) before a program stores data there. If any of these assertions fail, the program terminates.

Assertions are valuable, because programs don't always have control of how variables get set. For example, `pheap` and `index` could receive values from command line arguments, keyboard input, or from another function. Without assertions, programs may fail or execute improperly. With assertions, we detect the error as soon as possible.

There are no hard and fast rules about *when* to use an assertion. As we mentioned, it's a good idea to use assertions when you can't control how variables receive values. Perhaps the best advice is to use assertions in areas of your code where a run time error may produce disastrous results. On the other hand, you shouldn't use assertions to replace error checks and messages, either. Assertions are best suited for situations that should *never* occur. This takes experience. As you design software, make a habit of including assertions in places where it's important to detect a problem early.

## Assertions with Arrays

Let's put assertions to work now. In the following programs, we'll use assertions to check command line arguments and strings, but keep in mind that this is for demonstration only. In production code you'll most likely want to use assertions for more critical type applications.

The first program called `array1.c`, has two command line arguments. The first argument is an array subscript and the second argument is a value to store there. Here's the code.

**Program 5-8**

```
/* array1.c - array bounds without assertions */

#include <stdio.h>
#define MAX 10

main(argc, argv)
int argc;
char *argv[];
{
    int buf[MAX], index, value;

    if (argc != 3) {
        fprintf(stderr, "Usage: %s index value\n", argv[0]);
        exit(1);
    }
    index = atoi(argv[1]);          /* first argument */
    value = atoi(argv[2]);          /* second argument */

    buf[index] = value;
    printf("buf[%d] = %d\n", index, buf[index]);
}
```

The `array1.c` program is particularly prone to run time errors, since the first argument (index) may be any number.  The following test run, for example, made our XENIX 286 machine dump core.

```
$ cc array1.c -o array1
$ array1 12 99
Stack Overflow
Memory fault - core dumped
```

This appears explainable, since we're trying to store a value beyond the end of the array.

Note that `array1` does not always dump core, however.  Here's another run with a different subscript.

```
$ array1 25 99
buf[25] = 99
```

In this case, `array1` appears to work and the run time error goes undetected.

The next program is similar to `array1.c` but has an assertion.

**Program 5-9**

```
/* array2.c - array bounds with assertions */

#include <stdio.h>
#include <assert.h>
#define MAX 10

main(argc, argv)
int argc;
char *argv[];
{
    int buf[MAX], index, value;

    if (argc != 3) {
        fprintf(stderr, "Usage: %s index value\n", argv[0]);
        exit(1);
    }
    index = atoi(argv[1]);          /* first argument */
    value = atoi(argv[2]);          /* second argument */

    assert(index >= 0 && index < MAX);

    buf[index] = value;
    printf("buf[%d] = %d\n", index, buf[index]);
}
```

Here's a test run.

```
$ cc array2.c -o array2
$ array2 12 99
Assertion failed: file array2.c, line 20
```

This diagnostic message locates the failed assertion in your source code and displays *both* the line number *and* the filename. On some systems, the diagnostic message includes the assertion with the filename and the line number. If your system's message looks like ours, we show you how to make the message display the assertion later on. The Appendices also show you how assertions work with different UNIX and DOS C compilers.

## Assertions with Strings

Let's try assertions with strings. The following program, called string1.c, initializes two character arrays. It concatenates its first command line argument with the first string in the program. Here's the code.

**Program 5-10**

```
/* string1.c - strings without assertions */

#include <stdio.h>
#include <string.h>
#define MAX 15

main(argc, argv)
int argc;
char *argv[];
{
    static char s1[MAX] = "teststring";
    static char s2[20] = "another string";

    if (argc == 1) {
        fprintf(stderr, "Usage: %s string\n", argv[0]);
        exit(1);
    }
    printf("s2 = %s\n", s2);
    strcat(s1, argv[1]);            /* first argument */
    printf("s1 = %s\n", s1);
    printf("s2 = %s\n", s2);
}
```

The strcat() routine places the command line string at the end of s1. The program displays both strings.

Here's a test run of `string1.c`.

```
$ cc string1.c -o string1
$ string1 overflow
s2 = another string
s1 = teststringoverflow
s2 = ow
```

On our XENIX 286 machine, `string1.c` clobbers `s2`. The program concatenates `s1` and `"overflow"` correctly, but it overwrites `s2`. Here's an example of a C library function doing the damage and not a user program. This, of course, is not `strcat()`'s fault, since it works with character pointers and knows nothing about array bounds.

Let's see if an assertion helps.

**Program 5-11**

```c
/* string2.c - strings with assertions */

#include <stdio.h>
#include <string.h>
#include <assert.h>
#define MAX 15

main(argc, argv)
int argc;
char *argv[];
{
    static char s1[MAX] = "teststring";
    static char s2[20] = "another string";

    if (argc == 1) {
        fprintf(stderr, "Usage: %s string\n", argv[0]);
        exit(1);
    }
    assert(strlen(argv[1]) < MAX - strlen(s1));

    printf("s2 = %s\n", s2);
    strcat(s1, argv[1]);                /* first argument */
    printf("s1 = %s\n", s1);
    printf("s2 = %s\n", s2);
}
```

```
$ cc string2.c -o string2
$ string2 overflow
Assertion failed: file string2.c, line 19
```

As before, the program terminates before the damage is done. We know the file and line number where the assertion failed.

## Assertions with Pointers

Assertions help validate a pointer's address. Many run time bugs are caused by a corrupt pointer address or an uninitialized pointer. Assertions prevent core dumps and stop good data from being overwritten with bad data in memory. Let's explore several ways to use assertions with pointers.

First, assertions can check return values from storage allocator function calls. Suppose, for example, you need to allocate storage to hold a block of integers at run time. The following code reserves space on the heap to hold two lists of integers.

```
int *pheap;
 .  .  .  .
pheap = (int *) malloc(1000 * sizeof(int));
assert(pheap != (int *) NULL);
 .  .  .  .
pheap = (int *) malloc(50 * sizeof(int));
assert(pheap != (int *) NULL);
 .  .  .  .
```

We use an assertion to make sure `malloc()` has the room. If we run out of heap space, the program terminates. We may do this many places in our program, so the assertion helps tell us which allocator call fails.

Second, assertions help functions with pointers to arrays. The assertion verifies that a pointer's value is inside the bounds of an array. This works when the array and its upper bound are known inside the function. The following statements outline the approach.

```
#define MAX 100
double fval[MAX];
 .  .  .  .

servo(pd)
double *pd;
{
    assert(pd >= fval && pd < fval + MAX);
 .  .  .  .
}
```

The program declares `fval` as an array of doubles. Inside `servo()`, `pd` points to an array element. An assertion verifies that `pd`'s range is within the bounds of array `fval` before the function uses the pointer. Note that `fval` and MAX are available to the assertion because they are defined external to `servo()`.

Third, assertions apply to pointers that support *linked lists*. Suppose, for example, a program has the following declarations in a header file called `defs.h`.

```
$ cat defs.h
struct node {
    int data;
    struct node *fwd, *back;
};
struct node *phead, *ptail;
    . . . .
```

These declarations define a doubly linked circular list, as shown in Fig. 5-1.

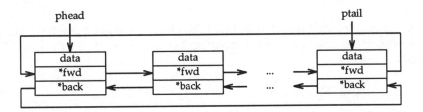

*Fig. 5-1.* Circular doubly linked list

Each node has an integer and a forward and backward pointer. The arrangement allows you to access data in the list quickly, since you can go forward or backward from any node. Here, `phead` points to the start of the list and `ptail` points to the end.

Let's examine a routine called `display_list()` that "walks" through the list, printing out data at each node. `display_list()` has pointer arguments for the starting and ending nodes to display. We could, for instance, display all the data in the list with

```
display_list(phead, ptail);
```

but we could print only parts of the list as well.

The `display_list()` routine traverses the list from a starting node (the first argument) to an ending node (the second argument). At the same time, the routine verifies that the list is intact; *i.e*, each node's forward pointer is pointing to a node whose backward pointer is pointing back to the current node. This is an example of using an assertion as a *consistency check*.

Here's the code for `display_list()`.

```
#include <stdio.h>
#include <assert.h>
#include "defs.h"

display_list(start, end);
struct node *start, *end;
{
    struct node *pnext;

    for (pnext = start; ;pnext = pnext->fwd) {
        assert(pnext == pnext->fwd->back);
        assert(pnext == pnext->back->fwd);
        printf("data = %d\n", pnext->data);
        if (pnext == end)
            return;
    }
}
```

We use `pnext` to walk forward in the linked list. We use an assertion at every node to check the `fwd` and `back` pointers before we print out the data. Note that the expression

```
pnext->fwd->back
```

evaluates left to right in C. This allows the program to look at the next node forward from `pnext` to verify that its backward pointer is the same address as `pnext`. We apply the same assertion to

```
pnext->back->fwd
```

## Deleting Assertions from Your Program

Although `assert()` appears to be a function, it's actually implemented as a *macro*. This means that assertions don't have function call overhead, but they do increase code size. Once your software becomes stable, you may wish to *delete* assertions from your source files. If run time errors appear, you can always reinsert assertions again.

The `-D` compiler option deletes assertions. The format is

```
$ cc -DNDEBUG . . .
```

where `NDEBUG` is a special name defined in `assert.h`. An assertion, therefore, is actually code which is conditionally compiled when the preprocessor symbol

NDEBUG is *not* defined. That's why compiling without the -DNDEBUG option automatically compiles assert() calls in your programs. To explore this further, we need to examine assert.h in more detail.

## How Assertions Work

Since an assertion is a macro, we can look at it in the file system. Here's the assert.h file from a typical UNIX system (DOS C compilers provide a similar file, also called assert.h).

```
1   /* assert.h */
2   /*
3   *       assert -- program verification
4   *
5   *       assert(expr);
6   *       int  expr;
7   */
8
9   #ifndef NDEBUG
10  #  define   assert(expr)\
11  if (!(expr)) {\
12      fprintf(stderr,"Assertion failed: file %s, line %d\n", \
13              _ _FILE_ _,  _ _LINE_ _);\
14      exit(1);\
15  }\
16  else
17  #else
18  #  define   assert(expr)
19  #endif
```

The line numbers don't appear in the header file. We've numbered them for reference. Your file may look different, but the concepts are similar. To see how assertions work, let's begin by following what happens when you delete assertions from your code.

Suppose you compile a program with -DNDEBUG to delete assertions. Line 9 uses #ifndef to see if NDEBUG is defined. Since it is, the preprocessor takes the #else path at line 17. The statement

```
18   #  define   assert(expr)
```

makes the preprocessor substitute *nothing* for assert() calls, effectively removing them from your program. After the preprocessor finishes, the C compiler never sees the assert() calls.

Now let's suppose you compile a program to include assertions. In this situation, NDEBUG is not defined, so the program defines an assertion starting at line 10. The preprocessor substitutes an assertion with the if statement shown on lines 11-16. This means that *every* assertion becomes an `if` statement of this form in your program. More importantly, the preprocessor substitutes the boolean expression from your assertion into the `if` statement where `expr` appears. After the preprocessor is through, the C compiler compiles the `if` statements as though they were part of your source file.

When your program runs, the `if` statement evaluates a boolean expression. If it's nonzero (TRUE), the `else` path executes at line 16. This means the assertion is valid and no error occurs. Otherwise, the `if` statement evaluates to zero (FALSE), and the assertion fails. In this case, lines 12-13 write a diagnostic message to standard error and line 14 terminates the program.

The `else` statement at line 16 is what allows assertions to have different formats. The format

```
assert(i >= 0 && i < MAX)    data[i] = 100;
```

for example, makes the preprocessor substitute

```
if (!(i >= 0 && i < 10)) { . . . } else data[i] = 100;
```

Note that this format makes the statement we are "asserting" become part of the `else` path. If, however, you use the format

```
assert(i >= 0 && i < MAX);
data[i] = 100;
```

the preprocessor substitutes

```
if (!(i >= 0 && i < 10)) { . . . } else ;
data[i] = 100;
```

and a NULL statement (`;`) follows the `else`. Regardless of which format you use, the result is the same.

Look closely at lines 12 and 13, where the names `_ _FILE_ _` and `_ _LINE_ _` appear. Typically these names are defined by the C preprocessor, but it's possible they could be part of the C compiler in some implementations. Here, we assume the preprocessor defines these names, which you can use in your programs. `_ _FILE_ _` becomes a string constant that contains the name of the source file being compiled, and `_ _LINE_ _` becomes an integer constant that contains the current line number in the file. The preprocessor assigns values to these constants before your program compiles. These special names are available to the assert macro and to your source files as well.

To demonstrate this, we compiled and ran the following program on our system.

**Program 5-12**

```
/* fline.c - display file and line
           numbers from the compiler */

main()
{
        printf("this is file %s\n", _ _FILE_ _);
        printf("line = %d\n", _ _LINE_ _);
        printf("line = %d\n", _ _LINE_ _);
        printf("line = %d\n", _ _LINE_ _);
        printf("line = %d\n", _ _LINE__ );
}
```

```
$ cc fline.c -o fline
$ fline
this is file fline.c
line = 6
line = 7
line = 8
line = 9
```

The program displays the name of the source file and a series of line numbers. Note that the preprocessor substitutes a new value for _ _LINE_ _ on each line.

You may want to use _ _LINE_ _ and _ _FILE_ _ in your own debugging routines. Be sure to check the exact symbol names because they may vary from system to system. Appendix E lists the special names available in ANSI C.

## Customizing Assertions

We've shown you the value of assertions and how they work. But there's more good news. It's possible to *modify* the standard assert macro or create your own version. We'll look at examples of both, starting with a custom one.

Assertion messages do not always have the same format. Some systems include the assertion in the error message along with the filename and line number. In other words, instead of displaying

```
Assertion failed: file pgm.c, line 12
```

you may see

```
Assertion failed: c >= '0' && c <= '9', file pgm.c, line 12
```

The second message is more informative than the first, so we'd like to modify the assert macro to produce this format if our system does not do it for us. To accomplish this, we create our own version of `assert.h`. Note that we'll need to use

```
#include "assert.h"
```

instead of the standard header file, however.

Here's our custom assert macro.

```
1    /* user-defined assert.h */
2
3    #ifndef NDEBUG
4    #   define   assert(expr)\
5    if (!(expr)) {\
6        fprintf(stderr, "Assertion failed: %s, ", "expr");\
7        fprintf(stderr, "file %s, line %d\n", _ _FILE_ _, _ _LINE_ _);\
8        exit(1);\
9    }\
10   else
11   #else
12   #   define   assert(expr)
13   #endif
```

As before, we've numbered the lines for reference. What makes this custom macro work is the expression

```
"expr"
```

in line 6. Here, the preprocessor substitutes your assertion between double quotation marks, making it a constant string, effectively. For example, an assertion that looks like

```
assert(ptr != NULL);
```

expands to

```
fprintf(stderr, "Assertion failed: %s, ", "ptr != NULL");\
```

after preprocessor substitution. Bear in mind that this technique will *not* work for expressions that have string constants. For example, the assertion

```
assert(strcmp(s1, "string1") == 0)
```

produces a compilation error because the preprocessor substitutes one constant string within another.

Furthermore, this technique does not work with all C compilers. On machines where the preprocessor does not substitute the assertion between double quotes, the word `expr` will appear. Chances are your compiler is ANSI C compatible, so consult the appendices for a solution with ANSI C compilers that provide *stringizing*.

Let's try our new assert macro with arrays. Here's the code for `array3.c`.

**Program 5-13**

```
/* array3.c - array bounds with custom assertion */

#include <stdio.h>
#include "assert.h"
#define MAX 10

main(argc, argv)
int argc;
char *argv[];
{
    int buf[MAX], index, value;

    if (argc != 3) {
        fprintf(stderr, "Usage: %s index value\n", argv[0]);
        exit(1);
    }
    index = atoi(argv[1]);          /* first argument */
    value = atoi(argv[2]);          /* second argument */

    assert(index >= 0 && index < MAX);

    buf[index] = value;
    printf("buf[%d] = %d\n", index, buf[index]);
}
```

Note that `array3.c` includes our custom macro (not the standard one), and it uses an assertion just like the previous version. Here's a test run.

```
$ cc array3.c -o array3
$ array3 25 99
Assertion failed: index >= 0 && index < MAX, file array3.c, line 20
```

We see the assertion that fails as well as the file and line number where the run time error occurs.

The next example suggests a change to the standard `assert.h` header file. Instead of terminating programs, the new assert macro calls a *user-defined* function. This approach gives executing programs more options. A program, for example, may continue to run if an error is not severe. Programs can automatically call a debugger or "pop up" an error window on the terminal. Alternatively, a program may display the same information as the standard version and terminate. Here's the new version.

```
/* new system-wide assert.h */

void (*assertf)();  /* pointer to user-defined function */

#ifndef NDEBUG
#   define   assert(expr)\
if (!(expr)) {\
        (*assertf)("expr", _ _FILE_ _, _ _LINE_ _);\
}\
else
#else
#   define   assert(expr)
#endif
```

The structure is the same as before, but the assert macro no longer displays an error message nor does it terminate a program. Instead, it uses a pointer called assertf to call a function. User programs provide this function and assign assertf to its address.

The user function has three arguments. The first argument is a pointer to a character string (the assertion), the second is a pointer to a character string for the filename (_ _FILE_ _), and the last argument is an integer for the line number (_ _LINE_ _). User functions may display this information in whatever form is appropriate.

The following program demonstrates the new assert macro. custom.c reads characters from standard input and places only lowercase letters in a buffer. If the input is invalid, an assertion calls the adump() routine from earlier in the chapter. Here's the program.

**Program 5-14**

```
/* custom.c - demonstrate new assert macro */

#include <stdio.h>
#include <assert.h>                 /* new macro */
#define MAX 100

char buf[MAX];
void dump();                        /* our function */
```

```
main()
{
   int c, index = 0;

   assertf = dump;                 /* have assert call dump() */

   while ((c = getchar()) != '\n') {
     assert(c >= 'a' && c <= 'z');
     buf[index++] = c;
   }
}

void dump(passertion, filename, lineno)
char *passertion, *filename;
int lineno;
{
   fprintf(stderr, "Assertion failed: %s, ", passertion);
   fprintf(stderr, "file %s, line %d\n", filename, lineno);
   adump(buf, MAX);
   exit(1);
}
```

Here, dump() is the name of our debug function. The program custom.c assigns assertf to dump()'s address. This makes the assert macro call dump() when an assertion fails. Each time the program reads a character, an assertion verifies that the character is a lowercase letter. If the assertion fails, dump() executes.

The dump() function displays the same debug information as the standard version using the new assert macro's arguments. The routine calls adump() after the error message.

We use the following file (called alpha) to test custom.c.

```
$ cat alpha
abcdefghijklmnopqrstuvwxyz4
```

Note that all characters are lowercase except for the last one. Here's the result.

```
$ cc custom.c adump.o -o custom
$ custom < alpha
Assertion failed: c >= 'a' && c <= 'z', file custom.c, line 17

000:   6162 6364 6566 6768 696a 6b6c 6d6e 6f70    abcdefghijklmnop
016:   7172 7374 7576 7778 797a 0000 0000 0000    qrstuvwxyz......
032:   0000 0000 0000 0000 0000 0000 0000 0000    ................
048:   0000 0000 0000 0000 0000 0000 0000 0000    ................
064:   0000 0000 0000 0000 0000 0000 0000 0000    ................
080:   0000 0000 0000 0000 0000 0000 0000 0000    ................
096:   0000 0000                                   ....
```

dump() displays the filename, the line number, and the assertion that fails. In addition, it displays the contents of the buffer using adump().


## ♦ Selective Debug Print Statements ♦

Up to this point, all the techniques we've shown require recompilation to display debug output. This can be very time consuming for large software systems with many modules. A technique we call *selective debug prints* allows you to display debug information *without* recompiling your system.

The approach is similar to command line flags. Debug calls have flags as arguments and may display nonaggregate data types (no arrays, structures, or unions). Selective debug prints, however, display as many variables as you want with one debug call. This is something we could *not* do with command line flags, since that technique uses a *macro* to display one variable at a time. Selective debug prints, on the other hand, must use a function because the number of arguments we pass to the debug function may vary.

You also provide a flags *file* to use selective debug prints. Flags could be set from the command line; however, we prefer the flags file approach. Rather than type in a long string of debug flags on the command line, we've found that it's easier to edit a file of flag numbers. For this reason, we present the flags file approach, but we leave a version using command line flags as an exercise for the reader. (See Exercise 5.)

There are a few more details. The first time you call the debug function, it checks to see if the flags file exists in your current directory. If it's not there, your system will *never* call the debug function again, even though there may be more debug calls. If there are flag numbers in the file, however, the debug function stores the flags into an array from the flags file. Subsequent calls to the debug function display debug statements on standard error if a flag is set.

Selective debug prints aren't for everyone, since there is overhead involved. Time-critical C programs, for example, may not be able to tolerate the overhead of working with a flags file. Furthermore, you may not want to have your system "react" to a debug file, either. The technique does have its advantages, however. For example, we recently used it on a large project with the UNIX compiler tools yacc and lex. It proved to be an invaluable tool during the development of a new language interpreter. Debug information from the parser, the lexical analyzer, and the code generator helped debug the interpreter while it processed statements.

The technique is nothing more than a small C program. As we've done throughout this chapter, we present an embedded driver to demonstrate it.

```
/*                  DBUG routine

    To test:  cc -DDRIVER dbug.c -o dbug
    To use:   cc -c dbug.c
              and link dbug.o with your libraries */

#include <stdio.h>
#include <assert.h>
#include <varargs.h>
#include "dbug.h"

#define TRUE   1
#define FALSE  0
#define MAXF 50        /* maximum flags allowed */

int Noflags;           /* set if no flags file */

#ifdef DRIVER
main()
{
    char broil        = 'M';
    short stuff       = 24680;
    int  rude         = 13579;
    float age         = 6.276;
    double talk       = 3.45e-12;
    long fellow       = 45678L;
    static char ge[10] = "low";
    char *coal        = "black";

    DBUG(1, "broil = %c\n", broil);
    DBUG(2, "stuff = %d\n", stuff);
    DBUG(3, "rude = %d\n", rude);
    DBUG(4, "age = %.3f\n", age);
    DBUG(5,  "talk = %g\n", talk);
    DBUG(6, "fellow = %ld\n", fellow);
    DBUG(7, "ge = %s\n", ge);
    DBUG(8, "coal's address = %x  coal = %s\n", coal, coal);
    DBUG(9, "broil = %c  rude = %d  age = %.3f  ge =%s  coal = %s\n",
            broil, rude, age, ge, coal);
    if (DBUG(10, "hello\n"))
        printf("goodbye\n");
    if (DBUG(11, ""))
        printf("end of debug output\n");
}
#endif
```

There are several new header files, which we'll return to shortly. Note that dbug.c includes the assert macro, since it uses an assertion.

The driver declares and initializes different C data types. Calls to DBUG have a flag followed by the same arguments that you would typically pass to printf(). If the flag is set in the flags file, debug output appears on standard error; otherwise, nothing happens. Since DBUG is a function, return values allow you to use it as a boolean expression in any C statement. DBUG returns the flag number if it's set, or zero if it's not.

Before we look at the debug function, let's compile it with the driver, run it, and see what happens.

```
$ cc -DDRIVER dbug.c -o dbug
$ dbug
$
```

Not very exciting. Nothing happens because a flags file doesn't exist. Let's provide one and try it again.

```
$ cat flags
1  2  3  4  5
$ dbug
broil = M
stuff = 24680
rude = 13579
age = 6.276
talk = 3.45e-12
$
```

Note that we didn't have to recompile the driver. When we set flag numbers in the flags file, debug output appears for the corresponding DBUG call.

Now let's set the rest of the flags.

```
$ cat flags
1  2  3  4  5
6  7  8  9 10 11
$ dbug
broil = M
stuff = 24680
rude = 13579
age = 6.276
talk = 3.45e-12
fellow = 45678
ge = low
coal's address = 2f4a   coal = black
broil = M   rude = 13579   age = 6.276   ge =low   coal = black
hello
```

```
goodbye
end of debug output
$
```

Flag numbers may be all on one line or on separate lines. Note that flags 8 and 9 make the debug function print more than one variable.

Flags 10 and 11 use DBUG as a boolean expression. Both calls use if statements that return TRUE if the flags file contains 10 or 11. In the call for flag 10, the driver prints the string "hello\n" followed by "goodbye\n". This format is useful for printing headers in front of a lot of debug output. For example, suppose flag 14 is set. The statement

```
if (DBUG(14, "symbol table\n"))
    dump_symtab();
```

displays the string "symbol table" before it calls dump_symtab() to print symbols.

The DBUG call for flag 11 prints only "end of debug output". This format is useful for executing several statements in a block. For example,

```
if (DBUG(15, "")) {
    int c;
    adump(buffer, MAX);
    printf("abort? ");
    c = tolower(getchar());
    if (c == 'y')
        exit(1);
}
```

calls adump() to display the contents of a buffer before it prompts to continue. If the user types 'y', the program terminates; otherwise the program continues. All this happens only if flag 15 is set in the flags file.

To eliminate debug output, simply remove the flags file.

```
$ rm flags
$ dbug
$
```

Before we look at the the debug function, let's examine the dbug.h header file.

```
$ cat dbug.h
/* dbug.h - Selective Debug Prints */

extern Noflags;
#define DBUG  !Noflags && dbug
```

Recall that we don't want to call the debug function repeatedly if there's no `flags` file. Consequently, the debug function sets a global flag called `Noflags` if the `flags` file doesn't exist. The preprocessor replaces all calls to `DBUG` with a statement that checks `Noflags` before it calls `dbug`. For example, the call

```
DBUG(4, "age = %.3f\n", age);
```

becomes

```
!Noflags && dbug(4, "age = %.3f\n", age);
```

Since `&&` is a sequence guarantee point, we never call `dbug` if `Noflags` is set. (We discuss sequence guarantee points in Chapter 4.)

Here's the debug function (`dbug()`) which is part of the same file as the driver.

```
int dbug(va_alist)              /* debug routine */
va_dcl
{
    va_list args;                   /* argument list */
    int flag;                       /* flag number */
    char *fmt;                      /* print format */
    FILE *fp;
    int f;
    static char readf = TRUE;
    static char flags[MAXF];        /* holds the flags */

    if (readf) {
        if ((fp = fopen("flags", "r")) == NULL) {
            Noflags = TRUE;
            return 0;
        }

        /* read in the flags */
        while (fscanf(fp, "%d", &f) != EOF) {
            assert(f > 0 && f < MAXF);
            flags[f] = TRUE;
        }
        fclose(fp);
        readf = FALSE;          /* done reading flags file */
    }
```

```
    va_start(args);                /* initialize argument list */
    flag = va_arg(args, int);      /* get flag number */
    fmt  = va_arg(args, char *);   /* get print format */

    if (flags[flag])
        vfprintf(stderr, fmt, args); /* display remaining args */

    va_end(args);                    /* cleanup argument list */

    return flags[flag] ? flag : 0;  /* return flag number or 0 */
}
```

The dbug() routine reads the flags file and displays the debug information. It also handles a variable number of arguments (va_list), which we will return to shortly. The array to hold the flags is internal to the debug function, and the static variable readf makes the function access the flags file only once. The function sets Noflags (from dbug.h) if the flags file doesn't exist.

The library routine fscanf() reads the flags file in a loop with an assertion to verify flag numbers. Flag 0 is invalid because dbug() returns FALSE if a flag is not set in the flags file. dbug() writes to standard error and returns a flag number if it's not zero.

For portability, dbug() uses the varargs technique discussed in Chapter 4 to handle a variable number of arguments. va_start() initializes the argument list and va_end() cleans up. The first call to va_arg() fetches the flag number and the second call grabs the format string. Note that the format string and args are all we need to display any number of remaining arguments with vfprintf().

Our next example is similar to a previous program (bytes.c) from the command line flags section. However, bytes2.c calls the debug function instead of the debug macro.

**Program 5-15**

```
/* bytes2.c - Use selective debug prints to
              display bytes with adump() */

#include <stdio.h>
#include "dbug.h"              /* Selective debug prints */
```

```
main(argc, argv)
int argc;
char *argv[];
{
    char *s1 = "Printable chars !@#$%^&*()_+={}?Unprintable ints";
    char *buf, *malloc();
    int i, num, nbytes, offset;

    if (argc == 1) {
        fprintf(stderr, "Usage: %s count\n", argv[0]);
        exit(1);
    }
    num = atoi(argv[1]);
    nbytes = strlen(s1) + num;
    DBUG(1, "buf size = %d\n", nbytes);
    buf = malloc(nbytes);
    if (buf == (char *) NULL) {
        fprintf(stderr, "Can't malloc from heap\n");
        exit(1);
    }
    strcpy(buf, s1);
    offset = strlen(s1);
    for (i = 0; i < nbytes; i++)      /* generate data */
        buf[i + offset] = i;

    adump(buf, nbytes);               /* display data */
}
```

The program includes dbug.h and calls DBUG to display the buffer size if flag 1 is set.

We can add a DBUG call in adump.c as well.

```
/* adump.c - ASCII to hexadecimal debug display */

#include <stdio.h>
#include "dbug.h"      /* Selective debug prints */
 . . . . . .
adump(p, size)          /* ASCII to hex dump */
char *p;
int size;
{
 . . . . . .
    for (i = 0; i < size; i += 16, q += 16) {
        DBUG(2, "\ni = %d\n", i);
 . . . . . .
    }
```

Here's how we compile `bytes2.c`:

```
$ cc bytes2.c adump.c dbug.c -o bytes2
```

To execute `bytes2` and display the buffer size, the `flags` file must contain a 1.

```
$ cat flags
1
$ bytes2 25
buf size = 73
```

```
000:    5072 696e 7461 626c 6520 6368 6172 7320    Printable chars
016:    2140 2324 255e 262a 2829 5f2b 3d7b 7d3f    !@#$%^&*()_+={}?
032:    556e 7072 696e 7461 626c 6520 696e 7473    Unprintable ints
048:    0001 0203 0405 0607 0809 0a0b 0c0d 0e0f    ................
064:    1011 1213 1415 1617 18                      .........
```

To display debug output from `adump()`, the `flags` file must contain 2.

```
$ cat flags
2
```

This generates many lines of output, so we save the output in a file called `dump`.

```
$ bytes2 25  2>  dump
```

To minimize output, we run `grep` to look at only `adump()`'s debug output.

```
$ grep "i = " dump
i = 0
i = 16
i = 32
i = 48
i = 64
```

To eliminate debug output, we remove the flags.

```
$ rm flags
$ bytes2 25
000:    5072 696e 7461 626c 6520 6368 6172 7320    Printable chars
016:    2140 2324 255e 262a 2829 5f2b 3d7b 7d3f    !@#$%^&*()_+={}?
032:    556e 7072 696e 7461 626c 6520 696e 7473    Unprintable ints
048:    0001 0203 0405 0607 0809 0a0b 0c0d 0e0f    ................
064:    1011 1213 1415 1617 18                      .........
```

All this was done without recompiling `bytes2.c`.

## ◆ Customized Memory Allocators ◆

Many of the standard C library routines have no error checking. When you use these routines and errors occur, you may want to report error information which the standard routines can't (or won't) provide. One way to get this extra level of error checking is to write *front ends* to the standard library routines. These custom routines check for errors and handle system specifics, then call the standard routines if they don't discover problems.

The dynamic storage allocators from the standard C library are good candidates for custom front ends. We've found that software systems that make heavy use of dynamic storage allocation are harder to debug. Calls to `malloc()`, `calloc()`, and `realloc()`, for example, provide some information about errors, but you rarely get enough to find the cause of the problem. What's worse, `free()` may destroy the integrity of the heap if its argument is not a heap address from a previous call to the allocator.

With a little effort and some overhead, we can improve this situation. In this section, we present front ends for `malloc()`, `realloc()`, and `free()`. A front end for `calloc()` is left as an exercise for the reader.

### The Technique

Programs include a file called `xalloc.h` to use the front end routines. The statement

```
#include "xalloc.h"
```

provides the interface. We will examine this file shortly.

Let's start with `xmalloc()`, a front end for `malloc()`. The use of `xmalloc()` allocates storage dynamically in the same way as `malloc()`. Suppose, for example, a file called `pgm.c` contains the following statements.

```
#include "xalloc.h"
 .  .  .  .
char *pheap;
 .  .  .  .
pheap = xmalloc(100);            /* 100 bytes */
 .  .  .  .
```

`xmalloc()` allocates 100 bytes of memory from the heap. If all is well, it's as if you called `malloc()`. If there is an error, however, the program terminates and displays the following message on standard error:

```
file pgm.c - line 56:  malloc error for 100 bytes
```

The error message shows the filename and line number where `malloc()` fails. This helps you locate the exact spot in your source file where the problem occurred.

The front ends `xrealloc()` and `xfree()` work in a similar way. Programs use these front ends with the same parameters as their C library counterparts. Note that none of the front ends require you to test the return value from an allocator call.

Here's what's inside the include file `xalloc.h`.

```
/* xalloc.h - header file for customized memory allocators */

#define xmalloc(N)      ymalloc(_ _FILE_ _, _ _LINE_ _, N)
#define xcalloc(N, S)   ycalloc(_ _FILE_ _, _ _LINE_ _, N, S)
#define xrealloc(P, N)  yrealloc(_ _FILE_ _, _ _LINE_ _, P, N)
#define xfree(P)        yfree(_ _FILE_ _, _ _LINE_ _, P)

char *ymalloc(), *ycalloc(), *yrealloc();
void yfree();
```

The header file reveals that the front ends are actually *macros* that call separate functions. Using the same technique as assertions, each macro passes a file name and a line number (using `_ _FILE_ _` and `_ _LINE_ _`, respectively). This allows each function to display an error message with a filename and a line number when a C library allocator routine fails.

Let's continue with our discussion of `xmalloc` and return to the others later. Note that `xmalloc()` (a macro) calls `ymalloc()` (a function). Here's the first version of `ymalloc()`.

```
/* ymalloc1.c - front end for malloc()   Version 1 */

#include <stdio.h>

char *ymalloc(file, lineno, nbytes)
char *file;
int lineno;
unsigned int nbytes;
{
    char *pheap, *malloc();

    pheap = malloc(nbytes);
    if (pheap == (char *) NULL) {
      fprintf(stderr,"file %s - line %d: malloc error for %u bytes\n",
                    file, lineno, nbytes);
      exit(1);
    }
    return pheap;
}
```

It's not very fancy yet, but there's more to come. At this point, ymalloc() calls malloc and checks the return pointer value. If there's an error, an error message appears on standard error and the program terminates.

Let's put xmalloc() to use. Suppose we want to maintain a symbol table of different data types. For simplicity, we limit data types to only strings and doubles. One way to handle different data types is with a union of pointers to the data. The following header file called defs.h, for example, defines a node (called Symbol) for a symbol table linked list.

```
/* defs.h - symbol table definitions */

#define STRING 1
#define DOUBLE 2

typedef struct Symbol {
      int dtype;
      union {
         char *pstring;
         double *pdouble;
      } val;
      struct Symbol *pnext;
} Symbol;
```

The pointer pnext links each symbol in the table to the next one. Suppose you declare

```
Symbol *p;              /* pointer to symbol table */
```

in a program. If p points to a symbol and p->dtype is equal to STRING, then p->val.pstring is a pointer to a string. Otherwise, p->val.pdouble points to a double.

The following program calls xmalloc() to create storage for a string symbol, a double symbol, and a large number of integers. For the symbols, the first call to xmalloc() allocates storage for a symbol, and the second call reserves storage for the data. We omit the details of linking the two symbols together. The last call to xmalloc() doesn't have anything to do with the symbol table, but it shows what happens if you try to allocate heap storage for too many objects. Here's the code and a test run.

**Program 5-16**

```
/* sym1.c - symbol table data types */

#include <stdio.h>
#include "xalloc.h"
#include "defs.h"
```

```
main()
{
    Symbol *p1, *p2;
    char *ps = "test string";
    int *p5;

    p1 = (Symbol *) xmalloc(sizeof(struct Symbol));
    p1->dtype = STRING;
    p1->val.pstring = xmalloc(strlen(ps) + 1);
    strcpy(p1->val.pstring, ps);

    p2 = (Symbol *) xmalloc(sizeof(struct Symbol));
    p2->dtype = DOUBLE;
    p2->val.pdouble = (double *) xmalloc(sizeof(double));
    *p2->val.pdouble = 6.7e-13;

    printf("%s\n", p1->val.pstring);
    printf("%g\n", *p2->val.pdouble);

    p5 = (int *) xmalloc(30000 * sizeof(int));
}
```

```
$ sym1
test string
6.7e-13
file sym1.c - line 26:  malloc error for 60000 bytes
```

The header file `defs.h` contains the definition of `Symbol`. The first `xmalloc()` allocates storage for a string symbol and assigns a heap address to pointer `p1`. The second `xmalloc()` allocates storage for the string member pointed to by `p1`. The program sets `p1`'s data type to STRING and copies the constant string `"test string"` pointed to by `ps` to the heap.

The third `xmalloc()` allocates storage on the heap for a double symbol and the fourth `xmalloc()` creates storage for a `double`. The program assigns a double precision constant (`6.7e-13`) to `p2`, whose data type is DOUBLE.

The last `xmalloc()` attempts to allocate 30,000 integers on the heap. On our XENIX 286 machine, the program fails because there's not enough room. The error message indicates which `xmalloc()` fails.

Before we move on to the front ends for `realloc()` and `free()`, let's include another level of error checking. This time we'll have the calls to `xmalloc()` and `realloc()` *save* heap pointers, so that `xfree()` can check them before it calls `free()`. With this arrangement, the front ends flag an error if a program tries to free an invalid heap pointer.

We need a data structure to hold heap pointers. For simplicity, we use an array that holds a maximum of 256 pointers. Here are the declarations.

```
#define MAXBUF 256          /* size of debug buffer */
static char *dbuf[MAXBUF];  /* debug buffer */
```

Next, we'll need to modify ymalloc to install the heap pointer in dbuf. Here's
the second version of ymalloc().

```
/* ymalloc2.c - front end for malloc()
              Version 2
*/

#include <stdio.h>

char *ymalloc(file, lineno, nbytes)
char *file;
int lineno;
unsigned int nbytes;
{
    char *pheap, *malloc();
    void install();

    pheap = malloc(nbytes);
    if (pheap == (char *) NULL) {
      fprintf(stderr,"file %s - line %d: malloc error for %u bytes\n",
                     file, lineno, nbytes);
      exit(1);
    }
    install(pheap);                /* place in debug buffer */
    return pheap;
}
```

All that's different from the first version is a call to install() to save the heap
pointers. Here's the code for install().

```
    /* store heap pointer in debug buffer */

    void install(pheap)
    char *pheap;
    {
        register char **pbuf;

        for (pbuf = dbuf; pbuf < dbuf + MAXBUF; pbuf++)
            if (*pbuf == (char *) NULL) {
                *pbuf = pheap;
                return;
            }
        fprintf(stderr, "No room left in debug buffer\n");
        exit(1);
    }
```

The `install()` routine searches the `dbuf` array for an empty spot (NULL). If none is found, the program exits with an error message that says the debug buffer is full. Otherwise, the heap pointer is stored in a vacant slot. For simplicity, we make a linear search through the `dbuf` array and terminate the program if it's full, but other approaches are possible (Exercises 8 and 9).

Recall that the macro `xrealloc()` calls the function `yrealloc()`, which is a front end to `realloc()`. `yrealloc()` verifies the pointer that's passed to it has been previously allocated on the heap, however. It checks the debug buffer for the pointer, and if it's there, calls the standard `realloc()` to replace it with a new pointer. Here's the code for `yrealloc()`.

```c
char *yrealloc(file, lineno, oldp, nbytes)
char *file, *oldp;
int lineno;
unsigned int nbytes;
{
    char *newp, *realloc();
    register char **pbuf;
    short found = 0;

    if (oldp != (char *) NULL)
        for (pbuf = dbuf; pbuf < dbuf + MAXBUF; pbuf++)
            if (*pbuf == oldp) {        /* find oldp's slot */
                found = 1;
                break;
            }
    if (!found) {
        fprintf(stderr,
            "file %s - line %d:  realloc error for address %x\n",
                    file, lineno, oldp);
        exit(1);
    }
    newp = realloc(oldp, nbytes);
    if (newp == (char *) NULL) {
        fprintf(stderr,
            "file %s - line %d:  realloc error for %u bytes\n",
                    file, lineno, nbytes);
        exit(1);
    }
    *pbuf = newp;           /* replace in debug buffer's old slot */
    return newp;
}
```

First, `yrealloc()` checks `oldp` to make sure that it's not NULL and in the buffer. Otherwise, the program displays an error message along with the illegal address and exits. If all is well, `yrealloc()` calls `realloc()` and verifies that the new heap pointer is not NULL. Before `yrealloc()` returns the heap pointer, the function installs the pointer in the same slot of the debug buffer as the old pointer.

The last front end is `xfree()`, which calls `yfree()` and verifies that a pointer has heap storage associated with it. This is the important level of error checking that's missing from the `free()` library routine. Here's the code for `yfree()`.

```
void yfree(file, lineno, pheap)
char *file, *pheap;
int lineno;
{
    void free();
    register char **pbuf;

    if (pheap != (char *) NULL)
        for (pbuf = dbuf; pbuf < dbuf + MAXBUF; pbuf++)
            if (*pbuf == pheap) {
                *pbuf = NULL;
                free(pheap);
                return;
            }
    fprintf(stderr,"file %s - line %d:  free error for address %x\n",
                    file, lineno, pheap);
    exit(1);
}
```

The `yfree()` routine displays an error message and exits if the heap pointer is not stored in `dbuf` or it is NULL. The error message displays the bad address. If the pointer contains a valid heap address, the routine makes the pointer's location in the `dbuf` array available (NULL), before it calls `free()`. This arrangement makes sure that you never free storage on the heap that hasn't been previously allocated.

Let's test these new routines by modifying our symbol table example. The program `sym2.c` reallocates the heap to hold a longer string for the string symbol and calls `xfree()` to free heap storage. Here's the new code and its output.

## Program 5-17

```c
/* sym2.c - more symbol table data types */

#include <stdio.h>
#include "xalloc.h"
#include "defs.h"

main()
{
    Symbol *p1, *p2;
    char *ps = "test string";
    char *ps2 = "much longer test string";

    p1 = (Symbol *) xmalloc(sizeof(struct Symbol));
    p1->dtype = STRING;
    p1->val.pstring = xmalloc(strlen(ps) + 1);
    strcpy(p1->val.pstring, ps);

    p2 = (Symbol *) xmalloc(sizeof(struct Symbol));
    p2->dtype = DOUBLE;
    p2->val.pdouble = (double *) xmalloc(sizeof(double));
    *p2->val.pdouble = 6.7e-13;

    printf("%s\n", p1->val.pstring);
    printf("%g\n", *p2->val.pdouble);

    p1->val.pstring = xrealloc(p1->val.pstring,
                                        strlen(ps2) + 1);
    strcpy(p1->val.pstring, ps2);
    printf("%s\n", p1->val.pstring);

    xfree((char *) p2->val.pdouble);
    xfree(ps2);                         /* free a bad pointer */
}
```

```
$ sym2
test string
6.7e-13
much longer test string
file sym2.c - line 31:  free error for address 2634
```

The first part of the program is the same as the previous version. However, `sym2.c` calls `xrealloc()` with the old pointer (p1->val.pstring) to allocate enough storage to accommodate a longer string (ps2). The program copies the longer string to Symbol `p1` on the heap and displays the new string.

Note that `sym2.c` calls `xfree()` twice. The first call works fine, since the pointer contains a valid heap address. The second call, however, displays an error message because `ps2` is not a heap pointer.

What about performance issues? Although the front ends give us error checking, be aware that these routines introduce additional overhead and may cause problems with time-critical software. There are several reasons. First of all, we are passing more parameters to the front end routines than the C library modules require. Secondly, it takes time to save heap pointers and search for them. What you have, therefore, is a trade-off between error checking and performance.

In the early stages of development, the front ends can help considerably during debugging. After the software becomes stable, you can always remove the front ends and return to the standard allocators. One way to do this is by modifying `xalloc.h` as follows.

```
/* xalloc.h - header file for standard memory allocators
              (No error checking)
*/

#define xmalloc(N)       malloc(N)
#define xcalloc(N, S)    calloc(N, S)
#define xrealloc(P, N)   realloc(P, N)
#define xfree(P)         free(P)

char *malloc(), *calloc(), *realloc();
void free();
```

This makes your code execute the C library calls instead of their front end counterparts. Bear in mind, however, that this approach does not check return values. See Exercise 10 for further discussion.

## ◆ Summary ◆

- The C compiler's -D option is handy for debugging. This command line option allows programs to conditionally compile debug code in source files.

- Embedded test drivers allow modules to test themselves.

- Signals allow users to type keyboard characters and make executing programs dump debug output.

- An assertion is a boolean expression that is expected to be true at run time.

- Assertions detect run time errors. If assertions fail, programs display error messages and terminate.

- Assertions help detect array out-of-bounds errors and check for invalid pointer values.

- Assertions are macros. Users may create their own assertions.

- The compiler option  -DNDEBUG deletes assertions from programs.

- The preprocessor substitutes the name of the current source file and the current line number for the symbols  _ _FILE_ _ and  _ _LINE_ _, respectively. The file name is a string constant and the line number is an integer constant. User programs may use this information in error messages.

- Selective debug prints allow programs to display debug output without recompiling modules.

- Front ends provide additional error checking for C library routines.

# ◆ Exercises ◆

1. Modify `adump.c` so that it produces an ASCII to octal dump. Include run time options to produce ASCII to hexadecimal dumps as well.

2. The calls to `DEBUG` for command line flags allow you to print only one variable at a time. Is there a way to modify the macro to allow a *variable* number of arguments?

3. Using the C library function `getopt()`, modify `DEBUGFLAGS` to process the command line flags in *any* order,

4. Devise a way to use a different signal than `SIGQUIT` for signal debugging. (*Hint*: use one of the user-defined signal names. You'll have to have a second process running to send this signal to your main program when you type a keyboard sequence, or use the `kill()` system call).

5. Instead of a `flags` file, modify the selective debug print technique to use command line flags. Use the DEBUGFLAGS approach from this chapter or the C library function `getopt()` to access the flags from the command line and store them in the `flags` array.

6. Selective debug prints allow a variable number of arguments. Can you think of a way to implement this technique as a macro? If so, create a header file to allow you to conditionally compile and remove all debug calls from your source files.

7. Implement `xcalloc()` using the same design methodology used with `xmalloc()` and `xrealloc()`.

8. The front ends for the storage allocators use a fixed size array (`dbuf`) to store heap pointers. Use `malloc()` to initially create the array and call `realloc()` to increase its size as necessary.

9. Instead of an array to store the heap pointers, implement a similar scheme to dynamically create and maintain a linked list on the heap. Note that this approach can handle any number of calls to the storage management routines. If possible, perform timing tests with the two approaches in a software system and compare the results.

10. Write a macro that allows you to switch back and forth from the standard C library storage allocators to your own. Implement it with a compile time option or with selective debug prints. Start with the preprocessor definitions for `xalloc.h` shown in the chapter.

♦ ♦ ♦ ♦ ♦ ♦
# 6

# A Memory Object Allocator

C programs call the library routines `malloc()`, `calloc()`, `real-loc()`, and `free()` to control a standard memory allocator (the heap manager). These routines offer portable solutions to programs that need to manage memory at run time. The basic philosophy behind the standard allocator is to allocate and deallocate *chunks* of heap memory. These memory blocks may be as small as a single byte or as large as the limitations of the hardware or operating system. The lowest level interface to the heap is a byte pointer. Programs may use larger objects by casting a byte pointer to an appropriate data type. This arrangement allows programs to superimpose structure on top of streams of bytes from heap memory.

The standard allocator is designed to hide implementation details from programs. Consequently, programmers do not typically concern themselves with how the allocator manages heap memory. Programmers can misuse the heap with the standard allocator routines, however. The symptoms of such problems are data corruption or the unexpected exhaustion of heap memory. The most likely culprits are programs that frequently allocate and free heap storage. Heap problems are frustrating because the symptoms are not always repeatable and often depend on seemingly unrelated events.

If you study the standard allocator closely, you'll discover the following:

Once the standard allocator returns a byte pointer address to a user
program that calls `malloc()`, `calloc()`, or `realloc()`,
the allocator *cannot* change the pointer.

This fact seems unimportant until you realize that it prevents the standard allocator from ever rearranging the heap. Actually, `realloc()` calls `malloc()` and copies data to a new area of the heap if it has to. In the most general sense, however, we're referring to moves of arbitrary data to and from any heap address.

Why is this important? Suppose a user program frequently allocates and frees different size blocks of heap memory. After a period of time, the heap becomes *fragmented*. There may be many "holes" between data chunks. Eventually, the standard allocator will be unable to allocate a chunk of heap memory, even though there may be enough unallocated bytes in the heap. If the allocator could remove the holes by rearranging the data (a technique appropriately called *garbage collection*), the allocator could satisfy further requests for heap memory and user programs would not fail. Of course, the heap allocator can't rearrange the data since the data's pointer would have to change.

In this chapter we apply the standard allocator to an application where its use *seems* appropriate. The application, however, requires an allocator that performs garbage collection. To solve this problem, we provide the design and source code for a memory object allocator (we call it a *mob*). The mob allows user programs to allocate and deallocate objects of any size and data type from the heap. The mob's user interface is similar to the standard allocator, except that mob routines return a pointer to an *object* instead of a byte pointer. This arrangement allows the mob to rearrange the heap when it becomes fragmented. Garbage collection becomes automatic and transparent to user programs.

Most of this chapter covers the mob's implementation in detail and discusses its advantages and disadvantages. You'll probably want to study the source code carefully, and several readings may be required. At the end of this discussion, we return to our initial application and present a practical solution with the mob. We have applied the mob design to several projects with good results. We hope you'll find it as useful as we have.

## ◆ Project ATL ◆

ATL (A Tape Language) allows application developers to write programs to read and write 9 track tapes. ATL is a structured language with user-defined functions and control constructs similar to DBASE III and BASIC. Nine track tape users work with strings of data in different formats (ASCII, EBCDIC, BCD, etc.), so ATL provides specific operators and functions for string manipulation. ATL relies on the UNIX tools `yacc` and `lex` for the grammar and parser. The rest of ATL is written in C, and it runs under XENIX and MS-DOS.

Of interest to this chapter is the implementation of dynamic strings in ATL. The following sample ATL program demonstrates several string manipulation features. We show string declarations, string assignment, and string output. The program also builds new strings dynamically with ATL string operators and built-in string functions.

**Program 6-1**

```
main
    string s1, s2, s3;      // declare 3 strings

    s1 = "Hello";           // string assignments
    s2 = "World";

    echo ( s1 - s2 );       // output s1, s2 with space in between

    s3 = dup ( "=", 61);    // assign to s3 a 61 char string of '='
    echo ( s3 );            // output s3

    // concat (+ is no space, - is with a space)
    s3 = left(s3, 25) + s1 - s2 + left(s3, 25); // string building
    echo (s3);
endmain
```

ATL programs use the keywords `main` and `endmain` to surround declarations and executable statements. All lines have free format and executable statements terminate with a semicolon. The notation `//` starts an ATL comment terminated automatically at the end of a line.

The program declares three strings `s1`, `s2`, and `s3`. All three have zero length initially. The program stores constant strings in `s1` and `s2` using the ATL string assignment operator (=). The expression

```
    s1 - s2
```

uses the ATL string operator `-` (dash). The result is a new string with a space between `s1` and `s2`. The built-in function `echo(s)` writes string `s` to the terminal screen with a newline. The program uses `echo(s1 - s2)` to display the string `"Hello World"`.

The built-in function `dup(c, n)` creates a string of the same character. `dup()`'s arguments are a character (c) and a count (n). The program calls `dup("=", 61)` to create a string of 61 `'='`. Using ATL string assignment, the program stores this new string in `s3`.

The line

```
s3 = left(s3, 25) + s1 - s2 + left(s3, 25);   // string building
```

demonstrates how easily ATL builds new strings. `left()`'s arguments are a string and the number of leftmost characters to extract. `left(s3, 25)` returns the first 25 characters from `s3`. This ATL statement, therefore, takes the first 25 characters of `s3`, concatenates it with `s1`, joins it with `s2` (a space in between), concatenates it again with the first 25 characters of `s3`, and stores the new string in `s3`. `echo()` displays `s3` on the screen.

The output of this ATL program is the following.

```
Hello World
================================================================
========================Hello World========================
```

ATL strings may contain tape data as well as ASCII characters. For example,

```
    readtape(s1);
```

uses the ATL built-in function `readtape()` to read a block of tape data into string `s1`. Tape records may contain `NULL` bytes as valid data.

## The Standard Approach

Suppose we attempt to implement ATL strings in C. The first problem to solve is how to handle string length. ATL cannot treat dynamic strings as C strings because NULL bytes are valid data. Since ATL strings live on the heap, one approach is to use *negative subscripts* to hold a string's length. With this technique, a call with a front end to the standard heap routines allocates room for an integer as well as the data. String length is stored in *front* of string data on the heap and is available with the heap pointer and a negative subscript. We present the technique in Chapter 3. This allows you to manipulate a string's length as it changes during program execution.

Using the standard allocator, the implementation must create storage for the strings and handle ATL string functions and operators. We need routines to provide string declarations, string assignment (from a constant string or another string variable), and string concatenation (with or without a blank). ATL also creates temporary strings, so we'll need to free string storage as well.

Suppose, for example, we outline the steps required to handle the ATL statement

```
    echo(s1 - s2);
```

ATL breaks this down into the following actions:

1. Create a temporary string variable, `stemp`.
2. Store `s1` into `stemp`.
3. Join `stemp` with `s2` with a blank in between.
4. Echo `stemp` to the terminal screen.
5. Free `stemp`.

Using the standard allocator, Step 1 uses `malloc()`. Steps 2 and 3 use `realloc()` to change the string's length. Step 5 uses `free()` to release string storage.

This type of behavior demonstrates the biggest obstacle to using the standard allocator for implementing ATL strings. The allocation requests will occur often and they will be handling small pieces of memory. When we allocate heap memory in small chunks like this and subsequently release it, we eventually fragment the heap. Unless the memory allocator can move data, allocation requests may fail even though enough unused memory exists. The routines `malloc()` and `realloc()` cannot manage memory efficiently when requests result in fragmentation, because they cannot rearrange or pack heap data to make larger chunks available.

### Garbage Collection

When we speak of dynamic strings, we're talking about strings that *change*. We don't care particularly how their contents change, but when their sizes change, it affects adjacent strings. When strings get longer, for example, data must relocate to provide additional room. It's possible to reallocate space using the standard allocator, but the standard allocator cannot move allocated data and collect unused space into a single resource. While this process is traditionally called *garbage collection*, what we really mean is *packing* existing data, so that the unused space can be used again. The standard memory allocator cannot do this.

The absence of built-in garbage collection in the standard allocator is not a design flaw. The standard allocator is meant to be a portable set of general purpose routines. If a programmer needs to dynamically allocate, resize, and free small chunks of memory frequently, he or she should manage heap memory with a separate allocator. This new allocator can manage smaller chunks of heap memory once it has called `malloc()` or `calloc()` to grab a large amount of memory to begin with. The new allocator keeps track of allocated memory, finds unallocated "holes," and packs heap data when necessary.

ATL dynamic strings require such an allocator. We present the following memory object allocator as both a solution for ATL dynamic strings and as a general purpose tool.

## ◆ The Object Allocator ◆

The memory allocator manages objects from heap memory. Each object is a structure containing a byte pointer to the data it refers to, the length of the data, and the amount of data in use. Both the objects and their data live in heap memory. User programs locate data with an *object pointer* instead of a byte pointer (as with the standard allocator). This arrangement allows the object allocator to rearrange the heap at any time without bothering an executing program.

The pointer to an object's data may change for several reasons. If a user program resizes an object's data, the object allocator may change the heap address. Garbage collection also changes object addresses. Deallocating an object frees an object structure and makes it available for reuse. Each object also has a field that indicates how much heap memory is in use for the data.

We present the source code for the object allocator from top to bottom, but we'll discuss it a section at a time. Let's start with the structures we use to control the memory allocator. This provides the interface to user programs. Following this, we'll examine allocation, deallocation, sizing, and packing.

## Memory Objects and Control Variables

The object allocator controls two separate areas of heap memory. The first area, called *object data space*, has a fixed size and contains object data. The second area holds the *object descriptors*. This space is partitioned into an array of structures containing variables that locate and control object data space. User programs call a routine to initialize the object allocator, which calls `malloc()` and `calloc()` to allocate both areas on the heap.

Here is the start of the code.

```c
/* objalloc.c - memory object allocator */

#include <stdio.h>
#include "obj.h"                 /* object definitions */
#include "dbug.h"                /* selective debug prints */

#define OBJSPACE 0x7000          /* max size of object data space */
#define OBJSIZE   512            /* max number of object descriptors */
```

We'll look at the header files `obj.h` and `dbug.h` shortly. OBJSPACE is the amount of heap memory we allocate for object data space. OBJSIZE is the number of object descriptors. This is the maximum number of objects that the allocator can handle. In this implementation, we use 7000 (hexadecimal) or 28,672 decimal bytes for object data space and 512 object descriptors. The application and available memory will affect these numbers.

Next, let's look at how we define objects. This information lives in the header file `obj.h` so user programs may access it.

```c
/* obj.h - object header */

typedef struct Object {         /* object descriptor */
    unsigned char *pobj;        /* base address of object */
    int len;                    /* memory allocated for object */
    int used;                   /* object's length, must be <= len */
    struct Object *prev;        /* pointer to prev object */
    struct Object *next;        /* pointer to next object */
} Object;
```

We store each memory object descriptor in a structure called `Object` that we `typedef` for convenience. Pointer `pobj` points to the base address of the object's data. `len` is the number of bytes allocated for the object in object data space, and `used` keeps track of the number of bytes that the object is actually using. We'll show you later why they are kept separately and why the value of `used` may vary between 1 and `len` without any other adjustments. The object allocator never increases `len` without checking the bounds of the next memory object. Object data, therefore, can never overlap.

Although the object descriptors are stored in an array, the *allocated* descriptors form an ordered *doubly linked list* (pointers link the list in both directions). The order is based on the value of `pobj`, which is the address of the object's data. Figure 6-1 shows the arrangement.

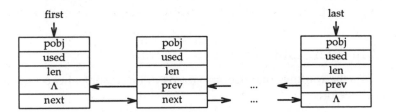

*Fig. 6-1.* Object descriptor linked list

Λ is the notation we use for a NULL pointer. `prev` points to the object descriptor that is immediately below the current descriptor in memory, and `next` points to the next highest descriptor. Pointers `first` and `last` point to the start and end of the list, respectively.

The object allocator traverses the list of object descriptors by following `prev` (going backwards from high address to low address) or `next` (going forwards from low address to high address). The order of the pointers is crucial to the design of the object allocator. The packing routines assume that the linked list is maintained in order of increasing memory locations (that is, the relative value of `pobj`). We'll see why this is important later.

The header file `dbug.h` provides debugging capability. We use the following code from Chapter 5 for selective debug prints.

```
/* dbug.h - selective debug prints */

extern Noflags;
#define DBUG  !Noflags && dbug
```

We embed `DBUG` calls inside the allocator to display pointer addresses and other information while it's running. Later in this chapter we show debug output for a sample user program.

Next, let's look at the static control variables for the object allocator.

```
static unsigned char *base;        /* address of object data space */
static long mavail, availend;      /* memory available counts */
static Object *objects;            /* address of first object */
static Object *first, *last;       /* start, end of objects */
static int nobj;                   /* number of object descriptors */
```

base points to the start of object data space.  mavail keeps track of how many bytes are currently available in object data space (including any holes of unused memory).  availend keeps track of how many bytes are available after the last allocated chunk.  objects points to the first object in the object descriptor array, and first and last point to the start and end of the ordered linked list, respectively.  nobj keeps track of how many objects are currently in use.

## Object Allocator Routines

Table 6-1 lists the routines that user programs call to manage heap memory with the object allocator.

**TABLE 6-1.  Object allocator routines**

| Routine | Meaning |
| --- | --- |
| void obj_init() | Initialize object allocator |
| Object *obj_alloc(len)<br>int len; | Return pointer to new object with len data bytes |
| void obj_free(p)<br>Object *p; | Release object p |
| void obj_size(p, len)<br>Object *p;<br>int len; | Resize object p for len bytes |
| void obj_check() | Consistency check |
| long obj_mavail() | Return number of bytes left in object data space |
| int obj_davail() | Return number of unallocated object descriptors |

`obj_init()` initializes the object allocator. `obj_alloc()` is like `malloc()`, except that it returns a pointer to an object (type `Object *`), rather than a byte pointer to heap data. Likewise, `obj_free()` is like `free()`, but it expects an object pointer for an argument. `obj_size()` is similar to `realloc()`. It expects an object pointer from a previous call to `obj_alloc()` (or possibly a previous `obj_size()`), and resizes an object's data to `len` bytes. These four routines form the core of the object allocator.

The remaining three routines perform allocator consistency checks or provide specific information to user programs. `obj_check()`, for example, loops through the object descriptor list to make sure that it's consistent. User programs may call this routine any time. `obj_mavail()` returns the number of bytes left in object data space and `obj_davail()` returns the number of unused object descriptors. User programs call these routines to find out how much heap memory is free.

## Initializing the Object Allocator

Before user programs manipulate objects, they must initialize the object allocator with `obj_init()`. This routine allocates heap memory for object data space and the object descriptor array. The routine also assigns values to the allocator control variables. Here is the code for `obj_init()`:

```
void obj_init()                       /* initialize object allocator */
{
  char *malloc(), *calloc();

  if ((base = (unsigned char *) malloc(OBJSPACE)) == NULL)
     obj_error("obj_init cannot malloc for Object Data Space");

  if ((objects = (Object *) calloc(OBJSIZE, sizeof(Object))) == NULL)
     obj_error("obj_init cannot calloc for Object Descriptors");

  objects[0].pobj = base;      /* first object's base address */
  first = last = &objects[0];  /* init to first object */
  nobj = 1;                    /* mark first object */
  availend = mavail = OBJSPACE; /* available space left */
}
```

`obj_init()` calls `malloc()` to allocate object data space from the heap and `calloc()` to allocate heap memory for the object descriptors. This is the only time that the object allocator uses the standard allocator library routines. The control variable `base` is set to the starting address of object data space, and `objects` points to the array of object descriptors. The object allocator does not release either area until a user program terminates.

Note that `obj_init()` calls `calloc()` (and not `malloc()`) for the object descriptors. This zero fills the array, which initializes pointers to NULL and lengths to zero. This is important for allocating new objects, as we will see shortly.

`obj_init()` also sets `object[0]` (the first object descriptor) to the base address of object data space. This is a *dummy object* because it does not point to real data. The object allocator wastes one descriptor to make the algorithms for packing simpler, and to keep from having to reinitialize the descriptor array if all objects become free. User programs never access the first object.

The rest of `obj_init()` sets control variables. Initially, `availend` and `mavail` contain the entire object data space and `nobj` is set to 1. `first` and `last` point to the first object descriptor and form the skeleton of the memory object descriptor linked list. Fig. 6-2 shows heap memory after initialization.

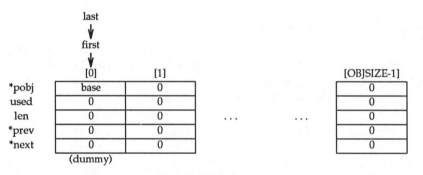

Memory object descriptors

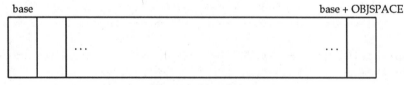

Memory object data space

*Fig. 6-2.* Heap memory after initializing the allocator

Object members are shown in brackets ([0], [1], etc.). All object structure members are set to zero at this point. `Object[0]` is the dummy object, and its `pobj` pointer contains the address of object data space. Variables `first` and `last` live in the data area.

`obj_init()` calls `obj_error()` when an error occurs. This makes the object allocator terminate after displaying a message on standard error. We will look at `obj_error()` later. For more generality, the object allocator could

return an error code and let the user program handle errors. (See Exercise 2.)
This is useful in a window based system, for example. If an error occurs, the
object allocator returns an error code, so the system can "pop up" an error window.

## Object Allocation

`obj_alloc()` allows user programs to allocate new objects from heap memory.
The routine expects one argument, the number of bytes of object data. Here is
the code for `obj_alloc()`:

```
Object *obj_alloc(len)              /* allocate a memory object */
int len;
{
    register Object *p;

    if (len > mavail || nobj >= OBJSIZE)
        obj_error("obj_alloc exceeds Object Data Space");

    nobj++;
    if (availend < len)              /* enough room at end? */
        pack();

    for (p = objects; ; p++) {    /* find free object descriptor */
        if (!p->pobj)                /* zero means unallocated */
            break;
    }

    p->pobj = last->pobj + last->len;   /* start of next buffer */
    p->len = len;
    p->used = 0;

    last->next = p;                     /* adjust the pointers */
    p->prev = last;
    p->next = 0;
    last = p;

    mavail -= len;                      /* adjust memory avail */
    availend -= len;                    /* adjust memory avail at end */
    DBUG(12, "obj_alloc: pobj = %x for %4d bytes  mavail = %x\n",
            p->pobj, len, mavail);
    return p;                           /* pointer to new object */
}
```

Before `obj_alloc()` allocates a new object it makes several checks. First, the
routine makes sure there is enough room for `len` bytes in object data space.

`mavail` contains the number of bytes available, including any holes left by freeing previously allocated objects. Second, `obj_alloc()` insures that the number of occupied slots in the descriptor array (`nobj`) is less than the maximum (`OBJSIZE`). If either condition fails, `obj_alloc()` calls `obj_error()` with an error message. Otherwise, `obj_alloc()` increments `nobj` to update the object descriptor count.

Next, the routine checks available memory at the end of object data space. If `availend` is less than `len`, `obj_alloc()` packs object data space to make room for the new object. We'll examine `pack()` later.

`obj_alloc()` finds an unused object descriptor with a linear search through the descriptor array, looking for the first `pobj` that is zero. Another way to implement free descriptors is with a *free list*. Using this method, all free object descriptors use their *next* pointers to form a linked free list. The allocator fetches a free descriptor from the free list instead of searching the descriptor array linearly. See Exercise 3 for more details.

`pobj` is set to zero at initialization and when the object allocator frees the descriptor. The statement

```
for (p = objects; ; p++) {    /* find free object descriptor */
```

loops through the object descriptor array looking for a free slot.   `p` is a register variable to make this loop execute as fast as possible. A zero value for `p->pobj` means the slot is free.

`obj_alloc()` installs a new descriptor at the end of the linked descriptor list. Recall that the order of the memory object descriptors in the linked list must correlate to the order of their memory object addresses (`pobj`). To ensure this, `obj_alloc()` installs the descriptor at the end of the descriptor list and allocates object data space after the last allocated object.

The lines

```
p->pobj = last->pobj + last->len;    /* start of next buffer */
p->len = len;
```

assign a heap address to the newly allocated memory object after the last object, and mark the object's length as `len` bytes.   `obj_alloc()` zeros the object's used field with

```
    p->used = 0;
```

`used` allows user programs to make small adjustments in its "used" memory without costly data movement. We'll see how this works when we apply the object allocator to ATL dynamic strings.

`obj_alloc()` installs the new descriptor at the end of the linked list with

```
    last->next = p;                    /* adjust the pointers */
    p->prev = last;
    p->next = 0;
    last = p;
```

After adjusting the memory available control variables `mavail` and `availend` by `len`, `obj_alloc()` returns a pointer to the newly allocated object.

Suppose a user program allocates two objects of 50 bytes and 75 bytes. Fig. 6-3 shows heap memory after two calls to `obj_alloc()`.

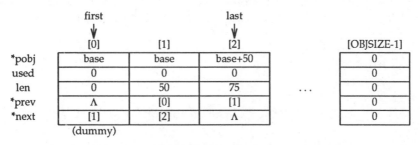

Memory object descriptors

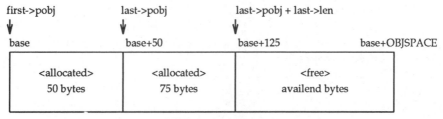

Memory object data space

*Fig. 6-3.* Memory allocation for *obj_alloc(50)* and *obj_alloc(75)*

In the object descriptor list, `object[1]` has 50 bytes of data and `object[2]` has 75 bytes. `Object[1]`'s data is at `base` and `object[2]`'s data is located at `base + 50`. We refer to objects as `object[1]` and `object[2]` using array subscripts for object descriptors. The allocator, however, accesses and maintains the object descriptors through the link list pointers. `Object[0]` (the dummy object) has no data in object data space (`len` is zero), but its `next` pointer links to `object[1]`. Likewise, `object[2]`'s `prev` pointer links to `object[1]`. `Object[2]`'s `next` pointer is zero, marking the end of the object descriptor list.

In object data space, `base + 125` is the next available memory address. `availend` is set to the number of free bytes shown in Fig. 6-3. The allocator uses variables `first` and `last` to locate object data and find the next available address.

## Object Deallocation

To free an object, user programs call `obj_free()` with an object pointer. Basically, all `obj_free()` does is mark the object free and delink it from the descriptor list. `obj_free()` makes several checks, however. First, it reports an error if a user program tries to free an object that's already free. Second, `obj_free()` sets control variables and adjusts pointers if the object is first or last in the descriptor list. Here's the code for `obj_free()`:

```
void obj_free(p)                    /* free a memory object */
Object *p;
{
    if (p->pobj == 0)
       obj_error("obj_free detects object already free");

    if (p == last) {                /* check for last object */
       availend += p->len;
       last = p->prev;
       last->next = 0;
    }
    else if (p == first) {          /* check for first object */
       first = p->next;
       first->prev = 0;
    }
    else {
       p->prev->next = p->next; /* adjust the pointers */
       p->next->prev = p->prev;
    }

    mavail += p->len;               /* increase available memory */
    DBUG(12, "obj_free:  pobj = %x for %4d bytes  mavail = %x\n",
             p->pobj, p->len, mavail);

    p->pobj = 0;                    /* 0 to free object descriptor */
    nobj--;                         /* decrement descriptor count */
}
```

An object is already free if `p->pobj` is 0; consequently, `obj_free()` reports an error. Otherwise, the routine checks if the object is the first or last one. `obj_free()` increments `availend` if it's the last object and sets `first` and `last` to the next object or the previous one, respectively. If the object is not the first or last one, the statements

```
    p->prev->next = p->next;    /* adjust the pointers */
    p->next->prev = p->prev;
```

remove the object from the descriptor list by changing its neighbors' pointers to

point "around" it.   obj_free() adjusts mavail to increase available
memory in object data space and decrements nobj for the the descriptor count.
obj_free() always increments mavail but only adjusts availend if the
freed object is the last one.

Fig. 6-4 shows object data space and the descriptor array after freeing the
50-byte memory object (object[1]).

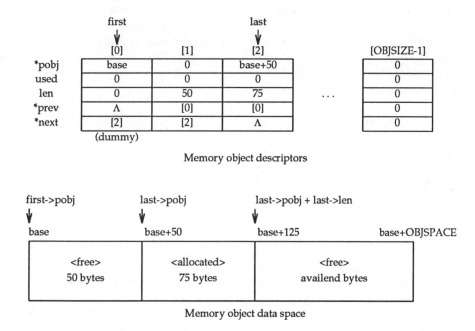

Memory object descriptors

Memory object data space

*Fig. 6-4.* Memory allocation after freeing object[1]

In this figure, we've updated the linked list to point around object[1].
Because this descriptor is no longer linked into the list, the values for len,
used, prev, and next are not meaningful.   pobj, however, is 0 and this
marks the descriptor as free. The values for first->next and last->prev
skip around the deallocated descriptor. Furthermore, there are 50 free bytes
since

```
50 == first->next->pobj - (first->pobj + first->len)
```

That is, the start of the next object allocated *less* the end of the current allocation
equals 50. The object allocator uses this fundamental relationship in the next
routine for object sizing.

## Object Sizing

Changing object data size is potentially an expensive operation. If the allocator needs to increase the data size beyond the boundaries of of the next object, it must move object data to make room in object data space. Obviously, a large object data space requires some time to have its data moved up or down.

User programs change the size of an object's data with `obj_size()`. The routine has two arguments: an object descriptor (`Object *`) and a new length (`len`). User programs typically call `obj_size()` to increase object data length, but a call to decrease the length is also possible. User programs may also change an object descriptor's `used` field to decrease the size. Manipulating `used` does not make the object allocator release memory. This arrangement prevents the object allocator from rearranging the heap too often (a condition called *thrashing*). Here's the code for `obj_size()`:

```
void obj_size(p, len)                    /* resize memory object */
Object *p;
int len;
{
    register Object *t;
    unsigned char *tmp;
    Object *new;
    int need, avail;

    if (p->pobj == 0)
        obj_error("obj_size detects object already free");

    DBUG(12, "obj_size: want %4d, (have %4d)\n", len, p->len);

    if (p->len >= len) {
        if (p == last)
            availend += p->len - len;
        mavail += p->len - len;       /* increase available buffer */
        p->len = len;
        DBUG(12, "obj_size:  pobj = %x for %4d bytes  mavail = %x\n",
                p->pobj, len, mavail);
        return;
    }

    need = len - p->len;
    if (need > mavail)
        obj_error("obj_size exceeds Object Data Space");
    avail = 0;
```

```
    if (p != last || need > availend) {
        /* don't pack if p at end */
        for (t = p, avail = 0; ;t = t->next) {
            if (t == last) {
                pack();
                break;
            }
            avail += t->next->pobj - (t->pobj + t->len);
            if (avail >= need)
                break;
        }
        while (t != p) {
            if (t == last) {
                tmp = t->pobj + t->len - 1 + need;   /* make room */
                availend -= need;
            }
            else
                tmp = t->next->pobj - 1;   /* top of mem for move */
            upmove(tmp, t->pobj + t->len - 1, t->len);
            tmp -= t->len;
            t->pobj = tmp + 1;
            t = t->prev;
        }
    }
    else
        availend -= len - p->len;
    mavail -= len - p->len;              /* decrease available buffer */
    p->len = len;
    DBUG(12, "obj_size:  pobj = %x for %4d bytes  mavail = %x\n",
            p->pobj, len, mavail);
}
```

obj_size() calls obj_error() if a user program tries to resize a free object.
If the requested length (len) is less than the object's allocated space (p->len),
the allocator does not have to pack data or check object boundaries. In this case,
obj_size() adjusts the object's len field to a new value and updates mavail
(available memory) and possibly, availend (available memory at the end).

   If len is greater than the object's allocated space, obj_size() checks to
see if additional object data space is available. A special situation exists if the
memory object is the last object and there is enough room in availend. This
means the allocator does not have to move data.

   It is possible that while there is enough free memory to handle the resizing,
memory objects must move to make room.  obj_size() moves objects in
object data space under these conditions. The routine starts at the requested
memory object and moves *up* through the object descriptor linked list until it
reaches the top (last), or it finds enough space in the holes to make up the

difference. If it reaches the top, it packs all the memory objects. To make room, it then moves upward all objects above the target object by the resize amount. If, on the other hand, `obj_size()` finds available space before reaching the last object, the routine stops and moves upward all objects without first repacking. Thus, `obj_size()` only packs when necessary.

  `obj_size()` does all this with two loops. The following `for` statement starts with `p` (the object that needs resizing) and loops through the linked descriptor list.

```
for (t = p, avail = 0; ;t = t->next) {
```

The local variable `avail` accumulates free space as we encounter it in the loop. The following statement increments `avail` by the amount in each unallocated area:

```
avail += t->next->pobj - (t->pobj + t->len);
```

We exit the `for` loop when we've accumulated enough space with

```
avail >= need
```

or when we've reached the end (top) of memory with

```
t == last
```

In the latter case `obj_size()` packs the memory object data space, since it did not find enough holes above the object to fill the request.

  The second loop (`while`) starts where the `for` loop leaves off. It moves *backwards* through the linked descriptor list, moving each successive memory object *up* in memory by the required amount (need). `upmove()` moves object data up in memory. `obj_size()` calls `upmove()` as follows:

```
upmove(tmp, t->pobj + t->len - 1, t->len);
```

`upmove()`'s first argument is a destination address and the second argument is a source. The third argument is the number of bytes to move. Careful study reveals that `tmp` and `t->pobj + t->len - 1` are the *ends* of the destination and source addresses, respectively. Moving from the end is necessary to prevent overwriting data as we move it if the source and destination arrays overlap.

## Data Packing

This section is particularly interesting because it involves time-critical code. Besides showing you the code that moves bytes in object data space, we also discuss some of the techniques we can (or can't) use to make the routines more efficient.

First let's look at `pack()`. `obj_alloc()` calls `pack()` when there is not not enough room at the end of object data space to accommodate a new object. `obj_size()` calls `pack()` if the number of unused holes above the object to be resized cannot accommodate the resize amount. `pack()`'s task is straightforward. It starts at the bottom of memory and looks for holes in allocated object data space. `pack()` moves object data *down* to fill unused holes. It steps through the entire linked descriptor list until it reaches the end (`last`), moving each memory object in turn. Here's the code for `pack()`:

```
static pack()           /* pack object data space to bottom */
{
    register Object *p, *tmp;
    void obj_check();

    for (p = first; p != last; p = p->next) {
        tmp = p->next;

        /* pack the block above this flush to the end */
        if (p->pobj + p->len < tmp->pobj) {
            downmove(p->pobj + p->len, tmp->pobj, tmp->len);
            tmp->pobj = p->pobj + p->len;
        }
    }
    if (DBUG(12, "pack: performing object check\n"))
        obj_check();
}
```

`pack()` relies on the fact that the linked descriptor list maintains memory objects in order of increasing heap addresses. Each time through the loop, `tmp` contains the address of the next object in object data space. If the statement

```
    if (p->pobj + p->len < tmp->pobj) {
```

evaluates to TRUE, there is a hole that is

```
    tmp->pobj - (p->pobj + p->len)
```

bytes long.

The call to `downmove()`

```
    downmove(p->pobj + p->len, tmp->pobj, tmp->len);
```

moves data in `tmp->pobj` *down* in memory so that it directly follows data that starts at `p->pobj`. `downmove()` has the same number of arguments and protocols that `upmove()` uses. The statement

```
tmp->pobj = p->pobj + p->len;
```

assigns the new memory address for the memory object just moved.

pack() also calls obj_check() for debug output. We'll return to this later when we discuss debugging the allocator.

Now let's look at upmove() and downmove(). Both routines take three arguments: to (a destination address), from (a source address), and cnt (the number of bytes to move). Here's the code:

```
static upmove(to, from, cnt)            /* move objects up */
register unsigned char *to, *from;
int cnt;
{
    DBUG(12, "upmove:     from = %x  to = %x for %4d bytes\n",
            from, to, cnt);

    while (cnt--)
        *to-- = *from--;
}

static downmove(to, from, cnt)          /* move objects down */
register unsigned char *to, *from;
int cnt;
{
    DBUG(12, "downmove:   from = %x  to = %x for %4d bytes\n",
            from, to, cnt);

    while (cnt--)
        *to++ = *from++;
}
```

All the work is done with while loops and compact pointer expressions. In upmove(), for example, the code

```
    while (cnt--)
        *to-- = *from--;
```

copies data from the *end* of the block first.   downmove(), on the other hand, starts at the *beginning* of the block with

```
    while (cnt--)
        *to++ = *from++;
```

and increments the pointers as each byte is copied.

Clearly, `upmove()` and `downmove()` require careful tuning to optimize run time performance. Not only does the object allocator call these routines frequently, but they may move the entire object data space. How can we increase performance? As long as the size of a pointer is the same as the size of an integer, the use of compact pointer expressions with register variables for `to` and `from` can help. However, register variables are machine dependent, and in some situations the compiler may not be able to provide a register variable, even if one is available. (See Appendix C for a discussion of `far` pointers with the INTEL 8086, 186, and 286 architecture.)

Perhaps the best approach is to implement `upmove()` and `downmove()` with the C library routine `memcpy()`. These routines are fast, since many versions are assembly language programs that use block move instructions. Some implementations of `memcpy()` do *not* allow moving overlapping memory blocks, however. Since the object allocator may have to rearrange heap memory that overlaps object data, be forewarned that if you implement the object allocator on your machine, make sure your version of `memcpy()` works properly. We left out calls to `memcpy()` intentionally, because `upmove()` and `downmove()` are more portable. If your machine supports `memcpy()` that works for overlapping arrays, replace the calls to `upmove()` and `downmove()` with `memcpy()`. The number of arguments and protocols are the same.

## Consistency Checks

Chapter 5 shows the value of designing custom debugging tools for complicated software systems. The object allocator is a good example of a program that may harbor subtle bugs. The allocation and deallocation of pointers, for instance, can be particularly troublesome, since the symptoms may not be repeatable. To combat this, we provide a routine called `obj_check()` that runs *consistency checks* of object data space and the object descriptor structures. User programs may call this routine at any time to check the integrity of the allocator.

Consistency checks are meant to check known relationships between certain variables and report discrepancies. The object allocator, for example, uses 0 in field `*pobj` to mark unused slots in the descriptor list. The number of slots whose value is not 0, therefore, should equal the number of used slots. Also, the sum of allocated memory and unallocated memory should total the size of object data space. And of course, no memory object's data should overlap another one.

`obj_check()` performs these consistency checks. Since they are time-consuming, user programs should call them only during program development and debugging. We recommend you remove them from production code with conditional compilation.

Here is the code for `obj_check()`:

```
void obj_check()              /* memory object consistency check */
{
    Object *p;
    register int i, cnt, len;

    for (cnt = len = i = 0; i < OBJSIZE; i++) {
        if (objects[i].pobj != 0) {
            cnt++;
            len+= objects[i].len;
        }
    }
    if (len + mavail != OBJSPACE)
        obj_error("obj_check error for Object Data Space");
    if (cnt != nobj)
        obj_error("obj_check error for Object Descriptors");

    for (i = 1, p = first; ;i++, p = p->next) {
        if (p == last || i > nobj)
            break;
        if (p->pobj + p->len > p->next->pobj)
            obj_error("obj_check error for Object Data Space overlap");
    }
    if (p != last || i != nobj)
        obj_error("obj_check consistency error");
}
```

obj_check() uses two for loops with the object descriptors. The first loop
traverses the descriptor array (not in link list order, but in subscript order),
counting the number of slots and the amount of allocated bytes. The statement

```
    if (len + mavail != OBJSPACE)
```

makes sure the total amount of allocated and unallocated memory is equal to the
entire object data space (OBJSPACE). Similarly, the statement

```
    if (cnt != nobj)
```

verifies that the total number of allocated slots (cnt) agrees with the current
number of object descriptors (nobj). If either case fails, obj_check() reports
an error and the program terminates.

In the next for loop, obj_check() traverses the descriptors in linked
list order. The loop stops when we've exceeded the number of allocated slots
(nobj), or we've reached the value of the last descriptor on the list (last).

With each descriptor, obj_check() makes sure that memory areas don't
overlap with the statement

```
    if (p->pobj + p->len > p->next->pobj)
```

Following the second `for` loop, `obj_check()` verifies that the loop terminated properly. This means we should be at the last object in the descriptor list, and the number of allocated objects should equal `nobj`. If either is not true, `obj_check()` reports an error and the program terminates.

The only object allocator routines left to examine are `obj_mavail()`, `obj_davail()`, and `obj_error()`. Here's the code for each one.

```
    /* amount of object data space left */
    long obj_mavail()
    {
        return mavail;
    }

    /* number of object descriptors left */
    int obj_davail()
    {
        return OBJSIZE - nobj;
    }

    /* display error message from allocator */
    static obj_error(msg)
    char *msg;
    {
        fprintf(stderr, "objalloc: %s\n", msg);
        exit(1);
    }
```

`obj_mavail()` returns control variable `mavail`. This lets user programs know how much object data space is left. Likewise, `obj_davail()` returns the number of unused object descriptors to a user program. `obj_error()`, on the other hand, is declared `static` and is never called from user programs. The object allocator calls it when errors occur. `obj_error()` reports all error messages on standard error and terminates the object allocator with an `exit(1)`.

## Allocator Driver

The previous routines make up the last part of the object allocator. We now discuss an embedded *driver* to test the allocator. As we showed in Chapter 5, the driver is part of the file that contains the source code for the allocator. The driver consists of a `main()` function that calls routines from the allocator and mimics a user program. We conditionally compile the driver with the `-D` option to test the allocator routines. Without the option, compilations create a relocatable file that we may link with other programs. When problems appear, we return to the driver to duplicate errors, as much as possible. This makes it easier to analyze what the allocator is doing.

The following driver contains a main program and a function prob-jects(). The main program calls obj_init() to initialize the allocator and allocates five memory objects. The program uses an array of object pointers to hold the objects. The driver shrinks, expands, frees, and resizes memory objects, calling obj_check() at appropriate places. probjects() displays the linked descriptor list, showing each object's pointer address, size, and unused space (if any) in front of the next object.

Here's the code for the driver.

```
#ifdef DRIVER
main()
{
    Object *p[5];
    int i;
    void obj_init(), obj_free(), obj_size(), obj_check();

    obj_init();              /* initialize structures */
    obj_check();

    p[0] = obj_alloc(100);
    p[1] = obj_alloc(200);
    p[2] = obj_alloc(300);
    p[3] = obj_alloc(400);
    p[4] = obj_alloc(500);
    probjects(stderr);

    obj_free(p[2]);                /* free object 3 */
    obj_check();

    obj_size(p[0], 64);            /* shrink object 1 */
    obj_size(p[3], 275);          /* shrink object 4 */
    probjects(stderr);
    obj_check();
    obj_size(p[1], 800);         /* expand object 2 */
    obj_check();

    probjects(stderr);
}
```

```
probjects(where)
FILE *where;
{
    Object *p;
    long obj_mavail();
    int nobj;

    fprintf(where, " OBJECT    ADDR    SIZE    UNUSED\n");
    for (nobj = 0, p = first; p != last; nobj++, p = p->next)
        fprintf(where, "%4d      %4x    %4d    %4d\n", nobj,
                p->pobj, p->len, p->next->pobj - (p->pobj + p->len));

    fprintf(where, "%4d      %4x    %4d\n", nobj,
                last->pobj, last->len);

    fprintf(where, "Object Data Space left: %7ld bytes\n",
                obj_mavail());
    fprintf(where, "Object Descriptors left: %6d\n",  obj_davail());
}
#endif
```

The main program allocates five objects, each with data sizes from 100 bytes to 500 bytes. The program frees the third object (p[2]) and calls obj_check() for consistency checks. main() calls obj_size() three times to resize objects. The first two calls shrink object data and the third call quadruples p[1]'s data size. main() calls probjects() several times to display object information.

probjects() writes to standard error from the driver, but it's designed to write to data files as well (using FILE *where). The routine uses a for loop to traverse the object descriptor list showing each object's pointer address, size, and unused space. Routine probjects() uses the familiar expression

```
p->next->pobj - (p->pobj + p->len)
```

to determine the unused number of bytes between the current object and the next one. The routine also calls obj_mavail() to display the amount of object data space remaining and obj_davail() for the number of used objects.

All that's left is to compile the allocator and run it. The name of the allocator source file is objalloc.c and we link it with the debugger. Chapter 5 contains the source for the debug routine dbug.c. Here's the output.

```
$ cc -c dbug.c
$ cc -DDRIVER objalloc.c dbug.o -o objalloc
$ objalloc
```

| OBJECT | ADDR | SIZE | UNUSED |
|--------|------|------|--------|
| 0 | 54b8 | 0 | 0 |
| 1 | 54b8 | 100 | 0 |
| 2 | 551c | 200 | 0 |
| 3 | 55e4 | 300 | 0 |
| 4 | 5710 | 400 | 0 |
| 5 | 58a0 | 500 | |

```
Object Data Space left:    27172 bytes
Object Descriptors left:     506
```

| OBJECT | ADDR | SIZE | UNUSED |
|--------|------|------|--------|
| 0 | 54b8 | 0 | 0 |
| 1 | 54b8 | 64 | 36 |
| 2 | 551c | 200 | 300 |
| 3 | 5710 | 275 | 125 |
| 4 | 58a0 | 500 | |

```
Object Data Space left:    27633 bytes
Object Descriptors left:     507
```

| OBJECT | ADDR | SIZE | UNUSED |
|--------|------|------|--------|
| 0 | 54b8 | 0 | 0 |
| 1 | 54b8 | 64 | 0 |
| 2 | 54f8 | 800 | 0 |
| 3 | 5818 | 275 | 0 |
| 4 | 592b | 500 | |

```
Object Data Space left:    27033 bytes
Object Descriptors left:     507
```

The driver calls probjects() three times, so the output appears in three sections. The first section shows the descriptor list after five objects have been allocated. Heap addresses are in hexadecimal, and the UNUSED column shows there are no holes. There is nothing printed in the UNUSED column for the last object because the rest of object data space is available. There are 506 object descriptors remaining (0 is the dummy slot).

The second section shows the descriptor list after the third object has been freed and the first and third objects have been resized. The UNUSED column displays the number of bytes in each hole. The output shows there are now 507 free object descriptors.

The last section shows the descriptor list after object two expands to 800 bytes. Since there is not enough room for the resize amount, the allocator packs object data space and rearranges the data. The UNUSED column shows there are no holes. The number of object descriptors does not change, and the amount of available data space decreases.

The driver is useful for studying the behavior of the allocator. As an exercise, try different parameters for each call to the object allocator and observe the output.

## Debugging the Allocator

Each object allocator routine contains embedded debug calls. Using the technique for selective debug prints from Chapter 5, we display debug information while the allocator executes. Typical debug calls have the form

```
DBUG(12, "obj_alloc: pobj = %x for %4d bytes  mavail = %x\n",
    p->pobj, len, mavail);
```

DBUG is a macro defined in dbug.h. This calls a debug function if flag number 12 appears in an ASCII file called flags in your current directory. If there is no file, the debugger runs silently. The technique allows you to observe debug information without recompiling modules.

Here's debug output from the driver. The information provides considerable insights into how the allocator behaves.

```
$ cat flags
12
$ objalloc
obj_alloc: pobj = 54b8 for  100 bytes  mavail = 6f9c
obj_alloc: pobj = 551c for  200 bytes  mavail = 6ed4
obj_alloc: pobj = 55e4 for  300 bytes  mavail = 6da8
obj_alloc: pobj = 5710 for  400 bytes  mavail = 6c18
obj_alloc: pobj = 58a0 for  500 bytes  mavail = 6a24
  OBJECT     ADDR     SIZE     UNUSED
    0        54b8        0        0
    1        54b8      100        0
    2        551c      200        0
    3        55e4      300        0
    4        5710      400        0
    5        58a0      500
Object Data Space left:    27172 bytes
Object Descriptors left:     506
obj_free:  pobj = 55e4 for  300 bytes  mavail = 6b50
obj_size: want   64, (have  100)
obj_size:  pobj = 54b8 for   64 bytes  mavail = 6b74
obj_size: want  275, (have  400)
obj_size:  pobj = 5710 for  275 bytes  mavail = 6bf1
  OBJECT     ADDR     SIZE     UNUSED
    0        54b8        0        0
    1        54b8       64       36
    2        551c      200      300
```

```
   3         5710       275         125
   4         58a0       500
Object Data Space left:     27633 bytes
Object Descriptors left:      507
obj_size: want  800, (have  200)
downmove:   from = 551c  to = 54f8 for   200 bytes
downmove:   from = 5710  to = 55c0 for   275 bytes
downmove:   from = 58a0  to = 56d3 for   500 bytes
pack: performing object check
upmove:     from = 58c6  to = 5b1e for   500 bytes
upmove:     from = 56d2  to = 592a for   275 bytes
obj_size:   pobj = 54f8 for   800 bytes   mavail = 6999
  OBJECT      ADDR      SIZE       UNUSED
    0         54b8        0          0
    1         54b8       64          0
    2         54f8      800          0
    3         5818      275          0
    4         592b      500
Object Data Space left:     27033 bytes
Object Descriptors left:      507
```

The output displays all parts of the allocator. This includes data packing, upmoves, downmoves, as well as object sizing, allocation, and deallocation. We leave it to you to interpret the output.

# ◆ Implementing Dynamic Strings ◆

Let's return to ATL. The C program that implements ATL has to handle string declarations, string assignments, string functions (such as concatenation and concatenation with a blank), and string output. This section examines C code that uses the object allocator to perform these operations.

ATL is a language interpreter that translates ATL statements to C statements. For example, ATL translates the statement

```
string s1;
```

to the C statement

```
s1 = string(0, NULL);
```

The C routine `string()` assigns a string of zero length to the string object `s1`. Likewise, ATL translates the statement

```
s1 = "Hello";
```

to the C function calls

```
sassign(s1, string(5, "Hello"));
```

In this case, `string()` creates the string constant `"Hello"` and the C routine `sassign()` assigns it to the string object `s1`. The details of how ATL generates these C statements don't concern us. Instead, we'll focus on how ATL uses the object allocator with string objects.

To see how this works, we use the same approach as we used with the allocator in the previous section. We'll go through a file of C routines for ATL dynamic strings, followed by an embedded driver that implements the sample ATL program from the start of the chapter.

Let's start with simple string declarations and string assignments, then work toward more complicated ways to build strings. Along the way, you'll see how the object allocator does most of the hard work.

Before we begin, let's look at several new definitions. Here's the start of our program (called `strmob.c`).

```
/* strmob.c - implement ATL dynamic strings with
               memory object allocator

     cc -DDRIVER strmob.c objalloc.o dbug.o -o strmob
*/

#include <stdio.h>
#include "obj.h"

#define obj_room 40          /* default string size */

typedef Object String;       /* objects are strings */
```

`strmob.c` includes a comment which explains how to compile it. The program implements strings as objects, using a `typedef` and the `obj.h` header file. `obj_room` is a constant (40) that we'll return to shortly.

## String Declarations

ATL allows two types of string declarations. Without initialization, ATL creates a string of zero length by default. Using a format similar to C, ATL strings may be declared and initialized to a constant string on the same line. The following statements

```
string s1;
string s2 = "Hello, World";
```

for example, declare s1 to be a string of zero length and s2 to be a string of 12 characters. The C routine for string declarations, therefore, must handle both formats.

Here's the code for a string declaration:

```
String *string(nc, s)            /* string declaration */
int nc;
char *s;
{
    String *p, *obj_alloc();

    p = obj_alloc(nc > obj_room ? nc : obj_room);
    p->used = nc;                /* amount used */
    if (s)
        memcpy(p->pobj, s, nc);
    return p;
}
```

string() takes two arguments: a count (nc) and a pointer to a C string (s). The routine returns a string (specifically, a pointer to a string). string() calls obj_alloc() to allocate heap space for the string. The routine allocates either obj_room or nc bytes, whichever is greater. This provides "elbow room" if resizing occurs later. string() sets p->used to nc. If s is not NULL, string() copies nc bytes from s into the newly allocated string. (We use memcpy() and not strcpy(), since ATL strings do not have NULL byte terminators.) Thus, the following call

```
s1 = string(0, NULL);
```

implements the default format for string declaration. The object allocator allocates 40 bytes (obj_room) of storage for the string. s1's length (p->used) is zero. The call

```
s2 = string(12, "Hello, World");
```

implements the second format. The object allocator also allocates 40 bytes, but only the first 12 bytes contain characters ("Hello, World"). p->used is 12 and p->len is 40 for s2.

## String Assignment

ATL supports string assignment between a string variable and a constant string or two string variables. For example, the lines

```
s1 = s2;
s2 = "Hello";
```

copy the contents of s2 to s1 and assign the constant string "Hello" to s2. Both formats require resizing strings. Here's the code for string assignment:

```
String *sassign(to, from)            /* string assignment */
String *to, *from;
{
    if (to->len < from->used)
        fix_size(to, from->used);
    memcpy(to->pobj, from->pobj, from->used);
    to->used = from->used;
    return to;
}
```

sassign()'s first argument is a string destination address and its second argument is a string source address. sassign() examines the length of the two strings first. If the destination's length (to->len) is less than the source's string length (from->used), sassign() calls fix_size() to increase the amount of memory allocated for the destination string. This routine uses len to compare the storage reserved for the destination object and used for the length of valid data used by the source string. After making sure that there is enough room for the new string, sassign() copies data with memcpy() and updates used.

Here's the code for fix_size(), which resizes strings.

```
fix_size(p, size)      /* resize with elbow room */
String *p;             /* previously allocated pointer */
int size;              /* make string at least this big */
{
    void obj_size();

    if (p->len < size)            /* need to resize */
        obj_size(p, size + obj_room);
    return size;
}
```

fix_size() calls obj_size() to resize strings. Rather than always call obj_size() to change a string's length, fix_size() makes sure there are at least size bytes available before it uses the object allocator to resize. When it's necessary to resize, fix_size() requests obj_room extra bytes. This small amount of extra work helps minimize packing when frequent small adjustments are likely.

## String Functions

Our sample ATL program contains the following statements:

```
echo (s1 - s2);
s3 = dup("=", 61);
s3 = left(s3, 5) + s1 - s2 + left(s3, 5);     // string building
```

ATL uses the following C functions to implement the previous ATL statements:

| | |
|---|---|
| sjoin | concatenate two strings |
| sjoinb | concatenate two strings with blank |
| sdup | create a string of duplicate chars |
| sleft | extract left substring of chars |
| secho | echo a string to the terminal |
| sfree | free a string |

As you look at the code for each routine, you'll discover none of them create new strings, because they work with strings that already exist. For example, sjoin() appends the contents of its second string argument to its first string argument. sjoinb() works similarly. sleft()'s first argument is the number of bytes to extract from its second string argument. The routine copies the new string of extracted bytes to its first argument. All routines explicitly avoid creating new strings so we may control string creation and destruction from a central part in our code. This is a design issue rather than a coding issue, since we can write string functions either way.

Keeping this in mind, let's look at the source for each routine. We begin with sjoin().

```
String *sjoin(to, from)                /* concatenation */
String *to, *from;
{
    int need = from->used + to->used;

    if (to->len < need)
        fix_size(to,need);
    memcpy(to->pobj + to->used, from->pobj, from->used);
    to->used = need;
    return to;
}
```

sjoin's arguments are the same as sassign(). The routine uses a local variable need to hold the amount of new storage required. If the destination's allocated space (to->len) is less than this amount, sjoin() increases string space with fix_size(). The routine copies the contents of the string it is appending (`from->pobj`) to the *end* of the destination string (`to->pobj + to->used`). `sjoin()` updates `to->used` to the new length before returning. `sjoin()` returns a pointer to its first argument (`to`).

Why does `sjoin()` return a string pointer? After all, we can access the same information with the first argument we called it with. By returning a pointer, we may use `sjoin()`'s return value in an expression. In particular, we may use `sjoin()` as an argument to another function, such as:

```
sleft(s3, sjoin(s1, s2), 10);
```

Here we append string `s2` to `s1` and then place the first 10 characters in string `s3`. We can accomplish the same thing with the more verbose

```
sjoin(s1, s2);
sleft(s3, s1, 10);
```

of course, but the previous version allows the ATL interpreter to generate more compact function calls.

`sjoinb()`, which is similar to `sjoin()`, concatenates two strings with an intervening blank. Here's the code for `sjoinb()`:

```
/* concat with a blank */

String *sjoinb(to, from)
String *to, *from;
{
    int need = from->used + to->used + 1;

    if (to->len < need)
        fix_size(to, need);
    to->pobj[to->used++] = ' ';
    memcpy(to->pobj + to->used, from->pobj, from->used);
    to->used = need;
    return to;
}
```

`sjoinb()` adjusts need to reserve an additional byte for the blank. The statement

```
to->pobj[to->used++] = ' ';
```

assigns a blank to the end of the destination string. The increment operator `++` updates `to->used` so that the following `memcpy()` statement copies the source string to the correct location.

Next, let's look at the routine for duplicating a character in a string. ATL calls `sdup()` with three parameters: a destination string (to), a character (ch), and a count (nc).

```
/* duplicate char ch nc times */

String *sdup(to, ch, nc)
String *to;
char ch;
int nc;
{
    if (to->len < nc)
        fix_size(to, nc);
    memset(to->pobj, ch, nc);
    to->used = nc;
    return to;
}
```

The routine checks that `to` has room for `nc` characters and calls `fix_size()`, if necessary. The C library routine `memset()` fills the string with the character ch. `sdup()` updates `to->used` and returns a pointer to the destination string, `to`.

The next string function is `sleft()`. This routine takes three arguments: a pointer to the destination string (to), a pointer to the source string (from), and the number of characters to extract. Like the others, `sleft()` returns a pointer to the destination string. Here's the code:

```
/* left nc chars from string */

String *sleft(to, from, nc)
String *to, *from;
int nc;
{
    if (to->len < nc)
        fix_size(to, nc);
    memcpy(to->pobj, from->pobj, nc);
    to->used = nc;
    return to;
}
```

`sleft()` makes sure the destination string has enough storage to hold the requested number of characters (nc) and calls `fix_size()` if it needs to increase storage. `memcpy()` copies the requested characters to the destination string. `sleft()` updates `to->used` and returns a pointer to the new string (to).

`secho()` displays characters from its string argument. Here's the code:

```
/* display string data */

secho(ps)
String *ps;
{
    unsigned char *start = ps->pobj;
    unsigned char *end = start + ps->used;
    register unsigned char *p;

    for (p = start; p < end; p++)
        putchar(*p);
    putchar('\n');
}
```

`secho()` uses `putchar()` to display each string character one at a time. It's not possible to use C string library functions here, because ATL strings have no NULL terminator byte.    `secho()` displays a newline before it returns.

The last routine is `sfree()`, which frees a string. Here's the code:

```
/* free a string */

void sfree(s)
String *s;
{
    obj_free(s);              /* free it */
}
```

The routine just passes its argument as an object address to `obj_free()`.

These routines demonstrate how easily the object allocator moves data in the heap without disturbing ATL's data structures. For example, if `sjoin()` needs more room, it calls `fix_size()`. `fix_size()` in turn, possibly calls `obj_size()` and `obj_size()` may call `upmove()`, `downmove()`, or both. All of the data movement is transparent to `sjoin()`.

`sjoin()` keeps track of strings with object descriptors. Descriptor locations never change, even though the fields in the descriptor change as objects move. Consequently, when `sjoin()` copies new data to the end of the destination string, the fields `to->pobj` and `from->pobj` may have new values, but `to` and `from` don't change.

# ◆ Putting It All Together ◆

As a final exercise, let's return to the original ATL sample program and use an embedded driver with the object allocator and string functions. This driver is different than the object allocator driver we looked at earlier, because it calls the string routines we just discussed as well as the object allocator routines.

The driver is nothing more than a simple test showing dynamic string manipulation in action. While this is a small part of the ATL Project, it's still an important aspect of resolving the implementation of dynamic strings without running out of memory through uncollected garbage. Here is the driver with the ATL sample program statements enclosed in comments.

```
#ifdef DRIVER
main()
{
  String *s1, *s2, *s3, *stemp1, *stemp2;
  void obj_init();

  obj_init();            /* initialize the allocator */

/* ATL string declaration
    string s1, s2, s3;
*/
    s1 = string(0, NULL);
    s2 = string(0, NULL);
    s3 = string(0, NULL);

/* ATL string assignment
    s1 = "Hello";
    s2 = "World";
*/
    sassign(s1, string(5, "Hello"));
    sassign(s2, string(5, "World"));

/* ATL string concatenation
    echo ( s1 - s2 );
*/
    stemp1 = string(0, NULL);
    sassign(stemp1, s1);
    secho(sjoinb(stemp1, s2));
    sfree(stemp1);

/* ATL string function
    s3 = dup("=", 61);
    echo(s3);
*/
```

```
    sdup(s3, '=', 61);
    secho(s3);

/* ATL string building
    s3 = left(s3, 25) + s1 - s2 + left(s3, 25)
    echo(s3);
*/
    stemp1 = string(0, NULL);
    stemp2 = string(0, NULL);
    sassign(stemp2, sleft(stemp1, s3, 25));
    sassign(s3, sjoin(sjoinb(sjoin(stemp1, s1), s2), stemp2));
    sfree(stemp1);
    sfree(stemp2);
    secho(s3);

    sfree(s1);
    sfree(s2);
    sfree(s3);
}
#endif
```

`s1`, `s2`, `s3`, `stemp1`, and `stemp2` are strings (pointers to objects). The driver calls `obj_init()` to initialize the object allocator.

To implement the ATL statement

```
    echo (s1 - s2);
```

ATL does need to create a temporary string variable. The statements

```
    stemp1 = string(0, NULL);
    sassign(stemp1, s1);
    secho(sjoinb(stemp1, s2));
    sfree(stemp1);
```

do the job. In this case, `stemp1` becomes the concatenated string that `secho()` displays. First we create the temporary string and fill it with `s1`'s data before we use `sjoinb()` to place a blank between it and `s2`. ATL frees `stemp` with `sfree()`.

The ATL statement

```
    s3 = left(s3, 25) + s1 - s2 + left(s3, 25)
```

shows the true power of the object allocator implementation. You'll have to look carefully at

```
sassign(stemp2, sleft(stemp1, s3, 25));
sassign(s3, sjoin(sjoinb(sjoin(stemp1, s1), s2), stemp2));
```

to see how all this works. ATL uses *two* temporary string variables here. `stemp2` holds the string returned from `sleft()` and `stemp1` holds an intermediate string. The object allocator handles all the resizing and data movements for these function calls.

Here's how you compile and run the program.

```
$ cc -c objalloc.c
$ cc -DDRIVER strmob.c objalloc.o dbug.o -o strmob

$ strmob
Hello World
==================================================================
=======================Hello World=========================
```

The ATL project's string functions comprise only one example of using the object allocator. With the `obj.h` header file and appropriate `typedef`'s, programs may use the object allocator for window based systems, databases, or other object oriented applications.

# ◆ Summary ◆

- C programmers use the standard allocator for dynamic memory allocation. The routines `malloc()`, `calloc()`, `realloc()`, and `free()` manage data from the heap.

- During program execution, the heap may become fragmented, containing holes of unused space between data.

- Garbage collection entails moving data to eliminate holes.

- The standard allocator does not perform garbage collection because user programs interface to heap data with a byte pointer. These pointers become invalid if the allocator moves data. It is possible, therefore, for allocation requests to fail even if sufficient unallocated heap memory exists.

- The memory object allocator is one solution to this problem. The object allocator returns a pointer to an object descriptor rather than a byte. Object descriptors contain pointers to heap data, and the object allocator performs garbage collection when necessary. Pointers to heap data may change, but pointers to object descriptors do not.

- The object allocator has routines to allocate, deallocate, resize, and free objects (see Table 6-1). Additional routines perform consistency checks and return memory size and object counts to user programs.

- The object allocator moves data either up or down in memory to make room for new objects.

- The object allocator routines that move data up or down in memory must be fast to make performance acceptable. Heap rearrangement involves moving blocks of data that may overlap.

- The object allocator is useful for handling dynamic variables.

- Custom debugging tools assist in the development, support, and maintenance of complex programs like the memory object allocator.

# ◆ Exercises ◆

1. Modify the memory object allocator so that it does not use the first slot in the object descriptor array for a dummy object. What routines are affected? Discuss the advantages and disadvantages of the new approach.

2. Eliminate the calls to `obj_error()` inside the object allocator and return error codes (integers) instead. The allocator routines in Table 6-1 that are `void` should now return 0 on success and a negative number on failure. Have `obj_alloc()` return NULL if it fails. Write a driver to test the new system.

3. Modify the object allocator to use a *free list*. Have `obj_init()` put all object descriptors in a free list. Use the `next` field to connect each free object descriptor to another one. In `obj_free()`, place free objects at the end of the free list. In `obj_alloc()`, fetch new object descriptors from the end of the free list. Implement such a scheme and test it with a driver. If possible, benchmark your new object allocator against the version from this chapter. How do the execution times compare?

4. Why can't we implement `upmove()` and `downmove()` with the fast array transfer technique from Chapter 4?

5. Substitute the following main program for the driver shown in this chapter.

```
main()
{
    Object *p[20];
    int i;
    void obj_init(), obj_free(), obj_size(),
        obj_check();

    obj_init();              /* initialize structures */
    obj_check();

    p[0] = obj_alloc(100);
    p[1] = obj_alloc(200);
    p[2] = obj_alloc(300);
    p[3] = obj_alloc(400);
    p[4] = obj_alloc(500);
    probjects(stderr);

    obj_free(p[3]);          /* free object 4 */
    obj_check();

    for (i = 5; i < 20; i++)
      p[i] = obj_alloc(10 * i);
```

```
    obj_check();

    obj_size(p[0], 50);    /* shrink object 1 */
    obj_check();
    obj_size(p[1], 350);   /* expand object 2 */
    obj_check();
    probjects(stderr);

    for (i = 5; i < 20; i += 4)
      obj_free(p[i]);
    obj_check();
    for (i = 6; i < 20; i += 4)
      obj_size(p[i], i * 10 + 200);
    obj_check();
    probjects(stderr);
}
```

Compile, run the program and study the output. Can you follow the allocator's behavior when objects are freed and resized? For additional information, enable debugging and rerun.

6. Write a string comparison routine for the custom memory allocator. The routine, called scmp() should have the following form:

```
int scmp(s1, s2)
String *s1, *s2;
```

scmp() returns 0 if strings s1 and s2 are equal, −1 if s1 is less than s2, and 1 if s1 is greater than s2. Remember to compare their contents (pointed to by s1->pobj and s2->pobj) as well as their lengths (s1->used and s2->used).

7. Write a string comparison *macro* that calls scmp() only if the first elements in each string match. Why would we want to do this?

8. ATL supports the following relational operators for dynamic strings.

| | | |
|---|---|---|
| = | equals | "radar" = "radar" |
| <> | not equals | "rotor" <> "radar" |
| < | less than | "symth" < "symthe" |
| > | greater than | "pa" > "PA" |
| <= | less than or equal to | "foot" <= "root" |
| >= | greater than or equal | "gag" >= "bag" |

Write C functions that implement these operators for ATL strings. Use scmp() as a starting point.

9. `sdup()` and `sleft()` have no error checking. Modify the routines to check for `nc = 0`. What should `sdup()` and `sleft()` do in the case of an error?

10. Combine `join()` and `joinb()` into one routine. Have the new routine take a third argument, which is the character to place between the two strings.

11. Write `right(s, nc)`, which extracts the last `nc` characters from string s. How would you implement the following ATL program which displays "part"?

```
main
    string s1, s2, s3;
    s1 = "department";
    echo(right(left(s1, 6), 4));
endmain
```

12. Discuss the implications of implementing the custom storage allocator under the Intel 286 medium or large memory models. The Microsoft C compiler provides the keyword `far` for accessing data outside the near segment. `far` pointers are 32 bits, `near` pointers are 16 bits.

13. Rewrite `obj_size()` so that it moves the object to be resized to the *end* of object data space before it frees the current object. Perform garbage collection only when space is not available. How does this impact performance?

# A P P E N D I X
♦   ♦   ♦   ♦   ♦   ♦   ♦   ♦
# A

# The Standard C Compiler
# Under UNIX

The standard UNIX C compiler (the  cc command) compiles programs in several steps.  These steps, in order, are the preprocessor, compiler, optimizer, assembler, and link editor (or linker).  The number of steps that  cc performs depends on the file names and compiler options that appear on the command line.  Table A-1 lists the file naming conventions used by  cc:

**TABLE A-1.  Command cc file naming conventions**

| File Name | Meaning |
| --- | --- |
| pgm.c | C source file |
| pgm.o | Object file (unlinked) |
| pgm.s | Assembly language source file |
| libx.a | Archive (library) file |

A list of  .o file names on the command line, for example, makes  cc invoke only the link editor.  Likewise,  .s files make  cc invoke the assembler in place of the C compiler.  Library files are typically named  libx.a, where $x$ appears with command line option  -l.

Table A-2 lists some common command line options that affect the steps performed by  cc:

**TABLE A-2.  Command line options affecting cc**

| Option | Meaning |
|--------|---------|
| -O     | Optimize step |
| -c     | Suppress link-edit step |
| -o     | Rename object file |

The  -O option makes the compiler perform optimization and  -c suppresses the link edit step.  Many  cc options are not compiler options at all (-o, for example, is a link editor option).

This appendix looks at useful  cc options for the standard UNIX C compiler.  Separate sections cover the compiler, link editor, and preprocessor.  Refer to Appendix B for a complete list of the options available on a typical UNIX system (Microport System V/AT).  This appendix also serves as a reference for all C compilers (specific C compilers appear in the remaining appendices).  The compiler options from this appendix should work in a similar way with your C compiler, but you need to consult your compiler's documentation as well.

## ◆ Compiler Options ◆

By default,  cc (without compiler options) invokes the preprocessor, compiler, and link editor automatically, producing an executable object file called  a.out. For example, the command

```
$ cc prog.c
```

compiles and links the C program  prog.c.  Typing  a.out executes the program.

```
$ a.out
```

Let's look at several compiler options that make  cc perform different actions.

### Separate Compilation: -c

The  -c option makes  cc suppress the link editor step.  The following command

```
$ cc -c objalloc.c dbug.c
```

creates two relocatable object files called  objalloc.o and  dbug.o, neither of which are executable. Suppose `prog.c`, for example, calls routines or references variables from either file. The following command makes `cc` compile `prog.c` and link all the files together.

```
$ cc prog.c objalloc.o dbug.o
```

The executable file is `a.out`. Files `objalloc.o` and `dbug.o` are not affected.

## Optimization: -O

The `-O` option (capital O) makes `cc` invoke the optimizer. Optimization techniques are often compiler dependent, but most compilers optimize programs for speed over size. The following command line, for example, compiles and optimizes `prog.c` and `sup1.c`, assembles `quick.s`, and links them with `dbug.o` to create an executable object module in `a.out`.

```
$ cc -O prog.c sup1.c quick.s dbug.o
```

The `-O` option has no affect on files `quick.s` or `dbug.o`.

## Assembly Language Listings: -S

The `-S` (capital S) option makes `cc` create an assembly language program. This option suppresses the link edit step. The command

```
$ cc -S -O idim2.c
```

for example, enables optimization and creates an ASCII file called `idim2.s` containing the assembly language instructions from the C compiler. This intermediate step allows you to investigate the assembly language instructions that the compiler generates from a C program. The `-S` option helps answer questions like:

1. Is the compiler generating a multiply instruction from the storage map equation?

2. Is the compiler *really* giving me a register in this declaration?

3. How does the compiler optimize this C code?

# ◆ Link Editor Options ◆

The `cc` command allows link editor options on the command line. Typical options name executable files, link special libraries, separate text and data space, and remove symbol tables from object code files. Let's look at several examples.

### Rename the Executable File: -o

Normally, you want the name of your executable file to be something other than `a.out`. The `-o` option (lowercase `o`) followed by a file name makes the link editor rename the executable object file. The following command line, for example, compiles `prog.c` and links it with `objalloc.o` and `dbug.o`, producing a file named `prog` instead of `a.out`.

```
$ cc prog.c objalloc.o dbug.o -o prog
```

Typing `prog` executes the program. The `-o` option and the file name may follow `cc` and appear before the rest of the file names.

### Name Libraries: -l

Command `cc` arranges to have the link editor search a standard set of libraries automatically. This is why you may use function calls from the standard C library (`printf()`, `malloc()`, `strcpy()`, etc.) without doing anything special on the command line. However, the link editor cannot search them all. The `curses` library and the `math` library are examples of special C libraries. The `-lx` option makes the link editor access `libx.a` for the library name. Suppose, for example, a C program (`servo.c`) calls `sqrt()` from the math library. The following command compiles `servo.c` and tells the link editor to search the math library.

```
$ cc servo.c -o servo -lm
```

`-lm` makes the link editor search the library `libm.a` in the directories `/lib` and `/usr/lib`. (While `-lm` is standard, the actual library name may be system dependent.)

### Sharing Text Space: -i

The `-i` option makes the link editor separate a C program's text and data segments. (This is the default on most UNIX systems.) The command

```
$ cc -i database.c -o database
```

for example, makes `database` a *pure* object code file. That is, the loader places the text and data segments in separate areas of memory.

Having separate text and data areas helps protect a program from inadvertently overwriting its instructions. Pure object files are also required for programs that *share* text space. Frequently used programs like the shell (/bin/sh) and the editor (/bin/vi) are compiled with the -i option (when it's not the default) because it's more efficient for UNIX. These programs have a read-only text space that user programs share from the same in-memory copy. Consequently, UNIX needs only to provide each user with its own data area, but not its own text area.

## Strip an Executable Object File: -s

Executable object files contain information from the link editor that is not needed to execute the program. This information is typically a program's symbol table and other relocatable data. Once a program is debugged, you may want to reduce the size of its executable object file. The -s (lower case s) option makes the link editor "strip" the relocation and symbolic information from an object file.

We can use the UNIX commands wc, size, and file to observe the effect of stripping an object file. wc -c, for example, produces a byte count for a program, and size displays the number of decimal bytes in a program's text, data, and BSS areas. file tells you if an object file has been stripped. Let's compile servo.c again, run these UNIX commands, and observe the results.

```
$ cc servo.c -o servo -lm
$ wc -c servo
  13757 servo
$ size servo
9768 + 1082 + 1566 = 12416 = 0x3080
$ file servo
servo:    executable not stripped
```

File servo's size is 13,757 bytes and its program areas total 12,416 bytes. It is an unstripped object file.

Now, let's recompile servo.c with the -s option to remove the linker information and run wc, size, and file again.

```
$ cc -s servo.c -o servo -lm
$ wc -c servo
  10978 servo
$ size servo
9768 + 1082 + 1566 = 12416 = 0x3080
$ file servo
servo:    executable
```

Now servo is only 10,978 bytes; however, the size of each program area doesn't change. Command file shows the object file has been stripped. (UNIX command strip performs the same function if you forget the -s flag at compilation time.)

# ◆  Preprocessor Options  ◆

The C compiler calls the preprocessor automatically.  Programs use the preprocessor to include files, expand macros, define symbols, and conditionally compile
C statements.  The preprocessor performs its duties behind the scenes most of the
time, so let's look at ways to use compiler options to find out more about what
it's doing and how it's doing it.

## Debugging the Preprocessor: -E

The  −E option makes the preprocessor display on standard output what it's
doing.  C comments disappear and  #include statements are replaced with the
text of the include file.  One simple use of this option, therefore, is to observe
how your program interacts with a system include file.  The  −E option's most
useful application, however, is for debugging *macros*.  Suppose, for example, we
compile and run the following program, which defines a macro to *set* a bit in a
word.

**Program A-1**

```
/* setbit1.c - bit set - incorrect */

#define SET(X,N) (X) |= 1 << (N)

main()
{
    int byte = 0x40;

    printf("%x\n", SET(byte, 0) + 8);
}

$ setbit1
140
```

The program should display 49, not 140.  Let's compile it with the  −E option to
find out how the preprocessor performs the macro substitution.

```
$ cc -E setbit1.c
 . . . .
main()
{
    int byte = 0x40;

    printf("%x\n", (byte) |= 1 << (0) + 8);
}
```

This display reveals that the compiler performs the addition before the left shift, due to C's precedence rules. We need to insulate the macro expression to make it evaluate correctly. Here's the correct version.

**Program A-2**

```
/* setbit2.c - bit set - correct */

#define SET(X,N) ((X) |= (1 << (N)))

main()
{
    int byte = 0x40;

    printf("%x\n", SET(byte, 0) + 8);
}

$ setbit2
49
```

The −E option shows the correct evaluation.

```
$ cc -E setbit2.c
 . . . .
main()
{
    int byte = 0x40;

    printf("%x\n", ((byte) |= (1 << (0))) + 8);
}
```

## Preprocessor File Output: -P

The −P option makes the preprocessor dump its output to a file, which is handy for debugging macros and large programs. The following command line

```
$ cc -P mdim2.c
```

for example, produces a file called mdim2.i, which contains C code after preprocessor substitutions and conditional compilation. To demonstrate, let's compile mdim2.c from Chapter 3 and follow what the preprocessor does for the macros that allocate and free two-dimensional arrays of any data type. Preprocessor output is often compressed and hard to follow, so here's mdim2.i after we run it through the UNIX C "beautifier" program cb:

```
$ cb mdim2.i
main(argc, argv)
int argc;
char *argv[];
{
    . . . . . . .
    {
        char *calloc();
        register int *pdata;
        int i;
        pdata = (int *) calloc(rows * cols, sizeof (int));
        . . . . . . .
        a   = (int **) calloc(rows, sizeof (int *));
        . . . . . . .
        for (i = 0; i < rows; i++) {
                a[i] = pdata;
                pdata += cols;
        }
    };
    . . . . . . .
    {
        char *calloc();
        register double *pdata;
        int i;
        pdata = (double *) calloc(rows * cols, sizeof (double));
        . . . . . . .
        b   = (double **) calloc(rows, sizeof (double *));
        . . . . . . .
        for (i = 0; i < rows; i++) {
                b[i] = pdata;
                pdata += cols;
        }
    };
    . . . . . . .
    {
        void free();
        free(*a);
        free(a);
    };
    {
        void free();
        free(*b);
        free(b);
    };
}
```

The output shows where the `calloc()` and `free()` library calls appear in the program after macro substitution.

## Preprocessor Defines: -D

Chapter 5 shows the utility of embedded *drivers* in C programs. Using preprocessor directives, the lines

```
#ifdef DRIVER
main ()
{
   . . . .
}
#endif
```

include a main routine and create an executable program for testing. The `-D` option compiles the driver. The following command, for example, prepares the debugger from Chapter 5 for testing.

```
$ cc -DDRIVER dbug.c -o dbug
```

Without the `-D` option, you can compile `dbug.c` with `-c` and link `dbug.o` with other modules. The following commands link the debugger and the object allocator (from Chapter 6) to the program `strmob.c`, which also contains a driver.

```
$ cc -c dbug.c objalloc.c
$ cc -DDRIVER strmob.c objalloc.o dbug.o -o strmob
```

We have to compile `objalloc.c` and `dbug.c` separately because they have embedded test drivers of their own. Compiling either `objalloc.c` or `dbug.c` with `-DDRIVER` enables their test drivers as well as `strmob.c`'s, creating more than one `main()` entry point.

You can also use the command line option `-D` to set constants. For example, the following C statement in your source file `dbug.c`

```
#define VERSION 5.0
```

is equivalent to using the following command line option:

```
$ cc -c dbug.c -DVERSION=5.0
```

## Preprocessor Include Files: -I

The -I option makes the preprocessor search for include files in a directory other than /usr/include. You supply a full pathname for the directory name after the -I option. The preprocessor searches these pathnames *before* /usr/include.

The -I option helps compile large systems that have many include files in one directory. Suppose, for example, objalloc.c and dbug.c use the include files obj.h and dbug.h from the directory /usr/atl/include. The following command compiles the two programs with the header files.

```
$ cc -c -O -I /usr/atl/include objalloc.c dbug.c
```

Both objalloc.c and dbug.c may use the notation

```
#include "obj.h"
#include "dbug.h"
```

to include the header files. If these files are not in the current directory, the preprocessor looks for them in the /usr/atl/include directory.

Another use of the -I option is to substitute your own macros and header files for the ones in /usr/include. Suppose, for example, dbug.c uses assertions from a custom version of the assert macro in a subdirectory called tools in your home directory. Without changing dbug.c, the following command compiles dbug.c and uses your assert macro in place of the system one:

```
$ cc -c -I $HOME/tools dbug.c
```

This works because the preprocessor searches your tools directory before /usr/include.

## ♦ Compiler Debugging Options ♦

UNIX provides tools to help you debug a C program and analyze its performance while it runs. These tools need special information that is not normally available in an object file. Before you can run these tools, you need to compile programs with special compiler options to gather the necessary information and prepare the object file. Let's look at the debugger and performance analyzer under UNIX System V.

## Symbolic Debugging: -g

UNIX System V provides a symbolic debugger called sdb that helps you track down bugs in C programs. (BSD systems provide a symbolic debugger called dbx.)   sdb provides features to trace a program's execution path, display program variables at run time, and pinpoint where a program is causing UNIX to dump core. The debugger accepts commands that use your program's variable and function names (in place of addresses), and sdb knows about line numbers and C *data types* (arrays, structures, etc.).

In order to use sdb, you must compile programs with the −g compiler option. The following commands, for example, prepare strmob for debugging with sdb.

```
$ cc -g -c objalloc.c dbug.c
$ cc -g -DDRIVER strmob.c objalloc.o dbug.o -o strmob
```

Note that we compile the object allocator and our debugger with −g as well as the main program strmob. To use sdb, we type

```
$ sdb strmob
*
```

## Performance Analysis: -p

UNIX System V also provides a tool called prof to study *where* a C program is spending its time and how many times your program calls each routine. This information tells you which routines you need to optimize to improve the performance of a program. Several steps are required to analyze a program's performance. First, you compile your system with the −p compiler option. Second, you run your program, which writes profiling information to a file called mon.out in your current directory. Third, you run prof to gather the profiling information and display it for you.

Let's do a performance analysis of the memory object allocator from Chapter 6. The following commands prepare our ATL test program (strmob.c) for prof.

```
$ cc -p -c objalloc.c dbug.c
$ cc -p -DDRIVER strmob.c objalloc.o dbug.o -o strmob
```

Program strmob contains an embedded driver for testing. Let's execute it and run prof.

```
$ strmob
Hello World
================================================================
=======================Hello World==========================
```

```
$ prof -g strmob
         name %time   cumsecs   #call   ms/call
         pack   0.0     0.10       2      0.00
       upmove   0.0     0.10       3      0.00
         dbug   0.0     0.10       1      0.00
     fix_size   0.0     0.10       2      0.00
         main   0.0     0.10       1      0.00
    obj_alloc   0.0     0.10       8      0.00
     obj_free   0.0     0.10       6      0.00
     obj_init   0.0     0.10       1      0.00
     obj_size   0.0     0.10       2      0.00
      sassign   0.0     0.10       5      0.00
         sdup   0.0     0.10       1      0.00
        secho   0.0     0.10       3      0.00
        sfree   0.0     0.10       6      0.00
        sjoin   0.0     0.10       2      0.00
       sjoinb   0.0     0.10       2      0.00
        sleft   0.0     0.10       1      0.00
       string   0.0     0.10       8      0.00
```

The display is much longer than we show and may look different on your system. Command prof lists system routines that you call as well as ones from your program; here, we show only our own routines. By default, prof only displays information about external routines. We use -g so prof includes statistics about static functions as well. (Some versions of prof use -a.) The first column lists the name of each routine and the second column shows the percentage of total time spent executing the routine (times smaller than a tenth of a second show up as 0.0). The third column is the cumulative time for execution, and the fourth column is the number of times the routine was called. The last column is the number of milliseconds per call. Although this display doesn't show it, prof orders the list of execution times from top to bottom (those at the top take more time).

# C Under Microport System V/AT

Microport provides UNIX System V products for both the 286 (System V/AT) and 386 (System V/386) Intel processors. The C compiler is an implementation of AT&T's Standard C Compiler on both systems. This appendix looks at the C compiler under Microport System V for the Intel 286 processor.

Microport's compiler produces **COFF** (Common Object File Format) object files that are compatible with the UNIX symbolic debugger, sdb. In the following list of compiler options for Microport's cc command, we follow each option with one or more letters designating the preprocessor (P), compiler (C), and link editor (L). Most of the compiler options are the same as the Standard C compiler's except for the differences relating to the Intel 286 architecture. We mark Microport specific compiler options with a †.

-a    Produce an absolute, executable file. Relocation information is stripped. *-a* is the default. (L)

-c    Produce .o file(s). (C)

-e *sym*
     Use *sym* as entry point address. (L)

-g    Include information for the symbolic debugger, sdb. (C)

-h *num*
     Define a *num*-byte header in the output file. (L)

-i    Produce a pure object file, one that has separate I (instruction) and D (data) spaces. (L)

-k *x* † Initially allocate *x* bytes for the stack. (L)

-l*name*
     Search library **lib***name***.a**, in directories /lib and /usr/lib. (L)

-m   Produce a link map and direct it to standard output. (L)

-o *outfile*
    Use *outfile* for output object file instead of `a.out`. (L)

-p   Produce code that counts the number of times each routine is called. If linking, use profile versions of `libc.a` and `libma.a`. Execution of object program produces file `mon.out`, which can be examined with `prof(1)`. (C/L)

-p[*nn*]
    † Generate a patch list. Use *nn* bytes of memory for patch sections. (L)

-r   Retain relocation entries for subsequent links. (L)

-s   Strip symbol table and line number information from the output object file. (L)

-t   Don't produce warnings about multiply defined symbols that are not the same size. (L)

-u *symbol*
    Place *symbol* as undefined in the symbol table. (L)

-x   Enter only external and static symbols in the output symbol table. (L)

-z   Do not place any data references at address zero. (L)

-B *nn*
    Create pad output sections of *nn* bytes each. (L)

-C   Do not strip C-style comments. (P)

-D*name*
    Define *name* to be `1` to the preprocessor. (P)

-D*name=str*
    Define *name* to be *str* to the preprocessor. (P)

-E   Run only the preprocessor and direct the result to standard output. (C/P)

-H   Display the full pathname of each include file on standard error. (P)

-I *pathname*
    Add *pathname* to the list of directories to be searched when an `#include` file is not found in the directory containing the source file. (P)

-L *dir*
    Look in *dir* for `libx.a` before looking in `/lib` and `/usr/lib`.   `-L` must precede the `-l` option on the command line. (L)

-M Complain when external definitions are multiply-defined. (L)

-Ms,-Ml
  † Generate small model (-Ms) or large model (-Ml) programs. These options apply only to the 286. Small model is the default. (C)

-O Perform object code optimization. This option does not affect .s files. (C)

-P Run only the preprocessor and place the output in the file *file*.i, where *file* is the base name of the C source file. (C/P)

-S Create an assembly language source listing in *file*.s, where *file* is the base name of the C source file. (C)

-T Force the preprocessor to use only the first eight characters of preprocessor symbols for backward compatibility. (P)

-U*name*
  Undefine preprocessor symbol *name*. (P)

-V Display version information for the compiler, optimizer, assembler, and/or link editor being used. (L)

-VS *num*
  Store *num* as a decimal version stamp in the a.out file header. (L)

-W*c,arg1[,arg2...]*
  Pass the arguments *arg1* ... to the compiler pass *c* where *c* is either p (preprocessor), 0 (compiler), 2 (optimizer), a (assembler), or 1 (link editor). (C)

-Y[p02albSILU],*dirname*
  Specify pathname *dirname* for the tools and directories named, as follows:

  p   preprocessor

  0   compiler

  2   optimizer

  a   assembler

  l   link editor

  b   basicblk

  S   directory for startup routines

  I   default include directory

  L   first library searched by ld

U   second library searched by `ld`

(C/P/L)

-#

-##

-###

Display `cc`'s steps (preprocessor, compiler, assembler, etc.)  as they
execute. -# displays the name of each program and -## displays absolute pathnames. -### displays the information without executing it.
(C/P/L)

# ◆ Memory Models ◆

The Intel 286 processor restricts memory accesses to 64-kilobyte chunks called
*segments*. Programs cannot view memory as contiguous bytes with addresses
from 0 to the amount of physical memory in the machine.  Instead, addresses
have two parts: a 16-bit *segment register* that specifies a 64-kilobyte segment and
a 16-bit *offset* that specifies the address within the segment.  The 286 processor
has specially named segment registers for accessing different memory segments.
These segment registers have the following names:   CS (code segment),  SS
(stack segment), DS (data segment), and ES (extra segment).  A C program running on Microport System V/AT has a *memory model* to conform to the 286's seg-
mented architecture.†

Chapter 2 shows UNIX programs have five program areas: initialized data,
uninitialized data (commonly called BSS), heap space (or dynamic data), the
stack, and text (or code).  The allocation of these program areas depends on the
memory model you specify during compilation.  Microport System V/AT
currently supports two memory models: small (the default) and large.

## Small Memory Model (Pure)

The small memory model allows up to 64K bytes for code (one segment) and a
*total* of 64K bytes (a different segment) for the stack, initialized data, BSS, and the
heap.  Object code files are *pure* because text and data are in separate segments.
Fig. B-1 shows how Microport System V/AT allocates the different program
areas in the small pure memory model.

---

† Memory models do not apply with C programs compiled with the 386 instruction set,
  but the 386 processor runs 286 object code files, which can have different memory
  models.

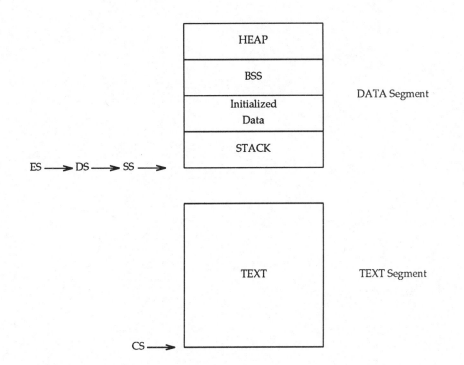

*Fig. B-1.* Small pure memory model

The CS register accesses the text segment. The DS, SS, and ES registers access the same data segment where the initialized data, BSS, heap, and stack reside. The compiler uses the ES register to move data from one section of memory to another. In the small pure memory model, these registers are loaded with values prior to execution and do not change as your program runs.

Consequently, data pointers in small model programs are always 16 bits, since the segment portion of the data pointer (register DS, SS, or ES) doesn't change. Text addresses (register CS) are 16 bits for the same reason. The small model allows programs to have a code size up to 64K bytes, but the amount of data a program can address is partitioned within one 64-kilobyte segment. The heap area starts with zero space and expands as your program runs. The size of the stack defaults to 8K bytes in the small model.

## Large Memory Model

In the large memory model, Microport System V/AT allocates separate segments for each program area. Fig. B-2 shows the arrangement.

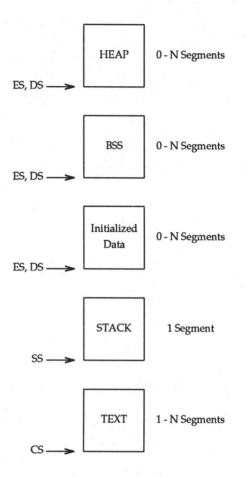

*Fig. B-2.* Large memory model

Initialized data, BSS, and the heap occupy zero or more segments. Text space may occupy more than one segment. The stack is limited to one segment, which defaults to 8K bytes and grows dynamically to a maximum of 64K bytes.

The size of a C program variable (such as an array) is limited to a single segment in the large model. This implies you cannot have an array (static or automatic) that is larger than 64K bytes. Furthermore, large model pointers are 32 bits (16 bits for the segment and 16 bits for the segment offset). The −Ml option creates large model programs.

## Choosing a Memory Model

Choosing a memory model under Microport System V/AT depends on the size of your program and the data it requires. In the small memory model, for instance, one 64-kilobyte segment accommodates the stack, initialized data, BSS, and the heap. A program that doesn't use the heap, for example, allows more space for the other program areas. If, on the other hand, the *total* amount of initialized data, BSS, stack, and heap exceeds 64K bytes, you'll need to upgrade to the large model. You'll also have to switch to the large model if your program's code size grows beyond 64K bytes.

Choosing the correct memory model is important. Large model programs make the compiler reload segment registers during execution. Consequently, large model programs typically run slower than small model ones. Large model programs also require the large model C library. Furthermore, large model pointers are 32 bits, and this affects how the compiler handles pointer operations. Pointers declared with storage class *register*, for instance, become automatic pointers in large model programs. The compiler performs 16-bit arithmetic with large model pointers. Although this helps make large model programs run faster (than using 32-bit arithmetic with pointers), a large model pointer cannot arbitrarily cross segment boundaries.

## ◆ Other Features ◆

## Compiler Pass Display

Microport provides cc options to display compiler pass information while your program is compiling. The  -# option, for example, displays the *name* of the step that's currently running.  -## displays the full pathname, and  -### displays the name of each step without executing it. To show this in action, suppose we compile pgm.c and follow the steps.

```
$ cc -# pgm.c
cc:   'cpp' 'pgm.c' '/tmp/ctm1AAAa00504' '-DSMALL_M' '-DiAPX286'
cc:   'comp' '-i' '/tmp/ctm1AAAa00504' '-o' '/tmp/ctm2BAAa00504' '-f'
cc:   'as' '-dl' '-o' 'pgm.o' '-Ms' '/tmp/ctm2BAAa00504'
cc:   'ld' '/lib/small/crt0.o' 'pgm.o' '-lc' '-la'
```

The output shows the preprocessor (cpp), compiler (comp), assembler (as), and link editor (ld) steps. The names of temporary files and libraries appear, as well as preprocessor definitions for the small memory model and the 286 target processor. The output reveals the Microport compiler *always* creates a pure object code file (-i option for  comp) to separate text and data space, even if you omit this option on the  cc command line.

Let's compile pgm.c again with optimization and link the math library (using the  -lm option).  Here is the result.

```
$ cc -# -O pgm.c -lm
cc:   'cpp' 'pgm.c' '/tmp/ctm1AAAa00531' '-DSMALL_M' '-DiAPX286'
cc:   'comp' '-i' '/tmp/ctm1AAAa00531' '-o' '/tmp/ctm2BAAa00531' '-f'
cc:   'optim' '-I' '/tmp/ctm2BAAa00531' '-O' '/tmp/ctm4CAAa00531'
cc:   'as' '-dl' '-o' 'pgm.o' '-Ms' '/tmp/ctm4CAAa00531'
cc:   'ld' '/lib/small/crt0.o' 'pgm.o' '-lm' '-lc' '-la'
```

The display shows the optimization step (optim).  The  -lm option appears in the link editor step (ld).

## Assertions

Chapter 5 presents a technique to customize the system  assert  macro to display the assertion that fails along with the line number and file name.  Microport System V/AT's assert macro displays this information by default.  Suppose, for example, we compile  array2.c from Chapter 5 as follows:

**Program B-1**

```
/* array2.c - array bounds with assertions */

#include <stdio.h>
#include <assert.h>
#define MAX 10

main(argc, argv)
int argc;
char *argv[];
{
    . . . .
    assert(index >= 0 && index < MAX);
    . . . .
}
```

Note that we include the system  assert macro and not our own.  Here's the result when we run the program.

```
$ cc array2.c -o array2
$ array2 12 99
Assertion failed: index >= 0 && index < MAX, file array2.c, line 20
```

Furthermore, Microport System V/AT supports macro parameter substitution between double quotes, as discussed in Chapter 5.  User-defined assertion macros are therefore possible, and  custom.c (from Chapter 5) runs on UNIX System V machines as well as Microport's.

# C

# C Under SCO XENIX System V

The C compiler for Santa Cruz Operations (SCO) XENIX System V is an adaptation of the Microsoft C compiler for MS-DOS. The C compiler runs under XENIX, but it's possible to produce object-compatible files for MS-DOS as well. The compiler produces Intel format object files for the Intel 8086, 186, 286 and 386 processors. Furthermore, the Microsoft C compiler has been "tuned" for these Intel processors. Compiler options handle different memory models for the Intel processors, and other options extend the language to accommodate different pointer sizes.

Most of cc's options are the same as the standard C compiler. The differences relate to memory models and compatibility with MS-DOS.

Here is the list of C compiler options for SCO XENIX 386. Note that memory models don't apply to the 386 instruction set, but SCO maintains compatibility with 8086, 186, and 286 object files; hence, you'll find memory model options in the 386 system. In the following list, (C) marks compiler options, (P) preprocessor options, and (L) link editor options.

-c    Produce .o file(s). (C)

-c *num*

Change the default target CPU symbol stored in the *x.out* header. *num* is one of [0123] indicating target 8086, 186, 286, or 386 processor respectively. This option only changes the default; linking in object modules with higher target processors overrides the default. (L)

-compat

Produces an executable file that is binary compatible with the following systems:

```
XENIX-286 System V
XENIX-386 System V
XENIX-286 3.0
XENIX-8086 System V
```

(C/L)

-d    Displays the preprocessor, compiler, and optimizer passes and their arguments before execution. (See also −z.) (C/P)

-dos

Creates an executable program for the MS-DOS system. (See also option −FP.)

-g    Includes information for the symbolic debugger, sdb. This is the same as option −Zi. (C)

-i    Produce a pure object file, one that has separate I (instruction) and D (data) spaces. (L)

-lname

Search library libname.a, in directories /lib and /usr/lib. (L)

-m name

Produces a link map file named name. (L)

-n    Create a pure object file (separate I and D space). This option is equivalent to −i. (C)

-n num

Truncates symbols to length num. (L)

-nl num

Truncates symbols to length num. (L)

-o outfile

Use outfile for output object file instead of a.out. (L)

-p    Produce code that counts the number of times each routine is called. If linking, use profile versions of libc.a and libma.a. Execution of object program produces file mon.out, which can be examined with prof(1). (C/L)

-pack

Pack structures. This option saves space, but execution will be slower because of the extra time required to access words that begin on odd-byte boundaries.

-r    Retain relocation entries for subsequent links. (L)

-s    Strip symbol table and line number information from the output object file. (L)

-u     Remove all manifest defines. (P)

-v *num*

     Specify the XENIX version number (2, 3, or 5). 5 is the default.

-w     Suppress compiler warning messages. This is the same as −W0. (C)

-z      Display the preprocessor, compiler, and optimizer passes and their arguments but do not execute them. (See also −d.) (C/P)

-A *num*

     Create a stand-alone program with load address of *num* (hexadecimal). (L)

-B *num*

     Set the text selector bias to the specified hexadecimal number. (L)

-C     Do not strip C-style comments. This option is only used with the −E or −P options. (P)

-C     Forces the link editor to ignore case of symbols. (L)

-CSON

     When optimization (−O) is also specified, enable "common subexpression" optimization. This optimization is enabled by default with the large memory model. (C)

-CSOFF

     When optimization (−O) is also specified, disable "common subexpression" optimization. This optimization is disabled by default with the small memory model. (C)

-D     Sets the data selector bias to the specified hexadecimal number. (L)

-D*name*

     Define *name* to be 1 to the preprocessor. (P)

-D*name=str*

     Define *name* to be *str* to the preprocessor. (P)

-E     Run only the preprocessor and direct the result to standard output. This options places a #line directive at the beginning of each file. (C/P)

-EP    Run only the preprocessor and direct the result to standard output. This option does not place a #line directive at the beginning of the file. (C/P)

-F *num*

     Create a program stack of *num* (hexadecimal) bytes. This option does not apply to a 386 object file and is incompatible with the −A option. (L)

-Fa, -Fa*name*

Create an assembly listing in *file*.L, where *file* is the base name of the C source file, or in the named file. The link edit step follows, if requested. (C)

-Fc, -Fc*name*

Create a merged assembler and C listing in *file*.L, where *file* is the base name of the C source file, or in the named file. (C)

-Fe*name*

Place the executable object file in file *name*. (L)

-Fl, -Fl*name*

Create a listing file in *file*.L, where *file* is the base name of the C source file, or in the named file. (C)

-Fm, -Fm*name*

Create a map listing in *file*.map, where *file* is the base name of the C source file, or in the named file. (L)

-Fo*name*

Name the object file name *name* instead of *file*.o, where *file* is the base name of the C source file. (C)

-FPa, -FPc, -FPc87, -FPi, -FPi87

Control the type of floating point code generated. Use these options in conjunction with −dos. (C)

-Fs, -Fs*name*

Create a C source listing in file *file*.S, where *file* is the base name of the C source file, or in the named file.

-I *pathname*

Add *pathname* to the list of directories to be searched when an #include file is not found in the directory containing the source file. (P)

-K    Remove stack probes from a program. Stack probes detect possible stack overflow conditions upon entry to program routines. (Stack probes do not apply to the 386) (C)

-L    Produce an assembler listing file with assembled code and assembly source in *file*.L, where *file* is the base name of the C source file. This option overrides option −S. (C)

-LARGE

Invoke the large model C compiler. (Note that this option affects the model of the *compiler*, not the resulting object module.) Use this when the compiler complains of "Out of heap space" during compilation. (C)

-M*string*

    Specify memory model parameters. *string* may combine any of the following, except *s, m, l, h* are mutually exclusive.

        s  Create a small model program (default).

        m  Create a middle model program.

        l  Create a large model program.

        h  Create a huge model program.

        e  Enable the `far, near, huge, pascal, fortran` keywords. Enable non-ANSI extensions.

        0  Generate 8086 code. This is the default for non-386 processors.

        1  Generate 186 code.

        2  Generate 286 code.

        3  Generate 386 code (386 processors only). This is the default for 386 processors.

        b  Reverse word order for `long` bytes (high order word is first). The default is low order word is first.

    t*num*

        Allocate all data items greater than *num* bytes to a new data segment. The default value for *num* is 32,767. This option can only be used in large model programs.

-ND *name*, -NM *name*, -NT *name*

    Change the data, module, and text segment name to *name*. (L)

-O, -O*string*

    Perform object code optimization, according to the default or to *string*.

        d Disable optimization (the same as not specifying `-O`).

        a Relax alias checking.

        s Optimize code for space.

        t Optimize code for speed. This is equivalent to `-O`.

        x Perform maximum optimization. This is equivalent to `-Oactl`.

        c Eliminate common expressions.

l Perform loop optimizations.

(C)

-P    Run only the preprocessor and place the output in the file *file*.i, where *file* is the base name of the C source file. (C/P)

-P    Disable segment packing. (L)

-R    Ensure that the relocation table is of nonzero size. (L)

-Rd *num*, -Rt *num*
     Specify the data segment and text segment relation offset (386 only) in hexadecimal. (L)

-S    Create an assembly language source listing in *file*.s, where *file* is the base name of the C source file. (C)

-U*name*
     Undefine preprocessor symbol *name*. (P)

-V *string*
     Copy *string* to the object file. This option is used for version control. (L)

-W0  Turn off all warning messages. This is the same as −w.

-W1  Display most warning messages (the default).

-W2  Display intermediate level warning messages. This includes additional messages not displayed with −W1.

-W3  Display the highest level of warning messages, including warnings about non-ANSI standard features and extended keywords. This includes additional messages not displayed with −W2. (C)

-Zi   Include information used by the symbolic debugger (*sdb*) in the output file. This option is equivalent to −g. (C)

-Zp1, -Zp2, -Zp4
     Align data structures on one, two, or four-byte boundaries. This option applies only to the 386. (C)

# • Memory Models •

The SCO XENIX C compiler supports five memory models: small impure, small pure, medium, large, and huge.

## Small Impure Model

The small impure model places a program's text, stack, BSS, initialized data, and heap in *one* segment. Fig. C-1 shows the arrangement.

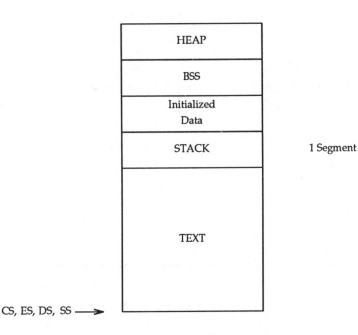

CS, ES, DS, SS ⟶

*Fig. C-1.* Small impure memory model

The model is impure because a program's code resides in the same segment as the data. Small impure is the default model for programs compiled under SCO XENIX. Text and data pointers are 16 bits.

## Small Pure Model

A program may *share* text under XENIX to utilize memory more efficiently. Programs that share text must be pure and have separate segments for text and data. Refer to Fig. B-1 of Appendix B for a diagram of the small pure model. The −i compiler option creates small pure model programs and makes program text sharable between users under XENIX. Text and data pointers are still 16 bits.

## Medium Model

The medium (or middle) model allows programs to use as many text segments as necessary but limits program data (stack, heap, initialized data, and BSS) to a single 64-kilobyte segment. Fig. C-2 shows the medium memory model.

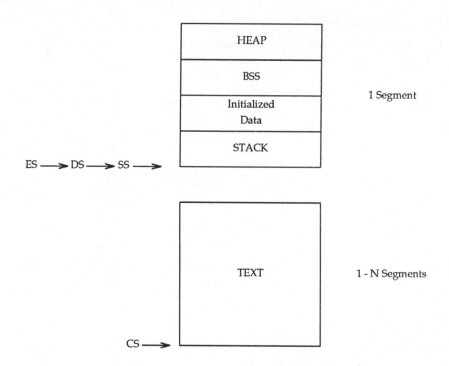

*Fig. C-2.* Medium memory model

A program's code size may be greater than 64K bytes, but its data must fit in 64K bytes or less. Data pointers remain 16 bits, but *text* pointers become 32 bits in size. The medium model, therefore, places additional overhead on pointers to functions and function calls and returns. The compiler option −Mm creates medium model programs, which are always pure.

## Large Model

The large model allocates more than one data segment for *both* text and data. Fig. C-3 shows the large memory model.

The number of data segments depends on your program's use of the heap, BSS, and initialized data. The stack appears in the default segment (segment 1). C objects (arrays, structures, unions) are limited to 64K bytes or less in size. In the large model, data pointers are 32 bits, but the compiler still performs 16-bit arithmetic with pointer operations. Programs typically run slower in large model because the compiler must reload segment registers as a program executes. The compiler option −Ml creates large model programs, which are always pure.

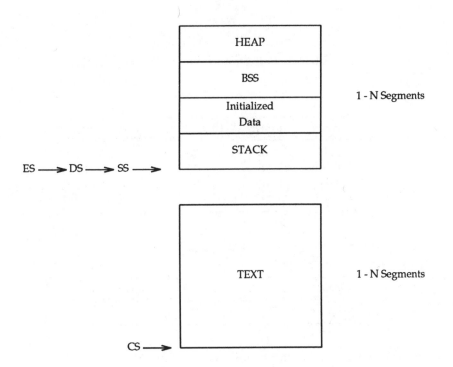

*Fig. C-3.* Large memory model

## Huge Model

Huge model programs may declare C arrays larger than 64K bytes. The huge model has the same memory arrangement shown in Fig. C-3. Structures, unions, and array *elements* must still be less than 64K bytes, however. The -Mh compiler option creates huge model programs, which are always pure.

Huge model pointers make the compiler perform 32-bit arithmetic with pointer operations, since the segment selector might change. Suppose, for example, ip is a character pointer. The statement

```
ip++;
```

generates one line of assembly code in a small, medium, or large model program. In the huge model, however, this statement generates 10 lines of 286 assembly code!

Table C-1 summarizes the sizes of integers and pointers in the different 286 memory models and on the 386.

**TABLE C-1. Pointer and integer sizes for XENIX**

XENIX 286

| Model | Integer | Text Pointer | Data Pointer |
|-------|---------|--------------|--------------|
| Small | 16 | 16 | 16 |
| Medium | 16 | 32 | 16 |
| Large | 16 | 32 | 32 |
| Huge | 16 | 32 | 32 |

XENIX 386

| Model | Integer | Text Pointer | Data Pointer |
|-------|---------|--------------|--------------|
| N/A | 32 | 32 | 32 |

On the 386, integers and pointers (text and data) are 32 bits.

## Keyword Extensions

Small model pointers are commonly referred to as *near* pointers. The compiler uses 16-bit arithmetic to compute pointer offsets within one 64-kilobyte segment. Large model pointers carry with them a segment selector and are commonly referred to as *far* pointers. Similarly, data that resides outside the default data segment is called *far data*, and functions that reside outside the default text segment are called *far functions*. While a far pointer is 32 bits, it always references the same 64-kilobyte data segment in a single operation; hence, the compiler still performs 16-bit arithmetic on far pointers. *Huge* pointers, however, make the compiler perform 32-bit arithmetic for all pointer operations.

The XENIX C compiler supports keyword extensions for these concepts. Programs may use the keywords `near`, `far`, and `huge` to reference data in the same segment or in different segments. The use of `far` in a small model program, for example, accesses data outside the current segment. Similarly, large model programs may use `near` to access data with just an offset. Programs use `huge` to declare an array greater than 64K bytes.

The following program shows several uses of these keywords for pointers in a C program.

**Program C-1**

```
/* keywords.c - keyword extensions */

main ()
{
    int near *np;      /* default data segment, 16-bit arithmetic */
    int far *fp;       /* any data segment, 16-bit arithmetic */
    int huge *hp;      /* any data segment, 32-bit arithmetic */
    int far *far *pfar;  /* far ptr to a far ptr to an integer */
    char (far *pf)();    /* far pointer to far function */

    printf("size of near pointer = %d\n", sizeof(np));
    printf("size of far pointer = %d\n", sizeof(fp));
    printf("size of huge pointer = %d\n", sizeof(hp));
    printf("size of far function pointer = %d\n", sizeof(pf));
}

char far func()                    /* far function */
{
}
```

Let's compile `keywords.c` in the small pure memory model and run it.

```
$ cc -Me keywords.c -o keywords
$ keywords
size of near pointer = 2
size of far pointer = 4
size of huge pointer = 4
size of far function pointer = 4
```

The `-Me` option enables keyword extensions. The program displays the different sizes of the pointers.

## Using the Preprocessor for Model Independence

You can use the preprocessor to support two versions of the same program that use near and far pointers. The following program, for example, declares an array and fills it with data using pointers.

**Program C-2**

```
/* ptop.c - pointer operations with model independence */

#include <stdio.h>

#ifdef FVERS
#define FAR far
#else
#define FAR
#endif

#define MAX 16384

int FAR big_array [MAX];

main()
{
    int FAR *ip;
    int FAR *head, FAR *tail;
    unsigned num_elem;

    head = big_array;
    tail = head + MAX;

    for (ip = head, num_elem= 0; ip < tail; num_elem++, ip++)
        *ip = num_elem;

    printf("num_elem = %u\n", num_elem);
    printf("size of ip = %d\n", sizeof(ip));
}
```

Suppose we compile and run this program as follows:

```
$ cc ptop.c -o ptop
$ ptop
num_elem = 16384
size of ip = 2
```

Program ptop is compiled in a small impure model. It declares an array of integers and three integer pointers. Preprocessor statements make the array and the pointers near.

Now, let's recompile and run the same program again, this time making the array and pointers `far`.

```
$ cc -i -Me -DFVERS ptop.c -o ptop
$ ptop
num_elem = 16384
size of ip = 4
```

The `-i` option creates a pure program and `-Me` enables keyword extensions. The `-DFVERS` option defines symbol `FVERS`, which makes the preprocessor create `far` pointers and a `far` array. The size of `ip` is 4 with this compilation.

# ◆ Function Calling Conventions ◆

Microsoft C's calling convention for functions places arguments on the stack in reverse order. The calling routine is responsible for cleaning up the stack when the function returns. The calling routine always knows how many arguments it pushes on the stack; hence, C functions may have a variable number of arguments. One disadvantage of this approach is that a program's code size becomes larger, since every function call must generate code to clean up the stack. An alternative is to have the *called* function perform this task, which reduces a program's code size and makes it compatible with other languages.

The XENIX C compiler provides special keywords to implement this approach. The keywords `pascal` and `fortran` make the compiler push function parameters on the stack in *forward* order and have the called function clean up the stack. Either keyword has the same effect. In addition, the XENIX C compiler changes all global PASCAL identifiers to uppercase and omits the initial underbar when placing them in the global namelist.

Why would we want to use this different convention in a C program? Here are several reasons:

- You may need to call an assembly language routine that assumes this calling convention.

- You might want to call routines written in another language that expect arguments on the stack in forward order.

- You may wish to reduce your code size.

The following program uses the `pascal` keyword to implement the forward calling convention to pass arguments on the stack.

**Program C-3**

```
/* forward.c - forward calling convention
               for functions */

#define FWDPUSH pascal

int FWDPUSH retval;

int FWDPUSH myfunc(a, b, c)
int a, b, c;
{
    return  a + b + c;
}

main()
{
    int i = 50, j = 33, k = 2;

    retval = myfunc(i, j, k);

    printf("retval = %d\n", retval);
}
$ cc -Me forward.c -o forward
$ forward
retval = 85
$ nm forward
 . . . .
003f:008c   T MYFUNC
 . . . .
```

The −Me option enables keyword extensions. Using the preprocessor, FWDPUSH makes the compiler use the forward calling convention. myfunc() is a C function that requires exactly 3 arguments on the stack. Parameter c is on top of the stack, since a is pushed first. The global namelist (from the nm command) contains the MYFUNC identifier instead of _myfunc.

# D

# Microsoft C 5.0 Compiler

Microsoft C 5.0 runs under the MS-DOS operating system and produces executable object files for MS-DOS. While it's possible to create MS-DOS compatible object files with the C compiler under XENIX (see Appendix C), the Microsoft C 5.0 compiler offers features not found in its XENIX cousin.

Microsoft C 5.0 is a package that includes a compiler, linker, and symbolic debugger (CodeView). You also get QuickC, an incremental compiler with its own built-in editor and debugger. The C compiler produces Intel format object code for the 8086, 186, and 286 Intel processors. Microsoft C 5.0 provides different levels of optimization and, like the C compiler under XENIX, contains options for compiling different memory models for the Intel processors. In addition, Microsoft 5.0 supports several new ANSI C features and has compiler options to extend the language to accommodate different pointer sizes and different function calling conventions. Microsoft C also provides interrupt functions (functions callable through a hardware interrupt).

Under DOS, command lines are different from the UNIX and XENIX examples in this book. The compiler's name, for instance, is CL and compiler options have a forward slash instead of the -option convention UNIX uses.† The following command, for example, compiles a program called FILE1.C.

```
> CL /c FILE1.C
```

The compiler option /c suppresses linking.

Here is the list of options for the Microsoft C 5.0 compiler. We denote compiler options with (C), preprocessor options with (P), and link editor options with (L).

---

† The Microsoft compiler does support command line options marked with a dash to remain compatible with XENIX. However, the documentation that comes with Microsoft 5.0 uses only the "forward slash" notation.

/c    Produce `.OBJ` file(s). (C)

/qc Use the Microsoft QuickC compiler instead of the optimizing compiler. (C)

/u    Remove all manifest defines. (P)

/w   Suppress compiler warning messages. This is the same as `/W0`. (C)

/AS Create a small memory model program (default). (C)

/AM Create a medium memory model program. (C)

/AC Create a compact memory model program. (C)

/AL Create a large memory model program. (C)

/AH Create a huge memory model program. (C)

/Aw Control the segment setup for C programs that interface with the Microsoft Windows operating system. (See also option `/Gw`.) (C)

/C    Do not strip C-style comments. This option is only used with the `/E`, `/EP`, or `/P` options. (P)

/D*name*
> Define *name* to be `1` to the preprocessor. (P)

/D*name=str*
> Define *name* to be *str* to the preprocessor. (P)

/E    Run only the preprocessor and direct the result to standard output. This options places a `#line` directive at the beginning of each file. (C/P)

/EP Run only the preprocessor and direct the result to standard output. This option does not place a `#line` directive at the beginning of the file. (C/P)

/F *num*
> Create a program stack of *num* (hexadecimal) bytes. The default stack size is 2048 bytes. (L)

/Fa, /Fa*name*
> Create an assembly listing in *file*`.ASM`, where *file* is the base name of the C source file, or in the named file. If the named file does not have an extension, use `.ASM`. (C)

/Fc, /Fc*name*
> Create a merged assembler and C listing in *file*`.COD`, where *file* is the base name of the C source file, or in the named file. If the named file does not have an extension, use `.COD`. (C)

/Fe*name*
> Place the executable object file in file *name*. (L)

/Fl, /Fl*name*
> Create an object listing file in *file*.COD, where *file* is the base name of the C source file, or in the named file. If the named file does not have an extension, use .COD. (C)

/Fm, /Fm*name*
> Create a map listing in *file*.MAP, where *file* is the base name of the C source file, or in the named file. If the named file does not have an extension, use .MAP. (L)

/Fo*name*
> Name the object file name *name* instead of *file*.OBJ, where *file* is the base name of the C source file. (C)

/FPa, /FPc, /FPc87, /FPi, /FPi87
> Control the type of floating point code generated. (C)

/Fs, /Fs*name*
> Create a C source listing in file *file*.LST, where *file* is the base name of the C source file, or in the named file. If the named file does not have an extension, use .LST. (C)

/G0  Generate code for the 8086/8088 processor (default). (C)

/G1  Generate code for the 186 processor. (C)

/G2  Generate code for the 286 processor. (C)

/Gc  Control a function's calling convention with extended keywords. fortran and pascal make functions push their arguments on the stack in left-to-right order and remove them before returning. cdecl makes functions have the C calling convention, which pushes function arguments right-to left on the stack and has the caller clean up the stack. (C)

/Gs  Remove stack probes from a program. Stack probes detect possible stack overflow conditions upon entry to program routines. (See also pragma check_stack.) (C)

/Gw The application will run in the Windows environment. (C)

/H *num*
> Restrict the length of external (public) names to *num* significant characters. The compiler ignores any extra characters in external names. This option is useful for producing portable programs. (C)

/HELP
> Display a list of the commonly used compiler options. (C)

/I *pathname*

> Add *pathname* to the list of directories to be searched when an #include file is not found in the directory containing the source file. (P)

/J   Change the type char from the default signed to unsigned. This prevents sign extension when assigning a type char variable to a type int variable. Declaring a variable type signed char overrides the /J command line option. (C)

/O*string*

> Perform object code optimization, according to *string*. (See also option /Gs.)

> > d   Disable optimization. (This is useful when debugging to prevent code rearrangement.)

> > a   Relax alias checking.

> > i   Enable intrinsic functions. Table D-4 lists the routines that have intrinsic forms. (See also pragma intrinsic.)

> > l   Enable loop optimization. (See also pragma loop_opt.)

> > p   Improves consistency of floating-point results.

> > s   Optimize code for space. (See also pragma function.)

> > t   Optimize code for speed. (This is the default.)

> > x   Perform maximum optimization. (Equivalent to /Oailt /Gs.)

> (C)

/P   Run only the preprocessor and place the output in the file *file*.I, where *file* is the base name of the C source file. (C/P)

/Sl *num*

> Set the linewidth to *num* for source listings. (Used only with option /Fs.)

/Sp *num*

> Set the pagelength to *num* for source listings. (Used only with option /Fs.)

/Ss *"subtitle"*

> Set the subtitle to *"subtitle"* for source listings. (Used only with option /Fs.)

/St *"title"*

> Set the title to *"title"* for source listings. (Used only with option /Fs.)

-S    Create an assembly language source listing in *file*.**ASM**, where *file* is the base name of the C source file. (C)

/Tc *sourcefile*

Tell the compiler that *sourcefile* is a C source file. Otherwise, the compiler considers only files with extension .C to be source files.

/U*name*

Undefine preprocessor symbol *name*. (P)

/V *string*

Copy *string* to the object file. This option is used for version control. (L)

*m*VARSTCK.OBJ

Link your program with the variable stack/heap versions of the heap allocation routines malloc, calloc, _expand, _fmalloc, nmalloc, realloc. Normally, stack and heap space are fixed. These routines allow the heap allocators to use unused stack space when the heap space is full. *m* specifies the memory model of the routines: S (small), M (medium), C (compact), and L (large or huge). (L)

/W0

Turn off all warning messages. This is the same as /w.

/W1 Display most warning messages (the default).

/W2 Display intermediate level warning messages. This includes additional messages not displayed with /W1.

/W3 Display the highest level of warning messages, including warnings about non-ANSI standard features and extended keywords. This includes additional messages not displayed with /W2. (C)

/X    Prevent the compiler from searching the standard places for include files.

/Za Disable all language extensions. (See also option /Ze.) Use this option for porting programs to a different system.

/Zd Create an object file with debugging information for the Microsoft debugger **SYMDEB**. (See also option /Od.) (C)

/Ze Enable language extensions (the default). (See also option /Za.) Extensions include:

- Keywords cdecl, far, fortran, huge, near, pascal.

- Allow casts to produce lvalues.

- Allow redefinitions of `extern` identifiers as `static`.

- Allow trailing commas rather than an ellipsis to indicate functions with variable-length argument lists.

- Allow certain `typedef` redefinitions.

- Allow mixed character and string constants in an initializer.

- Allow bit fields with base types other than `unsigned int` or `signed int`.

(C)

/Zg  Generate function declarations (function prototypes) for each function declared in the source file to standard output. If you include the output in your source file, the compiler checks each argument to a function call for type agreement with the function's declaration. (C)

/Zi  Include information used by the Microsoft debugger **CodeView** in the output file. Unless you also specify certain optimizations with /O, all optimizations that rearrange code are disabled. (See also option /Od.) (C)

/Zl  The compiler does not place the default library name in the object file, saving space. (C)

/Zp1, /Zp2, /Zp4
Align data structures on one, two, or four-byte boundaries. (See also pragma `pack()`.) (C)

/Zs  Process the source file for syntax errors only; don't produce an object file. This option can be used with option /Fs to create a source listing showing the syntax errors. (C)

## ◆ Memory Models ◆

Microsoft C 5.0 supports five memory models: small, medium, compact, large, and huge. Refer to Appendices B and C for an introduction to memory models on the Intel processors.

### Small Model

The small model creates separate segments for text and data. Fig. B-1 in Appendix B shows a diagram of the small model, which is always pure. A program's text and and data must each be less than 64K bytes, and text pointers and data pointers are 16 bits. Small model (compiler option /AS) is the default when you compile programs in Microsoft C 5.0.

## Medium Model

The medium or middle model allows more than one text segment but only one data segment. Fig. C-2 in Appendix C shows a diagram of the medium model, which is always pure. The medium model applies to programs that have a code size greater than 64K bytes, but whose data size is 64K bytes or less. Text pointers are 32 bits and data pointers are 16 bits. The compiler option /AM creates medium model programs.

## Compact Model

The compact memory model allocates multiple data segments but only one segment for text. Fig. D-1 shows the compact memory model.

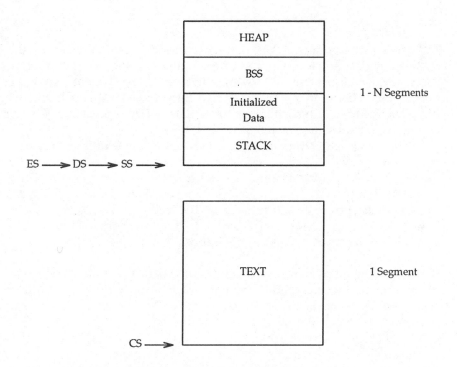

*Fig. D-1.* Compact memory model

Data pointers are *far* pointers (32 bits), and text pointers are 16 bits. The compact model minimizes function call overhead for a program that has a code size less than 64K bytes but a data area larger than 64K bytes. The compiler option /AC creates compact model programs.

In practice, the compact model is usually not necessary. Often you can compile a program in small model and define a set of far pointers to manipulate the data that has to live in another segment. With this arrangement, most of the data pointers in your program are near (16 bits), with the exception of the ones that you declare far. This is typically more efficient than compiling the same program in compact model, which would make *all* data pointers far.

## Large Model

The large memory model allocates multiple data segments for both text and data. Fig. C-3 in Appendix C shows a diagram of the large model, which is always pure. Any C object (arrays, structures, unions, etc.) cannot exceed 64K bytes. The large model applies to programs whose code size and data size cannot fit in a total of 128K bytes. Pointers are 32 bits, but the compiler performs 16-bit arithmetic for pointer operations. The compiler option /AL creates large model programs.

## Huge Model

The huge memory model has the same memory configuration as the large memory model shown in Fig. C-3 of Appendix C. Huge model programs may declare arrays larger than 64K bytes, however. Array elements, structures, and unions must be less than 64K bytes, and huge model pointers are 32 bits. The compiler performs 32-bit arithmetic for all data pointer operations. The compiler option /AH creates huge model programs.

The sizeof() operator and pointer subtraction is different in huge model programs. sizeof() normally returns an unsigned int, but in the huge model you need to *cast* sizeof()'s return value to a unsigned long. Suppose, for example, buf is a huge array (greater than 64K bytes). The following expression determines the correct size of buf using sizeof():

```
(unsigned long) sizeof(buf)
```

Similarly, subtracting two pointers of the same data type in C normally evaluates to an int. In huge model this becomes a long. Suppose p1 and p2 are huge pointers of the same data type, for example. The expression

```
(long) (p1 - p2)
```

evaluates to the correct number of items between the two huge pointers.

## Keyword Extensions

Microsoft C 5.0 supports the keywords near, far, and huge for text and data pointers. near pointers are 16 bits and far and huge pointers are 32 bits. The compiler performs 16-bit arithmetic on far pointers, which must always address an object within a 64-kilobyte segment. huge pointers can address multiple segments in the same operation; consequently, the compiler performs

32-bit arithmetic on pointer operations. See the program `keywords.c` from Appendix C for examples of these keywords.

## Summary

Table D-1 summarizes the sizes of integers and pointers in the different memory models for Microsoft C 5.0.

**TABLE D-1.** Pointer and integer sizes for Microsoft C

| Model | Integer | Text Pointer | Data Pointer |
|-------|---------|--------------|--------------|
| Small | 16 | 16 | 16 |
| Medium | 16 | 32 | 16 |
| Compact | 16 | 16 | 32 |
| Large | 16 | 32 | 32 |
| Huge | 16 | 32 | 32 |

# ◆  ANSI C Features  ◆

As of this writing, the ANSI C draft has not become the ANSI C standard, but it's "only a matter of time." The industry's compiler writers are busy taking steps to prepare their products to conform to this new standard. Microsoft and Borland International (see Appendix E for Turbo C) implement features that are currently in the ANSI C draft and are likely to be part of the standard. Let's look at several of Microsoft's new features for their 5.0 compiler and show you how to use them.

## Pragmas

ANSI C has new definitions for the C preprocessor as well as for the C language. A new preprocessor directive called a *pragma* is available in Microsoft C 5.0. Here's the syntax:

    #pragma *PRAGMA(arg1, arg2, ...)*

Pragmas are similar in syntax to a `#define` statement. A pragma affects a source file until you change it. Some pragmas are "toggles" (they may be turned on and off) and others have arguments. Table D-2 shows the Microsoft C pragmas and their meanings.

**TABLE D-2.  Microsoft C pragmas**

| Pragma | Meaning |
|---|---|
| loop_opt | Control loop optimization |
| intrinsic | Use inline version of some library routines |
| function | Use function version of some library routines |
| check_stack | Control stack probes |
| pack | Data structure alignment |
| same_seg | Specify variables in same segment |
| alloc_text | Specify functions in named segment |

Table D-3 lists a pragma's full definition and associated compiler option (if any).

**TABLE D-3.  Pragmas and associated compiler options**

| Pragma | Compiler Option |
|---|---|
| loop_opt (ON \| OFF) | /Ol, /Ox |
| intrinsic (f1, f2, ...) | /Oi |
| function (f1, f2, ...) | /Od |
| check_stack (ON \| OFF) | /Gs |
| pack (1 \| 2 \| 4) | /Zp1, /Zp2, /Zp4 |
| same_seg (var1 [var2, ...]) | No equivalent |
| alloc_text (text_segment, f1[f2, ...]) | No equivalent |

Let's apply pragmas to several of our programs and see how they work.

Loop optimization often makes nested loops execute faster.  The following program called `det.c` from Chapter 3 contains embedded `for` loops to calculate a determinant.  We use the `loop_opt` pragma to enable and disable loop optimization.

**Program D-1**

```
.  .  .  .
/* calculate determinant for n by n matrix */
double det(arg, n)
double *arg;
int n;
{
.  .  .  .
#pragma loop_opt(on)
    /* determinant algorithm using rows and columns */
    for (k = 0; k < n - 1; k++)
        for (i = k + 1; i < n; i++){
            x = a[i][k]/a[k][k];
            for (j = k; j < n; j++)
                a[i][j] = a[i][j] - x * a[k][j];
            }
#pragma loop_opt(off)
.  .  .  .
}
```

The compiler optimizes the loops only between the two pragma statements.

Microsoft C 5.0 supports pragmas to replace function calls with *inline* assembly code for many heavily used library routines. Table D-4 lists the routines that have intrinsic forms.

**TABLE D-4. Library routines that have intrinsic forms**

| Routine | Routine | Routine |
|---------|---------|---------|
| strcat | inp | asin |
| strcmp | outp | acos |
| strcpy | min | atan |
| strlen | max | atan2 |
| strset | abs | sinh |
| memcpy | pow | cosh |
| memcmp | log | tanh |
| memset | log10 | sqrt |
| _rotl | exp | floor |
| _rotr | sin | ceil |
| _lrotl | cos | fabs |
| _lrotr | tan | fmod |

The following program from Chapter 4 called str1.c, for example, joins character strings using C library string functions. The intrinsic pragma replaces
the function calls with inline assembly instructions and speeds up the program.

**Program D-2**

```
/* str1.c - join strings with an array
            of function pointers */

#include <stdio.h>
#include <string.h>
#include <malloc.h>

#pragma intrinsic(strlen, strcpy, strcat)
  . . . . .
char *join(s1, s2)          /* join s1, s2 */
char *s1, *s2;
{
   char *pnew;

   pnew = malloc(strlen(s1) + strlen(s2) + 1);
   if (pnew == (char *) NULL) {
      fprintf(stderr, "Can't malloc for heap space\n");
      exit(1);
   }
   return strcat(strcpy(pnew, s1), s2);
}

char *joinb(s1, s2)      /* join s1, s2 with blank */
char *s1, *s2;
{
   char *pnew;

   pnew = malloc(strlen(s1) + strlen(s2) + 2);
   if (pnew == (char *) NULL) {
      fprintf(stderr, "Can't malloc for heap space\n");
      exit(1);
   }
   return strcat(strcat(strcpy(pnew, s1), " "), s2);
}
```

Microsoft C 5.0 also supports a function pragma, which works the opposite from intrinsic. function pragmas force the compiler to call a library
routine instead of generating inline code. When you compile a program with the
/Oi compiler option (which enables intrinsics for those library routines that have
them), function pragmas may decrease a program's code size. The ATL

language interpreter from Chapter 6, for example, is a small model program under DOS. Compiling ATL with intrinsics (compiler option /Oi) increases the code size above the 64-kilobyte small model limit. Function pragmas in selective parts of the ATL code keep the code size within the small model limit. This solution demonstrates the trade-off between a program's code size (function calls) and its execution speed (intrinsics).

Compiler options (like /Oi) affect an *entire* source file. We can, for instance, use the /Ol compiler option to optimize all of the loops in the three-dimensional array program a3d.c from Chapter 3.

```
> CL /Ol /F 4096 a3d.c
```

To run a3d.c, we compile it with the /F option and create a stack of 4K bytes (2K bytes is the default). Without loop optimization, a3d.c generates multiply instructions in assembly code for the three-dimensional storage map equation. Microsoft C 5.0's loop optimization eliminates the multiply instructions and speeds up the program.

Likewise, we can use the /Oi compiler option to speed up the dynamic string program strmob.c from Chapter 6. Recall this program uses the C library calls memset() and memcpy(). The /Oi compiler option enables intrinsics for these library functions.

```
> CL /Oi -DDRIVER strmob.c objalloc.obj dbug.obj
```

## Stringizing and Token Pasting

Microsoft's preprocessor has additional features that improve macro expansion. A # before a macro argument makes the preprocessor place the argument inside double quotes, which creates a C string constant. This is called *stringizing*. The following macro called errmsg, for example, uses stringizing to display error messages on standard error.

```
#include <stdio.h>

#define errmsg(msg) fprintf(stderr, #msg "\n"), exit(1)
```

The comma operator forms a single statement inside the macro in place of a block. Here are two examples of calling errmsg:

```
if (p == NULL)
  errmsg(Pointer is not set);

if (c != '\n')
  errmsg(You must use a "newline" here);
```

This is how the preprocessor expands the macro calls:

```
if (p == 0)
  fprintf((&_iob[2]), "Pointer is not set" "\n"), exit(1);

if (c != '\n')
  fprintf((&_iob[2]), "You must use a \"newline\" here" "\n"), exit(1);
```

&_iob[2] is an internal buffer defined in stdio.h for standard error. The preprocessor automatically generates \" for the double quotes in the second macro call.

Microsoft C 5.0 uses stringizing in the assert macro (from Chapter 5). We'll return to stringizing later when we show you how Microsoft's assertions work.

Another preprocessor feature called *token pasting* uses ## between macro arguments to form a new token. Let's use token pasting with constant strings to eliminate the function calls from str1.c in Chapter 4, as follows.

**Program D-3**

```
/* str1.c - join strings using stringizing */

#include <stdio.h>
#define JOIN(word1, word2) (word1 ## word2)

main()
{
    printf("%s\n", JOIN("alpha", "bet"));
    printf("%s\n", JOIN("duck ", "soup"));
}

$ str1
alphabet
duck soup
```

The preprocessor expands the JOIN macro as follows:

```
printf("%s\n", ("alpha""bet"));
printf("%s\n", ("duck ""soup"));
```

## Function Prototyping

A powerful feature of the ANSI C draft aids C programmers in declaring functions and using them consistently. *Function prototyping* makes function declarations explicitly state their return data type and the name and data type of each of

their arguments. During compilation, the compiler verifies that a call to a proto-
typed function has a consistent number of arguments and their data types agree.

Before we discuss function prototyping, let's look at the "old" style of
declaring functions:

```
main()
{
    char *join();      /* appears before the
                          function is called */

    . . . .
}

char *join(s1, s2)     /* join s1, s2 */
char *s1, *s2;
{

  . . . .
}
```

Before you call `join()`, the compiler needs to know its return data type.
Although this arrangement documents the data type that `join()` returns, the
reader has no idea what `join()`'s arguments are or their data types. Function
declarations provide this information, but these statements may be in a different
file.

Now let's apply function prototyping to this example and see the difference.

```
main()
{
    char *join(char *s1, char *s2);   /* the prototype */
    . . . .
}

char *join(char *s1, char *s2);        /* join s1, s2 */
{

  . . . .
}
```

The prototype includes the data type of each function parameter as well as the
function's return data type. In the function declaration, arguments appear with
the function name and not on a separate line.

Additionally, Microsoft C 5.0 provides the `/Zg` compiler option to *create*
function prototypes from "old" style programs. We did this for the memory
object allocator and the dynamic string program from Chapter 6, as follows:

```
> cl /Zg objalloc.c > objalloc.dcl
> cl /Zg strmob.c > strmob.dcl
```

We use #include's in each program to define the function prototypes we just
created. Here's the contents of both files.

> **type objalloc.dcl**
```
extern void obj_init(void);
extern struct Object *obj_alloc(int len);
extern void obj_free(struct Object *p);
extern void obj_size(struct Object *p,int len);
static int pack(void);
static int upmove(unsigned char *to,unsigned char *from,int cnt);
static int downmove(unsigned char *to,unsigned char *from,int cnt);
extern void obj_check(void);
extern long obj_mavail(void);
extern int obj_davail(void);
static int obj_error(char *msg);
```

> **type strmob.dcl**
```
extern struct Object *string(int nc,char *s);
extern struct Object *sassign(struct Object *to,struct Object *from);
extern struct Object *sjoin(struct Object *to,struct Object *from);
extern struct Object *sjoinb(struct Object *to,struct Object *from);
extern struct Object *sleft(struct Object *to,struct Object *from,
                                                int nc);
extern struct Object *sdup(struct Object *to,char ch,int nc);
extern void sfree(struct Object *s);
extern int fix_size(struct Object *p,int size);
extern int secho(struct Object *ps);
```

Note that the files include the static and extern keywords where applicable.


## Keywords: void, const, volatile

The ANSI C draft defines new keywords that are making their way into commercial compilers. Function return types may be void when a function does not
return anything. Additionally, function prototypes may use void when a function has no arguments. In the object allocator, for example, the function prototype

```
void obj_init(void);
```

declares obj_init() as a function that doesn't return anything and has no
arguments.

void has a third use with *pointers* in Microsoft C 5.0. Suppose we declare a function prototype for the fast array transfer routine called bmove() from Chapter 4. The statement

```
void bmove(void *destptr, void *srcptr, unsigned count);
```

makes destptr and srcptr pointers to a void.† destptr and srcptr may point to any C object and programs that call bmove() don't need to cast pointers. The statements

```
static struct something s[100], t[100];
. . . .
bmove(&t[20], &s[20], 80 * sizeof(struct something));
. . . .
```

for example, call bmove() to copy 80 structures in memory starting from address s[20] to address t[20]. Here's the modified code for bmove() with void pointers.

```
/* bmove.c - block move function with function
            prototype and void pointers */

#define BSIZE 256

void bmove(void *destptr, void *srcptr, unsigned count)
{
    struct mblock {     /* block size */
       char a[BSIZE];
    };
    register unsigned char *dest = destptr;
    register unsigned char *src =  srcptr;

    while (count >= BSIZE) { /* transfer blocks */
       *(struct mblock *)dest = *(struct mblock *)src;
       dest += BSIZE;
       src  += BSIZE;
       count -= BSIZE;
    }

    while (count--)     /* transfer remaining bytes */
       *dest++ = *src++;
}
```

Except in assignment statements, void pointers produce compilation errors unless you cast them to a data type in pointer expressions. Routines bmove()

---

† Note that a verbal explanation may give people the wrong idea about pointers to a *void*.

assigns `destptr` and `srcptr` to the register pointers `dest` and `src` to avoid casting the pointer expressions to `unsigned char`. The assignment statements are convenient because `void` pointers may be assigned to or from a pointer of any C data type.

There are two additional keywords: `const` and `volatile`. `const`, which is for your benefit, keeps a module from changing a variable's value once you set it. The compiler reports an error if you try to change its value.

`volatile` has more to do with the compiler's actions than yours. Inside loops, for example, program variables like semaphores and memory mapped hardware locations may change their values asynchronously from your running program. The compiler might assume that a variable inside a loop that's used as an rvalue may never change. The `volatile` keyword makes the compiler reload `volatile` variables each time through the loop. Although Microsoft C 5.0 accepts the `volatile` keyword, it's currently unimplemented (as of this writing).

The following program demonstrates the `const` and `volatile` keywords.

**Program D-4**

```
/* key.c - const and volatile keywords */

#include <stdio.h>

const   int hrs  = 24;              /* global to other files */
static const int mins = 60;         /* local to this file */
static const int secs = 60;         /* local to this file */

main()
{
   static const int days = 7;       /* int constant */
   const int *ptime = &hrs;         /* ptr to int constant */
   static const int *const pt = &mins;  /* const ptr to const int */
   static char *const msg = "warning one";   /* const ptr to char */
   volatile int flag;               /* flag may change */

   ptime = &secs;                   /* ptr to int constant */
   strcpy(msg, "warning two");      /* same memory location */

   days++;                          /* illegal, doesn't compile */
   pt = &secs;                      /* illegal, doesn't compile */
   msg = "warning two";             /* illegal, doesn't compile */
}
```

`const` and `volatile` variables have storage classes just like other C variables. Variables `mins` and `secs`, for example, are local to this file but other files may reference hrs. Note that to initialize the const variables days, pt, and msg inside main(), you must declare them static, just like arrays and structures. Otherwise, they become automatic variables and you cannot initialize them following their declarations.

Since ptime is a pointer to a constant integer and not a constant itself, we may change where it points to as long as the object is a constant integer. Likewise, strcpy() may modify memory that msg points to, but we can't change msg's address. The remaining statements are all illegal because they try to change a const variable's value.

## Function Calling Conventions

Microsoft C 5.0 enables the keywords cdecl, fortran, and pascal for function calling conventions. Keyword cdecl specifies the C calling convention (the default), which pushes function arguments right-to-left on the stack and has the caller clean up the stack. Programs that use the keywords fortran or pascal make functions push their arguments left-to-right on the stack and remove them before returning. The program forward.c in Appendix C shows you an example of a PASCAL calling convention in a C program.

# ♦ Other Features ♦

## Automatic Run Time Arrays

Microsoft C 5.0 includes a library routine called alloca() that's similar to malloc(). alloca(), however, returns a pointer to *stack* space instead of the heap. Since stack space is automatically freed when a function returns, alloca() helps you create automatic arrays of any size at run-time.

To demonstrate, let's return to the mdim2.c program from Chapter 3, which creates two-dimensional arrays of arbitrary data types.

**Program D-5**

```
/* mdim2.c - two-dimensional arrays at run time */

#include <stdio.h>
#include "mdim.h"                      /* header file for macros */
```

```
main(argc, argv)
int argc;
char *argv[];
{
    int **a;                       /* 2D array of integers */
    double **b;                    /* 2D array of doubles */
    int rows, cols;
    . . . .
    DIM2(a, rows, cols, int);      /* create 2D array of integers */
    . . . .
    DIM2(b, rows, cols, double);   /* create 2D array of doubles */
    . . . .
    D2FREE(a);                     /* free 2D integer heap storage */
    D2FREE(b);                     /* free 2D doubles heap storage */
}
```

Recall that `DIM2` allocates heap storage for the arrays with `calloc()` and `D2FREE` releases the storage with `free()`. `DIM2` and `D2FREE` are both macros.

Here's the new header file for `mdim.h` using `alloca()` instead of `calloc()`:

```
/* mdim.h - header file for run time multidimensional arrays */

#define DIM2(prow,row,col,type) \
    {\
        char *alloca();\
        register type *pdata;\
        int i;\
        pdata = (type *) alloca(row * col * sizeof (type));\
        if (pdata == (type *) NULL) {\
            fprintf(stderr, "No stack space for data\n");\
            exit(1);\
        }\
        prow = (type **) alloca(row * sizeof (type *));\
        if (prow == (type **) NULL) {\
            fprintf(stderr, "No stack space for row pointers\n");\
            exit(1);\
        }\
        for (i = 0; i < row; i++) {\
            prow[i] = pdata;\
            pdata += col;\
        }\
    }
```

Calls to `alloca()` use the stack instead of the heap. If there's no stack space available, `alloca()` returns a NULL. The rest of the macro code doesn't change. This means you can remove the `D2FREE` statements from `mdim2.c`, since heap space was never allocated.

You should be careful with calls to `alloca()` in your programs. Functions that return heap pointers, for example, can't use `alloca()` because stack space is released when the function returns. For this reason, `alloca()` does not apply to `idim2.c` and `idim3.c` from Chapter 3. Routine `mdim2.c` can use `alloca()` because `DIM2` is a *macro* and not a function.

## Assertions

Here's what happens when you compile and run `array2.c` from the section on assertions in Chapter 5.

```
> cl array2.c
> array2 12 99
Assertion failed: index >= 0 && index < MAX, file array2.c, line 20

Abnormal program termination
```

The `assert` macro in Microsoft C 5.0 displays the assertion that fails as well as the file name and line number. Let's take a look at the `assert` macro to see how this is done.

```
. . . .

static char _assertstring[] =
                "Assertion failed: %s, file %s, line %d\n";

#define assert(exp) { \
  if (!(exp)) { \
    fprintf(stderr, _assertstring, #exp, _ _FILE_ _, _ _LINE_ _); \
    abort(); \
    } \
  }
. . . .
```

The `assert` macro uses *stringizing* to display the assertion that fails. The technique we show in Chapter 5 to customize assertions and display the assertion that fails is unnecessary in Microsoft C 5.0.

Stringizing means the compiler doesn't substitute macro parameters between double quotes, a technique we used in Chapter 5 to customize assertions. User defined assertion macros are still possible using stringizing, however. The program `custom.c` from Chapter 5 runs on Microsoft C 5.0 if you make the following change to the custom `assert.h` file.

```
/* new system-wide assert.h */

void (*assertf)();  /* pointer to user-defined function */

#ifndef NDEBUG
#  define   assert(expr)\
if (!(expr)) {\
      (*assertf)(#expr, _ _FILE_ _, _ _LINE_ _);\
}\
else
#else
#  define   assert(expr)
#endif
```

The header file uses #expr instead of "expr" to pass a constant string as a function parameter.

# E

# Turbo C

Turbo C runs under the MS-DOS operating system in two separate environments. The `tc` command runs the C compiler in a menu-driven environment with a text editor. The `tcc` command runs Turbo C as a stand-alone compiler and automatically calls the linker if a compilation is successful. Turbo C also supplies the `tlink` command to call the linker in a separate step. We discuss only the `tcc` command and its options in this appendix.

Turbo C targets programs for the Intel 8086 family of processors. Consequently, the compiler has options to create different memory models for programs and has keywords to specify 16-bit and 32-bit pointers. Turbo C also supports ANSI C features, such as pragmas, stringizing, token pasting, function prototypes, and PASCAL and C calling conventions (for more information, see Microsoft C 5.0 in Appendix D). Additionally, Turbo C provides MS-DOS interrupt routines, inline assembly code, and pseudo-variables (register names).

Before we look at these features, here's a list of options for for the Turbo C compiler command `tcc`. (C) marks compiler options, (P) preprocessor options, and (L) link editor options.

-1   Generate code for the 186/286 instruction set. (C)

-1-  Generate code for the 8088/8086 instruction set (default). (C)

-a   Align integer size variables and structure fields on a machine-word boundary.

-a-  Do not force integer size variables and structure fields to align to a machine-word boundary (default). (C)

-c   Produce (compile `.C` or assemble `.ASM`) `.OBJ` file(s). Do not call the linker. (C)

-d   Merge duplicate constant strings. (C)

-e*name*
     Create executable file *name*. (C/L)

-f  Specify 8087/287 floating point emulation (default). If the target hardware has an 8087/287 coprocessor installed, the program will call it for floating-point calculations. (C/L)

-f-  Do not use the floating-point libraries at link time. Use this option if your program does not contain any floating-point calculations. (C/L)

-f87

  Use inline 8087 instructions for floating point operations. Programs compiled with this option will not run on computers that lack the 8087/287 coprocessor. (C/L)

-g*num*

  Stop compiling after *num* compiler error and warning messages. (C)

-i*num*

  Set identifier size to *num* significant characters. The default is 32. Use this option to truncate identifier size. (C)

-j*num*

  Stop compiling after *num* compiler error messages. (C)

-m*x* Compile using one of six different memory models, where *x* is one of tsmclh. The memory models are as follows:

    t Create a tiny model program (sometimes called *impure* on other systems.)

    s Create a small model program (default).

    m Create a middle model program.

    c Create a compact model program.

    l Create a large model program.

    h Create a huge model program.

  (C)

-n*pathname*

  Create any .OBJ or .ASM files in directory *pathname*. (C)

-o*filename*

  Compile the name file, creating object file *filename*.OBJ. (C)

-p  Tell the compiler to use the "Pascal" calling convention for all function calls. Function arguments must match in number and type. Override option -p with keyword cdecl. (C)

-p-  Tell the compiler to use the "C" calling convention for all function calls (default). Functions may have a variable number of arguments and not necessarily match type with formal parameters. Override option -p- with keyword pascal. (C)

-r  Allow register variables (default). (C)

-r-  Disable register variables even though keyword `register` precedes the variable declaration. This option is useful when you want to call assembly language routines that do not preserve the SI and DI registers. (C)

-w  Display warnings (default). (C)

-w-  Do not display warnings. (C)

-w*str*

Enable the warning message associated with *str*. (C)

-w-*str*

Suppress the warning message associated with *str*. (C) Turbo C warning messages fall into four classes: ANSI Violations, Common Errors, Less Common Errors, and Portability Warnings. Of interest are the following warnings which under most compilers flag compilation errors.

> str  Either the named field is not part of the structure, or the named identifier is not a structure.

> stu  The named structure has no definition.

> zst  A structure has zero length.

> nod  No declaration for function.

(C)

-zX*name*

Changes the name or class of the segment specified by X to *name*.

-zX*

Uses the default name or class of segment specified by X. X can be one of:

> A  Code segment class (default is _CODE).

> B  Uninitialized data segments class (BSS) (default is class _BSS).

> C  Code segment name (default is _TEXT).

> D  Uninitialized data segment name (default is name _BSS).

> G  Uninitized data segments group name (default is name DGROUP).

> P  Code group name for the code segment.

> R Initialized data segment name (default is name _DATA).
>
> S Initialized data segments group name (default is group DGROUP).
>
> T Initialized data segment class name (default is class _DATA).

(L)

-A Allow ANSI-compatible language constructs. Ignore extended keyword set. (C)

-B Call the assembler to process inline assembly code. (C)

-C Allow nested comments. (P)

-D*name*
   Define *name* to be 1 to the preprocessor. (P)

-D*name=str*
   Define *name* to be *str* to the preprocessor. (P)

-G Optimize for speed rather than size. (C)

-I *pathname*
   Add *pathname* to the list of directories to be searched when an #include file is not found in the directory containing the source file. (P)

-K Create char type variables with attribute unsigned by default. (C)

-K- Create char type variables with attribute signed by default (default). (C)

-L*pathname*
   Search directory *pathname* for the Turbo C library files and the object file start-up routine instead of the current directory. (L)

-M Produce a link map file. (L)

-N Generate code for stack probes upon entry to functions (the default). (C)

-O Perform object code optimization. (C)

-S Create an assembly language source listing in *file*.ASM, where *file* is the base name of the C source file. (C)

-U*name*
   Undefine preprocessor symbol *name*. (P)

-Y Generate a standard stack frame useful for debugging. (C)

-Z Optimize register load operations by suppressing them when the register contents are unchanged. (C)

# ♦ Memory Models ♦

Turbo C supports six memory models: tiny, small, middle, compact, large, and huge. Refer to Appendices B, C, and D for more information about memory models and the placement of data, stack, text, and heap program areas in memory.

## Tiny Model

The tiny model groups all the program areas into one 64-kilobyte segment, making object code files impure. Fig. C-1 in Appendix C shows a diagram of the tiny model. Text pointers and data pointers are 16 bits. The −mt compiler option creates a tiny model program.

## Small Model

The small model creates separate segments for text and data. Fig. B-1 in Appendix B shows a diagram of the small model, which is always pure. Text pointers and data pointers are 16 bits, and a program's text and and data must each be less than 64K bytes. The −ms compiler option creates small model programs and is the default in Turbo C.

## Middle Model

The middle or medium model has more than one text segment but only one data segment. Fig. C-2 in Appendix C shows a diagram of the medium model, which is always pure. Text pointers are 32 bits and data pointers are 16 bits. The −mm compiler option creates middle model programs.

## Compact Model

The compact model has more than one data segment but only one text segment. Fig. D-1 of Appendix D shows the compact memory model, which is always pure. Data pointers are 32 bits and text pointers are 16 bits. The −mc compiler option creates compact model programs.

## Large Model

The large memory model has multiple data segments for both text and data. Fig. C-3 in Appendix C shows a diagram of the large model, which is always pure. Large model pointers are 32 bits, but the compiler performs 16-bit arithmetic for pointer operations. The −ml compiler option creates large model programs.

## Huge Model

The huge memory model has the same memory configuration as the large memory model shown in Fig. C-3 of Appendix C. Huge model pointers are 32 bits, and the compiler performs 32-bit arithmetic for pointer operations. The −mh compiler option creates huge model programs.

## Keyword Extensions

Turbo C also supports the keywords near, far, and huge for text and data pointers. near pointers are 16 bits and far and huge pointers are 32 bits. The compiler performs 16-bit arithmetic on far pointers, which must always address an object within a 64-kilobyte segment. huge pointers can address multiple segments; consequently, the compiler performs 32-bit arithmetic on pointer operations. See the program keywords.c from Appendix C for examples of these keywords.

## Summary

The following table summarizes the sizes of integers and pointers in the different memory models for Turbo C.

**TABLE E-1. Pointer and integer sizes for Turbo C**

| Model | Integer | Text Pointer | Data Pointer |
|-------|---------|--------------|--------------|
| Tiny | 16 | 16 | 16 |
| Small | 16 | 16 | 16 |
| Medium | 16 | 32 | 16 |
| Compact | 16 | 16 | 32 |
| Large | 16 | 32 | 32 |
| Huge | 16 | 32 | 32 |

# ◆ ANSI C Features ◆

Turbo C supports several new ANSI C draft features, some of which we looked at in Appendix D for Microsoft C 5.0. Let's take a closer look at these new features to see how they work.

## Pragmas

Pragmas are preprocessor directives. Turbo C recognizes the following pragmas:

```
#pragma inline
#pragma warn option
```

The `inline` pragma, which should be placed at the beginning of a source file, tells the compiler that the file contains inline assembly code. The `-B` compiler option has the same effect. We'll return to inline assembly code in C programs later.

The `warn` pragma controls the compiler's warning messages. Parameter *option* has the following three forms:

```
+www        Turn on warning www
-www        Turn off warning www
.www        Restore warning www to the value it had
            when compilation began
```

*www* warnings are three letter abbreviations that warn you of ANSI Violations, common errors, and portability problems. The `warn` pragma helps you enable or disable warning messages for different modules in one source file.

## Stringizing and Token Pasting

Turbo C supports ANSI C stringizing and token pasting. Refer to Appendix D for how they work and examples of their use.

## Keywords: void, const, volatile

Turbo C supports the keywords `void`, `const`, and `volatile` from the ANSI C draft. The program `key.c` in Appendix D shows examples of their use. The Turbo C compiler implements all three keywords.

Note that Turbo C allows you to initialize a `const` variable inside a function, without declaring it `static`. In `key.c`, for example, the statement

```
static const int days = 7;              /* int constant */
```

compiles as well as the statement

```
const int days = 7;                        /* int constant */
```

in Turbo C.

## Function Prototyping

Appendix D discusses function prototypes in detail. Suppose we define a function prototype for `bmove()` from Chapter 4 as follows:

```
void bmove(void *destptr, const void *srcptr, size_t count);
```

The keyword `const` in the second parameter declaration prevents `bmove()` from modifying `srcptr`. Argument `size_t` is an `unsigned int` in the ANSI C standard.

## Function Calling Conventions

Turbo C supports the function calling conventions for FORTRAN and PASCAL, which is different from C. Appendices C and D provides more information about these calling conventions.

Turbo C has compiler options that make *all* routines use either the PASCAL calling convention (-p option) or the default C convention (-p- option). The `pascal` keyword specifies the PASCAL calling convention, and the `cdecl` keyword makes the compiler use standard C conventions. The Turbo C library header files contain the keyword `cdecl` so that programs using the PASCAL calling conventions may use C library routines with the C convention. The program `forward.c` in Appendix C shows you an example of a PASCAL calling convention in a C program.

## Macro Names

Turbo C supports the following built-in macro names:

```
_ _LINE_ _        Current source line number
_ _FILE_ _        Current file name
_ _DATE_ _        Date of compilation
_ _TIME_ _        Time of compilation
_ _STDC_ _        (1) Indicates standard C
```

Chapter 5 shows uses of _ _LINE_ _ and _ _FILE_ _ with assertions and customized memory allocators. Here is a Turbo C program that displays them all.

**Program E-1**

```
/* mac.c - example showing predefined ANSI macro names */

main ()
{
    printf("This line is %d\n", _ _LINE_ _);
    printf("This line is %d\n", _ _LINE_ _);
    printf("This file is %s\n", _ _FILE_ _);
    printf("This file was compiled on %s at %s\n",
                  _ _DATE_ _, _ _TIME_ _);
    printf("A %d means standard C\n", _ _STDC_ _);
}
```

To compile and run mac.c type:

```
> tcc -A mac.c
> mac
This line is 5
This line is 6
This file is mac.c
This file was compiled on Mar 04 1988 at 15:18:17
A 1 means standard C
```

The −A compiler option enables ANSI C compatible constructs.

## Functions with Variable Arguments

Chapter 4 shows you how to write a function that accepts a variable number of arguments with different data types. The technique uses macros defined in varargs.h. In Chapter 4, mypass.c calls a function mypass() with a variable number of arguments to fetch each argument from the stack.

Turbo C provides the stdarg.h header file in place of varargs.h. This changes things slightly, so let's look at the differences under ANSI C. Here's the first part of mypass.c.

**Program E-2**

```
/* mypass2.c - pass variable number of data types to
               one function ANSI C compatible
*/

#include <stdio.h>
#include <stdarg.h>                          /* ANSI C */

main()
{
    static char buf[] = "string of data";
    int num = 44;
    char c = 'X';
    float f = 6.72;

    mypass("%s", buf);
    mypass("%s %d", buf, num);
    mypass("%s %d %c", buf, num, c);
    mypass("%s %d %c %f", buf, num, c, f);
    mypass("%f %c %d %s", f, c, num, buf);
    mypass("%x", num);
}
```

The only line that's different is the #include statement, which includes the new ANSI C header file.

The rest of the program is the function mypass(). Routine mypass()'s argument is a character pointer in ANSI C.  va_start() has two arguments (the old version had one), and its second argument is the character pointer you pass to mypass(). Otherwise, the rest of the code doesn't change, and the output looks like what we showed you in Chapter 4.

The debugger in Chapter 5 (dbug.c) also uses varargs.h. This code won't run under Turbo C either, unless you convert it to stdargs.h like we did for mypass().

```
mypass(fmt)
char *fmt;
{
    va_list args;                    /* argument list */
    char *p;
    int inum;                        /* for integers */
    double fnum;                     /* for floats, doubles */
    char *ps;                        /* for strings */
    int ch;                          /* for a character */

    va_start(args, fmt);             /* initialize argument list */
```

```
    printf("\nmypass called with format %s\n", fmt);

    for (p = fmt; *p; p++ ) {           /* loop over format line */
        if (*p == '%')
            switch (p[1]) {
                case 's':
                    ps = va_arg(args, char *);           /* string */
                    printf("    string    = %s\n", ps);
                    break;
                case 'd':
                    inum = va_arg(args, int);            /* integer */
                    printf("    integer   = %d\n", inum);
                    break;
                case 'c':
                    ch = va_arg(args, int);              /* character */
                    printf("    character = %c\n", ch);
                    break;
                case 'f':
                    fnum = va_arg(args, double);         /* double */
                    printf("    double    = %g\n", fnum);
                    break;
                default:
                    printf("    %c is an illegal format\n", p[1]);
                    break;
            }
    }
    va_end(args);                       /* clean up argument list */
}
```

# ♦ Low Level Support ♦

Turbo C has special features for low level operations. C programs may declare interrupt functions, and inline assembly code instructions may appear with C statements. Turbo C also lets you directly access the contents of machine registers while your program is running.

## Pseudo-Variables

Turbo C provides special names called *pseudo-variables* to access CPU registers. You may load pseudo-variables with values or access data from them just like a C variable. Of course, pseudo-variables have limitations. Their data types are unsigned int or unsigned char, and if you arbitrarily modify the contents of certain pseudo-variables you may crash your program. Furthermore, you can't always be sure a pseudo-variable's data will remain valid, since the compiler may change it when executing assembly instructions. And, since registers do not have an address, you can't take the address of a pseudo-variable with the & operator.

Turbo C has both 8-bit and 16-bit pseudo-variables. Table E-2 lists the Turbo C 16-bit pseudo-variables and their meanings.

**TABLE E-2. 16-bit pseudo-variables**

| Pseudo-variable | Usual Purpose |
|---|---|
| _AX | General/Accumulator |
| _BX | General/Indexing |
| _CX | General/Looping |
| _DX | General/Holding data |
| _CS | Code Segment Address |
| _DS | Data Segment Address |
| _SS | Stack Segment Address |
| _ES | Extra Segment Address |
| _SP | Stack Pointer |
| _BP | Base Pointer |
| _DI | Register Variable |
| _SI | Register Variable |

Pseudo-variable _AX, for example, represents register AX, and so on. All 16-bit pseudo-variables are unsigned int. Turbo C uses _DI and _SI for register variables in C programs.

Table E-3 lists the Turbo C 8-bit pseudo-variables and their meanings.

**TABLE E-3. 8-bit pseudo-variables**

| Pseudo-variable | Usual Purpose |
|---|---|
| _AH | General/Accumulator |
| _AL | General/Accumulator |
| _BH | General/Indexing |
| _BL | General/Indexing |
| _CH | General/Looping |
| _CL | General/Looping |
| _DH | General/Holding data |
| _DL | General/Holding data |

Pseudo-variable _AH, for example, is the high byte of register AX and _AL is the low byte, and so on. All 8-bit pseudo-variables are unsigned char.

The following C program uses pseudo-variables to display the contents of all its CPU registers and tells you a lot about the program's run time environment as well.

**Program E-3**

```
/* pseudo.c  - example showing pseudo-variables */

main ( )
{
    register int i = 25;                /* Register _SI */
    register int j = 35;                /* Register _DI */

    printf("Current Machine Registers\n");
    printf("AX = %x\n", _AX);
    printf("BX = %x\n", _BX);
    printf("CX = %x\n", _CX);
    printf("DX = %x\n", _DX);

    printf("Code Segment Address (CS) = %x\n", _CS);
    printf("Data Segment Address (DS) = %x\n", _DS);
    printf("Stack Segment Address (SS) = %x\n", _SS);
    printf("Extra Segment Address (ES) = %x\n", _ES);

    printf("Stack PTR = %x\n", _SP);
    printf("Base PTR = %x\n", _BP);

    printf("i is %d because Register SI = %d\n", i, _SI);
    printf("j is %d because Register DI = %d\n", j, _DI);
}
```

The program declares two register variables i and j and displays their values with the pseudo-variables _SI and _DI, respectively. The program also prints out the segment registers and the stack and base pointer registers.

Here's the output after we compile the program.

```
> tcc pseudo.c
> pseudo
Current Machine Registers
AX = 1a
BX = fffd
CX = fffd
DX = 0
Code Segment Address (CS) = ef0
Data Segment Address (DS) = ff7
Stack Segment Address (SS) = ff7
Extra Segment Address (ES) = ff7
Stack PTR = ffd0
Base PTR = ffde
i is 25 because Register SI = 25
j is 35 because Register DI = 35
```

We display the contents of each register in hexadecimal format except for _SI and _DI. Here we use decimal format to show that their contents match the program's register variables i and j.

## Inline Assembly Instructions

Turbo C handles assembly language instructions within C source files. When you use this feature, the compiler invokes the Microsoft Macro Assembler (MASM). C files that use inline assembly instructions should be compiled with the -B compiler option or include the directive

```
#pragma inline
```

at the beginning of the file. (Actually, if you forget to do either of these, the compiler issues a warning and then *restarts* itself with the –B option.)

Turbo C implements inline assembly instructions with the keyword asm. Here's the format:

asm *opcode operands*

Each asm statement is terminated by a return or a semicolon.  asm statements cannot continue to the next line.  opcode is a valid 8086 instruction with its operands, which may reference C constants, variables, and labels. The compiler produces assembly source (.ASM) when it sees inline assembly instructions and automatically calls the assembler by running masm.exe. This means you must have the MASM assembler (version 3.0 or later) on your system, since Turbo C doesn't provide it.

Let's look at a simple program that has inline assembly instructions. inline.c calls a C function sum2() to add its command line arguments and return the result.

**Program E-4**

```
/* inline.c - example showing inline assembly
              & inline pragma */

#include <stdio.h>
#pragma inline

static int sum2(int v1, int v2)
{
    asm mov ax, v1
    asm add ax, v2
    return _AX;                    /* This is a C statement */
}

main (argc, argv)
int argc;
char *argv[];
{
    register int i;
    register int j;

    int total;

    if (argc != 3) {
        fprintf(stderr, "Usage: %s num1 num2\n", argv[0]);
        exit(1);
    }

    i = atoi(argv[1]);             /* First number */
    j = atoi(argv[2]);             /* Second number */

    total = sum2(i, j);

    printf("Total = %d\n", total);
}
```

The program uses a `#pragma inline` in its source file, so we don't need to compile `inline.c` with `-B`. Inside `sum2()`, `asm` statements perform the addition, and `sum2()` returns the value with a C `return` statement. Here's the result when we compile `inline.c` and run it.

```
> tcc inline.c
> inline 300 500
Total = 800
```

In practice, inline assembly is handy for low-level IO operations, such as `bloc-kin()` and `blockout()` C functions that read and write blocks of data from a programmed I/O controller board. These functions cannot use C library routines because they must issue read and write commands directly to a controller.

## ♦  Other Features  ♦

### Duplicate Strings

Usually, C compilers place constant strings in the static data area. Chapter 2 reveals that duplicate constant strings in C programs often have *separate* copies in the data area. This can waste memory.

Turbo C has a compiler option (-d) that *merges* duplicate constant strings. This makes programs smaller, although you should be careful about using it. To demonstrate, let's compile and run `dup2.c` from Chapter 2 under Turbo C.

**Program E-5**

```
/* dup2.c - duplicate strings */

main()
{
    char *p, *q;

    p = "string";
    q = "string";

    p[3] = 'o';
    printf("%s %s\n", p, q);
}

> tcc dup2.c
> dup2
strong string
```

The output proves separate copies of `"string"` live in the data area. Now let's recompile `dup2.c` with -d to merge duplicate strings and run the program again.

```
> tcc -d dup2.c
> dup2
strong strong
```

Only one copy of "string" lives in the data area. Modifying it, therefore, may produce side effects.

## Assertions

Here's what happens when you compile and run array2.c from the section on assertions in Chapter 5.

```
> tcc array2.c
> array2 12 99
Assertion failed: file array2.c, line 20
```

Turbo C's assert macro displays only the file name and line number when an assertion fails. Chapter 5 shows you how to customize the assert macro to display the assertion that fails along with the file name and line number. The approach, which substitutes macro parameters between double quotes, doesn't work in Turbo C, but you can use stringizing to accomplish the same thing. Here's a custom assert macro that does the job for you.

```
/* assert.h - assertion macro for Turbo C */

#ifndef NDEBUG
#   define   assert(expr)\
if (!(expr)) {\
    fprintf(stderr,"Assertion failed: %s, file %s, line %d\n", \
            #expr, _ _FILE_ _, _ _LINE_ _);\
    exit(1);\
}\
else
#else
#   define   assert(expr)
#endif
```

To test it, let's compile and run array3.c from Chapter 5 which includes our custom macro instead of Turbo C's:

```
> tcc array3.c
> array3 25 99
Assertion failed: index >= 0 && index < MAX, file array3.c, line 20
```

Stringizing also makes custom.c from Chapter 5 run on Turbo C. Refer to Appendix D for the changes.

## Preprocessor Caveats

As of this writing, #include statements of the form

    #include <*filename*>

look for *filename* in your current directory before searching the system include directory. This implies that Turbo C programs that contain

    #include <assert.h>

will include a custom assert macro if you place one in your current directory.

Turbo C also does not support the preprocessor options -E and -P for writing preprocessor output to the screen or to a .i file, respectively.

## Initializing Automatic Variables

As of this writing, Turbo C allows you to initialize automatic arrays but not automatic structures. Inside a function, the declaration

    char name[] = "Turbo C";

allocates storage for 8 bytes on the stack containing the NULL terminated string "Turbo C". Likewise, the declaration

    int buf[10] = { 2, 4, 6, 8 };

inside a function allocates storage for 10 integers on the stack at run time. The first four elements have initial values and the rest are set to zero.

# Index

## Programming in C, Revised Edition

*Stephen G. Kochan*

This timely revision provides complete coverage of the C language, including all language features and over 90 program examples. The comprehensive tutorial approach teaches the beginner how to write, compile, and execute programs and teaches the experienced programmer how to write applications using features unique to C. It is written in a clear instructive style and is ideally suited for classroom use or as a self-study guide.

Topics covered include:

- Introduction and Fundamentals
- Writing a Program in C
- Variables, Constants, Data Types, and Arithmetic Expressions
- Program Looping
- Making Decisions
- Arrays
- Functions
- Structures
- Character Strings
- Pointers
- Operations on Bits
- The Preprocessor
- Working with Larger Programs
- Input and Output
- Miscellaneous and Advanced Features
- Appendices: Language Summary, ANSI Standard C, Common Programming Mistakes, The UNIX C Library, Compiling Programs under UNIX, The Program LINT, The ASCII Character Set

464 Pages, 7½ x 9¾, Softbound
ISBN: 0-672-48420-X
**No. 48420, $24.95**

## Programming in ANSI C

*Stephen G. Kochan*

This comprehensive programming guide is the newest title in the Hayden Books C Library, written by the series editor Stephen G. Kochan. A tutorial in nature, the book teaches the beginner how to write, compile and execute programs even with no previous experience with C.

The book details such C essentials as program looping, decision making, arrays, functions, structures, character strings, bit operations, and enumerated data types. Examples are complete with step-by-step explanations of each procedure and routine involved as well as end-of-chapter exercises, making it ideally suited for classroom use.

Topics covered include:

- Introduction and Fundamentals
- Writing a Program in ANSI C
- Variables, Data Types, and Arithmetic Expressions
- Program Looping
- Making Decisions
- Arrays, Functions, Structures
- Character Strings, Pointers
- Operations on Bits
- The Preprocessor
- More on Data Types
- Working with Larger Programs
- Input and Output
- Miscellaneous Features and Topics
- Appendices: ANSI C Language Summary, The UNIX C Library, Compiling Programs Under UNIX, The Program LINT, The ASCII Character Set

450 Pages, 7½ x 9¾, Softbound
ISBN: 0-672-48408-0
**No. 48408, $24.95**

## Inside the AMIGA® with C, Second Edition

*John Berry, The Waite Group*

Everyone who has recently upgraded their AMIGA computer system, or is thinking about doing it, needs this revised edition of *Inside the AMIGA with C*. The book covers the AmigaDOS™ operating system in greater detail, and is compatible with the new AmigaDOS 1.2. Paying particular attention to the AMIGA 500, the book presents special AMIGA graphics features including sprites, Genlock, and blitter objects, with updated information on Intuition™

Like the original book, code listings in each chapter are carefully constructed both as practical routines and as instructional examples for beginning to intermediate C programmers. The new edition features several new programs that demonstrate the use of color palettes and registers.

Topics covered include:

- The AMIGA Programming Environment
- Using Intuition
- Process Control and AmigaDOS
- Drawing in Intuition
- Animating the Sprites
- Programming Sound
- Artificial Speech
- Programming with Disk Files

400 Pages, 7½ x 9¾, Softbound
ISBN: 0-672-22625-1
**No. 22625, $24.95**

## Topics in C Programming

*Stephen G. Kochan and Patrick H. Wood*

Here is the most advanced and comprehensive coverage of the maturing C market. This sequel to *Programming in C* describes in detail some of the most difficult concepts in the C language—structures and pointers. It also explores the standard C library and standard I/O library, dynamic memory allocation, linked lists, tree structures, and dispatch tables.

Experienced C programmers can examine the UNIX System Interface through discussions on controlling processes, pipes, and terminal I/O. *Topics in C Programming* also explains how to write terminal-independent programs, how to debug C programs and analyze their performance, and how to use "make" for automatic generation of a programming system.

Topics covered include:

- Structures and Pointers
- The Standard C Library
- The Standard I/O Library
- UNIX System Interface
- Writing Terminal-Independent Programs with the "curses" Library
- Debug and Performance Analysis of C Programs
- Generating Program Systems with "make"

528 Pages, 7½ x 9¾, Softbound
ISBN: 0-672-46290-7
**No. 46290, $24.95**

**Visit your local book retailer or call**
**800-428-SAMS.**

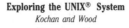

Use this form to order the booklet containing all of the exercise solutions or two companion diskettes with the source code to all of the programs and exercise solutions in *Advanced C: Tips and Techniques*. The booklet is over 100 pages in length and contains explanations and discussions of each exercise solution. The diskettes are 5-1/4″ floppies prepared for IBM-compatible personal computers running under DOS 2.0 or higher.

The booklet and diskettes sell for $19.95 (U.S.) each. Or, you may order both the booklet and diskettes for $29.95 (U.S.). Orders must include a check or money order made out to "Anderson Software Company". (No cash, please.) Add $2.00 for shipping and handling and $5.00 for foreign orders. California residents please add 6.5% sales tax.

Send this form with your payment to:

Paul and Gail Anderson
c/o Howard W. Sams & Company
4300 West 62nd Street
Indianapolis, IN 46268

*Howard W. Sams & Company assumes no liability with respect to the use or accuracy of the information contained in these diskettes.*

---

### Diskette/Booklet Order Form

Anderson, *Advanced C: Tips and Techniques*, #48417

| | |
|---|---|
| Name | Company |
| Address | |
| City | State/Zip |
| Phone (   ) | Date |
| ☐ Diskettes: $19.95 | ☐ Booklet: $19.95 |
| ☐ Diskettes and Booklet: $29.95 | ☐ Shipping/Tax: $ |
| ☐ Total Amount Enclosed: $ | |
| ☐ Check number | ☐ Money order number |